Primer for Translating Daoist Literature

道文翻譯入門

ALSO BY THE AUTHOR

Cultivating Perfection

Handbooks for Daoist Practice

The Way of Complete Perfection

The Daoist Tradition

Taming the Wild Horse

Entering Stillness

Primer for Translating Daoist Literature

真文翻譯入門

Louis Komjathy

伏轉

purple cloud press

Primer for Translating Daoist Literature (Dàowén fānyì rùmén 道文翻譯入門)

Copyright © 2022 by Louis Komjathy

Published by Purple Cloud Press 紫雲出版社. All rights reserved. No portion of this book, except for brief review, may be reproduced, stored in a retrieval system, or transmitted in any form or by any means electronic, mechanical, photocopying, recording, or otherwise without the written permission of the publisher.

All translations by Louis Komjathy. Translations of the Zhuāngzǐ 莊子 (Book of Master Zhuang) have benefited from and at times closely follow Burton Watson's *The Complete Works of Chuang Tzu* (1968).

For more information visit www.purplecloudinstitute.com

LIBRARY OF CONGRESS CATALOGING-IN-PUBLICATION DATA

Komjathy, Louis.
Primer for translating Daoist literature / by Louis Komjathy 康思奇.
First print edition | New Zealand: Publisher, 2022.
ISBN 978-1-99-117071-2 (hardcover : alk. paper)
ISBN 978-1-99-117070-5 (paperback : alk. paper)
1. Daoism/Taoism   2. Daoist literature   I. Komjathy, Louis, 1971-
BL1920.K812 2022
299.51482-dc23

FRONT COVER ART
Jennifer King • www.jenniferkingstudio.com

COVER CALLIGRAPHY
Chén Yěmèng 陳業孟

COVER DESIGN
Anne-Maree Taranto • contact@rhapsodica.com

LAYOUT DESIGN
Barbara Tada • www.pixelgardendesign.com

十九八七六五四三二一

Daoist Adept Meditating before the Sānqīng 三清 (Three Purities)
SOURCE: *Dàozàng* 道藏 (Daoist Canon), frontispiece (author's collection)

「古之人與其不可傳也死矣。然則君之所讀者，古人之糟粕已夫。」

"When the people of antiquity died, they took what could not be transmitted with them. Thus, what you are reading is nothing but the chaff and dregs of the people of antiquity."

—Wheelwright *P͡ʕer (Biǎn) 扁

學書之道，不可尋文而亂目。當宜採意以合心。捨書探意採理。捨理採趣。採趣則可以收之入心。

The way to study texts is not to strive after literary merit, and thereby confuse your eyes. Instead, you must extract the meaning as it harmonizes with the heart-mind. Abandon texts after you have extracted their meaning and grasped their principle. Abandon principle after you have realized the fundamental ground. After you realize the fundamental ground, then attend to it until it enters the heart-mind.

—Wáng Zhé 王嚞 (Chóngyáng 重陽 [Redoubled Yang]; 1113–1170)

Preface

THE PRESENT BOOK IS A primer for translating Daoist (Taoist) literature. It is the first such book and the first bilingual Daoist sourcebook. In addition to a robust introduction that discusses Daoist literature and translation, it contains twenty-eight "lessons" from a wide variety of Daoist texts with accompanying, supplemental materials. Each selection includes a brief contextual and framing introduction that includes essential information on the text in question and the relevant linguistic dimensions for developing fuller translation facility. The latter includes lesson-specific classical Chinese grammar and Daoist vocabulary. Derived from most of the major periods and movements of Daoist history, the selections cover alchemy, dietetics, ethics, health and longevity practice, hermeneutics, meditation, monasticism, principles, view, and so forth. While primarily intended for individuals interested in reading Chinese Daoist primary texts in the original, it also may be used to develop bilingual engagement with Daoism and as a sourcebook of Daoist literature. In the process, *Primer for Translating Daoist Literature* offers not only a new model for Daoist Studies, but also the aspirational possibility of "Daoist translation." It envisions a Daoist scholar-practitioner approach (SPA) and study-practice model (SPM), including one rooted in critical adherent discourse (CAD). This is study informed by practice, and practice informed by study, including translation work potentially inspired by and infused with Daoist commitments, principles, qualities, and values.

Contents

Preface ix
Acknowledgments xv
Tables & Illustrations xxi
Abbreviations xxiii

Introduction: Approaching Daoist Literature 1

Lessons

  Lesson 1: Examples of Daoist Text Titles with Abbreviations 65

  Lesson 2: Chapter Titles of the *Zhuāngzǐ* 莊子
  (Book of Master Zhuang) 71

  Lesson 3: Chapter Titles of the *Bàopǔzǐ nèipiān* 抱朴子內篇
  (Inner Chapters of Master Embracing Simplicity) 79

  Lesson 4: The Nine Practices
  From the *Tàishàng Lǎojūn jīnglǜ* 太上老君經律
  (Scriptural Statutes of the Great High Lord Lao) 87

  Lesson 5: Of Knobs & Pendants
  Xíngqì yùpèi míng 行氣玉佩銘
  (Jade Ornament Inscription on Circulating Qi) 97

  Lesson 6: Daoist Apophatic Meditation I
  From the *Nèiyè* 內業 (Inward Training) 105

  Lesson 7: Dao-as-Mystery
  From the *Lǎozǐ* 老子 (Book of Venerable Masters) 115

  Lesson 8: Daoist Apophatic Meditation II
  From the *Zhuāngzǐ* 莊子 (Book of Master Zhuang) 127

  Lesson 9: Primordial Nondifferentiation & Cosmic Emanation
  From the *Huáinánzǐ* 淮南子 (Book of the Huainan Masters) 139

  Lesson 10: Cosmological Attunement
  From the *Huángdì nèijīng sùwèn* 黃帝內經素問
  (Yellow Thearch's Inner Classic: Basic Questions) 153

Lesson 11: Daoist Alchemical Symbology
  From the *Zhōuyì cāntóng qì* 周易參同契
  (Token for the Kinship of the Three According to
  the *Changes* of the Zhou Dynasty) 167

Lesson 12: Daoist Subtle Anatomy & Physiology
  From the *Tàishàng huángtíng wàijǐng yùjīng* 太上黃庭外景玉經
  (Jade Scripture on the Outer View of the
  Yellow Court from the Most High) 179

Lesson 13: Entering the Mountains & Making Elixirs
  From the *Bàopǔzǐ nèipiān* 抱朴子內篇
  (Inner Chapters of Master Embracing Simplicity) 187

Lesson 14: Principles of Yǎngshēng 養生 (Nourishing Life)
  Bǎoshēng míng 保生銘 (Inscription on Protecting Life) 199

Lesson 15: Dietary Guidelines
  From the *Yǎngxìng yánmìng lù* 養性延命錄
  (Record of Nourishing Innate Nature and Extending Life-Destiny) 211

Lesson 16: The Way of Heaven
  From the *Huángdì yīnfú jīng* 黃帝陰符經
  (Yellow Thearch's Scripture on the Hidden Talisman) 221

Lesson 17: Returning to the Dao
  From the *Tàishàng Lǎojūn shuō cháng qīngjìng miàojīng*
  太上老君說常清靜妙經
  (Wondrous Scripture on Constant Clarity and Stillness,
  as Spoken by the Great High Lord Lao) 231

Lesson 18: Emptiness & Forgetfulness
  From the "Zuòwàng piān" 坐忘篇 (Treatise on Sitting-in-Forgetfulness) . . 241

Lesson 19: Alchemical Transmutation
  Lǚzǔ bǎizì bēi 呂祖百字碑 (Ancestor Lü's Hundred Character Stele]) 253

Lesson 20: Activating the Daoist Alchemical Body
  From the *Zhōng-Lǚ chuándào jí* 鍾呂傳道集
  (Anthology of the Transmission of the Dao from Zhong to Lü) 263

Lesson 21: Studying Immortality
  From the *Wùzhēn piān* 悟真篇 (Treatise on Awakening to Perfection) 273

Lesson 22: Dǎoyǐn 導引 (Guided Stretching) & Ànmó 按摩 (Self-Massage)
  From *Zázhù jiéjìng* 雜著捷徑 (Shortcuts from Various Authors) 281

Lesson 23: Daoist Living & Spiritual Companionship
  From the *Chóngyáng lìjiào shíwǔ lùn* 重陽立教十五論
  (Redoubled Yang's Fifteen Discourses to Establish the Teachings) 289

Lesson 24: Ethical Cultivation & Monastic Protocol
  From the *Chūzhēn jiè* 初真戒 (Precepts of Initial Perfection) 301

Lesson 25: Titles of Chapters 1–18 of the *Lǎozǐ zhāngjù* 老子章句
(Chapter-and-Verse Commentary on the *Laozi*) 311

Lesson 26: Governing the Country, Regulating the Self
From the *Lǎozǐ zhāngjù* 老子章句
(Chapter-and-Verse Commentary on the *Laozi*) 323

Lesson 27: Precept Study & Application
From the *Lǎozǐ xiǎng'ěr zhù* 老子想爾注
(Commentary Thinking through the *Laozi*) 333

Lesson 28: Reflections from Dragon Gate
From the *Dàodé jīng huìyì* 道德經會義
(Assembled Meaning of the Scripture on the Dao and Inner Power) 341

Appendices

Appendix 1: Chinese Character Radicals 357
Appendix 2: Important Chinese Character Radicals for Daoist Studies 365
Appendix 3: Foundational Classical Chinese Grammar 369
Appendix 4: Pinyin to Wade-Giles Romanization Conversion Chart 373
Appendix 5: Wade-Giles to Pinyin Romanization Conversion Chart 379
Appendix 6: Daoist Character Etymology 383
Appendix 7: Principles of Daoist Translation 397
Appendix 8: Towards a Dictionary of Daoist Classical Chinese 401
Appendix 9: Foundational Readings of Daoist Literature in Translation 419
Appendix 10: Texts Included in *Primer for Translating Daoist Literature* 435

Bibliography 439
About the Author 463

Acknowledgments

A BOOK LIKE THIS IS about the past and the future. Perhaps the future-past, or perhaps the present-future. It is about work that has been done and work yet to be done. It is about lives of commitment. Individuals who have given and continue to give their (our?) lives to something else. It is about received artifacts, enduring transmissions, and great dreams. Offerings rooted in vision.

In terms of the past, I would like to begin again by recognizing and expressing gratitude to the individuals who have been most central in my long journey, something like a mountaineering expedition, to learn and master classical Chinese. To gain the knowledge and skills necessary to realize my 命 of becoming a translator of Daoist literature, to advance what I increasingly think of as "Daoist translation" (*dàojiào fānyì* 道教翻譯). Wading across and carrying over. 登涉.

Many, many years ago now (1991–1993), Wai-lim Yip 葉維廉 (University of California, San Diego) inspired a deep early and lasting engagement with the Chinese literary tradition, especially Chinese landscape poetry in general and Wáng Wéi 王維 (699–759) in particular.

空山新雨後，天氣晚來秋。

晚年唯好靜，萬事不關心。

Hiding the universe in the universe. Wáng Chiēn 王堅 (Mingyuan Evergreen Chinese School 明遠中文學校; Seattle), my first formal Chinese teacher (1994–1996) who bestowed my ordinary Chinese name Kāng

Sìqí 康思奇 (via 康思齊), and Chāng Hsiǎo-chìh 張曉至 (Boston University), who taught me advanced modern Chinese (1999–2001) and brushed my first piece of Daoist calligraphy, inspired deep appreciation for Chinese character etymology and were ever patient and kind with my frequent questions.

非淡泊無以明志，非寧靜無以致遠。

夫唯病病，是以不病。

They set the foundation.

    I also am grateful for my two years of foundational graduate-level classical Chinese language training (1998–2000) at Harvard University under Paul Rouzer 羅吉偉, now at the University of Minnesota. He generously granted access, encouragement, and support in an institution and milieux based on the opposite. One never truly knows what seeds have been planted, or how they will germinate and come to fruition. One never knows what will be done with offerings graciously bestowed.

行到水窮處，坐看雲起時。

誰能超世累，共坐白雲中。

As I complete this *Primer for Translating Daoist Literature*, it is interesting to think back to those four courses/semesters when we used a manuscript version of what would become his *A New Practical Primer of Literary Chinese* (2007). This established a root for my intensive mentorship (1998–2005) under Livia Kohn 柯恩, then at Boston University and a leading translator of Daoist literature. I remain grateful to her, as my dissertation advisor, for sharing her knowledge and expertise, even as our paths diverged years later and ago.

ACKNOWLEDGMENTS xvii

<blockquote>
信者道之根；敬者德之蒂。
</blockquote>

<blockquote>
靈臺無物為之清，一念不起為之靜。
</blockquote>

During my graduate studies, I also benefited from a literary translation seminar conducted by Rosanna Warren, American poet-scholar and daughter of Robert Penn Warren (1905–1989). These meetings involved reading and discussing translation theory as well as developing our own translation projects. Each of these individuals made major contributions to my maturation as a translator, often in ways beyond the solely linguistic.

Since that time, and prior to my departure from and renunciation of mainstream academia (officialdom and technocracy) in 2019, my translation work benefited from participation as a senior contributor in two seminars, namely, the Classical Chinese Reading Group (CCRG) at the University of California, San Diego (2010–2016) and the *Daode jing* Translation Seminar (DDJTS) at Brown University (2017–2019). The former was originally initiated by Suzanne Cahill 柯素芝 and then facilitated by Sarah Schneewind 施珊珊.

<blockquote>
學而時習之，不亦說乎？
</blockquote>

<blockquote>
天下無道，戎馬生於郊。
</blockquote>

Our collaborative translation work and discussion clarified by own translation principles and methodology, including with respect to "Daoist linguistics." The Brown seminar was established and overseen by Harold Roth 羅浩 and myself. In addition to helping to advance my forthcoming *Dàodé jīng* 道德經: *A Contextual, Contemplative, and Annotated Bilingual Translation*, this work reconfirmed my own Daoist commitments and contemplative vision, beyond academic careerism and political calculus.

上士聞道，勤而行之。

———

內靜外敬，能反其性。

It also helped me re-member energetic presence beyond mere breathing. So many translational acts between and among so many languages, often non-linguistic ones. 忘息聽氣. 忘名聽性.

These relationships and experiences locate me in multiple, intersecting "translation lineages." These sometimes converge, and sometimes diverge. There is indirect connection with Edward H. Schafer 薛愛華 (1913–1991) through Cahill and Kohn, and with A.C. Graham 葛瑞漢 (1919–1991) through Roth. To these, I would add an affinity with the scholar-practitioners Michael Saso 蘇海涵 (b. 1930) and Kristofer Schipper 施舟人 (1934–2021), who represent different "fates" within Daoist Studies. It appears I am now located more clearly in the former trajectory, but perhaps beyond both. Combining these three lines, I see a new possibility of accurate literary and scholarly translation informed by, perhaps even rooted in and infused with, Daoist values and commitments. This, of course, would be the end of Sinological (Orientalist) Daoist Studies and perhaps academia more generally. 修道、體道、傳道。

This book also benefitted and received refinement through my facilitation of the 2021 Daoist Studies Summer Seminar through the Daoist Foundation 道教基金會. I am grateful to the eighteen participants for their suggestions, encouragement, and support. I also look forward to using this version in future offerings.

I am further grateful to Johan Hausen 李誠材 of the Purple Cloud Institute 紫雲學會 and Kate Townsend 唐鄉恩/抱靜 of the Daoist Foundation 道教基金會 for their assistance, encouragement, and vision. They provided important suggestions for accessibility, improvement, and revision. I am especially grateful to Johan for encouraging and supporting this publication, which perhaps only another Daoist could recognize. And I am especially grateful to Kate for reminding me of what's real, and, of course, for saving my life and convincing me to live.

Other key individuals who contributed to my survival, rebirth, and eventual flourishing include Frank Biancalana, Susan Cox, Jon Dodds, Paul Duffy, Jacque Godoy, Aaron Gross, Joel Gruber, Connell Linson, Chad Mattos, Fay McGrew, Cheryl Plaza, Steve Plaza, Takota, and Drew Wilkins. I also am grateful to Nicola Marae Allain and Joseph Bruchac, the Plazas, and various other anonymous benefactors for supporting my work in/as court-exile. I thank you all for helping me to remember and to forget.

Finally, in terms of book design and production, I wish to thank Chén Yèmèng 陳業孟 for his refined cover calligraphy, Jennifer King for her beautiful cover painting, Barbara Tada for her tireless layout work, Anne-Maree Taranto for her fitting cover design, as well as Oscar Idelji-Tehrani, Alex Leskiewicz, and Paweł Raszkiewicz for their excellent copy-editing. Each of you has ensured that this book became better than it would have been otherwise.

Here, among the returning birdsong and opening oak buds in the advancing spring, I sit in my studio surrounded by an opus of annotated scholarly translations of Daoist literature, some forty-plus Daoist texts, that I have completed and published to date. This includes various accompanying catalogues and research guides. And I think of a future of maybe eighteen more. As I now work on behalf of the Center for Daoist Studies 道學中心, including an aspirational physical location for research and translation, and facilitate the recently-established Daoist Translation Committee 道教翻譯學會, I am grateful to you, dear reader, for your openness and interest in this primer. Perhaps you will become part of its imagined and unimaginable future.

道炁長存

Louis Komjathy 修靜
Xiūjìng zhāi 修靜齋
Qīngmíng 清明 Day
Rényín 壬寅 Year

Tables & Illustrations

Frontispiece: Daoist Adept Meditating before the Sānqīng 三清 (Three Purities) iii
Figure 1: Examples of Historical Forms of 鼎 ("Tripod/Crucible") 3
Figure 2: Examples of Seal Script for 道 ("Way") 4
Figure 3: Comparative Pronunciations of 道 ("Way") 5
Figure 4: Calligraphic Rendering of Chapter 1 of the *Dàodé jīng* 道德經 (Scripture on the Dao and Inner Power) by Cáo Zhìhóng 曹志洪 15
Figure 5: Daoist Cosmic Script 18
Figure 6: Five Língbǎo 靈寶 (Numinous Treasure) Talismans 20
Figure 7: Examples of Movement-Specific Daoist Textual Corpuses 23
Figure 8: Reproduction of Opening Woodblock Page of the First Text in the Received *Dàozàng* 道藏 (Daoist Canon) 28
Figure 9: Genres of Daoist Literature and Categories of Daoist Writing 32
Figure 10: Some Important Daoist Scholar-Practitioners 45
Figure 11: Transmission of Daoist Scriptures 61
Figure 12: *Xíngqì yùpèi míng* 行氣玉佩銘 (Jade Ornament Inscription on Circulating Qi) 100
Figure 13: *Wújí tú* 無極圖 (Diagram of Nondifferentiation) 151
Figure 14: Illustration of Huàshān 華山 (Mount Hua) 186
Figure 15: "Lǎojūn rùshān fú 老君入山符" (Lord Lao's Talismans for Entering the Mountains) 189
Figure 16: Ten Elements of Yǎngshēng 養生 (Nourishing Life) 200
Figure 17: Section Titles of the *Yīnfú jīng* 陰符經 (Scripture on the Hidden Talisman) 222
Figure 18: Seven Steps to the Dao 242
Figure 19: *Mèngxiān cǎotáng tú* 夢仙草堂圖 (Dreaming of Immortality in a Thatched Hut) 252
Figure 20: Three Stages of Internal Alchemy 254
Figure 21: *Nèijīng tú* 內經圖 (Diagram of Internal Pathways) 261
Figure 22: Seated Eight Brocades Dǎoyǐn 導引 (Guided Stretching) 284

Figure 23: Section Titles of the *Chóngyáng shíwǔ lùn* 重陽十五論
   (Redoubled Yang's Fifteen Discourses) 290
Figure 24: Three Lóngmén 龍門 (Dragon Gate) Ordination Ranks 302
Figure 25: Illustrations of the Valley Spirit and Original Female 349
Figure 26: List of the 214 Kāngxī 康熙 Character Radicals 357

Abbreviations

abbrev.	abbreviated
b.	born
BCE	Before the Common Era
c.	century
ca.	circa
CE	Common Era
Chn.	Chinese
d.	died
dat.	dated
DDJ	*Dàodé jīng* 道德經 (Scripture on the Dao and Inner Power)
DH	*Dūnhuáng dàozàng* 敦煌道藏 (Dunhuang Daoist Canon)
dis.	discovered
du	dates unknown
DZ	*Dàozàng* 道藏 (Daoist Canon)
Jpn.	Japanese
JY	*Dàozàng jíyào* 道藏集要 (Collected Essentials of the Daoist Canon)
lit.	literally
LZ	*Lǎozǐ* 老子 (Book of Venerable Masters)
LZ*	*Lǎozǐ jíchéng* 老子集成 (Collection on the *Laozi*)
NY	*Nèiyè* 內業 (Inward Training)
r.	ruled
Skt.	Sanskrit
STIDC	"Supplements to *Title Index to Daoist Collections*"
SW	*Huángdì nèijīng sùwèn* 黃帝內經素問 (Yellow Thearch's Inner Classic: Basic Questions)
TIDC	*Title Index to Daoist Collections*
TK	*Tonkō dōkei* 敦煌道經 (Dunhuang Daoist Scriptures)
trad.	traditional
trl.	translated
ZH	*Zhōnghuá dàozàng* 中華道藏 (Chinese Daoist Canon)
ZW	*Zàngwài dàoshū* 藏外道書 (Daoist Texts Outside the Canon)
ZZ	*Zhuāngzǐ* 莊子 (Book of Master Zhuang)

Introduction

Approaching Daoist Literature

The present book is a primer in translating Daoist (Taoist) literature. It is the first such book and the first bilingual Daoist sourcebook. It consists of twenty-eight "lessons" from a wide variety of Daoist texts with accompanying, supplemental materials. While primarily intended for individuals interested in reading Chinese Daoist primary texts in the original, it also may be used to develop bilingual engagement with Daoism and as a sourcebook of Daoist literature.

In this introduction, I first provide some preliminary guidance for beneficial and effective application of the book, specifically with respect to assumed knowledge and related resources. I then move on to discuss Daoist literature more generally. This is followed by a series of reflections on the challenges and opportunities of translation in general and of translating Daoist literature in particular, including the possibility of "Daoist translation." I conclude with an overview of the book as a whole.

Beginning the Inquiry

This book aspires to assist interested individuals in developing a foundational Daoist translation vocabulary and familiarity with representative Daoist literature, perhaps with a resultant skillset for conducting deeper study and translation work. Both may be independent and/or collaborative. I assume at least some elementary knowledge of classical Chinese (*gǔwén* 古文; lit., "ancient writing"), which also is referred to as literary Chinese. While often synonymous, "classical Chinese" is sometimes used in a more technical sense to designate the language of traditional Chinese literature from the end of the Spring and Autumn period (770–480 BCE) to the end of the Eastern/Later Hàn 漢 dynasty (25–220 CE). In a parallel and accompanying manner, "literary Chinese" refers to the form of written Chinese used from the end of the Eastern Hàn dynasty to the early twentieth century, when it was replaced by vernacular written Chinese. We may thus think of literary Chinese as the written language of the educated elite for most of Chinese and East Asian history. This language stands in contrast to "modern Chinese" (*pǔtōnghuà* 普通話; *guóyǔ* 國語), including in the form of the modern mainland Chinese (PRC) use of simplified Chinese characters (*jiǎntǐ zì* 簡體字; *jiǎnhuà zì* 簡化字). Although not an exact correlation, we might think of the relationship of classical Chinese/modern Chinese as akin to Latin/English, or at least Old English/modern English. There are different grammars and often radically different vocabularies, including context-specific technical meanings in the case of Daoist literature. This means that it is possible to read the latter without understanding, let alone interpreting or translating it.

The matter is complexified by historical phonetics. Although so-called "Mandarin" (*guānhuà* 官話 [lit., "officials' speech"]; *pǔtōnghuà* 普通話 [lit., "common speech"]), via the Portuguese *mandarim* ("minister") and associated with "Běijīng dialect" (*Běijīng huà* 北京話; a.k.a. "Pekingese") (see, e.g., Ramsey 1987; Chen 1999), is the official dialect and *lingua franca* of mainland China as well as the international standard, there are both historical phonetics and diverse regional dialects. Here I simply draw attention to the existence of reconstructed phonology for Old Chinese (*shànggǔ Hànyǔ* 上古漢語) (see Karlgren 1957; Schuessler 2009; Baxter and Sagart 2014) and for Middle Chinese (*zhōnggǔ Hànyǔ* 中古漢語) (see Pulleyblank 1984). Old Chinese, also referred to as Archaic Chinese, corresponds to the written language especially associated with ancient oracle bone inscriptions (*jiǎgǔ wén* 甲骨文), bronze inscriptions (zhōngdǐng wén 鐘鼎文), and seal scripts (zhuànshū 篆書) (see fig. 1). These are materials from the Shāng 商 (ca. 1600–ca. 1046 BCE) and Zhōu 周 (ca. 1046–256 BCE) dynasties.

FIGURE 1: Examples of Historical Forms of 鼎 ("Tripod/Crucible")

The time period of Old Chinese roughly corresponds to 1250 BCE to 25 CE, although the rhymes are based on early poetry. Middle Chinese, formerly known as Ancient Chinese, is the historical variety of Chinese recorded in the Qièyùn 切韻 rhyme dictionary first published in 601. The time period of Middle Chinese roughly corresponds to the fifth to twelfth centuries CE, that is, the Northern and Southern Dynasties (386–589) to the middle of the Sòng dynasty (960–1279). Historically speaking, there also are many seal scripts and calligraphy styles (see fig. 2), which is beyond the confines of our work here, but which we will briefly explore in Lesson #5.

In addition, classical Japanese (Rìběn yǔ 日本語 [Nihongo]), specifically as utilizing Chinese characters (Hànzì 漢字 [Kanji]), and classical Korean (Hányǔ 韓語 [Han-eo]), specifically as utilizing Chinese characters (Hànzì 漢字 [Hanja]), were derived from literary Chinese, but employ different pronunciations (see fig. 3). This means that the "same" written language could and can be read with multiple verbal significations.

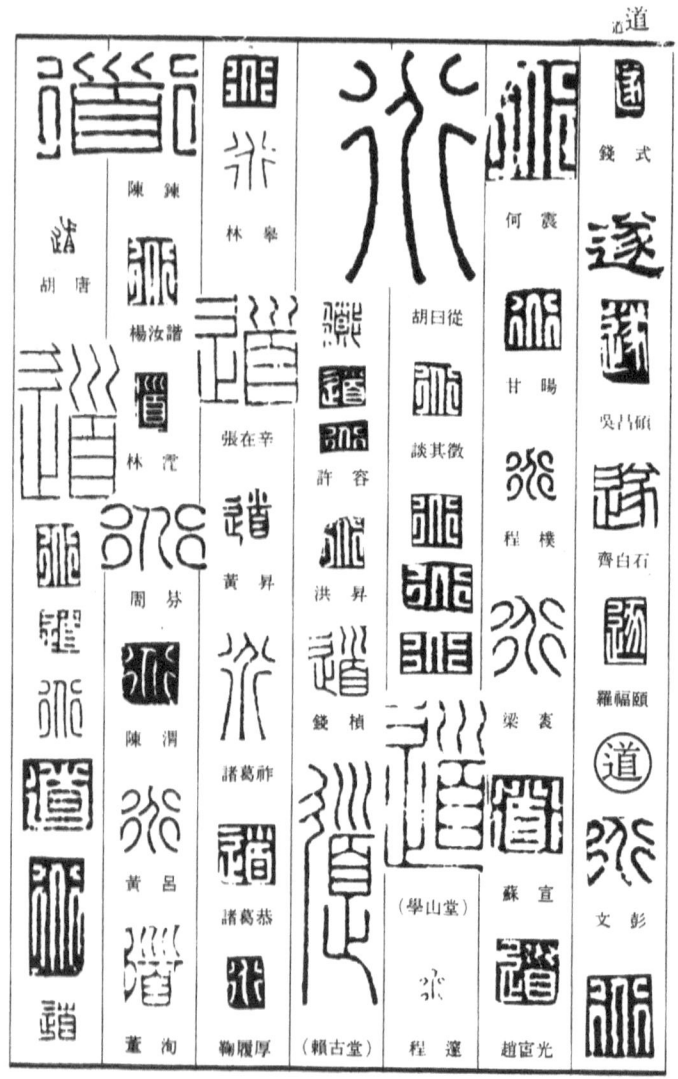

FIGURE 2: Examples of Seal Script for 道 ("Way")
SOURCE: *Zhuànkē zìdiǎn* 篆刻字典
(Seal Engraving Character Dictionary; 1988, 675)[1]

---

[1] For examples of Chǔ 楚 script with modern equivalents for the so-called Guōdiàn 郭店 *Lǎozǐ* 老子 (Book of Venerable Masters), the oldest extant manuscript (dat. ca. 300 BCE; dis. 1993), see Henricks 2000; Cook 2012.

INTRODUCTION: APPROACHING DAOIST LITERATURE

Old Chinese	Middle Chinese	"Mandarin"	"Cantonese"	Japanese	Korean
*kə.lˤuʔ	dawˣ	dào	dou⁶	dō	do

FIGURE 3: Comparative Pronunciations of 道 ("Way")[2]

In the case of the present book, few of the texts would have been read with phonetics resembling modern "Mandarin." While less relevant for our work here, this fact may inspire sufficient pause with respect to assumed rhyme patterns (e.g., in the *Kə.lˤuʔ-*tˤək *k-lˤeŋ 道德經 [*Dàodé jīng*]) or practices utilizing vocalizations (e.g., in the luwk-dzih kwɛt̚ 六字訣 [*liùzì jué*]). It also opens up the possibility of reading without the accompanying modern "Mandarin" pronunciations.

In any case, this book is neither a primer in literary Chinese nor in Chinese language more generally. We are focusing on what might be understood as "Daoist classical Chinese" and "Daoist translation" (see below). I am assuming some familiarity with basic grammar and vocabulary, character composition (including radicals), the ability to work with Chinese dictionaries, and ideally some engagement with the larger Chinese literary tradition.

乾元亨利貞

學而時習之不亦說乎

我善養吾浩然之氣

砍柴挑水

If these are familiar to you, if you can decipher them with a Chinese dictionary, or if they at least have some recognizable characters, then

---

[2] My Romanization for Old Chinese follows Baxter and Sagart 2014, which also is available online in searchable PDF format. For Middle Chinese, I follow Pulleyblank 1984.

this primer will probably be accessible and utilizable. If they are so foreign as to cause anxiety, bewilderment, or alienation, then you may want to begin with some preparatory work, preliminary readings, and background resources. Here I recognize that many readers will be more familiar with modern Chinese and simplified characters, so I simply encourage you to be patient with yourself and focus on gradual progress. We also can work on moving back and forth between traditional and simplified Chinese characters, although I obviously privilege and prefer the former. In terms of developing a basic root in classical Chinese, readers might begin with *Classical Chinese for Everyone* (Van Norden 2019). This may be supplemented with and strengthened by consultation of Michael Fuller's 傅君勱 *An Introduction to Literary Chinese* (2004) and Paul Rouzer's 羅吉偉 *A New Practical Primer of Literary Chinese* (2007), both of which are reliable textbook introductions intended for university courses. As mentioned in the acknowledgments, I received foundational classical Chinese language training at Harvard University (1998–2000) under Rouzer, during which we used a draft manuscript of said textbook.[3] That work thus has a special place in my own memory-palace. A more technical introduction focusing on translating classical Chinese medical literature was published by Paul Unschuld 文樹德 (1988) and on translating Chinese Buddhist texts by Graham Lock and Gary Linebarger (2018). I also have prepared a wide variety of reference materials, many of which I cite later herein and most of which are listed in the bibliography. For the moment, I would recommend familiarizing yourself with Daoist Studies Guides #4: Classical Chinese, which includes a section on foundational classical Chinese grammar and which is included as Appendix #3. This may be utilized in concert with the lessons in the

---

[3] Here I also should mention that my undergraduate degrees were in Literature and Philosophy from the University of California, San Diego (UCSD), with specific interests in English Romanticism, American Transcendentalism, as well as European Existentialism and Phenomenology. In addition, I received the Burkhardt Prize for Literature (1993) for my senior honors thesis, which was a poetry collection titled *Alluvial Fans*. These details may provide some context for understanding my lifelong interest in language and literary theory, interests that helped make me an outlier in mainstream Daoist Studies, though perhaps not in the Daoist tradition itself.

present book. As discussed below, while I do not provide a complete grammar discussion in each "lesson," I emphasize important and paradigmatic elements. I also suggest beginning to memorize some radicals (see Appendix #1 and #2), including stroke count, in order to expedite the use of traditional and modern Chinese-to-Chinese dictionaries. Two of the key ones are the *Shuōwén jiězì* 說文解字 (Discussing Writing and Explaining Characters; dat. 100/121 CE) and the *Hànyǔ dà cídiǎn* 漢語大詞典 (Major Dictionary of Chinese Language; 13 vols.; dat. 1986–1994) (see, e.g., Wilkinson 2018).

Here I also will say that I strongly encourage aspiring Daoist translators to develop manual skills and organic dexterity, to remain intact ("analog"), specifically through the ability to engage *physical texts and actual radical-based dictionaries*. As someone committed to tradition-based Daoist study-practice (*xuéxíng* 學行), with Neo-Luddite leanings, I believe that it is important to find ways of retaining our embodied being and to resist the technopoly, including in the form of corporatized "education" populated by bureaucrats and technocrats. While digitalized texts and electronic dictionaries are helpful and convenient, they should not replace material literature and physical dictionaries, thus the importance of the Daoist Studies Archive 道學檔案館 and Center for Daoist Studies 道學中心 of the Daoist Foundation 道教基金會. We need to be aware of how technology creates patterns of dependency and may become a major liability, including unanticipated alterations of consciousness. 君子不器. In the language of Daoism, perhaps such "contemplative reflections" may inspire a deeper commitment to "nourishing life" (*yǎngshēng* 養生). One also thinks of the Daoist gardener's rejection of a "well-sweep" (*gāo* 槔) and the associated "machine-heart" (*jīxīn* 機心) in chapter twelve of the anonymous/pseudonymous fourth-second century BCE *Zhuāngzǐ* 莊子 (*Chuāng-tzǔ*; Book of Master Zhuang). To maintain and continue the Daoist tradition of reading, and translation by extension, we need to remain attentive to embodiment, community, material culture, and place. This involves developing a greater sense of connection (*tōng* 通), again in multiple forms. There is an aesthetics and art of Daoist translation beyond merely moving signifier-to-signifier. At some point, we may find ourselves in a room at a Daoist translation center with fellow translators engaging in collaborative translation. How and who will we be together? In addition, how will we continue this work when the grid goes down, either temporarily or permanently? (And, yes, the grid will go down.) While this may sound apocalyptic and conspiratorial, it is, in fact, informed by Daoist history and "reading the signs." What would we be reading and translating if Daoists had not preserved and transmitted Daoist manuscripts through the chaos of the Warring States period (480–222 BCE), the book-burning campaigns of the *Dzin (Qín) 秦 (222–206 BCE) and Mongol-Yuán 元 (1279–1368) dynasties, and the "anti-tradition" projects and socio-political instability of the early modern period (1912–1978)? This sense of the vagaries of human-primate history is made all the more intense when we consider the *single* Báiyún guàn 白雲觀 (White Cloud Monastery; Běijīng) copy of the *Dàozàng* 道藏 (Daoist Canon), which became the basis of *all* modern editions (see below). In the words of the *Zhuāngzǐ*, "When the world is without the Dao, the sage survives" (*tiānxià wúdào* 天下無道, *shèngrén shēngyān* 聖人生焉) (ch. 4).

Additionally, I assume basic religious literacy about Daoism, including key figures, movements, and scriptures. I would thus suggest that readers familiarize themselves with the contours of Daoism as documented in my *The Daoist Tradition: An Introduction* (Komjathy 2013b). This includes movement-specific revelations and associated textual corpuses, which we will explore briefly below and in the lessons herein. It also involves adopting and applying what I refer to as the "continuity of tradition" and "lineal view" of Daoism, which centers on the Seven Periods and Four Divisions. My proposed interpretive framework, utilized herein, replaces the outdated and inaccurate bifurcated/Leggean view and truncated/Strickmannian view. The former, centering a division between so-called "philosophical Daoism" [sic] and so-called "religious Daoism" [sic], is epidemic among non-specialists, while the latter, centering on the Tiānshī 天師 (Celestial Masters) movement and related institutional forms of Daoism, is dominant among conventional Sinologists. My book-length discussion may, in turn, be supplemented by various electronic materials, including the Daoist Studies Guides (DSG) on Daoism, Daoist Studies, and Daoist literature, on my Alternate Homepage (www.louiskomjathy.com).

Let us now begin our inquiry proper with an initial Chinese learning exercise and series of linguistic reflections. I have chosen *Dàowén fānyì rùmén* 道文翻譯入門 as the Chinese correlate of *Primer for Translating Daoist Literature*. For native Chinese speakers, *dàowén* 道文 may be somewhat surprising, as it is a bit idiosyncratic. While the phrase primarily is intended to invoke *dàojiào wénxiàn* 道教文獻 ("Daoist literature"), this is not the whole story. As herein employed, *dàowén* (lit., "Dao-pattern") brings attention to the varied forms in which the Dao manifests, including, as we will explore momentarily, cosmic scripts and more material forms such as written literature. It thus connects to *dàojiào wénhuà* 道教文化 ("Daoist culture"), of which literature is only one, albeit a major expression. Here one thinks of the honorific name of the legendary Yǐn Xǐ 尹喜, the Guardian of the Pass, as Wénshǐ 文始 (Literary Beginning). The latter refers to the legendary transmission of the *Dàodé jīng* from Lǎozǐ 老子 ("Master Lao") to Yǐn as the supposed beginning of Daoist literature as such. I also hope that we will begin to imagine translation as a larger process and exercise (see below), with *wén* 文 again suggesting "patterns." In fact, the oracle-bone and bronze-inscription versions of the character (𠆢 / 𠁥) depict a person with a painted or tattooed chest. *Wén* suggests both imprinting and being imprinted, markings and being marked. As we will see, it also might invoke "Daoist criminality" and "Daoist dissidence." In any case, a more conventional "reverse-translation" choice for the title might have utilized *dàojīng* 道經 (lit., "Dao-classic") or *dàoshū* 道書 (lit., "Dao-book"). This would have resulted in *Dàojīng fānyì* 道經翻譯 ("Daoist Scripture Translation") or *Dàoshū fānyì* 道書翻譯 ("Daoist Textual Translation"). However, again as we will discover, many of the texts contained herein are neither "books" nor "classics/scriptures." Another potential alternative would have been *dàojiào* 道教 (lit., "teachings of the Dao") or *dàoxué* 道學 (lit., "study of the Dao"). *Dàojiào* 道教 is one of the primary names for the Daoist tradition as a whole. More technically, it corresponds to "organized Daoism," which is referred to as so-called "religious Daoism" [*sic*] in outdated and inaccurate Orientalist constructions. However, this primer covers the entire Daoist tradition, including *dàojiā* 道家 (lit., "family of the Dao"), or "classical Daoism." That is, we will examine Daoist literature from its earliest beginnings in the mid Warring States period (480–222 BCE), perhaps before, and into the Qīng dynasty (1644–1912). While from a Daoist perspective *dàojiào* encompasses and includes *dàojiā*, this is not necessarily the case in modern Chinese, especially in "non-Daoist" contexts. The second alternative, *dàoxué*, is sometimes used to refer to "Daoist Studies," which is more conventionally designated as *dàojiào yánjiū* 道教研究. However, as the phrase *dàoxué* also refers to late medieval Ruism ("Confucianism"), especially so-called "Neo-Confucianism" as "Way-Learning," this too might have created confusion. More specifically, either of these choices would have resulted in something closer to *Introduction to Daoist Translation*. That is, that title could have been taken to refer to "translating Daoism" and/or "Daoist translation," rather than translating Daoist *literature* as such. *Fānyì* 翻譯 (lit, "turn over and interpret") is the standard Chinese phrase for "translating/translation." *Fān* 翻 consists of *fān/pān* 番 ("repeat") and *yǔ* 羽 ("wings/flutter"), while *yì* 譯 consists of *yán* 言 ("speak/speech") and *yì* 睪 ("spy"). Both *fān*-repeat and *yì*-spy are usually read as phonetics. Understood from a Chinese etymological perspective, *fānyì*/translation involves repeatedly turning over, a circling, a soaring, a crossing, and perhaps even a reversing. As *yì*-interpret suggests, language is involved, although *yán* tends to refer to spoken language (cf. *huà* 話; *yǔ* 語), while *wén* 文 refers to written language. Finally, *rùmén* 入門 (lit., "enter the gates") is sometimes used in the sense of "introduction." A more conventional choice would have been *jièshào* 介紹 (lit., "assisting connection") or *yǐnlùn* 引論 (lit., "guiding discourse"), both of which are used for "introduction." A Daoist selection may have been *zhǐnán* 指南 (lit., "pointing south"), which is used for "guide/guidance." However, I chose *rùmén* not only for its poetic, evocatory quality, but also because of its Daoist associations. The phrase is often employed to refer to formal initiation and even ordination as well as to formal Daoist affiliates (e.g., "disciples"). That is, through this book, one may become an "initiated Daoist translator." Moreover, there are so many "doors," "gates," and "portals" in Daoism, with perhaps the most influential appearing in chapter one of the anonymous fourth-second century BCE *Dàodé jīng* 道德經 (*Tào-té chīng*; Scripture on the Dao and Inner Power):

玄之又玄，
眾妙之門。

Mysterious and again more mysterious,
The gateway to all that is wondrous.

This becomes the inspiration for Xuánmén 玄門 (Mysterious Gate), another, later Daoist name for "Daoism." Thus, *rùmén* suggests entering into the mysteriousness and wondrousness of the Dao itself. The phrase also may be connected to doorsills (*ménkǎn* 門檻; *hùkǔn* 戶梱). Measuring about twelve inches/thirty centimeters high, these are the bottom part of doorframes in traditional Daoist architecture, temples and monasteries in particular. They divide Daoist sacred space/time from ordinary space/time. They also require intentionality and awareness to cross. They establish a threshold and sacred demarcation, creating a different space with a different purpose. Combining these Daoist senses of portals, "entering the gate" may involve a sense of reverence, especially in Daoist translation as such (see below). Finally, for me, as an initiatory process, *rùmén* invokes *zhújī* 築基 (lit., "establishing a foundation") and *chūbù* 初步 (lit, "initial steps"), which generally means "elementary" and/or "preliminary," as well as my own affinity for walking and travel. Applied in Daoist training contexts, *bù* 步 often refers to "stages," with the associated connotation of *jìnbù* 進步 (lit., "advancing steps"), or "making progress." It thus encourages us to move forward with intentionality and to understand translation as gradual progress. For this, commitment, gentleness, patience, and perseverance are necessary companions.

The title in turn not only suggests "translating Daoism," but also "Daoist translation." It brings our attention to the fact that a religious tradition is involved. Our approach may be informed by, and perhaps inspired by and infused with, Daoist principles, qualities, and values. Along these lines, chapter twenty-two of the anonymous mid-fourth century BCE *Nèiyè* 內業 (Inward Training) is especially applicable: "Inwardly still; outwardly reverent" (*nèijìng wàijìng* 內靜外敬). While reverence may be too lofty of a request or requirement at this point, it relates to various other "respect" characters/qualities, including *chóng* 崇 ("esteem"), *guì* 貴 ("honor"), *lǐ* 禮 ("ritual propriety"), *zūn* 尊 ("venerate"), and so forth. These are often associated with the Fire (*huǒ* 火) phase, and with the heart-mind (*xīn* 心) and spirit (*shén* 神) by extension. Translation, especially *with respect to* scriptures (sacred texts) and religious literature, may require a higher degree of decorum and formality. Here one also thinks of the Daoist emphasis on "tradition" (*chuántǒng* 傳統 [lit., "transmit and unite"]) as centering on the external Three Treasures (*wài sānbǎo* 外三寶), namely, the Dao 道 (Tao/Way), scriptures (*jīng* 經), and teachers (*shī* 師) (in this order). In certain respects, the scriptures are manifestations (*shì* 示; *xiàn* 現) and vessels (*qì* 器; *xiàng* 象) of the Dao's numinous presence (*líng* 靈). They provide access points to that sacred Mystery and to the Daoist tradition. Ideally speaking, teachers are aligned with the Dao and informed by the scriptures. This is the Daoist community as a historical and energetic continuum. Translation, understood both literally and symbolically, is one way in which these become joined and mutually infusing.

Daoist Literature

Daoist literature (*dàowén* 道文) refers to literature composed by Daoists, revealed to and/or by Daoists, and revered in the Daoist tradition (*dàotǒng* 道統).[4] Daoist literature is an important element of Daoist culture (*dàojiào wénhuà* 道教文化), specifically related to Daoist hermeneutics, material culture, and scholasticism. Traditionally speaking, Daoist literature was composed and transmitted in/as manuscripts hand-written using calligraphy, and later through woodblock-printed editions and collections. As we will explore momentarily, it was written in classical/literary Chinese (*gǔwén* 古文) with traditional Chinese characters (*fántǐzì* 繁體字; *zhèngtǐzì* 正體字) from top-to-bottom and right-to-left. As mentioned, literary Chinese is the pre-modern literary language of the educated elite.

The history of Daoist literature, including the associated material culture, compositional contexts, and transmission lines, is complex (see, e.g., Komjathy 2013b, 225–42, 286–89). Early manuscripts were written on bamboo (*jiǎn* 簡 [*zhú* 竹]) and then silk (*bó* 帛 [*sī* 絲]) (see Tsien 2004), with hand-woven paper (*zhǐ* 紙) becoming more common from the Eastern/Later Hàn 漢 dynasty (25–220 CE) onward. Although the character for *zhǐ*-paper contains the *mì* 糸/糹 ("silk") radical, also pronounced *sī* (絲), early Chinese paper employed diverse materials, including silk rags, hemp fibers, mulberry bark, worn-out fishing nets, and a variety of other natural materials. The highest quality materials for early paper included plant fibers such as hemp, jute, flax, ramie, and rattan; tree bark of mulberry; grasses, such as bamboo, reeds, and stalks of rice and wheat; and other fibers (Tsien 2004, 161). These details thus bring our attention to the actual materiality of Daoist "book culture" and

---

[4] *Dàotǒng* 道統, literally, "tradition of the Dao," is herein used to encompass the more common (and misunderstood) *dàojiā* 道家 (lit., "family of the Dao") and *dàojiào* 道教 (lit., "teachings of the Dao"). Although *dàotǒng* is most often used to refer to late medieval *Dàoxué* 道學 (Way-Learning; so-called "Neo-Confucianism"), here I engage in a Daoist act of reverse appropriation and of historical and interpretive retrieval. It is Daoism, not Ruism (so-called "Confucianism"), that is the Tradition of the Dao.

the extraordinariness of textual survival. We might pause and consider all of the hands through which Daoist texts passed to reach these hands, my hands and your hands. The earliest extant Daoist manuscripts are the so-called "Bamboo *Lǎozǐ* 老子," from Guōdiàn 郭店 (dat. ca. 300 BCE; dis. 1993; abbrev. GD; see Henricks 2000; Cook 2012), and the early "silk manuscripts" of the same text, specifically from Mǎwángduī 馬王堆 (lit., "Tomb of King Ma"; dat. ca. 168 BCE; dis. 1973; abbrev. MWD; see Henricks 1989; Mair 1993; also Harper 1998). The GD manuscripts were written in Chǔ 楚 script, that is, the writing style associated with the state of *S.ra? (Chǔ) (704–223 BCE) before the standardization of Chinese writing under the *Dzin (Qín) dynasty.⁵ MWD A is written in "small seal script" (*xiǎozhuàn* 小篆) calligraphy (see figs. 1 and 2 above), which was an old style of writing abandoned in the Hàn dynasty, while MWD B uses "clerical script" (*lìshū* 隸書), which was a contemporaneous style. I mention these details to increase our appreciation of and sensibility to various potential reading experiences, beyond the standardization utilized in the present book.

Along these lines, I will again mention calligraphy (*shūfǎ* 書法). Pre-Táng 唐 dynasty (618–907) Daoist literature would have been written, read, and transmitted in calligraphic renderings; manuscripts remained central in much Daoist history; and calligraphy also continues to be a central dimension of modern Daoist aesthetics and culture (see fig. 4). For example, the early Shàngqīng 上清 (Highest Clarity) revelations/scriptures (364–370) were transcribed by the spirit-medium Yáng Xī 楊羲 (330–386) and members of the aristocratic Xǔ 許 family using calligraphy that reportedly appeared numinous (*líng* 靈) and infused with spirit (*shén* 神) (see Robinet 1984, 1993; Komjathy 2022c). Later, after the original manuscripts were distributed to various members and families of the Shàngqīng community, Táo Hóngjǐng 陶弘景 (Tōngmíng 通明 [Pervasive Illumination]; 456–536), the Ninth Shàngqīng Patriarch,

---

⁵ Traditional accounts date the founding of *S.ra? (Chǔ) to around 1030 BCE. Such dating is complex in terms of the degree of socio-political organization and coherence being emphasized.

accomplished herbalist and alchemist, relative of both the Xǔ 許 and Gé 葛 families, as well as eventual community-elder of the Máoshān 茅山 (Mount Mao; near Nánjīng, Jiāngsū) community, sought to collect them.

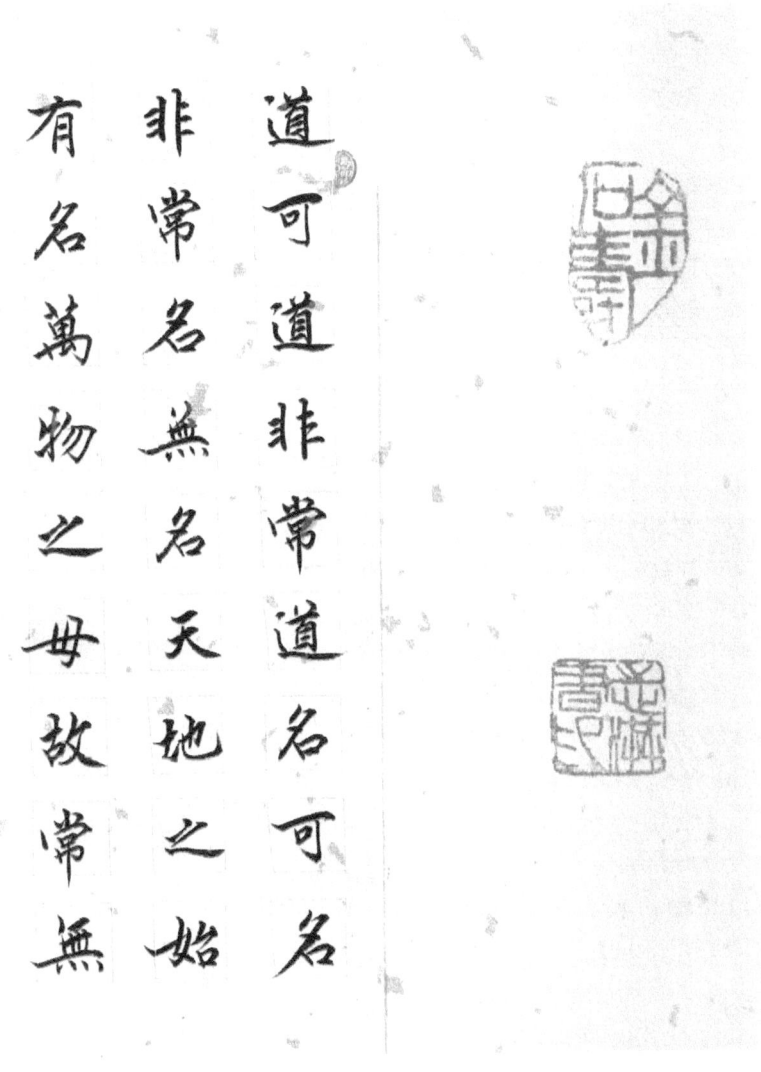

FIGURE 4: Calligraphic Rendering of Chapter 1 of the *Dàodé jīng* 道德經 (Scripture on the Dao and Inner Power) by Cáo Zhìhóng 曹志洪

SOURCE: Author's collection

He developed what might be thought of as an indigenous Chinese Daoist "text-critical method" for distinguishing authentic materials based on calligraphy-style.

> 三君手迹，楊君書最工。不今不古，能大能細。大較雖祖效郄【郗】法，筆力規矩，並於二王，而名不顯者，當以地微。兼為二王所抑故也。掾書乃是學楊，而字體勁利。偏善寫經畫符，與楊相似。鬱勃鋒勢，追非人功所逮。長史章草乃能，而正書古拙，符又不巧。故不寫經也。隱居昔見張道恩善別法書。歎其神識。今睹三君跡，一字一畫，便望影懸了。自思非智藝所及。特天假此監，令有以顯悟爾。

Considering the handwriting of the Three Lords, Lord Yáng's calligraphy is the most skilled. It is neither contemporary nor archaic, and it can be large or thin. Comparatively speaking, although the ancestor imitates the model of Chī 郗, the formal quality of his brushwork is equal to the two Wángs 王. And yet, his renown remained unmanifest because of his humble background and because he was concurrently impeded by the two Wángs. The calligraphy of the Accounts Clerk [Xǔ Huì], then, was learned from Yáng, and his character-structure is powerful and sharp. It was particularly good for copying scriptures and writing talismans, just like Yáng's. Lush and vigorous, with pointed form, it is not something that could be achieved through human effort. The seal and grass [script] of the Chief Secretary [Xǔ Mì], then, was capable, but his normal writing was archaic and clumsy. His talismans also are not skillful. Consequently, he did not copy scriptures.

While living in seclusion, I once met Zhāng Dào'ēn 張道恩, who excelled at distinguishing exemplary calligraphy. He praised their divine markers (*shénshì* 神識). Today, as I observe the traces (*jī* 跡) of the Three Lords, [attentive to] each character and every stroke, I catch a glimpse of presences (yǐng 影) suspended here. I personally think that this is not something that cleverness and artistry could reach; [rather,] the matched heavens lent this mirror so that there would be a means to display awakening (xiǎnwù 顯悟). (Zhēn'gào 真誥 [Declarations of the Perfected], DZ 1016, 19.6ab; cf. Bokenkamp 2021, 47; also Ledderose 1984, especially 258)[6]

Here we may note a Daoist energetic view of "material culture," including a numinous presence in the authentic early Shàngqīng calligraphy. Significantly, according to Táo Hóngjǐng, the "energetic imprint" and "spiritual signature" are still present *even more than a century later*. The passage also interestingly alludes to the famous, contemporaneous master-calligrapher Wáng Xīzhī 王羲之 (303–361), who apparently had some connection with early Shàngqīng, as he brushed a calligraphic rendering of the anonymous third-century CE *Huángtíng jīng* 黃庭經 (Scripture on the Yellow Court; DZ 332; ZH 897) (see Little 2000, 338–39; also Huang 1987–1990; Lesson #12). This piece of calligraphy, dated to 356, is still extant and housed in the Gùgōng bówùyuàn 故宮博物院 (Palace Museum; Běijīng). Like various paintings and poems in the larger contours of traditional Chinese cultural history, this artifact helps to reveal important connections, including Daoist influences and inspiration (see Little 2000; Komjathy 2013b, 281–86).

Along these lines, and especially relevant for thinking about translation from a Daoist perspective, we may briefly consider Daoist views of language and scripture. We will explore "Daoist linguistics" and "Daoist lexigraphy," including what I refer to as "Daoist etymology," throughout the present book. For the moment, I would like to bring attention

---

[6] The "Three Lords" (sānjūn 三君) are Yáng Xī, Xǔ Mì 許謐 (303–376), and his son Xǔ Huì 許翽 (341-ca. 370). The latter are referred to in the passage as the Chief Secretary (zhǎngshǐ 長史) and Accounts Clerk ([jì]yuàn [計]掾), respectively. Chī refers to the scholar-official Chī Yīn 郗愔 (313–384), the father of Chī Chāo 郗超 (336–377) and friend of the forthcoming. The "two Wangs" refer to the calligraphers Wáng Xīzhī 王羲之 (303–361) and his son Wáng Xiànzhī 王獻之 (344–388), to whom we will return momentarily. Zhāng Dào'ēn is otherwise unidentified.

to esoteric Daoist language, Daoist character-styles in particular. This includes things like "Brahma-language" (fànyǔ 梵語),[7] "cloud-seals" (yúnzhuàn 雲篆) and "cloud-script" (yúnzhāng 雲章), "incantations/invocations" (zhòu 咒/呪), and talismans (fú 符). These, in turn, relate to "effulgences" (jǐng 景), "immortality/transcendence" (xiān 仙), "numinosity" (líng 靈), "perfection" (zhēn 眞/真), "spirit/divinity" (shén 神), "subtle breath/energy" (qì 氣/炁), and associated experiences, qualities, and states. As depicted in the twelfth-century Língbǎo dàfǎ 靈寶大法 (Great Rites of Numinous Treasure; DZ 1221, 15.6ab; cf. DZ 22; DZ 1223), these are "stylized" Daoist characters related to cosmic scripts and primordial ethers (see fig. 5).

FIGURE 5: Daoist Cosmic Script
SOURCE: Língbǎo dàfǎ 靈寶大法 (Great Rites of Numinous Treasure; DZ 1221), 15.6ab (author's collection)

---

[7] This script obviously developed indirectly under Indian, specifically Hindu views and applications of Sanskrit. See, e.g., Zürcher 1980; Bokenkamp 1983, 1997; Capitanio 2018; also Sharf 2005; Mollier 2008.

The selected section, which is titled "Yùzhuàn liùshísì zì 玉篆六十四字" (Sixty-four Characters of the Jade Seal Script), illustrates the enlarged Daoist characters with the standard Chinese characters underneath.

真	化	通	空	妙	炁
zhēn	huà	tōng	kōng	miào	qì
perfect	transform	pervade	empty	wondrous	qi

This resembles a primer in Daoist vocabulary and attendant states: Perfected transformation, pervasive emptiness, and wondrous qi. The specifically Daoist languages of talismans and the like are, in turn, an extremely complex topic, both in terms of lived/living Daoist practice and Daoist Studies. They are among the most advanced constituents of translating Daoist literature on a "masters-level" and far beyond our current concerns and project. However, this dimension of the Daoist tradition in general and Daoist scriptures in particular offers an important opportunity for reflecting more deeply on the work of Daoist translation.

With respect to talismans (*fú* 符) (see Lessons #13 and #16), also referred to as "contracts/tallies" (*qì* 契) (see Lesson #11), these originally were objects used in ancient China for agreements and communication. Technically speaking, they consist of two pieces from an originally intact object, the breaking of which results in two unforgeable and uniquely related objects. In terms of Daoism, talismans consist of a "celestial" (*tiān* 天) part and "terrestrial" (*dì* 地) counterpart, also referred to as "numinous" (*líng* 靈) and "treasure" (*bǎo* 寶), respectively. When rejoined, they reveal original unity and result in efficacious influence. Two of the more famous examples are the Perfect Forms of the Five Marchmounts (*wǔyuè zhēnxíng* 五嶽真形) (DZ 441/ZH 281) and the Five Numinous Treasure Talismans (*língbǎo wǔfú* 靈寶五符) (DZ 388/ZH 222) (see fig. 6; Komjathy 2013b, 269–71).

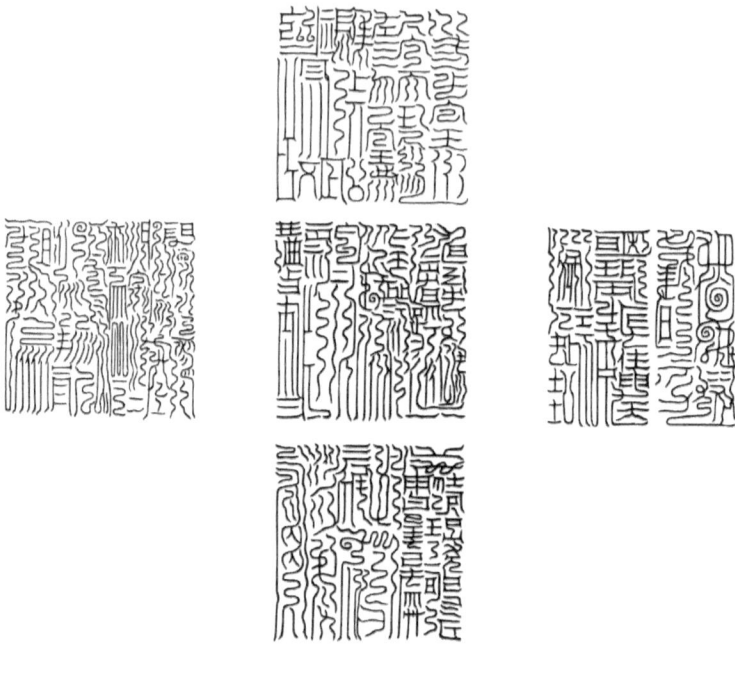

FIGURE 6: Five Língbǎo 靈寶 (Numinous Treasure) Talismans (Southern Orientation)

SOURCE: *Língbǎo wǔfú xù* 靈寶五符序 (Explanations of the Five Numinous Treasure Talismans), DZ 388, 3.9b-12b (author's collection)

We may, in turn, think of Daoist translation as talismanic: It links us to something larger than ourselves, perhaps unseen presences and influences. The "talisman of translation" also involves finding a close connection between the source-language (Chinese herein) and the target-language (English herein), which I will discuss in more detail momentarily.

Thus, Daoist scriptures are talismanic, at least on some level. Traditionally speaking, Daoists also tend to view scriptures as more than merely material. As we saw with the previous example from Táo Hóngjǐng and Shàngqīng Daoism, Daoist languaging and composition may be revelatory, in an ongoing sense. These and other examples may inspire sufficient pause concerning the possibility of alteration, connection, opening, and transformation through reading Daoist literature in the original, and perhaps in "talismanic translation" as well. From a Daoist perspective, this includes the possibility that there are "ethereal editions" and "celestial counterparts" of physically-manifested scriptures.

此諸天中大梵隱語、無量之音。舊文字皆廣長一丈。天真皇人昔書其文，以為正音。有知其音，能齋而誦之者，諸天皆遣飛天神王，下觀其身，書其功勤。上奏諸天。

These are the Inexhaustible Tones of the Hidden Language (*yǐnyǔ* 隱語) of the Great Brahma of All-the-Heavens. Formerly, the ancient graphs were all one *zhàng* square. In the past, the Sovereign of Celestial Perfection wrote out this script [in terrestrial characters] in order to reveal the correct pronunciations (*zhèngyīn* 正音). For those who know the pronunciations and who can go into retreat (*zhāi* 齋) and recite (*sòng* 誦) them, the various heavens will send down divine kings who fly through the heavens to keep watch over their bodies and record their meritorious diligence. The former will be reported back to the heavens. (*Dùrén jīng* 度人經 [Scripture on Salvation], DZ 1, 4.18a; cf. Bokenkamp 1997, 430; see also DZ 1016, 19.9b)

尋道家經誥，起自三元；從本降跡，成於五德。以三就五，乃成八會。其八會之字，妙氣所成。八角垂芒，凝空雲篆。太真按筆，玉妃拂筵；黃金為書，白玉為簡。秘於諸天之上，藏於七寶玄臺。有道即見，無道即隱。蓋是自然天書。

Examining the scriptures and declarations of the Family of the Dao (*dàojiā* 道家), they arose from the Three Primes (*sānyuán* 三

元). As descended traces (*jī* 跡) from the Source (*běn* 本), they developed into the Five Virtues (*wǔdé* 五德). Combining three with five, they then became the Eight Assemblies (*bāhuì* 八會). The characters of the Eight Assemblies were formed out of wondrous qi (*miàoqì* 妙氣). The Eight Corner-points (*bājiǎo* 八角) sent forth rays that coalesced in the Void as cloud-seals. The great Perfected pressed the brushes and the jade maidens swept the mats. [They used] yellow gold to make writs and pure jade to make tablets. They concealed them above the various heavens; they stored them in the Mysterious Tower of Seven Treasures. If one has the Dao, they manifest; if one is without the Dao, they remain hidden. Generally speaking, they are spontaneously revealed (*zìrán* 自然) celestial books. (*Yúnjí qīqiān* 雲笈七籤 [Seven Slips from a Cloudy Satchel], DZ 1032, 3.2b; cf. Wang 2010, 776; see also Lessons #7 and #9)[8]

Thus, Daoist scriptures are more than "books," especially in their more primordial and early "material" forms. Again, this helps us consider what is actually, or might be, involved in "translation."

Moving beyond these general points, which are informed by materials associated with a variety of Daoist movements and historical periods, we may briefly consider the history of Daoist literature, both with respect to textual affiliations and the larger, integrated tradition (see Komjathy 2013b, 17–36, 225–42; Komjathy 2022f; bibliography herein). Just as there is no single founder or primary community in the Daoist tradition, so too there is no single central scripture. Different Daoist adherents and communities privilege different scriptures. While the

---

[8] The Three Primes are synonymous with the Sānqīng 三清 (Three Purities), anthropomorphic representations of the three primordial cosmic ethers. Here the Five Virtues are place-holders for the Five Phases (*wǔxíng* 五行). Based on context, the Eight Assemblies most likely refer to the eight trigrams (*bāguà* 八卦). The Eight Corner-points are another name for the Eight Boundaries (*bāyú* 八隅) and Eight Poles (*bājí* 八極), that is, the four cardinal and four ordinal directions. The opening part of the passage is thus discussing Daoist cosmogonic emanation, specifically through the process of yin-yang differentiation and interaction.

anonymous fourth-second century BCE *Lǎozǐ* 老子 (*Lǎo-tzǔ*; Book of Venerable Masters), more commonly referred to with its honorific title of *Dàodé jīng* 道德經 (*Tào-té chīng*; Scripture on the Dao and Inner Power; see Komjathy forthcoming), is probably the most influential and consistently privileged text in Daoist history, it is an oversimplification to think of that text as the central scripture of Daoism.⁹ In fact, when speaking about texts in the Daoist tradition from a historical perspective, we should first discuss movement-specific textual corpuses (see fig. 7). Moreover, different scriptures occupy a central position in different Daoist movements and lineages.

Inner Cultivation Lineages	Tàiqīng 太清 (Great Clarity)	Quánzhēn 全真 (Complete Perfection)
Lǎozǐ 老子 (Book of Venerable Masters; DZ 664; ZH 552) and *Zhuāngzǐ* 莊子 (Book of Master Zhuang; DZ 670; ZH 616)	*Jīnyè jīng* 金液經 (Scripture on Potable Gold; in DZ 917; ZH 704); *Jiǔdān jīng* 九丹經 (Scripture on the Nine Elixirs; DZ 885; ZH 702); and *Tàiqīng jīng* 太清經 (Scripture of Great Clarity; in DZ 883; ZH 694)	*Dàodé jīng* 道德經 (Scripture on the Dao and Inner Power; DZ 664; ZH 552); *Qīngjìng jīng* 清靜經 (Scripture on Clarity and Stillness; DZ 620; ZH 350); and *Yīnfú jīng* 陰符經 (Scripture on the Hidden Talisman; DZ 31; ZH 642)

FIGURE 7: Examples of Movement-Specific Daoist Textual Corpuses¹⁰

---

⁹ Regrettably, we also must note the systematic appropriation, distortion, and exploitation of this *Daoist text* across the entire spectrum of "connoisseurs of Daoism," from scholars of so-called "Chinese philosophy" (*zhōngguó zhéxué* 中國哲學)/"Daoist (disembodied) thought" (*dàojiào sīxiǎng* 道教思想) through hybrid spiritualists. This includes what may be referred to as the "Tao Te Ching Translation Industry" (TTCTI). See Komjathy 2004, 2014b, forthcoming; also Hardy 1998; LaFargue and Pas 1998; Siegler 2010; Carmichael 2017. As we will explore, in addition to originating in the inner cultivation lineages of classical Daoism, which was a series of contemplative and mystical communities, the text became and is recognized as having sacred standing in the larger Daoist tradition, often accompanied by distinctive Daoist ways of reading, interpreting, and applying this key Daoist scripture. See below; Lessons #7 and #25–28.

¹⁰ Here *jīnyè* 金液 is translated in the more technical Tàiqīng outer alchemical (*wàidān* 外丹) sense of "potable gold," that is, liquified gold that is ingested as an ingredient of immortality. In inner cultivation contexts, especially internal alchemy (*nèidān* 內丹), the phrase is an esoteric name for saliva and thus better translated as "golden fluids" or "golden liquid."

These are representative and instructive. The textual corpus of the inner cultivation lineages of classical Daoism (4th-2nd c. BCE), which from a revisionist perspective actually consists of a much larger collection (see Lessons #6–9), were anthologies of the teachings and practices of various anonymous, pseudonymous, and occasionally named elders and teachers. These were loosely related master-disciple communities with a shared approach, practice repertoire, and worldview, including soteriology (ultimate purpose) and theology (sacred). Along with other, related works (e.g., *Lièzǐ* 列子 [Book of Master Lie]), usually from later historical periods, these texts eventually received the honorific designation of *jīng* 經 and were engaged in diverse ways in the later periods of Daoist history. The earliest known actual Daoist *jīng*, a specific literary genre that we will explore momentarily, were revealed and composed in early Daoism (2nd c. CE). This led to the distinct revelations and associated scriptures of early medieval Daoism (3rd-6th c. CE), including Tàiqīng 太清 (Great Clarity). Although most often associated with Gé Hóng 葛洪 (Bàopǔ 抱朴 [Embracing Simplicity]; 283–343) (see Lessons #3 and #13), there actually were three earlier works considered to be the scriptural core of the Tàiqīng sub-tradition. Here we should mention that the associated manuscripts and their derivatives were extremely rare and prized. Possession of them indicated lineal connection, and these were often transmitted during formal initiation and/or ordination (*chuánshòu* 傳授) rituals.

受之者以金人金魚投於東流水中以為約，啑血為盟。無神仙之骨，亦不可得見此道也。合丹當於名山之中，無人之地。結伴不過三人。先齋百日，沐浴五香，致加精潔。勿近穢汙，及與俗人往來。又不令不信道者知之，謗毀神藥，藥不成矣。

For those who do receive this, they must throw a gold human and gold fish [statue] into an eastward-flowing waterway as an oath and smear their lips with blood as a covenant. Without the bones of a divine immortal, it will indeed be impossible to encounter this Way. Preparing the elixir should be undertaken in an uninhabited place on a famous mountain. The number of companions should not exceed three. First purify yourself for one hundred days and bathe yourself with the five fragrances so that you reach essential cleanliness. Do not approach anything that pollutes or associate with ordinary people. In addition, do not allow those who do not trust in the Dao (xìndào 信道) to know about this, as [if] they besmirch the divine medicine, the medicine will not complete. (Bàopǔzǐ nèipiān 抱朴子內篇 [Inner Chapters of Master Embracing Simplicity], DZ 1185, 4.6b)

Such key scriptures also later became incorporated into a standardized and systematized ordination hierarchy with corresponding textual corpuses (see Benn 1991; Kohn 2003, 2004c; Komjathy 2013b, 57–60). While the Tàiqīng, Shàngqīng, and Língbǎo movements had their own tradition-specific *jīng*, Quánzhēn 全真 (Complete Perfection), the most influential movement of late medieval Daoism (7th-14th c.), did not. Instead, Quánzhēn adopted earlier, independent Daoist scriptures from various historical periods as its foundational scriptures (see Lessons #16 and #17). Interestingly, the senior representatives of early Quánzhēn Daoism preferred what might be thought of as "occasional" and "context-specific" teachings and writings, specifically in the form of poetry (*shīcí* 詩詞), including as collected in anthologies (*jí* 集), and discourse records (*yǔlù* 語錄) (see Lesson #23). These were adapted and adaptable to the needs and capacities of a given student or community.

These various movement-specific textual corpuses were eventually collected in what became known as the *Dàozàng* 道藏 (Daoist Canon; abbrev. DZ), which became authoritative beginning in the eleventh century and remains the primary Daoist textual collection. Literally meaning "storehouse of the Dao," and intimately connected to the predecessor Three Caverns (*sāndòng* 三洞) cataloguing system of Lù Xiūjìng 陸修靜 (Yuándé 元德 [Primordial Virtue]; 406–477), a major Daoist compiler, ritualist, and organizer in fifth-century south China, the principal codifier of the Língbǎo corpus of scriptures, and a central figure in the medieval Buddho-Daoist debates, *Dàozàng* actually refers to a variety of historical *canons*, or Daoist collectanea. Prior to the Míng-dynasty textual collection, there were four antecedent Daoist Canons. The first two of these were compiled during the Northern Sòng 宋 dynasty (960–1127), followed by one during the Jurchen-Jīn 金 dynasty (1115–1234) and another during the Mongol-Yuán 元 dynasty (1279–1368). They were as follows:

1. *Dà Sòng tiāngōng bǎozàng* 大宋天宮寶藏 (Precious Canon of the Celestial Palace of the Great Song Dynasty; dat. 1019; lost)

2. *Zhènghé wànshòu dàozàng* 政和萬壽道藏 (Daoist Canon for the Endless Longevity of the Zhenghe Reign Period; dat. 1119; lost)

3. *Dà Jīn xuándū bǎozàng* 大金玄都寶藏 (Precious Canon of the Mysterious Metropolis of the Great Jin Dynasty; dat. 1191; lost)

4. *Xuándū bǎozàng* 玄都寶藏 (Precious Canon of the Mysterious Metropolis; dat. 1244; lost), perhaps more accurately referred to as the *Dà Yuán xuándū bǎozàng* 大元玄都寶藏 (Precious Canon of the Mysterious Metropolis of the Great Yuan Dynasty; lost)

The "received *Dàozàng*" was compiled during the Míng 明 dynasty (1368–1644). Technically speaking, it consists of the *Dà Míng dàozàng jīng* 大明道藏經 (Scriptures of the Daoist Canon of the Great Ming Dynasty), which is more commonly referred to as the *Zhèngtǒng dàozàng* 正統道藏 (Daoist Canon of the Zhengtong Reign Period), and its Wànlì 萬曆 reign (1573–1620) addition titled *Xù dàozàng* 續道藏 (Supplement to the Daoist Canon). As received, it consists of 1,487 titles, sometimes including multiple individual works, in 5,558 scrolls (*juǎn* 卷) (abbrev. "j.")

and consisting of 1,120 fascicles (*cè* 冊) (abbrev. "fasc.") in traditional stitch-bound editions. Here we should note that *juǎn*-scroll is a counting unit and paper classifier for traditional Chinese books, often resembling a designation for a length of paper. These two terms may create confusion for a variety of reasons. Daoist *juǎn* may be of varying lengths; Daoist texts may consist of multiple *juǎn*; and some *juǎn* contain multiple texts. In some items, *juǎn* corresponds to "chapters" (see Lesson #3 herein), more technically referred to as *piān* 篇 or *zhāng* 章. Additionally, *juǎn* is sometimes translated as "fascicle" and "volume," which may create confusion with *cè*-fascicle. Similarly, the latter is also used to refer to modern "volumes." For clarity's sake, I prefer "scroll" and "fascicle," respectively, while rendering *juǎn* as "chapter" in specific cases.

There is no need to rehearse the history and complex organization of the received *Dàozàng* here (see, e.g., Komjathy 2002; Schipper and Verellen 2004; bibliography herein). However, we should be aware of some details, especially as most of the passages explored in this primer derive from texts preserved and contained in the *Dàozàng*. First, like all such Daoist culture-preserving activities, the collection effort was overseen by Daoists, in this case members of the Zhèngyī 正一 (Orthodox Unity) movement. Two key project-leaders were Zhāng Yǔchū 張宇初 (1361–1410), the 43rd Celestial Master, and Zhāng Yǔqīng 張宇清 (d. 1426), the 44th Celestial Master. Second, the possibility and completion of these Daoist Canons in general and the Míng-dynasty *Dàozàng* in particular were directly connected to developments in print technology and book production, specifically the invention of woodblock printing (*diāobǎn yìnshuā* 雕版印刷; *mùbǎn yìnshuā* 木版印刷) in the Táng dynasty (618–907) (see Tsien 2004; Komjathy 2013b, 286–89). Allowing greater textual dissemination, woodblock printing and the production of woodblock editions involve a process of reproduction with ink on paper or other surfaces from a reverse or negative image. On a material culture level, it contains at least three essential elements: a flat surface, originally cut in relief, containing a mirror image of whatever is to be printed; the preparation of the mirror image; and the transfer of the impression of this image onto the surface to be printed (Tsien 1985, 132–33). In the case of woodblock printing, hand-written calligraphy must be carved on woodblocks, which are then dipped in ink and pressed on paper. For stitch-bound editions, each page is then folded in half, stacked, and finally stitched into fascicles. Thus, when we open the received *Dàozàng* and read the texts reproduced therein, we are seeing reproductions of earlier woodblock editions (see fig. 8).

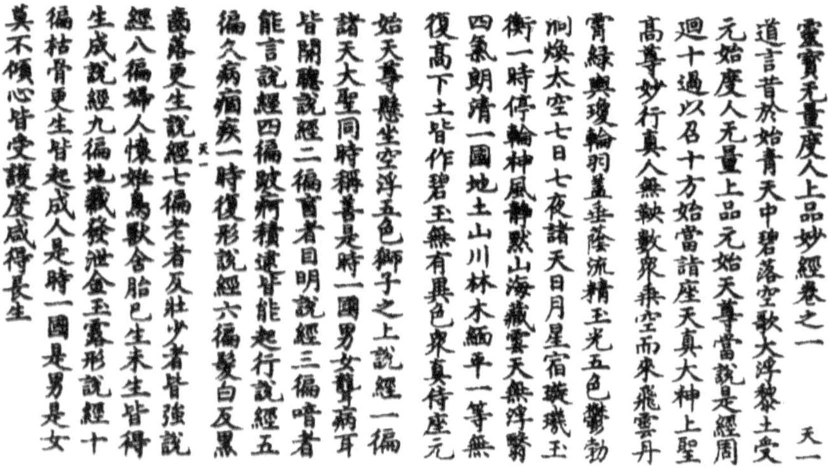
天一
靈寶无量度人上品妙經卷之一
道言昔於始青天中碧落空歌大浮黎土受
元始度人无量上品元始天尊當說是經周
迴十過以召十方始當詣座天真大神上聖
高尊妙行真人無鞅數衆乘空而來飛雲丹
霄綠輿瓊輪羽蓋垂蔭流精玉光五色鬱勃
洞煥太空七日七夜諸天日月星宿璇璣玉
衡一時停輪神風靜默山海藏雲天無浮翳
四氣朗清一國地土山川林木緬平一等無
復高下土皆作碧玉無有異色衆真侍座元
始天尊懸坐空浮五色獅子之上說經一徧
諸天大聖同時稱善是時一國男女聾病耳
皆開聰說經二徧盲者目明說經三徧瘖者
能言說經四徧跛疴積逮皆能起行說經五
徧久病痼疾一時復形說經六徧髮白反黑
天一
齒落更生說經七徧老者反壯少者皆強說
經八徧婦人懷姙鳥獸含胎已生未生皆得
生成說經九徧地藏發泄金玉露形說經十
徧枯骨更生皆起成人是時一國是男是女
莫不傾心皆受護度咸得長生

FIGURE 8: Reproduction of Opening Woodblock Page of the First Text in the Received *Dàozàng* 道藏 (Daoist Canon)
SOURCE: *Dùrén jīng* 度人經 (Scripture on Salvation), DZ 1, 1.1ab (author's collection)

As mentioned, Daoist texts, following pre-modern Chinese writing and reading practices, are traditionally printed from top-to-bottom and right-to-left. Here we may recall and perhaps be inspired to deepen our engagement with Chinese calligraphy. Said texts also are unpunctuated in a conventional Western sense, except for occasional grammatical characters (e.g., *ér* 而, *gù* 故, *hū* 乎, *yě* 也, *zāi* 哉) (see Appendix #3). High-quality reprintings in turn include the traditional page numbers on the upper ledger, while more economical, "reduced editions" exclude these. In looking at a DZ page, the center white "dots" are residual traces of the originary material artifact: They show the paper-piercings from stitch-binding and fold-markings of the page. The standard DZ citation method utilized in Daoist Studies involves noting the folio/page (*yè* 頁) number first, followed by "a" and "b" for the *recto* (right/front) and *verso* (left/back) side of a given woodblock page, respectively. If the text consists of more than one scroll, as in the above example, one records the scroll number first. Thus, if we were citing the second half of this page, it would read 1.1b. Along these lines, we should at least be somewhat sensitive to the fact that modern digitalized editions, usually reproduced using Western-style formatting (left-to-right, top-to-bottom) with Western punctuation, bring one much closer to *simulacra* (copies without an original), and farther away from the source, especially with respect to Daoist aesthetics, embodied being, material culture, reading experiences, transmission, and so forth. Third and finally, only one known complete copy of the Míng-dynasty *Dàozàng*, that of Báiyún guàn 白雲觀 (White Cloud Monastery; Běijīng; abbrev. BYG), survived the onslaughts of modern Chinese history, although the actual printing-blocks were destroyed during the Boxer Rebellion in 1900. The BYG copy became the basis of all modern editions (see Komjathy 2022f). This might again inspire sufficient pause: Without the efforts of so many Daoists, named and unnamed, apparently including underground and covert actions, a major source of Daoist culture would have been lost, and Daoist Studies as we know it would not exist. The same might be true of tradition-based global Daoism.

The Míng-dynasty Daoist Canon has, in turn, been thoroughly catalogued in the *Historical Companion to the Daozang* (abbrev. HCDZ), which is a key collaborative reference work for Daoist Studies that was edited by Kristofer Schipper 施舟人 (1934–2021) and Franciscus Verellen 傅飛嵐. The catalogue follows the earlier standardized numbering system of Schipper and his colleagues (1975; see also Shī and Chén 1996; cf. Rèn and Zhōng 1991; Komjathy 2002), which is abbreviated "CT" or "DZ" and is now standard in Daoist Studies. Although monumental and comprehensive, the three-volume work is not definitive. As the editors themselves note, "We kept fast to the idea that we should aim to say the first word about a given text, not the last" (47). The contributors have obviously done much more than that. For present purposes, one noteworthy and helpful contribution is the distinction between "texts in general circulation" and "texts in internal circulation," or public/outer texts and private/inner texts. At the same time, there are a variety of issues, especially for our project as outlined herein. Specifically, the individual entries often lack English translations of the original Chinese text titles, frequently only offering a paraphrase. The work also fails to establish standardized abbreviated titles (cf. Komjathy 2007, 2022b; herein), which represents a major lost opportunity. In addition, many of the categorizations and textual families are debatable, if not inaccurate; one of the most problematic categories is "philosophy," which many, if not most of said works are not (cf. Komjathy forthcoming). Finally, some of the entry authors are not reliable authorities, and many relevant academic publications are excluded or intentionally omitted. The latter practice unfortunately perpetuates various dysfunctional patterns in the larger (smaller) Sinological field, especially as what may be labelled "politicized Daoist Studies." One of the most egregious is the failure to cite the *Title Index to Daoist Collections* (TIDC; 2002), while at the same time apparently consulting and perhaps utilizing that work. This is particularly regrettable because the latter cross-indexes DZ texts with other editions. Here we also should note that, partially due to the date of the received Daoist Canon, there has been general neglect of late imperial Daoism, especially during the Qīng 清 dynasty (1644–1912), and into the modern period. This is especially lamentable because of the emergence and expansion of the Lóngmén 龍門 (Dragon Gate) lineage of the Quánzhēn monastic order during this time.

Although the Míng-dynasty *Dàozàng* 道藏 remains the primary source for accessing Daoist canonical writings utilized in Daoist Studies, there are many "extra-canonical" and "supplemental" textual collections, which are sometimes miscategorized and miscatalogued as "subsidiary."

These have been catalogued in *Title Index to Daoist Collections* (abbrev. TIDC), which is the definitive and standard work on the subject.[11] I also have continued my cataloguing and indexing work in the more recent electronic series titled "Supplements to *Title Index to Daoist Collections*" (abbrev. STIDC) (2022-), with the associated introductions providing background information and brief discussion of the relevant contents. In addition, each individual catalogue provides standardized abbreviations and numbering systems in a manner paralleling Kristofer Schipper et al.'s earlier DZ catalogue. As appearing herein, I follow those abbreviations and numbers, with notes supplied at the first appearance. These various materials, including an updated, comprehensive and comparative DZ index, will eventually be published under the tentative title *Catalogue of Daoist Textual Collections*. Here I also would recommend that readers familiarize themselves with my various Daoist Studies Articles Online (DSAO) and Daoist Studies Guides (DSG). Most relevant for the moment are "Research Guide to Daoist Studies," "Daoist Literature," and "Catalogue of Daoist Compendia, Collectanea, and Encyclopedias" (see bibliography herein), which are posted on my Alternate Homepage.

Paralleling the Míng-dynasty *Dàozàng* with respect to Daoist textual collections, *jīng* 經 are the most important, authoritative, and venerated genre of Daoist literature. The character consists of the *mì* 糸 / 糹 ("silk") radical, also pronounced *sī* (絲), and *jīng* 巠 ("underground stream"). Although the latter is conventionally understood as a phonetic, from a Daoist perspective it suggests something else and something more (see Appendix #6 herein). *Jīng* are threads and watercourses forming and reforming networks of connection. While often translated as "classic" in terms of Ruism ("Confucianism") and "sutra" in terms of Buddhism, "scripture," in the sense of sacred text with authoritative status, is the best choice for Daoist literature. This includes with respect to classical Daoist texts (see Komjathy 2013b, forthcoming), which are often mischaracterized and misrepresented as "philosophy." Daoist

---

[11] Again, among scholars and intellectuals, not politicians and technocrats.

jīng-scriptures are usually anonymous and considered revealed and/ or inspired (see above; Lessons #1, #10, #12, #16, #17, *passim*). As they usually lack specific historical details, this genre of Daoist literature is notoriously difficult to date and determine provenance. While much of our work in this primer will focus on important and representative Daoist scriptures, there are many other genres of Daoist literature and categories of Daoist writing (see fig. 9).

biǎo 表 (announcements)	piān 篇 (treatises)
fāng 方 (formulas)	shī 詩 (poetry)
fú 符 (talismans)	sòng 頌 (hymns/odes)
gē 歌 (songs)	tú 圖 (charts/diagrams)
jì 記 (records)	wén 文 (writs)
jí 集 (anthologies/collections)	yìn 印 (seals)
jiè 戒/誡 (precepts)	zàn 讚 (elegies/eulogies/memorials)
jiě 解 (explanations)	zhāng 章 (petitions)
jué 訣 (instructions)	zhì 志/誌 (records)
lù 錄 (records)	zhòu 咒/呪 (incantations/invocations)
lù 籙 (registers)	zhù 註/注 (commentaries)
lùn 論 (discourses)	zhuàn 傳 (biographies/hagiographies)
míng 銘 (inscriptions)	zǐ 子 (masters/teachers)

FIGURE 9: Genres of Daoist Literature and Categories of Daoist Writing

Translating Daoist Literature

Translation is an art, a discipline, and a practice. Translation involves commitment, actually a variety of commitments. While commonly framed as derivative, and even parasitic, skillful and elegant translation is its own unique undertaking and achievement. A new, albeit related composition is created, and this work deserves recognition and respect as such. As we will explore momentarily, if well-executed with "right" intention and motivation, translation may be considered an offering and a transmission. The English word "translation," in turn, derives from the Latin *trānslātiō* (via *trānsferō*), which comes from *trāns* ("across") and *ferre* ("carry"). Thus, translation is a "carrying across" and "carrying over." This involves moving from a given source-language (Chinese herein) to a specific target-language (English herein), ideally with attentiveness, intentionality, and fidelity. Along these lines, as we traverse this path, we should note that Daoist literature is increasingly being "translated" (commodified and monetized) by individuals who do not know Chinese. Technically speaking, these are not "translations," which requires advanced language facility and bilingualism, perhaps multilingualism; rather, in terms of "translation studies" (see below), they most often are "versions" or "adaptations." In the case of Daoist texts, the former usually involves using other translations to create new pseudo-translations in conformity to dominant cultural values and audience expectations, while the latter involves creating new compositions, often with little or no connection to the original text.[12] As here we are considering and engaging in actual translation in a bilingual manner, and ideally avoiding cognitive imperialism, linguistic hegemony, and Orientalism, we also should recall *fānyì* 翻譯 (lit, "turn over and interpret"), which is the standard Chinese phrase for "translating/translation." Again, *fān* 翻 consists of *fān/pān* 番 ("repeat") and *yǔ* 羽 ("wings/flutter"), while *yì* 譯 consists of *yán* 言 ("speak/speech") and *yì* 睪 ("spy"). Both *fān*-repeat and *yì*-spy are usually read as phonetics. Understood from a Chinese etymological perspective, *fānyì*/translation involves repeatedly turning

---

[12] With(out) respect to the *Dàodé jīng*, Stephen Mitchell and Ursula LeGuin are (unfortunately) influential versions, while Wayne Dyer is (unfortunately) an influential adaptation. Despite their broad appeal, these are not translations, but popular appropriations and commodifications of the *Dàodé jīng*, and thus are personal interpretations unmoored to direct knowledge of Chinese language, traditional Chinese culture, or classical Daoism as such. For critical discussions see Hardy 1998; LaFargue and Pas 1998; Komjathy 2004, 2014a; Siegler 2010; Carmichael 2017. There also are more extreme examples of cultural appropriation, banalization, and distortion like that of Benjamin Hoff. No, Daoists are not idiotic bears. For a potential lesson in counter-virtue, see Hoff's recent online reflections on his experience with commercial publishing. Not surprisingly, Hoff also has recently (2021) published his own version on "the philosophical [sic] masterwork of Taoism and its relevance today," while the actual "Daoist question" remains unaddressed. The main point here is that when individuals read these types of modern Western cultural productions, they are not reading approximations of the Daoist writings, let alone Daoist source-texts as such. Again, compare Komjathy forthcoming.

over, a circling, a soaring, a crossing, and perhaps even a reversing. *Fān* also may mean "change," "climb," and "multiply," while *yì* may also mean "decipher" and "decode." Thus, from a Chinese and thus Daoist linguistic perspective, translation also involves interpretation and transformation, a decoding leading to recoding. It also may enable us to travel to and in other culturescapes and mindscapes, perhaps even somascapes.

We may think of translation as a bridge. What kind of bridge are we building or crossing? Is it stable and reliable? Do we trust its construction and support? Does it provide ease of access to both sides? Does it, perhaps, resemble the Magpie Bridge (*quèqiáo* 鵲橋) of ancient Chinese mythology? This represents the annual formation of an astronomical and celestial connection between the Cowherd (*niúláng* 牛郎; Altair) and Weaving Maiden (*zhīnǚ* 織女; Vega). Or, drawing upon the Daoist tradition, does it more closely appear like the bridge (*liáng* 梁 [樑]) across the Háo 濠 River that Zhuāng Zhōu 莊周 ("Master Zhuang"; ca. 370-ca. 290 BCE) crossed with his friend and foil Huìzǐ 惠子 (Master Hui)? This is where the former observed the Joy of Fish (*yú zhī lè* 魚之樂). Or is it more like the Yùxiān qiáo 遇仙橋 (Bridge for Encountering Immortals)? This name commemorates the mystical experience of Wáng Zhé 王嚞 (Chóngyáng 重陽 [Redoubled Yang]; 1113–1170) with the immortals Zhōnglí Quán 鍾離權 (Zhèngyáng 正陽 [Aligned Yang]; 168?-256?) and Lǚ Dòngbīn 呂洞賓 (Chúnyáng 純陽 [Pure Yang]; b. 796?), during which he received secret transmissions. Or is it like the famous Zhàozhōu 趙州 Bridge? While often marveled at as an unsurpassed architectural feat, this is where Hǎo Dàtōng 郝大通 (Tàigǔ 太古 [Grand Antiquity]/ Guǎngníng 廣寧 [Expansive Serenity]; 1140–1213) lived and practiced under for six years (1175–1181). Or is it the bridge of blindmen brushed, no less than eight times, by the Rinzai Zen Buddhist Hakuin Ekaku 白隱慧鶴 (1686–1769)? Can we see the other shore and maintain our commitment and orientation?

With respect to translating Daoist literature, and translating Daoism by extension, there are many unique opportunities and challenges. For studying and understanding Daoism, the ability to engage the tradition through its source-language and source-literature in the original results in deeper insights and more sophisticated interpretation. On a practical and applied level, especially for individuals engaging in Daoist practice and following a Daoist way of life, Daoist technical vocabulary and associated scriptures offer clarification and nuance, often with accompanying, perhaps unexpected openings and even awakenings. As I will suggest, this might include a "contemplative approach" to "Daoist Chinese" itself and to the activity of reading, translating, and interpreting. Recalling the external Three Treasures (see above), both scholarly and applied approaches to Daoist literature and translation also provide a deeper root in the tradition as such. This allows us to develop our own, more direct understanding, to draw on primary Daoist materials to support our views, and, frankly, to protect ourselves against nonsense. Such nonsense takes many forms with(out) respect to Daoism, including in careerist academic accounts, Orientalist constructions, as well as popular appropriations and commodification. In terms of challenges, one major issue centers on Daoist technical terminology, with the accompanying lexicon often having context-specific meaning and sometimes varying according to movement and time-period. Some examples include the following:

dào 道: Dao (Tao/Way)	shì 士: adept/practitioner
dé 德: inner power/virtue	shǒu 守: guard/guarding
dìng 定: absorption (Skt.: *samādhi*)	wúwéi 無為: non-action
guān 觀: observe/observation (Pali: *vipassanā*; Skt.: *vipaśyanā*)	xiān 仙: immortal/immortality
	xiāoyáo 逍遙: being carefree/carefree ease
jǐng 景: effulgences	xíng 行: practice
jìng 境: mental projections	xìng 性: innate nature
jìng 靜: still/stillness	xiū 修: cultivate/cultivation
liàn 煉/鍊: refine/refinement	zhāi 齋: fast/purification/retreat
mìng 命: life-destiny	zhēn 眞/真: perfect/perfected/perfection
pǔ 樸/朴: unhewn simplicity	
qì 氣: qi (subtle/vital breath)	zhǐ 止: cessation (Pali: *samatha*; Skt.: *śamatha*)
qīng 清: clear/clarity	
shàn 善: adept/adeptness	

In addition to the obvious, these terms and my translations inspire a variety of questions. Should we aim to create one-to-one equivalencies? Do some Chinese terms require more in English translation? We obviously will focus on such questions through the lessons herein. Another issue is the insular, politicized and smallminded nature of mainstream Sinological Daoist Studies, the academic field dedicated to research and education on the Daoist tradition. More often than not, this involves presenting Daoism as a historical artifact via textual reconstructions. As articulated and perpetuated in its dominant Western European and North American modes, Daoist Studies has been and remains elitist and factional; perhaps somewhat surprisingly, though actually not at all, it is largely about power, prestige, and privilege. It is more about ego, fame, and reputation than Daoism as such. Why? Because most of the individuals in question are Sinologists, scholars of China, rather than Daologists per se. Here we might pause and consider the "scholars" in question and what they translate. It is no coincidence that these tend to overlap: Mainstream Sinologists, perhaps better understood as "contemporary nineteenth-century Orientalists," tend to focus on institutional history, ecclesiastical authority, political relationships, and ritual power. Along these lines, we should note the tendency of many of these academics to function like "surrogates of tradition," often with accompanying sectarian views. While they frequently have contributed to knowledge *about* Daoism, they should not be misidentified as adherents, let alone representatives *of* Daoism. This often involves failure to engage the deeper dimensions of the tradition, including its systems of inner cultivation and spiritual transformation. Simply stated, academic Daoist Studies is the place where scholars (and possibly human beings) go to die, though perhaps they died long before/ago.

In place of the resultant dominant and domineering approach, the received injurious and dysfunctional "model of scholarship" (not really a scholarly model at all), we may cultivate and embrace something else. One possible remedy involves reflecting on and applying Daoist commitments, principles, qualities, and values themselves.

bàopǔ 抱樸: embrace simplicity	shǒuzhōng 守中: guard the Center
guǎyù 寡欲: decrease desire	tóngchén 同塵: unite with dust
guīgēn 歸根: return to the root	xiànsù 見素: appear plain
jiěfēn 解紛: untie the knots	xiūjìng 修靜: cultivate stillness
shǎosī 少私: lessen selfishness	wàngmíng 忘名: forget name

This might also be understood as "nourishing life" (*yǎngshēng* 養生), or knowledge in the *service of life*. As I have worked for my entire "career" (life-trajectory), it is possible to take Daoism seriously on its own terms, to be informed and inspired by Daoist commitments and principles, and to follow a Daoist way of life. This results in a different approach to scholarship and translation: It is study informed by practice, and practice informed by study. It is a work-based and community-centered approach, which might replace the received court-based and egocentric one. It also inspires us to imagine and perhaps experience Daoism as a lived and living tradition. As this book evidences, I also am interested in facilitating and supporting a more egalitarian and open field, one that welcomes people from diverse backgrounds and with diverse interests. Along these lines, we may think of Daoist Studies as *dàoxué* 道學, which more literally means "study of the Dao" or "Way-Study" for short, rather than the conventional *dàojiào yánjiū* 道教研究, which more literally means "research on Daoism." Although *dàoxué* has historically been used to refer to late medieval Ruism (so-called "Neo-Confucianism"), like my invocation of *dàotǒng* 道統 (lit., "tradition of the Dao"), I am engaging in a variety of Daoist retrievalist and visionary projects. For the moment, I will just say that Daoist Studies, as documented herein and in my associated reference materials, may be more than merely academic, in every sense of the word. It may be *intellectual and scholarly* beyond mainstream academia (officialdom and technopoly). This vision opens up the possibility of independent Daoist schools and research/translation centers, and it makes space for individuals without formal institutionalized academic training (e.g., Ph.D.s) and unaffiliated with the so-called "professoriate" and so-called "higher" education.[13] Perhaps it is a project with which you have affinity. It definitely offers the possibility of something beyond impending (ongoing) institutional collapse. As discussed below, it also is informed by indigenous Chinese Daoist models of scholarship, specifically what may be understood as traditional "Daoist scholar-practitioners" (DSP). Recall our previous consideration of Lù Xiūjìng, Táo Hóngjǐng, Zhāng Yǔchū, and Zhāng Yǔqīng.

Translating Daoist literature is not simply a matter of bilingualism, of "knowing Chinese" and developing an English (or other) approximation. This is a superficial and simplistic understanding of translation. Just as I have advocated for developing Daoist Studies informed by Animal Studies, Contemplative Studies, and Religious Studies (see, e.g., Komjathy 2007, 2013b, 2017a, 2022f), translators of Daoist literature should have at least some familiarity with "translation criticism" and "translation studies," that is, theory and method related to translation as such (see, e.g., Biguenet and Schulte 1989; Schulte and Biguenet 1992; Barnstone 1993; Venuti 2000; Pym 2014; bibliography herein). What *type* of translation do we aspire to create? What are our commitments and values? As documented in my own advanced translation work (see, e.g., Komjathy 2007, 2008 [2003], 2013a, 2017a, forthcoming), and as articulated herein, I am most interested in *complete* annotated scholarly and literary translation. This would stand in contrast to other styles of related translation, including purely Sinological or popular renderings. The former tends to lack literary sensibility and readability, while the latter tends to domesticate and distort the texts in question. The former also tends to create historical artifacts, while the latter creates modern cultural ones. Here I also should mention that many earlier Sinological translations often insert assumed information in the translation and/or change names in order to increase accessibility, often resulting in deviation from the Chinese source-texts. In contrast, scholarly translation

---

[13] Here we also should note that, at least in the case of the United States, so-called colleges and universities have largely become corporations, with the primary purpose of creating debt-slaves ("students") and future wage-slaves ("workers/professionals").

is attentive to source-culture and context-specific technical meanings, while literary translation is attentive to language and readability. Combining these approaches, we aspire for elegant and refined English informed by the associated communities and contexts.

To this, we may add the importance of annotation. Annotation enables us to explicate technical meaning and to supply additional relevant information. From my perspective, it also may be understood as a form of close textual analysis, perhaps even representing a quasi-commentary. As in any translation, there also is the question of audience. As various commercial presses have communicated to me, there apparently is a very restricted "market" for this type of translation in terms of publication prospects. I am not convinced. More importantly, profit motives and market concerns, including popular "tastes," are irrelevant for this work and associated projects. My (our?) intended audience consists of individuals interested in reading Daoist literature in reliable translation, specifically with a commitment to deepening their/our understanding of tradition-based Daoism in an accurate and sophisticated manner. This requires weaning oneself from modern consumptive reading practices and demands for ease and accessibility. Along these lines, as we traverse this path, we may reflect on how accessible these texts were, and how accessible they should be in contemporary English. For example, the American translation theorist Lawrence Venuti (1995) speaks of, and in fact advocates for, "tactics of resistance" in translation. Should the radical unfamiliarity and occasional incongruence of the original be preserved? How much should one "polish away" problems and issues in the original?

I also would like to envision, advocate for, and facilitate an approach that might be labelled "Daoist translation" (*dàojiào fānyì* 道教翻譯) (see above), which represents a decolonial and deOrientalist methodology (see King 1999; Smith 2012). This is translation informed by, and perhaps inspired by and infused with, Daoist commitments, principles, qualities, and values. In addition, such translations aim to maintain greater connection to the original, in all of its layers, and to offer translational approximations of and access to the source-text. This means that "non-Chinese" readers might encounter a Daoist text in a new language. In its fullest expression, "Daoist translation" involves Daoist translators translating Daoist texts in order to create Daoist translations. This is Daoist literature as a living presence and ongoing transmission. Daoist translation also is translation informed by Daoist practice, and vice versa. It is rooted in and offered to/for the Daoist community and larger Daoist tradition. It may be thought of as an announcement (biǎo 表) and petition (zhāng 章), perhaps even an offering (jiào 醮) in the larger "ritual of translation." We have already encountered some approximations and hints above. First, Daoist translation recognizes the sacred standing of these texts in the Daoist tradition, especially jīng-scriptures as one of the external Three Treasures. For this, we may follow the principle of "inwardly still; outwardly reverent." Translation may be a sacred vocation. Second, Daoist translation involves discovering and ideally maintaining connection (tōng 通), perhaps "numinous pervasion" (língtōng 靈通) and "divine connection" (shéntōng 神通). Recall the "Daoist etymology" of jīng-scriptures: Threads and watercourses forming and reforming networks of connection. This relates to the Daoist community and Daoist tradition as a numinous thread, with committed Daoists connected to each other as a historical, energetic, and perhaps transtemporal continuum. Daoist translation thus, at least ideally speaking, involves transmission (chuán 傳).

       Affinity   Connection   Transmission

Other possible informing Daoist principles and guidelines include "returning to the root(s)" (guīgēn 歸根). This is not simply about having Chinese language facility and access to the deeper layers of a given text. It also is about constantly returning to that root throughout the translation process and beyond. In Daoist terms, the resultant translation ideally maintains the talismanic connection (see above). Like realized Daoist being, efficacious Daoist translation may re-present and facilitate such connection. This may be further linked to translation as an alchemical process involving "refining the elixir" (*liàndān* 煉丹/鍊丹) and "reversion" (*fǎnfù* 反復/反覆). We work to refine away impurities, and we constantly return to the original, perhaps even a transmuted distillation. The "alchemy of translation" also may result in "harmonizing brightness" (*héguāng* 和光). Along these lines, the Daoist Translation Committee 道教翻譯學會, a translation collective which is being facilitated by me through the Daoist Foundation 道教基金會, composed "Principles of Daoist Translation" (see Appendix #7), which also is available online. I invite you to read and reflect on it.

Daoist translation is, in turn, connected to Daoist ways of reading and Daoist hermeneutics. Hermeneutics refers to the art, theory and practice of interpretation. On a more general level, modern hermeneutics often involves "meta-reflection" on interpretation itself, textual interpretation in the present case. Much has been made of Paul Ricœur's (1913–2005) distinction between the "hermeneutics of faith" and "hermeneutics of suspicion" (see Ricœur 1970). Recognizing the contributions and sometime-relevance of the latter, it has become an academic vogue, especially in the form of deconstruction and hyper-skepticism. The latter includes endless careerist and opportunist dismissals of "traditional attribution" without evidential grounds. In place of this exegetical trajectory, various individuals have attempted to advance a "hermeneutics of generosity," "hermeneutics of retrieval," and "hermeneutics of hope." This is not to deny the value of both suspension of belief/disbelief and critical reflection on received views; rather, it aspires towards and inspires "sympathetic readings" of the materials under consideration, including "other people's myths" with some degree of meta-awareness (see, e.g., Doniger O'Flaherty 1995; Doniger 1998; Eliade 1998 [1963]). To these, I would add a "hermeneutics of the imaginal," one in which we move beyond received interpretive tendencies and conventional (mandated?) readings (see Komjathy forthcoming). Daoist translation is one such trajectory.

There are, in turn, diverse Daoist views concerning Daoist literature and scripture study (*jīngxué* 經學) (see book epigraphs; Komjathy 2008 [2003]; 2013b, 225–42; forthcoming). Based on the present undertaking, we obviously are located on the intellectual and scholarly side of the debate, at least to some extent. Thus, here I will assume affinity and aspiration, perhaps inspiration. In addition to the previously explored insights from Daoist texts themselves, we should note that Daoists have engaged and continue to engage in close reading and textual application. This has included composing and consulting commentaries (*zhù* 註/注) (see Lessons #25–28 herein). There are *Daoist ways of reading and interpreting Daoist texts*. These utilize uniquely Daoist approaches, concerns and orientations, informed by Daoist views and aspirations, which often diverge from "non-Daoist" motivations. One obviously does not need to be a Daoist to translate/interpret Daoist texts, and "Daoist translation" does not necessarily assume or require Daoist adherence. However, I want to suggest that there are alternative, perhaps more radical approaches and commitments. One important contribution involves "contemplative reading." This is more process-orientated than outcome-based. It is more about presence than production. It involves participation over objectification. In my way of understanding and engaging in contemplative reading, it involves reading, interpreting, and translating characterized by attentiveness, awareness, intentionality, interiority, presence, stillness, and so forth. Like breathing in meditation and associated contemplative states, it is long, slow, and deep. We follow the openings, and we allow space/time for additional awakenings and insights to occur. As mentioned, this may include annotations as an additional interpretive opportunity and exercise, as a deeper form of close reading. The resultant translation may, in turn, be infused by the associated contemplative silence and presence. In terms of my own translation methodology, I work to establish a deeper connection with a given text in terms of language and source. The latter includes author (if applicable), community, historical period, and so forth. I then compose an initial draft translation. This is followed by annotations. I then revise and refine the translation. Finally, I return to the source-text and compare the translation with the original Chinese. 歸根/反復. This approach may be condensed into the following four states/stages: connection, translation, revision, return. To this I would add that such a contemplative approach recognizes Daoist hermeneutics and Daoist translation as derived from and relevant to Daoist lifeways. That is, Daoist translation is a lived and living process, one that may contribute to the ongoing transmission of Daoism in/to the modern world, including in new forms and new places. In this way, it also may be thought of as "discoursing on the Dao" (*lùndào* 論道), in the sense of an ongoing and perhaps transtemporal communal dialogue. Daoist translation contributes to the emergence and development of global Daoism as characterized by multilingualism, reciprocity, and mutuality.

We may further connect Daoist translation and Daoist hermeneutics with Daoist scholasticism. As a Daoist scholar-practitioner/practitioner-scholar, I am constantly looking for pre-modern Chinese Daoist representatives and models. Although relatively small compared to other religious traditions (e.g., Buddhism and Catholic Christianity), and although Daoism is often (mis)characterized as "anti-intellectual," there is, in fact, a noteworthy and vibrant Daoist scholastic sub-tradition. Here I should mention a few dimensions of the classical and foundational Daoist emphasis on "non-knowing" (*wúzhī* 無知). Contrary to the claims of modern "intellectual historians" (more of the latter than the former), who tend to emphasize things like "arationality," "nihilism," "relativism," "skepticism," and the like, it is not that Daoists and Daoist communities are *anti*-rational, rather they/we are better understood as *trans*-rational. Rationality is only one dimension and expression of consciousness, and, while possibly helpful for solidifying identity and building bridges, it is deficient for other undertakings, especially contemplative and mystical modes of being in the world.

知者不言，言者不知。

One who knows does not speak;
One who speaks does not know.

知不知上；不知知病。

To know that you do not know is best;
Not to know that you are knowing is sickness.

This is not about "not-knowing"; it is about "non-knowing" (*wúzhī* 無知). It is about contemplative silence and resultant spiritual discernment and insight. Furthermore, there is an assumed distinction between *zhī* 知 as "knowing" (rational limitation) and as "gnosis" (spiritual realization) (see Komjathy 2017b, forthcoming). The former often hinders the latter, and the latter often transcends and encompasses the former. This is being beyond knowing. Thus, there are alternate or transformed Daoist modes of being and perceiving. These relate to a variety of other Daoist technical terms and related states. In addition to various Daoist "beyond/non-states" (*wú* 無), here non-knowing may be elucidated as *shǒucí* 守雌 ("guarding the feminine"). Technically another name for Daoist apophatic and quietistic (emptiness-/stillness-based) meditation (see Lessons #6 and #8), and paralleling *shǒuyī* 守一 ("guarding the One"), this refers to a "yin" mode and state centering on open receptivity, on letting be. One allows space for unfolding.

In any case, there are a variety of earlier Daoists, who may be engaged as precedents and models for our present undertaking. Some key figures include the following (in chronological order):

Wáng Bì 王弼 (226–249)	**Qín Zhìān** 秦志安
Guō Xiàng 郭象 (252–312)	(Tōngzhēn 通真 [Pervading Perfection]; 1188–1244)
Gé Hóng 葛洪 (Bàopǔ 抱朴 [Embracing Simplicity]; 283–343)	**Lǐ Dàoqiān** 李道謙 (Héfǔ 和甫 [Harmonious Beginning]; 1219–1296)
Lù Xiūjìng 陸修靜 (Yuándé 元德 [Primordial Virtue]; 406–477)	**Wáng Chángyuè** 王常月 (Kūnyáng 崑陽 [Paradisiacal Yang]; 1622?–1680)
Táo Hóngjǐng 陶弘景 (Tōngmíng 通明 [Pervasive Illumination]; 456–536)	**Liú Yīmíng** 劉一明 (Wùyuán 悟元 [Awakening-to-the-Source]; 1734–1821)
Sūn Sīmiǎo 孫思邈 (581–682)	**Chén Yīngníng** 陳攖寧 (Yuándùn 圓頓 [Complete Suddenness]; 1881–1969)
Sīmǎ Chéngzhēn 司馬承禎 (Zhēnyī 貞一 [Pure Unity]; 647–735)	**Mǐn Zhìtíng** 閔智亭 (Yùxī 玉溪 [Jade Rivulet]; 1924–2004)
Dù Guāngtíng 杜光庭 (Guǎngchéng 廣成 [Expansive Completion]; 850–933)	**Michael Saso** 蘇海涵 (b. 1930)
Liú Chángshēng 劉長生 (Chǔxuán 處玄 [Abiding Mystery]; 1147–1203)	**Kristofer Schipper** 施舟人 (1934–2021)

FIGURE 10: Some Important Daoist Scholar-Practitioners

Here we might also recall, contra popular constructions, that the legendary Lǎo Dān 老聃/儋 (trad. dat. 6th c. BCE), also known as "Lǎozǐ 老子" ("Master Lao"), is remembered in the Daoist tradition and the larger parameters of Chinese history as the "Archivist of Zhōu." For all intents and purposes, this position was something like head librarian. Observant readers also will note that there are no female Daoists in the above list. Although women have played a major role in and made major contributions to the Daoist tradition (see Despeux and Kohn 2003), and while Daoism tends to be gender-inclusive and even committed to female empowerment, I am unfamiliar with any female Daoists with the scholastic standing of the above male Daoists. One possible exception is the Daoist priestess Liǔ Mòrán 柳默然 (773–840) (see Jia 2018), who was involved in the transmission of the *Zuòwàng lùn* 坐忘論

(Discourse on Sitting-in-Forgetfulness; DZ 1036; ZH 992) (see Lesson #18 herein). I hope that further research will provide additional details that may supplement this apparent traditional deficiency and/or correct my own. And I, of course, look forward to a day, perhaps beyond my own horizon, when female Daoist scholar-practitioners compose new translations and studies.

Needless to say, it would take a tremendous amount of space to elucidate the associated contributions of earlier Daoists. Here I simply want to bring attention to *models*, including for those of us interested in both following a scholar-practitioner path and developing a study-practice approach. Let me be clear: This is not "academic" in the conventional sense of politicized knowledge, insular discourse, and technocratic specialization. The majority of academics, especially in the case of Daoist Studies and Sinology, are politicians and technicians masquerading as scholars and intellectuals. Thus, in place of "academic" (and academia), I propose "scholarly" (and scholarship). The latter is based on free and open inquiry, with attentiveness to excellence and merit beyond pedigree or affiliation. From my perspective, it ideally should include recognition and support for creativity, innovation, insight, radicalness, and the like. In Daoist terms, this is Daoist community outside and beyond the court and officialdom, with its positions, titles, and protocols, not to mention knee-bending and ring-kissing (to be polite). Again in the language of Daoism, it requires embracing the path of "namelessness" (*wúmíng* 無名), with *míng* referring to ordinary name, fame, reputation, and familial and social identity by extension. This represents a new model for Daoist Studies, one in which the primary emphasis is on *Daoist*. This is what the Center for Daoist Studies 道學中心 and the Daoist Translation Committee 道教翻譯學會 represent. Of course, we cannot expect conventional and mainstream academics to understand and recognize, let alone accept or support, this undertaking, but that is not our concern.

> 井蛙不可以語於海者，拘於虛也；
> 夏蟲不可以語於冰者，篤於時也；
> 曲士不可以語於道者，束於教也。

> You cannot discuss the ocean with well-frogs—they're limited by the space they live in.
> You cannot discuss ice with summer-insects—they're bound to a single season.
> You cannot discuss the Way with cramped scholars—they're shackled by their doctrines.
> (*Zhuāngzǐ* 莊子 [Book of Master Zhuang], ch. 17)

And, "Because they could not be recognized, we feel compelled to describe them." We aspire for something else and something more. This includes the possibility of "alternative centers" and "Daoist academies," perhaps something along the lines of "super-schools." Again, there are some models in the pre-modern Chinese Daoist tradition. One important example appears in the teacher-student communities of classical Daoism.

> 申徒嘉，兀者也，而與鄭子產同師於伯昏無人。子產謂申徒嘉曰：「我先出，則子止；子先出，則我止。」其明日，又與合堂同席而坐。子產謂申徒嘉曰：「我先出，則子止；子先出，則我止。今我將出，子可以止乎，其未邪？且子見執政而不違，子齊執政乎？」申徒嘉曰：「先生之門，固有執政焉如此哉？子而說子之執政而後人者也！聞之曰：『鑑明則塵垢不止，止則不明也。久與賢人處，則無過。』今子之所取大者，先生也，而猶出言若是，不亦過乎！」

Shēntú Jiā 申徒嘉 (Extended Disciple Excelling), who had lost a foot, was studying under Bóhūn Wúrén 伯昏無人 (Elder Obscurity Beyond-Humanity) along with Zǐchǎn 子產 (Adept

Chan) of Zhèng 鄭. Zǐchǎn addressed Shēntú Jiā saying, "If I go out first, you wait; if you go out first, I'll wait."

The next day the two of them were sitting together on the same mat (xí 席) in the hall (táng 堂). Zǐchǎn said to Shēntú Jiā, "If I go out first, you wait; if you go out first, I'll wait! Now I will go out. Are you going to wait or aren't you? When you see a prime minister, you don't even get out of the way—do you think you're equal to a prime minister?"

Shēntú Jiā said, "Within the gates (mén 門) of the master, is there any such thing as prime minister? You delight in being a prime minister and pushing people behind you. But as I've heard, 'If the mirror (jiàn 鑑) is bright, dust does not settle; if dust settles, it isn't bright. When you live around worthy people for a long time, you'll be free of faults.' Today you regard the master as great, and yet you talk like this—it isn't right, is it?" (Zhuāngzǐ 莊子 [Book of Master Zhuang], ch. 5; adapted from Watson 1968, 70; see also Lessons #2 and #8)

There are many interesting elements of this passage, especially with respect to the inner cultivation lineages of classical Daoism (see Lessons #6–9), but I want to draw attention to a few details relevant for our current concern, namely, the possibility of independent and intentional Daoist scholarly communities and training centers. Shēntú Jiā, who had his foot amputated in conformity with the ancient Chinese punishment (for theft in this case), was a criminal on some level, while Zǐchǎn refers to Gōngsūn Qiáo 公孫僑 (d. 522 BCE), who was the Prime Minister of the ancient vassal-state of *Dreŋ-s (Zhèng) 鄭 (806–375 BCE). The latter's presence here is presumably an invented literary device, but it is still tantalizing with respect to Daoist social participation and demographics. In any case, Shēntú Jiā's "deformity," literally marking him as an enemy of the state and "undesirable," and his attendant lack of social status leads to assumed inferiority/superiority on the part of Zǐchǎn, including demands for ritual protocol based on position. However, in the context of Bóhūn Wúrén's Daoist community, one must leave one's social identity and hierarchal thinking "outside the gates." One must practice meditation on the same mats and in the same hall as every person, presumably understanding and ideally realizing shared innate nature as the Dao manifesting through individual being-in-the-world. This, of course, is beyond the comprehension, let alone the practice of politicians and bureaucrats.

Other possible Daoist models include the Jìxià 稷下 Academy, the Daoist theocracies of the early Tiānshī 天師 (Celestial Masters) movement and later of Kòu Qiānzhī 寇謙之 (365–448), the above-mentioned Máoshān community associated with Shàngqīng, as well as the Tang-dynasty (618–907) Chóngxuán xué 崇玄學 (School of the Exalted Dao), conventionally referred to as the "College of Daoist Studies." For me, the "Daoist associations" (dàohuì 道會), or "Way-Gatherings" for short, of early Quánzhēn 全真 (Complete Perfection) are especially inspiring (see Lesson #23 herein). To this, we may add more institutional forms of Daoist organization, including Daoist temple/monastic networks, the late imperial Dàolù sī 道錄司 (Daoist Registrar), and the contemporary Dàojiào xuéyuàn 道教學院 (Daoist College/Seminary) of Báiyún guàn 白雲觀 (White Cloud Monastery; Běijīng), although the latter has a complex place in the political landscape of contemporary mainland China and thus Daoist history as such.[14] This is not to mention the various other "studios" (zhāi 齋) and quasi-salons, both known and unknown, that have functioned and continue to function as Daoist gathering places and study centers.[15] The point here is that we do not need

---

[14] As one Chinese Daoist monastic friend commented, "The Daoist College and Chinese Daoist Association are where Daoists go to die." Although rarely recognized outside of mainland China, the Zhōngguó dàojiào xiéhuì 中國道教協會 (Chinese Daoist/Taoist Association) is technically part of the Bureau of Religious Affairs, an administrative unit of the Chinese Communist state. Along these lines, the required curriculum includes the history of Communist (Marxist-Maoist) thought, with its accompanying view of religion as the opiate of the masses. Thus, use of *xiéhuì* indicates PRC-affiliation. A more traditional Daoist designation would be *dàohuì* 道會 (lit., "meeting of the Dao").

[15] As we will partially explore in ch. 8, *zhāi* 齋 may mean "fast," "purify," and "retreat." In the fully developed Daoist liturgical tradition, it may refer to ritual purity as well as a specific form of Daoist public ritual, namely, *zhāi*-purifications, which also are referred to more technically as levée (via French *lever* ["rise"]) in the sense of formal court audiences. At the same time, Daoists sometimes

authorized and legitimizing institutions, with their degree-systems and credentializing, to do the real work of Daoist Studies and Daoist translation. I say this as someone who has had and renounced them all, especially as preserved and perpetuated in institutionalized and corporate forms. We may, in turn, imagine new Daoist academies and communities, including independent research and translation centers.

Finally, although the *Dàodé jīng* and the *Zhuāngzǐ* to a lesser extent have received incessant and unnecessary translation, often in what I refer to as "Tao Te Ching Translation Industry" (TTCTI) and now the "Zhuangzi Philosophy Industry" (ZZPI), a large amount of Daoist literature actually has been published to date. Unfortunately, this remains largely unknown outside of specialized scholarly circles. This is because much of said translations have been published in academic journals or scholarly monographs, with the latter often being prohibitively expensive for "ordinary readers." As I will discuss in the next and last section, here we are focusing on specific genres, corpuses, topics, and vocabulary related to Daoist literature. However, interested readers may consult the following supplemental reference pieces that I have composed: "Daoist Literature" and "Daoist Literature in Translation: An Annotated Catalogue." The latter is an updated, revised, and expanded version of my earlier "Daoist Texts in Translation" (2004), which has received wide circulation on the internet and been translated into a five-part Chinese article (2007–2009). Both of these are annotated catalogues of Daoist literature translated to date. They include English translations of the original Chinese text titles, standardized title abbreviations, catalogue numbers, and associated bibliographical information. I also document popular translations, indicated by (P). I have included a distillation most relevant to present purposes in Appendix #9 herein.

As documented in that article and the associated "Research Guide to Daoist Studies," there are now three general scholarly anthologies of

---

have used *zhāi* to refer to private studios or residences.

Daoist literature (Kohn 1993; Komjathy 2008 [2003]; Robson 2014);[16] four theme-based anthologies (Kohn 2004b, 2009, 2014; Pregadio 2019); and three movement-specific anthologies (Bokenkamp 1997; Miller 2008; Komjathy 2013a).[17] Each has its contributions and limitations, which I again consider in the previously-discussed reference materials. This is not to mention translations and studies of individual texts. As these and accompanying translation work indicate, the four leading contemporary scholar-translators of Daoist literature are Stephen Bokenkamp 柏夷, Livia Kohn 柯恩, Louis Komjathy 康思奇, and Fabrizio Pregadio 玄英. The present primer is, in turn, the first bilingual installment, and it may be used as a Daoist sourcebook for a variety of purposes. It also sets a foundation for a future projected, theme-based *Readings in Daoist Literature*, intended as a companion-volume to my *The Daoist Tradition: An Introduction* (2013).

We may, then, recognize that while much has been completed, much remains to be done. This includes the need for new translations to replace earlier outdated and inaccurate ones (see Lessons #3, #13, and #26). Especially in the form of "Daoist translation," such translations may provide connection and transmission. This is particularly necessary to enable individuals without Chinese language facility to access Daoist literature in reliable translations. We may, by extension, recognize that translating Daoist texts also involves "translating Daoism," and vice versa. Various translational acts are involved. This is Daoism as both within and beyond texts. And, as we have seen, there are "texts" beyond texts.

---

[16] There also are four outdated, unreliable, and popular anthologies: Balfour 1894; Legge 1962 [1891]; Cleary 1991(P); Wong 1997(P).

[17] Ideally, any future anthologies should follow the model set forth in Komjathy's *The Way of Complete Perfection* (2013a) and herein and include an appendix with a list of the relevant primary source-texts.

On Primers and Priming

The present book is a primer in translating Daoist literature. It aspires to assist interested individuals in developing the necessary Chinese language facility and skills. It consists of twenty-eight "lessons" from a wide variety of Chinese Daoist texts with accompanying, supplemental materials. Each lesson provides a representative selection from an original Chinese Daoist text with accompanying English translation and vocabulary. I also have prepared a supplemental online PDF, which is available on the Purple Cloud Institute website (www.purplecloud-institute.com) and on my Alternate Homepage (www.louiskomjathy.com). Titled *Electronic Supplement to Primer for Translating Daoist Literature: Source-Editions of Daoist Texts Therein*, the collection includes the texts from their original Daoist editions in the traditional format, that is, written from top-to-bottom and right-to-left in unpunctuated form (see above). This allows readers to decide how they wish to learn. The most basic approach involves reading the included punctuated version in concert with my translation and vocabulary. On an intermediate level, one may attempt to read the punctuated passage with or without the vocabulary, while covering up the English translation. The most advanced approach, which approximates actual specialist work in Daoist Studies, involves attempting to read the DZ editions with a classical Chinese dictionary. Of course, beyond this is the translation of previously untranslated Daoist literature, which is many steps, and many peaks and valleys, beyond here. In any case, we will move from more basic and accessible examples to more advanced ones, while building skills and vocabulary along the way. This ideally involves moving from familiarity through proficiency to fluency, and perhaps eventually to mastery. As mentioned, I am focusing more on specialized Daoist vocabulary than grammar, so again I recommend constantly consulting Appendix 3: Foundational Classical Chinese Grammar herein. Each lesson also aims to be self-contained, so there is some vocabulary overlap. The most commonly occurring vocabulary is contained in Appendix 8:

Towards a Dictionary of Daoist Classical Chinese. For the most part, I do not necessarily assume that readers have retained technical terms from earlier lessons. I also attempt to highlight relevant principles and insights along the way. This may be thought of as an applied meta-reflection on translation, especially Daoist translation, itself.

We will begin with examples of Daoist text titles with abbreviations (#1), followed by two lists of chapter titles from larger works (#2 and #3). While this may not appear to be "lessons" per se, they are included in this order in order to approximate and prepare us for the actual reading of Daoist texts. When we open up a Daoist text in the original Chinese, we first encounter and must decipher the title, including the most relevant details. We then must determine the overall structure and organization. If we are fortunate, a given text includes chapter or section divisions, and if we are even more fortunate, accompanying titles. As I will suggest in Lessons #2, #3, and #25, contemplative engagement with such titles may result in not only deeper understanding of textual content, but also unexpected insights and perhaps even practical applications. The selections proper begin with Lesson #4. Generally speaking, these are organized chronologically. However, at times (e.g., #4, #14, #19) I deviate from this practice in order to introduce more foundational materials first. From a scholarly perspective, this is technically anachronistic and has the potential to create historical confusion. However, it is done with attentiveness and intentionality. Most of the passages are selections extracted from larger texts, often quite long. I have made the selections based on a more comprehensive understanding of the associated text, with the aspiration to provide a representative sampling. I have, however, included two complete texts (#14 and #19). This was possible because they are relatively brief and integral. We also move towards more technical works and longer selections in later lessons. In each case, the framing introduction utilizes a tripartite structure, namely, (1) brief contextualist background to the given text, (2) important grammatical points and distinctive Daoist technical vocabulary, and (3) foundational references to key specialist studies and scholarly translations, if applicable.

One issue, no doubt of particular concern for other specialists and future specialized translation projects, centers on the texts selected and associated terminology. While foundational and representative, and thus aligned with the aspirations and purpose of this primer, the selections are just that, *a selection*. While informed by lifelong study and comprehensive knowledge of the Daoist tradition, my choice evidences a specific set of concerns and interests. I am more interested in "inner cultivation" materials, especially Daoist literature that discusses Daoist views, practices (including specific techniques), and experiences on a deeper level. In the language of Daoism, this relates to "cultivation and refinement" (*xiūliàn* 修煉) and "experiential confirmation" (*zhèngyàn* 證驗), and thus to my previous points about Daoism as a lived and living tradition and as a way of life. They also relate to my own areas of expertise, including embodiment, hermeneutics, meditation, and mysticism. I have, in turn, provided examples from most of the major Daoist movements, specifically the inner cultivation lineages, Tiānshī 天師 (Celestial Masters), Tàiqīng 太清 (Great Clarity), Shàngqīng 上清 (Highest Clarity), and Quánzhēn 全真 (Complete Perfection), including its later Lóngmén 龍門 (Dragon Gate) lineage. Two major omissions are Tàipíng 太平 (Great Peace) and Língbǎo 靈寶, both of which are more advanced topics. There are a variety of other neglected areas, which overlap with genre and movement affiliation (see above). Given current academic trends, two of the more conspicuous "omissions" are hagiography (*zhuàn* 傳) and ritual (*lǐ* 禮; *yíshì* 儀式), including in its various forms and associated musical compositions. My response is multi-perspectival. First, this primer will provide a foundation for more advanced translation work, including even more technical lexigraphy. Second, interested individuals may consult associated translations in concert with the original Daoist source-texts. Again, I direct them/you to my "Daoist Literature in Translation." Third, I aspire to engage the largest possible audience. This includes not only aspiring "scholars," but also "practitioners," and ideally "scholar-practitioners," or at least "student-practitioners" and "scholar-teachers." As a scholar-practitioner myself, I also want to provide committed Daoists with resources for deepening their/our (your?) understanding and practice. Regardless of the accompanying aspiration for "translating Daoist literature," or lack thereof, this primer offers an opportunity to engage and develop a bilingual approach. Along these lines, my selection is informed by and informs Daoist practice. It includes passages on alchemy, dietetics, ethics, health and longevity practice, hermeneutics, meditation, monasticism, principles, view, and so forth. In this way, it may be read as not only a primer in Daoist translation, but also a guidebook to foundational Daoist practice.

I also have included ten appendices:

1. Chinese Character Radicals
2. Important Chinese Character Radicals for Daoist Studies
3. Foundational Classical Chinese Grammar
4. Pinyin to Wade-Giles Romanization Conversion Chart
5. Wade-Giles to Pinyin Romanization Conversion Chart
6. Daoist Character Etymology
7. Principles of Daoist Translation
8. Towards a Dictionary of Daoist Classical Chinese
9. Foundational Readings of Daoist Texts in Translation
10. Texts Included in *Primer for Translating Daoist Literature*

Of these, #6 is the most controversial and potentially problematic. It relates to the ways in which Chinese characters are interpreted by Daoists and applied in Daoist contexts. These often differ from historical Chinese linguistics and philology (see, e.g., Wieger 1965 [1927]; Wu 2015), although that too is by no means unproblematic. In fact, many claims about "phonetics" are simply absurd and do not hold up to deeper analysis and reflection. One danger here is giving free reign to fantastical projections, unmoored to the actual character history and composition. This is *not* what I am doing or advocating. What I refer to as "Daoist etymology" (*dàojiào cíyuán* 道教詞源) involves Daoist readings of Chinese characters, especially from an applied and lived perspective. Such an approach may be used as yet another form of Daoist contemplative inquiry, with many deeper insights emerging in/as/through practice. In any case, these technical materials may again be supplemented with my various online reference articles.

In terms of conventions, the original Chinese passages are formatted using Western left-to-right and top-to-bottom layout and Western punctuation. The latter was prepared by me and may be open to interpretation and amendment. As mentioned, the texts use traditional Chinese characters accompanied by modern "Mandarin" pronunciations using Pinyin Romanization with tone diacritics (see Appendix #4 and #5). Each selection begins with the Chinese text title in Pinyin Romanization with Chinese characters, followed by my English translation and the associated catalogue number. As most of the texts derive from the received *Dàozàng* 道藏 (Daoist Canon; dat. 1445/1607) (see above), I include the DZ number, which follows my *Title Index to Daoist Collections* (abbrev. TIDC) (2002) and parallels the earlier numbering system of Kristofer Schipper et al. (1975; also Shī and Chén 1996; Schipper and Verellen 2004), and the ZH number, which refers to the *Zhōnghuá dàozàng* 中華道藏 (Chinese Daoist Canon; dat. 2003) and follows my standardized numbering system (2014b). For other "extra-canonical" and "supplemental" Daoist textual collections, abbreviations and numbers follow my *Title Index to Daoist Collections* and more recent "Supplements to *Title Index to Daoist Collections*" (abbrev. STIDC) (2022-). These will be noted at first appearance. Many of the texts are, in turn, available online via the Chinese Text Project ("ctext") (www.ctext.org). The latter includes modern punctuated editions, often with a side-link to the DZ (or other) source-text. However, readers should note that the former often include character mistakes due to the use of optical character recognition (OCR) software. Ctext electronic editions may be further compared to those on the Kanseki Repository 漢籍リポジトリ (www.kanripo.org) and Shànshū túshūguǎn 善書圖書館 (www.taolibrary.com). Here some additional points need to be made. First, while digitalization of texts is positive in certain respects, including accessibility and democratization, we should ideally consult the actual text in question. In the case of the *Dàozàng*, many texts often are only extant in that single edition. Second, use of electronic texts created through OCR can be a source of frustration, confusion, and discouragement in the early stages of translation work. This is because one often struggles with character mistakes, assuming that it is one's own deficiency, rather than textual corruption. Simply stated, do not assume that it is your fault that a given passage is difficult to decipher. Along these lines and finally, DZ texts are not pristine and free from errors, including those made by scribes who created said transcriptions (see above). This perhaps helps to explain the Daoist admonition concerning utmost care and potential negative consequences for mistakes. Unfortunately, there are very few text-critical editions of Daoist texts, and some such work, which has been undertaken primarily by Japanese and secondarily by Chinese scholars, lacks discernment about actual semantic variants. Instead, these works often list *all* variants, with many of the latter often simply being character variants, or even transcription errors. Again, for guidance see Schipper and Verellen 2004; Komjathy 2022a, forthcoming.

Readers also may benefit from consulting various other reference works. In addition to those cited above and in the bibliography herein, we may add the foundational literary Chinese dictionary by Robert Henry (R.H.) Mathews 馬守真 (1943) and the more recent, supplemental dictionary by Paul Kroll 柯睿/號慕白 (2017) and grammar outline by Edwin Pulleyblank 蒲立本 (1996). There also are the specialized dictionaries on Chinese Buddhism by William Edward Soothill 蘇慧廉 and Lewis Hodous 何樂益 (1937) and on Chinese medicine by Nigel Wiseman 魏迺傑 and Féng Yè 馮燁 (2014). In addition, there are the three primary reference works of Western Daoist Studies: (1) *Daoism Handbook* (Kohn 2000; abbrev. DH); (2) *Historical Companion to the Daozang* (Schipper and Verellen 2004; abbrev. HCDZ); and (3) *Encyclopedia of Taoism* (Pregadio 2008; abbrev. EOT). There also are a variety of Chinese and Japanese dictionaries and encyclopedias of Daoism. Other Daoist technical glossaries may be found in my various translations (Komjathy 2007, 2008, 2013a, 2017a; Appendix #8 herein). For additional guidance see my *Title Index to Daoist Collections* (2002) and more recent "Research Guide to Daoist Studies" (2022).

To conclude (begin), I would offer the same advice about translation as about solo backcountry travel and mountaineering. Develop map and compass skills. Learn the terrain. Be careful. Listen to yourself. Don't give up. And then, along the way, perhaps you will encounter unexpected vistas and meet reliable companions. Perhaps you also will discover the transmission both within and beyond words.

道炁長存

FIGURE 11: Transmission of Daoist Scriptures
SOURCE: *Wǔdǒu sānyī tújué* 五斗三一圖訣 (Illustrated Instructions on the Three Ones of the Five Bushels), DZ 765, 17b (author's collection)

Lessons

Lesson 1

Examples of Daoist Text Titles with Abbreviations

The titles of Daoist texts often offer important insights into genre, associated content, primary concern, corresponding community, and revelatory source. The latter most often occurs in the titles of Daoist scriptures (*dàojīng* 道經), a specific genre of Daoist literature. With this first lesson, we move into our initial reading encounter with Daoist texts, namely, titles. Generally speaking, Daoist text titles are read in reverse: from end to beginning. As briefly mentioned in the general introduction herein, these usually help us first identify the specific literary genre and then, ideally, the source, affiliation, and primary concern of the text in question. While the *Dàozàng* is now more accessible with the various specialist reference works in Daoist Studies, this is not the case with less well-known and post-1607 works. Thus, we need to develop the ability to read Daoist text titles as a foundational linguistic skill for preliminary encounter and fuller translation work.

The present installment is bilingual with accompanying Pinyin Romanization, so let us simply consider some general insights. The titles of the *Lǎozǐ* and *Zhuāngzǐ*, later canonized as *jīng*, locate them in a larger "masters literature" (*zǐshū* 子書) of the Warring States (480–222 BCE) and Western/Early Han dynasty (206 BCE–9 CE). The *Huángdì nèijīng sùwèn* directs us to its association with the legendary Huángdì 黃帝 (Yellow Thearch/Yellow Emperor), with *dì*-thearch here indicating a divine ruler. We will return to this figure in Lessons #10 and #16. The

Língbǎo wúliàng dùrén shàngpǐn miàojīng indicates that it is a *jīng*-scripture associated with the Língbǎo 靈寶 (Numinous Treasure) movement and focused on salvation (*dùrén* 度人). As the *Tàishàng Lǎojūn shuō cháng qīngjìng miàojīng* is one of the most complex titles in the present sourcebook, let us consider it as instructive for using the standard methodology just articulated. The work is a *jīng*-scripture, here described as *miào* 妙 ("wondrous"), but with *zhēn* 眞/真 ("authentic perfect/true") being more common. It was "spoken" (*shuō* 說), here probably better understood as "revealed," by Lǎojūn 老君 (Lord Lao), the deified Lǎozǐ 老子 ("Master Lao"), high god of early Daoism, and personification of the Dao. Lǎojūn is one of the most commonly occurring figures in the larger Daoist tradition, including in its literary expressions. We will return to him in Lessons #4, #7, #12, and #17. The text in turn focuses on clarity and stillness (*qīngjìng* 清靜). However, what it rarely recognized, especially when the text is presented in its standard abbreviated title of *Qīngjìng jīng*, is that it is not just clarity and stillness, but *constancy* (*cháng* 常) of these Daoist contemplative states and traits that one aspires to realize (see Lesson #17). There are, in turn, a variety of commentaries (*zhù* 註/注) on this and other key Daoist scriptures, with the *Dàodé jīng* receiving the most attention. This brings our attention to a genre of Daoist literature that is derivative and based on Daoist *jīng*-scriptures as such. We will examine three key works in the final lessons (#25–28) of this primer. One interesting dimension of Daoist commentaries on a text-critical level, which is far beyond our current undertaking, centers on different editions of the associated source-text (see, e.g., Komjathy forthcoming). With Daoist commentaries, we also face another translation issue and challenge, namely, how to render the titles into English. In general, I prefer to keep the source-text in Pinyin Romanization. Thus, *Dàodé jīng zhù* 道德經註 would be "Commentary on the *Daode jing*," but one might rather choose "Commentary on the *Scripture on the Dao and Inner Power*." However, some distinction must be made between the commentary as such. With respect to citing Daoist texts more generally, an additional challenge involves deciding on viable title abbreviations.

The *Língbǎo wúliàng dùrén shàngpǐn miàojīng* is often abbreviated as *Dùrén jīng*. However, the *Chóngyáng lìjiào shíwǔ lùn* is variously abbreviated as *Chóngyáng shíwǔ lùn*, *Lìjiào shíwǔ lùn*, or just *Shíwǔ lùn*.

For guidance on these various texts readers may consult the reference works discussed in the general introduction herein, with additional assistance offered by Louis Komjathy's 康思奇 "Research Guide to Daoist Studies" (2022). Unfortunately, the matter of standardization is complicated by resistance among specialists in Daoist Studies and the absence of such titles in the authoritative *Historical Companion to the Daozang* (Schipper and Verellen 2004), which also often only provides English paraphrases of the Chinese titles rather than actual translations. For guidance on translations see Komjathy's "Daoist Literature in Translation" (2022) and Appendix #9 herein.

Primary Text

Lǎozǐ 老子
(Book of Venerable Masters)
Dàodé zhēnjīng 道德眞經 (DZ 664; ZH 553)
(Perfect Scripture on the Dao and Inner Power)

Zhuāngzǐ 莊子
(Book of Master Zhuang)
Nánhuá zhēnjīng 南華眞經 (DZ 670; ZH 616)
(Perfect Scripture of Master Nanhua [Southern Florescence])

Huángdì nèijīng sùwèn 黃帝內經素問 (DZ 1018; ZH 884)
(Yellow Thearch's Inner Classic: Basic Questions)[18]
Abbreviated: *Sùwèn* 素問 (Basic Questions)
Cf. *Língshū* 靈樞 (Numinous Pivot; DZ 1020; ZH 886)

Língbǎo wúliàng dùrén shàngpǐn miàojīng 靈寶無量度人上品妙經 (DZ 1; ZH 1282)
(Wondrous Scripture of the Upper Chapters on Limitless Salvation from Numinous Treasure)
Abbreviated: *Dùrén jīng* 度人經 (Scripture on Salvation)

Tàishàng Lǎojūn shuō cháng qīngjìng miàojīng 太上老君說常清靜妙經 (DZ 620; ZH 350)
(Wondrous Scripture on Constant Clarity and Stillness as Spoken by the Great High Lord Lao)
Abbreviated: *Qīngjìng jīng* 清靜經 (Scripture on Clarity and Stillness)

---

[18] There are technically at least four known *Huángdì nèijīng* 黃帝內經 (Yellow Thearch's Inner Classic) texts: *Língshū* 靈樞 (Numinous Pivot), *Míngtáng* 明堂 (Hall of Light), *Sùwèn* 素問 (Simple Questions), and *Tàisù* 太素 (Great Foundations), with the *Sùwèn* being most important and influential. See, e.g., Unschuld 1985.

Chóngyáng lìjiào shíwǔ lùn 重陽立教十五論 (DZ 1233; ZH 1010)
(Chongyang's [Redoubled Yang's] Fifteen Discourses to Establish the Teachings)
Abbreviated: *Chóngyáng shíwǔ lùn* 重陽十五論, *Lìjiào shíwǔ lùn* 立教十五論, or *Shíwǔ lùn* 十五論

Tàishàng Lǎojūn shuō cháng qīngjìng jīng sòngzhù 太上老君說常清靜經頌註 (DZ 974; ZH 354)
(Recitational Commentary on the *Taishang Laojun shuo chang qingjing jing*)
Abbreviated: *Qīngjìng jīng zhù* 清靜經註

Vocabulary

nèijīng 內經 (adj./n.)	"inner classic/inner scripture." Although often used as an abbreviation for a key work of classical Chinese medicine and mistranslated as "classic on internal medicine," the phrase is not text-specific. Rather, it points to an "inner" or "esoteric" work. From a Daoist perspective, there are many "inner scriptures," which often relates to "oral instruction" (kǒujué 口訣), "secrecy" (bì [mì] 秘/祕; mì 密), and "transmission" (chuán 傳)
dùrén 度人 (v./n.)	"salvation." Literally, "measuring/carrying humans." Also translated as "liberation." Usually indicates Mahāyāna 大乘 (Greater Vehicle) Buddhist influence, especially the bodhisattva (púsà 菩薩) ideal of universal salvation
qīngjìng 清靜 (n./n.)	"clarity and stillness." May also appear and be used in an adjectival sense: "clear and still." Also translated as "clear stillness" and "purity and tranquility." Interrelated and interdependent contemplative states/traits. Thus better thought of as "clarity-and-stillness." Also used in ascetic and monastic contexts to refer to celibacy (no sex), whether temporary or permanent
lùn 論 (n.)	"discourse." Invokes the Daoist emphasis on lùndào 論道 ("discoursing on the Dao"). Often relates to "oral instruction" (kǒujué 口訣). Here carries the connotation of "essay." Other related genres include piān 篇 ("treatise"), also translated as "folio" and "chapter," and yǔlù 語錄 ("discourse record"), also translated as "recorded sayings" and especially associated with Chán 禪 (Zen) Buddhism
zhù 註/注 (n.)	"commentary." Another major genre of Daoist literature. Especially focused on exegesis of jīng-scripture, thus revealing not only the Daoist practice of scripture study (jīngxué 經學), but also a vibrant Daoist scholastic sub-tradition

Lesson 2

Chapter Titles of the Zhuāngzǐ 莊子

(Book of Master Zhuang; DZ 670; ZH 616)

With this lesson and the next one, we move from our initial encounter with Daoist texts in terms of titles to the next preliminary form of engagement, namely, organization. If we are fortunate, Daoist texts have internal divisions or sections, and if we are even more fortunate there are chapter and/or section titles. This is the case for the *Zhuāngzǐ*. Also known by its honorific title *Nánhuá zhēnjīng* 南華眞經 (Perfect Scripture of Master Nanhua [Southern Florescence]; DZ 670; ZH 616), the *Zhuāngzǐ* 莊子 (*Chuāng-tzǔ*; Book of Master Zhuang; abbrev. ZZ) is an anonymous/pseudonymous multivocal anthology consisting of historical and textual layers dating from at least the fourth to the second century BCE. Often miscategorized as "philosophy" (i.e., disembodied ideas), it contains the teachings and practices associated with various anonymous, pseudonymous and named elders of the inner cultivation lineages of classical Daoism. The text consists of thirty-three prose chapters in the received (Guō Xiàng 郭象 [252–312 CE]) redaction. The so-called Inner Chapters (chs. 1–7) are generally accepted as containing the teachings and writings of the text's namesake, the historical Zhuāng Zhōu 莊周 ("Master Zhuang"; ca. 370-ca. 290 BCE). Although conventionally divided into the so-called Inner Chapters, Outer Chapters (chs. 8–22), and Miscellaneous Chapters (chs. 23–33), revisionist scholarship by A.C. Graham 葛瑞漢 (1919–1991), Liú Xiàogǎn 劉笑敢, Victor Mair 梅維恆, and Harold Roth 羅浩 identifies at least five distinct lineages or "schools" associated with a variety of chapters, which leads to a reorganization of the received text. In addition to providing entertaining stories and profound philosophical reflection, the text contains important information on the classical Daoist inner cultivation lineages, including specific inner cultivation techniques, apophatic and quietistic meditation in particular.

「魚相造乎水，人相造乎道。相造乎水者，穿池而養給；相造乎道者，無事而生定。故曰：魚相忘乎江湖，人相忘乎道術。」

"Fish thrive in water; humans thrive in the Dao. For those who thrive in water, dig a pond and they will find nourishment enough. For those who thrive in the Dao, don't bother about them and their lives will be secure. So it is said, fish forget each other in rivers and lakes; humans forget each other through the techniques of the Dao (*dàoshù* 道術)." (ch. 6; adapted from Watson 1968, 87)

For readers familiar with this Daoist text on a deeper level, the invocation of "techniques of the Dao," also translated as "arts of the Way," in concert with "forgetting" (*wàng* 忘) immediately connects to the germinal passage on a specific meditation method, namely, sitting-in-forgetfulness (*zuòwàng* 坐忘) (see Lesson #8). Another dimension of the text, rarely engaged in a more complete manner, centers on master-disciple dialogic exchanges. The latter became a major influence on the development of the Chán 禪 (Zen) Buddhist *yǔlù* 語錄 ("discourse record/recorded sayings") literary genre. The chapter titles themselves may be engaged as a contemplative exercise, offering insights into classical Daoist concerns as well as dimensions of classical and foundational Daoist practice-realization. For example, through carefree wandering (1), making things equal (2), and letting be, leaving alone (11), we may attune ourselves with the Great Ancestor (6) and the Way of Heaven (13).

Then we may overcome ingrained opinions (15), mend innate nature (16), and find utmost joy (18) as knowing wanders north (22). Perhaps, along the way, we sit and listen to the teachings of Gēngsāng Chǔ (23) and other key Daoist elders.

On a deeper language level and as we saw in Lesson #1, the earliest title locates the *Zhuāngzǐ* in the larger "masters literature" (*zǐshū* 子書). In addition, the received tripartite framework of "inner" (*nèi* 內), "outer" (*wài* 外), and "miscellaneous" (*zá* 雜) chapters draws our attention to one, foundational meaning of *piān* 篇, which contains the *zhú* 竹/⺮ ("bamboo") radical. Here meaning something like "chapter," this character later became used for a specific genre of Daoist literature, namely, "treatises" (see Lessons #3, #18, and #21). Along these lines and developing our engagement with *lùn* 論 in Lesson #1, as employed in the title of chapter two it means something like "discourse" or "discussion," but also suggests the possibility of "on [the topic of]" (see also Lessons #10 and #23). Moving further into the chapter titles themselves, ten in particular stand out for deeper foundational Daoist classical Chinese language facility. These are chapters one, two, three, five, six, twelve, thirteen, sixteen, twenty-six, and thirty-three (see vocabulary herein). Here I want to point out a number of larger connections and insights. First, each of the three characters in the title of chapter one contains the *chuò* 辵/辶 ("walk/move") radical. From a Daoist perspective, this suggests threefold or pure movement and further connects with the great Péng 鵬 bird at the opening of the chapter, the epitome of "being carefree" (*xiāoyáo* 逍遙). The latter may be paired with and possibly assumes *wúwéi* 無為 ("non-action") and *zìrán* 自然 ("suchness"). While these phrases are most often associated with the *Lǎozǐ* 老子 (Book of Venerable Masters) (see Lesson #7), they also appear in the *Zhuāngzǐ* itself (see chs. 1, 4–7, 10–17, 18, 21–25, 31, and 33). In medieval Daoism, both *wúwéi* and *xiāoyáo* become identified as major "fruits of the Dao" (*dàoguǒ* 道果), that is, signs of successful training. In the title of chapter three, the reference to *yǎngshēng* 養生 ("nourishing life"), which later becomes used to refer to health and longevity practice (see Lessons #14, #15, and

#22), is interesting, as it involves an explicit critique of excess concern for one's personal life. This further connects with the fuller critique in chapter fifteen, which refers to Dǎoyǐn 導引 (Guided Stretching) and respiratory methods, and again emphasizes apophatic meditation as the defining Daoist practice (see Lessons #6, #8, and #18). Along these lines, it is noteworthy that the title of chapter sixteen contains *xìng* 性 ("innate nature"). While commonly (and inaccurately) assumed to represent later "Buddhist" influence and to be a later Daoist concern, the character already appears in chapter twenty-two of the probably mid-fourth century BCE *Nèiyè* 內業 (Inward Training) (see Lesson #6).

內靜外敬，
能反其性。

Inwardly still and outwardly reverent,
You can return to innate nature.

Wài 外 ("external/outer") in the title of chapter twenty-six is straightforward. However, as a Daoist technical term related to contemplative practice, it also may be a verb in the sense of "externalizing." In fact, this very phrase *wàiwù* 外物, "externalizing things" and perhaps "beyond thinghood," appears among the seven contemplative states and stages emphasized by the female Daoist elder Nǚyǔ 女偊 (Woman Yu) in chapter six. Finally, in the title of chapter thirty-three, *tiānxià* 天下 (lit., "under-sky") is often translated as "all-under-heaven" and refers to the "whole world," usually in the sense of the human socio-political "world." This sometimes stands in contrast to both *shìjiè* 世界 ("world") and *yǔzhòu* 宇宙 ("space-time/universe") (see Lesson #9). However, on a more technical level and along with the cosmological chapters (chs. 12–14), it inspires us to consider what the "world" is from a classical and perhaps foundational Daoist perspective. Specifically, as we move into the chapter, we once again discover that "Daoists" are those committed to the above-mentioned "techniques of the Dao," with an accompanying self-conscious sense of Daoist community and emerging tradition.

There are three primary reliable English translations of the *Zhuāngzǐ*, namely, those of Burton Watson 華茲生 (1925–2017) (1968; complete), A.C. Graham 葛瑞漢 (1919–1991) (2001 [1981]; partial), and Victor Mair 梅維恆 (1998 [1994]; complete). Watson is the most commonly cited translation in Daoist Studies. However, Graham is helpful for comparing English renderings of classical Daoist technical terms, while Mair is especially helpful for deciphering names. There also is what may be referred to as the "Zhuangzi Philosophy Industry" (ZZPI), which publishes incessant independent studies and edited volumes that lack interpretive attention to the core contemplative and mystical dimensions of the text, its connection to the larger classical Daoist textual corpus, and its affiliation with the Daoist tradition as a whole. Interested individuals may consult the "Self-Study Guide to the *Zhuāngzǐ*" circulated by the Daoist Foundation 道教基金會.

Primary Text

Chapter #	Title	Translation
1	Xiāoyáo yóu 逍遙遊	Carefree Wandering
2	Qíwù lùn 齊物論	On Making Things Equal
3	Yǎngshēng zhǔ 養生主	Essentials of Nourishing Life
4	Rénjiān shì 人間世	The Human World
5	Déchōng fú 德充符	Talisman of Virtue Complete
6	Dà zōngshī 大宗師	The Great Ancestral Teacher
7	Yìng dìwáng 應帝王	Responding to Rulers and Kings
8	Piánmǔ 駢拇	Webbed Toes
9	Mǎtí 馬蹄	Horses' Hooves
10	Qūqiè 胠篋	Ransacking Coffers
11	Zàiyòu 在宥	Letting Be, Leaving Alone
12	Tiāndì 天地	Heaven and Earth
13	Tiāndào 天道	The Way of Heaven
14	Tiānyùn 天運	Celestial Revolutions
15	Kèyì 刻意	Ingrained Opinions
16	Shànxìng 繕性	Mending Innate Nature
17	Qiūshuǐ 秋水	Autumn Floods
18	Zhìlè 至樂	Utmost Joy
19	Dáshēng 達生	Understanding Life
20	Shānmù 山木	The Mountain Tree
21	Tiánzǐ Fāng 田子方	Adept Square Field
22	Zhī běiyóu 知北遊	Knowledge Wanders North
23	Gēngsāng Chǔ 庚桑楚	Gēngsāng Chǔ (Western Mulberry Cane)
24	Xú Wúguǐ 徐無鬼	Ghostless Xú
25	Zéyáng 則陽	Zéyáng (Sudden Yang)
26	Wàiwù 外物	External Things
27	Yùyán 寓言	Imputed Words
28	Ràngwáng 讓王	Abdicating Kingship
29	Dào Zhí 盜跖	Thief Zhí
30	Yuèjiàn 說劍[19]	Delighting in Swords
31	Yúfù 魚父	An Old Fisherman
32	Liè Yùkòu 列禦寇	Liè Yùkòu
33	Tiānxià 天下	All-under-Heaven

---

[19] Also Romanized as "Shuōjiàn 說劍" (Discussing Swords).

Vocabulary

xiāoyáo 逍遙 (adj./adj.)	"carefree ease." Also translated as "being carefree," "free and easy," etc. Both characters contain the *chuò* 辵/辶 ("walk/move") radical. Taken in context, threefold movement. Closely related to *wúwéi* 無為 ("non-action"), *zàiyòu* 在宥 ("letting be, leaving alone"), and *zìrán* 自然 ("suchness"). Later becomes one of the major "fruits of the Dao" (*dàoguǒ* 道果), that is, signs of successful training
qíwù 齊物 (v./n.)	"making things equal." *Qí* 齊 also may mean "identical," "level," "uniform," etc. Contextually related to *wàiwù* 外物 ("externalizing things")
yǎngshēng 養生 (v./n.)	"nourishing life." *Yǎng* 養 is one of a number of key Daoist technical terms utilizing an animal husbandry analogy. The character consists of *yáng* 羊/⺶ ("sheep") above *shí* 食 ("feed"). Cf. *xù* 畜 ("tend"). While Yǎngshēng is later used to refer to health and longevity practice, classical Daoists emphasize *shēng* 生 ("aliveness/life/vitality") as consisting of *jīng* 精 ("vital essence") and *qì* 氣 ("subtle breath") and as a natural state and outcome of apophatic meditation
dé 德 (n.)	"inner power." Also appears as 惪. Also translated as "integrity," "potency," and "virtue." The way in which the Dao manifests in/as/through embodied human activity and being in the world, especially beneficial and transformative presence, behavior and influence
zōng 宗 (n.)	"Ancestor." Another name for the Dao 道. Thus, overlaps with other, parallel designations, including Mother (*mǔ* 母), Root (*běn* 本/*gēn* 根), and Source (*yuán* 元/原/源). That from which everything emerges and to which everything returns

tiāndì 天地 (n./n.)	"heaven and earth." *Tiān* 天 more literally refers to the "sky" and "cosmos" by extension. The translation of "Heaven" should be avoided as it may inaccurately invoke Christocentric views and lead to confusion. As paired characters 天 and 地 also appear as *qián* 乾 ☰ (pure yang) and *kūn* 坤 ☷ (pure yin), *yuán* 圓 ("circle") and *fāng* 方 ("square"), as well as *xuán* 玄 ("dark") and *huáng* 黃 ("yellow"), respectively. Taken together, they point to the universe as experienced by human beings on a phenomenological level
tiāndào 天道 (adj./n.)	"Way of Heaven." Both the universe as transformative process (*zàohuà* 造化) based on yin-yang differentiation and interaction as well as associated human cosmological attunement. See also LZ 9, 47, 73, 77, 79, and 81; ZZ 12–14; and SW 2
xìng 性 (n.)	"innate nature." From a Daoist perspective, one's original and inherent connection to the Dao. Especially associated with the heart (*xīn* 心). In classical Daoism, sometimes used synonymously with *mìng* 命 ("fate/life-destiny") without the clear distinction utilized in the later Daoist tradition
wàiwù 外物 (adj./n.)	"external things." Read as adjective/noun, straightforwardly refers to animals, objects, etc. as encountered and experienced. Thus, basically synonymous with *wànwù* 萬物 ("ten thousand beings/things"). However, also used in a more technical contemplative sense as "externalizing things" and perhaps even "beyond thinghood"
tiānxià 天下 (n./prep.)	"all-under-heaven." More literally, "under-sky." Also translated as "whole world." Usually refers to the human socio-political "world." Cf. *shìjiè* 世界 ("world") and *yǔzhòu* 宇宙 ("space-time/universe")

LESSON 3

CHAPTER TITLES OF THE *BÀOPǓZǏ NÈIPIÀN* 抱朴子內篇

(INNER CHAPTERS OF MASTER EMBRACING SIMPLICITY; DZ 1185; ZH 980)

CONTINUING TO DEVELOP OUR ENGAGEMENT with textual organization from the previous lesson, here we focus on the chapter titles of the *Bàopǔzǐ nèipiān*. The *Bàopǔzǐ nèipiān* 抱朴子內篇 (Inner Chapters of Master Embracing Simplicity; DZ 1185; ZH 980; abbrev. BPZ) is a key work of early medieval Daoism and a *summa* of fourth-century religious traditions and related methods. It was written by Gé Hóng 葛洪 (Bàopǔ 抱朴 [Embracing Simplicity]; 283–343), a Daoist alchemist, paternal grandnephew of Gé Xuán 葛玄 (164–244), and systematizer of the Tàiqīng 太清 (Great Clarity) movement. Although not part of the three primary Tàiqīng scriptures, the text offers important insights into the views of its key representative and systematizer. Here we also should note that Gé Hóng's Daoist name Bàopǔzǐ 抱朴子 has been inelegantly translated as "The Master Who Embraces Simplicity," which, in addition to evidencing a "tin ear," lacks contextual imagination and understanding of Daoist naming traditions "on the ground." Significantly, the name derives from chapter nineteen of the anonymous fourth-second century BCE *Dàodé jīng* 道德經 (Scripture on the Dao and Inner Power):

見素抱樸；
少私寡欲。

Appear plain and embrace simplicity;
Lessen selfishness and decrease desires.[20]

Interestingly, Gé himself invokes similar commitments for following an alchemical path (*dāndào* 丹道).

故窮富極貴，不足以誘之焉，其餘何足以悅之乎。直刃沸鑊，不足以劫之焉，謗讟何足以戚之乎。常無心於眾煩，而未始與物雜也。

Thus, since extreme riches or the highest honors are insufficient to lure them, how could other things beguile them? Since exposed blades and boiling cauldrons are insufficient to coerce them, how could defamation aggrieve them? They are constantly unaffected by various vexations, and they never mix with things. (DZ 1185, 1.3b; see also 1.2b, 2.4b)

Gé's name in concert with the accompanying Daoist principles and the focus of two chapters (chs. 1 and 9) on the Dao/Mystery, coupled with the intertextuality throughout, reveals important connections between classical Daoism and early medieval Daoism. The current work is, in turn, called "inner" because its chapters deal with more esoteric and important matters. As there is an associated *Bàopǔzǐ wàipiān* 抱朴子外篇 (Outer Chapters of Master Embracing Simplicity; DZ 1187; ZH 981; part. trl. Sailey 1978), which is more Ruist ("Confucian") in orientation and covers socio-political aspects of the Jìn 晉 dynasty (265–420) and the contemporaneous Ruist tradition, neither should technically

---

[20] Note the pronunciation of 見 here as *xiàn* ("appear"), rather than the more common *jiàn* ("see"). One is manifesting, not perceiving, said quality.

be abbreviated as simply *Bàopǔzǐ* (BPZ) (see also Lesson #10). Nonetheless, the latter most often refers to our current text. Dating to 320, but first completed around 317 and revised around 330, the *Bàopǔzǐ nèipiān* consists of twenty individually titled chapters. This Daoist text provides information on the production of elixirs (*dān* 丹) through external alchemy (*wàidān* 外丹), also referred to as "laboratory/operational alchemy," which is the highest religious pursuit according to Gé. The text includes information on Tàiqīng, including key figures, texts, methods, and so forth. It also is loosely linked with the Gé family lineage, which later connects to the Língbǎo 靈寶 (Numinous Treasure) movement. The text also details contemporaneous contemplative, dietetic, exorcistic, and hygienic techniques. In addition to developing a foundational understanding of Daoist *wàidān*, the chapter titles provide a window into some of Gé's central concerns, including his engagement with and, in fact, critiques of contemporaneous Daoist movements such as Xuánxué 玄學 (Profound Learning; so-called "Neo-Daoism" [*sic*]).

五千文雖出老子，然皆泛論較略耳。其中了不肯首尾全舉其事，有可承按者也。但暗誦此經，而不得要道，直為徒勞耳。又況不及者乎 … 至使末世利口之奸佞，無行之弊子，得以老莊為窟藪，不亦惜哉。

Even if the *Wǔqiān wén* 五千文 (Five Thousand [Character] Composition) [*Dàodé jīng*] come from Lǎozǐ, they are only a general discussion and a rough outline of our topic [alchemy and immortality]. The contents in no way allow a complete exposition of the matter from beginning to end that could be employed as support for our pursuit. Merely to recite this scripture blindly without securing the essential Way would be to undergo useless toil. How much worse in the case of inferior texts….Is it not regrettable that the eloquent rogues and base scoundrels of these later days should be allowed refuge in Lǎo and Zhuāng? (DZ 1185, 8.5b-6a; see also 14.2b-3a, 16.4b)

Sounds familiar.

In terms of literary genre, the *Bàopǔzǐ*, like the *Zhuāngzǐ*, appears to present itself as part of the "masters literature" (*zǐshū* 子書). However, as received, it is further identified as *nèipiān* 內篇, here rendered more straightforwardly as "inner chapters," but also translatable as "inner treatise." As we saw in Lessons #1 and #2, *piān* 篇, which contains the *zhú* 竹/⺮ ("bamboo") radical, may mean "chapter" and/or "folios," but later became used for a specific genre of Daoist literature, namely, "treatises" (see Lessons #3, #18, and #21). Interestingly, also like the *Zhuāngzǐ*, but differing from other classical and early Daoist works (see Lessons #9 and #10), each BPZ chapter is unique, lacking a framing character (e.g., *lùn* 論). At the same time, the matter of *piān* as "chapter" becomes complexified here because each chapter corresponds to one "scroll" (*juǎn* 卷), of varying lengths. As we saw in the general introduction, *juǎn* refers to a specific paper measurement, but here is used for a given chapter. Do we need to use different technical terms (e.g., "folios" and "scrolls"), respectively? In terms of more technical lexigraphy and moving further into the chapter titles themselves, five in particular stand out (chs. 1, 2, 4, 9 and 18), although the *Bàopǔzǐ nèipiān* may require more antecedent religious literacy. In any case, the titles of chapters one and nine again draw our attention to the central importance of the Dao 道, here also referred to as Mystery (*xuán* 玄), as the sacred and ultimate concern of Daoists (see Lesson #7). Significantly, the text *begins with the Dao*, as perhaps should any and all Daoist works. This again challenges *assumed* bifurcations and dichotomies about, within, and across the diverse communities and movements of the Daoist tradition. The title of chapter four, Jīndān 金丹, may mean "Golden Elixir," or refer to the separate alchemical substances, namely, gold (Au) and cinnabar (HgS). However, as a technical term and as utilized by Gé Hóng, Jīndān refers to "alchemy" more generally, while *dān* may refer to "elixirs." This chapter thus connects to the titles of chapters eleven and sixteen and prepares us, at least hypothetically, to encounter specific alchemical ingredients/substances (*wù* 物) and associated elixir formulas (*fāng* 方). Various other chapters (2–3, 7–8, 12–13, 15, and 20), in turn, reveal the communal and dialogic dimensions of the text, including the accompanying "principles" (*lǐ* 理) and "decrees" (*zhǐ* 旨). The ultimate aspiration and culmination of alchemical transmutation is "immortality" (*xiān* 仙) (ch. 2) and "perfection" (*zhēn* 眞) (ch. 18). Finally, as was the case with the *Zhuāngzǐ* in Lesson #2, we may engage the chapter titles as a Daoist contemplative exercise. Perhaps, after penetrating the Mystery (ch. 1), we may discuss immortals and immortality (ch. 2). Then, perhaps, we will fully embrace the Golden Elixir (ch. 4), while resolving obstructions (ch. 8), diligently seeking (ch. 14), ascending and fording (ch. 17), and ultimately allaying doubts (ch. 20). For Daoists, this relates to "constancy" (*cháng* 常), "stability" (*dìng* 定) "trust" (*xìn* 信), and the like. That is, the text itself may mirror the alchemical path, in which one searches, dialogues, studies, and ideally becomes completely transformed into a different kind of being. One enters the transpersonal and transtemporal community of immortals.

The definitive Western language study of the Tàiqīng movement is Fabrizio Pregadio's 玄英 *Great Clarity* (2005), with important information also contained in Robert Campany's 康若柏 *To Live as Long as Heaven and Earth* (2002) and *Making Transcendents* (2009). A complete, but dated and often problematic English translation was published by James Ware 威厄/魏魯男 (1901–1977) as *Alchemy, Medicine, and Religion in China of A.D. 320: The Nei P'ien of Ko Hung* (1966). While relatively reliable on the literary elements and alchemical ingredients, it is deficient on other Daoist technical materials, including tradition-specific terminology. The *Bàopǔzǐ nèipiān* is currently being translated in a complete, annotated literary and scholarly edition by the Daoist Translation Committee 道教翻譯學會, under the editorial direction of Louis Komjathy 康思奇.

Primary Text

Chapter #	Title	Translation
1	Chàngxuán 暢玄	Penetrating the Mystery
2	Lùnxiān 論仙	Discussing Immortals
3	Duìsú 對俗	Responding to the Ordinary
4	Jīndān 金丹	The Golden Elixir
5	Zhìlǐ 至理	Ultimate Principles
6	Wēizhǐ 微旨	Subtle Decrees
7	Sāinán 塞難	Countering Objections
8	Shìzhì 釋滯	Releasing Obstructions
9	Dàoyì 道意	The Meaning of "Dao"
10	Míngběn 明本	Illuminating the Foundations
11	Xiānyào 仙藥	The Medicine of Immortality
12	Biànwèn 辨問	Discerning Questions
13	Jíyán 極言	The Ultimate Words
14	Qínqiú 勤求	Diligently Seeking
15	Záyīng 雜應	Miscellaneous Responses
16	Huángbái 黃白	Yellow and White [Gold and Silver]
17	Dēngshè 登涉	Ascending and Fording
18	Dìzhēn 地眞	Terrestrial Perfection
19	Xiálǎn 遐覽	Broad Overview
20	Qūhuò 祛惑	Allaying Doubts

Vocabulary

xuán 玄 (n.|adj.)	"mystery|mysterious." Also translated as "darkness/dark." Here used as a Daoist (non)name for the Dao 道, in the sense of Mystery. Thus, overlaps with other, parallel designations, including Darkness (*mò* 默), Silence (*jì* 寂), Subtle (*wēi* 微), and Wondrous (*miào* 妙). Like "Dao," these are placeholders for that which transcends any and all names and conceptions
xiān 仙 (n.)	"immortal." Also translated as "ascendent" and "transcendent." Usually appears as *xiānrén* 仙人. Along with *zhēnrén* 真人 ("Perfected"), the primary spiritual ideal of later Daoism
Jīndān 金丹 (adj./n.)	"Golden Elixir." More literally, "gold and cinnabar." In technical usage, refers to "alchemy," external alchemy (*wàidān* 外丹) in the present case
lǐ 理 (n.)	"principles." A complex, multivalent character, with the meaning varying depending on context. Most frequently used as a cosmological concept related to yin-yang differentiation and interaction. Technically, distinguished from "form" (*xíng* 形), "function" (*yòng* 用), "substance" (*tǐ* 體), and so forth. Here used in a broader sense of "principles" or "guidelines." Cf. *yuánzé* 原則
zhēn 眞/真 (n.|adj.)	"Perfected|perfect." Also "perfection." Also translated as "authenticity/authentic," "reality/real," and "truth/true." Here used in the sense of *zhēnrén* 眞人/真人 ("Perfected"). Along with *xiānrén* 仙人 ("immortal"), the primary spiritual ideal of later Daoism
huò 惑 (n.|v.)	"doubt|doubt." May also refer to "confusion" and/or "delusion." One of the major obstacles to Daoist practice. Often contrasted with "determination" (*zhì* 志) and "trust" (*xìn* 信), in the sense of confidence and resolution

LESSON 4

THE NINE PRACTICES
FROM THE *TÀISHÀNG LǍOJŪN JĪNGLÜ* 太上老君經律
(SCRIPTURAL STATUTES OF THE
GREAT HIGH LORD LAO; DZ 786; ZH 540)

THE NINE PRACTICES (*JIǓXÍNG* 九行), also translatable as the Nine Activities and even Nine Movements, are the earliest known Daoist "precepts" (*jiè* 戒/誡), although they are better understood as foundational Daoist principles, qualities, and values, and perhaps secondarily as conduct guidelines. They may be thought of as a primer or distillation of a foundational Daoist view. As the name indicates, they are nine principles derived from the anonymous fourth-second century BCE *Lǎozǐ* 老子 (Book of Venerable Masters), also known as the *Dàodé jīng* 道德經 (Scripture on the Dao and Inner Power; DZ 664; ZH 553). The Nine Practices may, in turn, be read as a quasi-commentary on that classical Daoist text (see Komjathy forthcoming). They are specifically associated with the early Tiānshī 天師 (Celestial Masters) movement, also known as Zhèngyī 正一 (Orthodox Unity). This means that they are roughly third-century BCE Daoist principles systematized in the present form possibly in the third century CE. The Nine Practices are extant in the opening section (1a) of the *Tàishàng Lǎojūn jīnglü* 太上老君經律 (Scriptural Statutes of the Great High Lord Lao; DZ 786; ZH 540; abbrev. *Lǎojūn jīnglü*), which is a sixth-century Tiānshī precept anthology. Paralleling the discussion in Lesson #1, they are presented as inspired and possibly revealed by Lǎojūn 老君 (Lord Lao), the deified Lǎozǐ 老子 ("Master Lao"), high god of early Daoism, and personification of the Dao. "He" in turn became the most important revelatory source for the entirety of the larger Daoist tradition (see, e.g., Seidel 1969; Kohn 1998a). In addition to the Nine Practices, that text includes the Twenty-Seven Xiǎng'ěr 想爾 Precepts (1b-2a) and the 180 Precepts of Lord Lao (2a-12b). On a text-critical level, it is important to note that the corresponding headings of the Nine Practices and Twenty-Seven Xiǎng'ěr Precepts, namely, "Precepts from the Venerable Scripture on the Dao and Inner Power" and "Xiǎng'ěr Precepts on the Venerable Scripture on the Dao and Inner Power," have been reversed in the received DZ edition. In any case, the Twenty-Seven Xiǎng'ěr Precepts derive from the probably third-century *Lǎozǐ xiǎng'ěr zhù* 老子想爾注 (Commentary Thinking through the *Laozi*; DH 55; TK 56; ZH 557), while the 180 Precepts of Lord Lao also are extant in another Dūnhuáng 敦煌 manuscript titled *Lǎojūn shuō yībǎi bāshí jiè* 老君說一百八十戒 (180 Precepts Spoken by Lord Lao; DH 87; TK 78; ZH 542).[21] The 180 Precepts date to at least as early as 350 CE and are intended for libationers (*jìjiǔ* 祭酒), high-ranking members of the Celestial Masters religious community equivalent to something like "parish priests." Connecting these various dates with the relative complexity of the three precept lists, the Nine Practices may actually date to the formative moments of this sub-tradition and are intended for the religious community as a whole. For example, as expressed in the *Lǎozǐ xiǎng'ěr zhù*, which is attributed to the third Celestial Master Zhāng Lǔ 張魯 (d. 215 CE),

> Whenever human beings wish to undertake some action, they should first gauge it against the precepts of the Dao (*dàojiè* 道誡), considering it calmly to determine that the principles of their

---

[21] "DH" refers to the *Dūnhuáng dàozàng* 敦煌道藏 (Dunhuang Daoist Canon; dat. 1999), while "TK" designates the *Tonkō dōkei* 敦煌道經 (Dunhuang Daoist Scriptures; dat. 1978–1979). Numbers follow my "Title Index to the *Dūnhuáng dàozàng* 敦煌道藏" (STIDC #4; 2022). "TK" replaces my earlier use of "DH" for that collection in my *Title Index to Daoist Collections* (2002).

action do not contravene the Dao. Only then should they gradually pursue it, so that the way of life does not depart from them. (see Lesson #27)

While it is impossible to know for certain, it may be that the Nine Practices are the primary "precepts of the Dao" mentioned and advocated by Zhāng Lǔ. In addition to providing insights into key Daoist values, including as a potential foundation of an early Daoist theocracy, the text is noteworthy for again revealing connective strands between classical Daoism and early Daoism. Especially significant is Practice #4 (qīngjìng 清靜), which is a key constituent of the Daoist tradition as a whole.

On a language level, we may also note the use of shàng 上 ("high/above"), zhōng 中 ("middle"), and xià 下 ("low/below"), which are often used in the sense of "first/second/third." There is a corresponding interpretive question about simple sequencing and/or hierarchal ordering. The list does appear to move from the most important/primary to the less important/secondary (or tertiary in this case), at least as articulated by members of the early Tiānshī community. We also note the use of Daoist ternary numerology (3x3=9), which might be further connected to the received Dàodé jīng itself (9x9=81). Grammatically speaking, the Nine Practices are quite simple, basically consisting of nine sets of a single verb-character followed by a specific Daoist quality to be cultivated. With the exception of Practice #8, each principle consists of two Chinese characters preceded by xíng 行 ("practice"), here functioning like a directive, even admonition. What the Nine Practices allow us to do, and thus the challenge and opportunity that they represent for aspiring translators, involves beginning to develop a tradition-specific Daoist lexigraphy. Particularly interesting are the various "beyond/non-states" (wú 無), specifically Practice #1, #4, and #7. This deeper structure raises an additional interpretive question as well: Should the associated, proceeding principles and practices be taken as an elucidation of the opening, framing ones?

The Nine Practices have been translated by Stephen Bokenkamp 柏

夷 (1997, 49–50), Louis Komjathy 康思奇 (2008 [2003], v. 5), and again by Louis Komjathy and Kate Townsend (2022) and Louis Komjathy (forthcoming). They thus represent one of the foundations of Daoist practice-realization as undertaken and taught within the Daoist Foundation 道教基金會. The more recent titles by Komjathy discuss them from a lived Daoist perspective as well as their connection to the *Lǎozǐ/Dàodé jīng*, respectively. An online lecture by Komjathy also is available. Finally, there is an interesting "Western Daoist" adaptation of Bokenkamp by Liú Míng 劉明 (Charles Belyea; 1947–2015) (1998)[P], a self-identified Daoist priest and former leader of Orthodox Daoism in America (ODA).

Primary Text

《道德尊經戒》

行無為，行柔弱，行守雌，勿先動。
　　　　　　　　此上最三行。

行無名，行清靜，行諸善。
　　　　　　　　此中最三行。

行無欲，行知止足，行推讓。
　　　　　　　　此下最三行。

Precepts from the Venerable Scripture on the Dao and Inner Power

Practice non-action.
Practice softness and weakness.
Practice guarding the feminine. Do not initiate actions.
> *These are the highest three practices.*

Practice being nameless.
Practice clarity and stillness.
Practice being adept.
> *These are the middle three practices.*

Practice being desireless.
Practice knowing how to stop and be content.[22]
Practice yielding and withdrawing.
> *These are the lower three practices.*

---

[22] Or, "how to stop with sufficiency/contentment."

Vocabulary

Lǎojūn 老君 (name/title)	"Lord Lao." The deified Lǎozǐ 老子 ("Master Lao"), high god of early Daoism, and personification of the Dao
lǜ 律 (n.)	"statute." Rules and codes. Conduct guidelines. Often synonymous with *jiè* 戒 ("precept")
dàodé 道德 (n./n.)	"Dao and inner power." Also translated as "Way and virtue." *Dào* 道 (Tao/Way) is the sacred and ultimate concern of Daoists. *Dé* 德 ("inner power"), also translated as "integrity," "potency" and "virtue," is the way in which the Dao manifests in/as/through embodied human activity and being in the world, especially beneficial and transformative presence, behavior and influence. Here the paired characters refer to the title of the *Dàodé jīng* 道德經 (Scripture on the Dao and Inner Power), which is conventionally divided into the so-called *dàojīng* 道經 ("Dao section"; chs. 1–37) and so-called *déjīng* 德經 ("inner power section"; chs. 38–81)
jiè 戒 (n.)	"precept." Also translated as "admonition." The most general Daoist term for rules and regulations. Contains the *gē* 戈 ("halberd") radical. Conduct principles and guidelines
xíng 行 (v.)	"practice." More literally means "walk/move/travel." Also later used in the Buddhist-influenced sense of "good deeds"
wúwéi 無為 (neg./v.)	"non-action." Literally, "without acting/doing." Also translated as "not-acting/not-doing." Effortlessness. Also understood as non-interference and non-intervention
shǒu 守 (v.)	"guard." Key classical and foundational Daoist term for "meditation," especially apophatic and quietistic (emptiness-/stillness-based) forms. Some common names include *shǒujìng* 守靜 ("guarding stillness"), *shǒuyī* 守一 ("guarding the One"), and *shǒuzhōng* 守中 ("guarding the Center"), with *shǒuyī* being most influential. The latter eventually became a general term for Daoist meditation, even including visualization (*cúnxiǎng* 存想 [lit., "maintain thought"])

cí 雌 (n.)	"female." Also translated as "feminine." Technically, a small female bird (zhuī 隹) (e.g., sparrow). *Not human* (nǚ 女). Basically synonymous with pìn 牝 ("female [ox]"). Usually corresponds to yin 陰
qīngjìng 清靜 (n./n.)	"clarity and stillness." May also appear and be used as adjectives: "clear and still." Also translated as "clear stillness" and "purity and tranquility." Interrelated and interdependent contemplative states/traits. Thus better thought of as "clarity-and-stillness." The characters also appear separately and as 清淨
míng 名 (n.)	"name." May also mean "fame" and "reputation." One's personal name given by one's parents. Corresponds to familial and social identity. Cf. shēn 身 ("body/self") and sī 私 ("personal/selfish")
shàn 善 (adj.|n.)	"adept|aptitude." Conventionally means "good/goodness/to be good at." While may refer to conventional morality, more often used in Daoist contexts in the sense of skill, excellence, and even mastery developed through practice. E.g., Cook Dīng 丁
zhǐ 止 (v.)	"stop." Also translated as "pause." Originally, "footprint." A key Daoist approach and practice. Related to other directive characters, including guǎ 寡 ("decrease"), shǎo 少 ("lessen"), and sǔn 損 ("decrease")
zú 足 (adj.|n.|n.)	"enough|sufficiency|contentment." Literally means "foot," and "leg" by extension. May also mean "abundance/affluence." Taken in combination with zhǐ 止, double awareness of and presence in one's activities

Lesson 5

Of Knobs & Pendants
Xíngqì yùpèi míng 行氣玉佩銘
(Jade Ornament Inscription on Circulating Qi)

THE ARTIFACT EARLY ON LABELLED *Xíngqì yùpèi míng* 行氣玉佩銘 (Jade Ornament Inscription on Circulating Qi) and now simply *Xíngqì míng* 行氣銘 (Inscription on Circulating Qi) by Chinese archaeologists is an excavated object of unclear provenance and disputed date.[23] Possibly dating to around 380 BCE and discovered around 1953, it has been conjectured that it may have an origin in the ancient Chinese state of *Gar (Hán) 韓 (403–230 BCE), specifically near present-day Luòyáng 洛陽, Hénán, or in the ancient Chinese state of *Dzej (Qí) 齊 (386–221 BCE), which occupied present-day Shāndōng and Héběi provinces.[24] The original purpose of the object is unclear, but it may have been the knob of a staff, hilt of a weapon, handle attached to the wooden bar of a scroll painting, or a writing tablet. In keeping with revisionist views of classical Daoism, and perhaps too radically, the first hypothesis may point to a Daoist community elder. In any case, the *Xíngqì míng* is not a "Daoist text" per se, as it probably pre-dates or at least is roughly contemporaneous with the earliest hypothetical inner cultivation lineages

---

[23] In Western-language publications, the artifact also is referred to as the "Duodecagonal Jade Tablet Inscription on Breath Circulation" and "Twelve-sided Jade Knob Inscription" due to its material qualities and layout, namely, twelve sides consisting of three characters each (36 characters total).

[24] *Gar and *Dzej are the Baxter-Sagart Old Chinese phonetic reconstructions of the modern "Mandarin" Hán and Qí, respectively. See general introduction herein.

of classical Daoism (ca. 350 BCE). It is currently housed in the Tiānjīn lìshǐ bówùguǎn 天津歷史博物館 (Tianjin History Museum) and also disseminated as epigraphic (inscription) reproductions. On a material culture level, the object brings our attention to not only other materials beyond later woodblock texts, but also the reality of different character scripts and calligraphic styles (see general introduction). That is, this is Chinese before the various stages and forms of "standardization."

On a language level and in terms of grammar, the "text" is interesting for using a simple conditional structure, namely, ☐ 則 ☐ (A then B).²⁵ In more "standard" classical Chinese, this structure appears as 如/若…則… (If…then…) (see also Appendix #3). More liberally, we may think of it as ☐ leads to/results in ☐. When consisting of a longer series of sequential statements, this is sometimes referred to as a "sorites/sortie argument." On an interpretive level, the framing phrase and assigned title *xíngqì* 行氣 brings our attention to the multiple meanings of qi. The latter, which contains *qì* 气 ("steam/vapor") and has a sense of "atmosphere," is a traditional Chinese and thus Daoist cosmological term that may refer to both physical respiration and/or a more subtle current/presence. Both are viable here, but the former is more debatable. In addition to contextual meaning, this is partially because there are specific characters indicating actual breathing, such as *hūxī* 呼吸 (lit., "exhale and inhale") (see Lesson #2), with both characters containing the *kǒu* 口 ("mouth") radical. That is, unlike actual physical respiration and breath, which involve nose (*bí* 鼻), mouth (*kǒu* 口), and lungs (*fèi* 肺), qi does not. In keeping with my larger views about these and related materials, I understand qi as "subtle" or "vital breath" here. Along these lines, it is open to interpretation whether the artifact points towards cosmological attunement, seated meditation, and/or movement practice. If it is the latter, the *Xíngqì míng* would represent the earliest known evidence for what would later become known as

---

²⁵ Here and in similar examples of grammatical constructions ☐ indicates any inserted character. Such "empty boxes" also are used in Chinese text-critical work to indicate missing characters.

Yǎngshēng 養生 (Nourishing Life), or health and longevity techniques, and related *fúqì* 服氣 ("qi ingestion") practices in particular (see Lessons #2, #14–15, and #22). It may be further connected with the so-called *Dǎoyǐn tú* 導引圖 (Illustrations of Guided Stretching; ca. 168 BCE) (see Harper 1998; Kohn 2008) as early source-points for the later Daoist Yǎngshēng sub-tradition.

The *Xíngqì míng* has been translated by Hellmut Wilhelm 衛德明 (1905–1990) (1948, 385 [German]), Joseph Needham 李約瑟 (1900–1995) et al. (1956, 242), and Harold Roth 羅浩 (1999, 162–63). Note that the latter, as is the case with his scholarship in general, problematically claims that this relates to the "practice of breath meditation."

Primary Text

FIGURE 12: *Xíngqì yùpèi míng* 行氣玉佩銘
(Jade Ornament Inscription on Circulating Qi)

行氣：深則蓄，蓄則伸，伸則下，下則定，定則固，固則萌，萌則長，長則退，退則天。天機舂在上；地機舂在下。順則生；逆則死。[26]

---

[26] Harold Roth (1999, 162–63) makes the following emendations: *tūn* 吞 ("swallow") for *shēn* 深 ("deep") and *fù* 复 ("return") for *tuì* 退 ("retreat").

For circulating qi,
Deepening leads to accumulation;
Accumulating leads to expansion;
Expanding leads to descent;
Descending leads to stability;
Stabilizing leads to solidity;
Solidifying leads to germination;
Germinating leads to development;
Developing leads to retreat;
Retreating leads to becoming celestial.
The Celestial Pivot is refined through ascent;
The Terrestrial Pivot is refined through descent.
According with this results in life;
Opposing this results in death.

Vocabulary

xíngqì 行氣 (v./n.)	"circulating qi." Also translated as "moving the breath." Later also appears as *yùnqì* 運氣
qì 氣 (n.)	"qi." Also translated as "energy," "subtle/vital breath," and "pneuma" (Greek). May refer to both physical breath and a more subtle current/presence. The fundamental cosmic (non)material substance
pèi 佩 (n.)	"ornament." Technically refers to a "belt pendant," and "to wear" by extension. Also translated as "knob." The original purpose of the object here is unclear, but it may have been the knob of a staff, hilt of a weapon, handle attached to the wooden bar of a scroll painting, or a writing tablet. In keeping with revisionist views of classical Daoism, the first hypothesis may point to a Daoist community elder
zé 則 (conj.)	"then." Indicates conditional ("if/then") relationships. Here translated more liberally as "leads to/results in"
dìng 定 (adj.|v.|n.)	"stable|stabilize|stability." Also translated as "concentration," "settle," and most technically "absorption"
gù 固 (adj.|v.|n.)	"solid|solidify|solidity." May also mean "firm/firmly" and "strong/strengthen." Contains the *wéi* 囗 ("enclosure") radical. Later becomes an important Daoist character indicating psychosomatic integrity and stability
méng 萌 (adj.|v.|n.)	"germinating|germinate|germination." Also translated as "sprout/sprouting," and "beginning" by extension. Contains the *cǎo* 艸/艹 ("grass") radical
tuì 退 (v.|n.)	"retreat|retreat." May also mean "ebb," "recede," "retire," "return," and "withdraw." Contains the *chuò* 辵/辶 ("walk/move") radical. Later becomes an important Daoist approach and practice. For example, LZ 41 tells us, "Advancing in the Dao seems like retreat." See also chs. 9, 61, 67, and 69

tiānjī 天機 (adj./n.)	"Celestial Pivot." *Jī* 機 more literally refers to a "trigger," and "mechanism" by extension. Sometimes translated as "workings." Often used synonymously with *shū* 樞 ("pivot"). The contextual meaning here is unclear, but may have an astronomical/cosmological sense and refer to the moving power of the heavens. May also have a microcosmic sense of the head region. A classical Daoist occurrence appears in ZZ 6. Later sometimes used in Daoism to refer to the Northern Dipper and/or the heart
chōng 舂 (v.)	"refine." Literally, "pound on grains to remove the husk" and "grind in a mortar." Distinguish from *chūn* 春 ("spring")
dìjī 地機 (adj./n.)	"Terrestrial Pivot." *Jī* 機 more literally refers to a "trigger," and "mechanism" by extension. Sometimes translated as "workings." Often used synonymously with *shū* 樞 ("pivot"). The contextual meaning here is unclear, but may have an astronomical/cosmological sense and refer to the moving power of the earth. May also have a microcosmic sense of the lower torso region. Coupled with the previous Celestial Pivot, suggests axes and polar alignment
shùn 順 (v.)	"accord." May also mean "follow" and "obey." Has the sense of following the correct path and being in harmony. Contains *chuān* 川 ("river")
nì 逆 (v.)	"oppose." May also mean "disobey," "go against," "rebel," and "reverse." The opposite and negative counterpart of the previous *shùn* 順. Has the sense of obstruction and disharmony. Contains the *chuò* 辵/辶 ("walk/move") radical. Later used in Daoism, especially in alchemy, in a positive sense related to various "inversion/reversion" characters, including *diāndǎo* 顛倒, *fǎnfù* 返復/*fùfǎn* 復返, and *huán* 還

LESSON 6

DAOIST APOPHATIC MEDITATION I
FROM THE *NÈIYÈ* 內業
(INWARD TRAINING)

THE *NÈIYÈ* 內業 (INWARD Training; abbrev. NY), which may also be translated as "Inner Cultivation" and "Inner Work," is a recently rediscovered, anonymous classical Daoist text dating to around 350 BCE. It has been preserved as chapter forty-nine of the received *Guǎnzǐ* 管子 (Book of Master Guan), a "miscellaneous" (*zá* 雜) textual collection traditionally ascribed to Guǎn Zhòng 管仲 (d. 645 BCE), but edited by Liǔ Xiàng 柳向 (77–6 BCE) around 26 BCE. It is often grouped together with three other texts that are collectively referred to as the "Techniques of the Heart-mind" (*xīnshù* 心術) chapters, namely, "Xīnshù shàng 心術上" (Heart-Mind Techniques I; ch. 36), "Xīnshù xià 心術下" (Heart-Mind Techniques II; ch. 37), "Báixīn 白心" (Purifying the Heart-Mind; ch. 38), and *Nèiyè* (technically "Nèiyè" as the chapter in question). The *Nèiyè* may be, in turn, be thought of as a more technical companion to the *Lǎozǐ* 老子 (Book of Venerable Masters) (see Lesson #7), with the core of the latter text being roughly contemporaneous. The categorization of the *Nèiyè* as "Daoist" is somewhat problematic, as its context of composition and later dissemination are unclear and as it is not included in the received *Dàozàng* 道藏 (Daoist Canon; dat. 1445/1607). A more creative view is that members of the inner cultivation lineages of classical Daoism intentionally hid the work in the *Guǎnzǐ* in order to protect it from the socio-political fate and misuse of "public texts" like the *Lǎozǐ* and to ensure that it would survive the onslaughts of Chinese history. From this perspective, it is an "esoteric" or "inner text." As far as current research goes and outside of contemporary reengagements, the *Nèiyè* apparently exerted little influence on the larger Daoist tradition.[27] However, one significant clue appears in chapter twenty-three of the *Zhuāngzǐ*, which is titled "Gēngsāng Chǔ 庚桑楚" (Western Mulberry Cane) and associated with the Anthologists.

「衛生之經，能抱一乎？能勿失乎？能無卜筮而知吉凶乎？能止乎？能已乎？能舍諸人而求諸己乎？能翛然乎？能侗然乎？能兒子乎？」

"Let us consider the principle of preserving life. Can you embrace the One? Can you keep from losing it? Can you, without resorting to divining by tortoise or milfoil, recognize the auspicious and the inauspicious? Can you stop? Can you cease? Can you not seek it in others, but rather realize it in yourself? Can you be swift? Can you be plain? Can you become the Newborn Child?"

In addition to attributing these teachings to Lǎozǐ 老子 ("Master Lao") in the context of a master-disciple training session and documented in the *Zhuāngzǐ* itself, the passage combines key teachings and practices now contained in various chapters of the received *Lǎozǐ* and the *Nèiyè*. Specifically, *bàoyī* 抱一 ("embracing the One") is discussed in chapters ten and twenty-two of the former, while the divination and "stopping" (*zhǐ* 止) lines appear in chapter nineteen of the latter. Significantly, NY 19 is one of the most technical chapters and further connects with ZZ 4 (see Lesson #8 herein). This suggests that contemporaneous Daoists may have been reading the *Nèiyè*, or at least may have been familiar with oral teachings incorporated into that text. Significantly, it appears that Daoists were involved in the compilation of the received *Guǎnzǐ* at the

---

[27] A brief discussion of potential later influences appears in Kirkland 2004, 40–52.

Jìxià 稷下 (lit., "below the Ji Gates") Academy (Línzī 臨淄, Shāndōng; fl. ca. 320-ca. 260 BCE). At the very least, the above passage appears to indicate that said Daoists were part of a self-conscious religious community with an emerging sense of tradition. In any case, the *Nèiyè* is a manual of Daoist self-cultivation emphasizing dietetics, quietistic meditation, and mystical realization of the Dao. Like the texts of the inner cultivation lineages of classical Daoism in general, primary emphasis is placed on emptiness- and stillness-based meditation. It is especially important for providing supplemental information on the more technical dimensions of inner cultivation, including physical posture and contemplative psychology.

On a language level and in terms of grammar, the *Nèiyè* is relatively straightforward, even when compared to the *Lǎozǐ*. An interesting and important occurrence in terms of classical Chinese grammatical constructions and sentence patterns is the conjunction *ér* 而 (lines 1–4, 7) (see also Appendix #3). A more technical classical Chinese understanding is "under the condition of (utc)," and/but it is often translated as "and" or "but." Both are viable here, but each choice alters the meaning considerably. The crux in the present chapter is line seven, which speaks of a relationship between being "relaxed" (*kuān* 寬) and "unwound" (*shū* 舒) and "caring" (*rén* 仁), more commonly translated in the Ruist ("Confucian") sense of "humaneness" or "kindness." Is it that being relaxed and unwound allows one to care, or that one remains caring even while disengaged and non-attached? In terms of Daoist vocabulary, particularly interesting in the present selection of chapter twenty-four is the reference to *shǒuyī* 守一 ("guarding the One") (line 4), a classical Daoist technical term for apophatic meditation that also appears in chapter eleven of the *Zhuāngzǐ* and parallels the use of *bàoyī* 抱一 ("embracing the One") in the previously mentioned *Lǎozǐ* chapters, which may be further connected to *dàoshù* 道術 ("techniques of the Dao/ arts of the Way") (see Lesson #2). The term *shǒuyī* later became used by Daoists to refer to "meditation" more generally (see Kohn 1989; Komjathy 2013b). The present chapter also brings our attention to the polyvalent, contextual connotations of *shēn* 身 (line 8), which may mean "body," "person," and/or "self" depending on context. For example, 「及吾無身，吾有何患？」 in chapter thirteen of the *Lǎozǐ* 老子 has been mistranslated, often via unrecognized Christocentric assumptions or Buddhist influence, as "if I did not have a body, what calamities would I have?" when here *shēn* refers to a personal self, resulting in "if I did not have a self, what calamities would I have?" Translating *shēn* as "body" rather than "self" here gives the false impression of a body-negating and world-negating view, when the text is, in fact, emphasizing the disorientation that occurs from a mistaken sense of separate personhood. This further connects to classical Daoist uses of *míng* 名 ("personal name/fame"), with the sense of reputation and social identity. The possibility of a Daoist transpersonal (non)identity, in turn, relates to other "beyond/non-states," including "desirelessness" (*wúyù* 無欲), "formlessness" (*wúxíng* 無形), "namelessness" (*wúmíng* 無名), "no-thingness" (*wúwù* 無物), "selflessness" (*wúsī* 無私), and so forth. We must, in turn, be constantly attentive to not only contextual nuance, but also unrecognized assumptions and possible unintended consequences in translation work, including with respect to reader reception.

In Western Daoist Studies, the potential significance of the *Nèiyè* was first emphasized by the late A.C. Graham 葛瑞漢 (1919–1991) (1989, 100–5, 112, 188–245) and Isabelle Robinet 賀碧來 (1932–2000) (1997 [1992], 39–41). It has been translated by W. Allyn Rickett 李克 (1985/1998, 2.39–55), Harold Roth 羅浩 (1999), Louis Komjathy 康思奇 (2008 [2003], v. 1), and Romain Graziani 葛浩南 (2011 [French]). Roth's interpretive study also includes a text-critical Chinese edition, which divides the text into twenty-six individual chapters that I follow here. Readers should again note that Roth often problematically interprets references to qi as related to "breathing techniques."

Primary Text

二十四

1   大心而放，*paŋ-s
    寬氣而廣。*kʷˤaŋʔ
    其形安而不移，*laj
    能守一而棄萬苛。*kʰˤajʔ
5   見利不誘，
    見害不懼。
    寬舒而仁，*niŋ
    獨樂其身。*niŋ
    是謂運氣。
10 意行似天。*l̥ˤin²⁸

---

[28] These are Old Chinese phonetic reconstructions based on the simplified Baxter-Sagart system, which relies on the International Phonetic Alphabet (IPA) for pronunciation. I have only included them for rhymes. Rickett (1985/1998) and Roth (1999) also include phonetic reconstructions based on the older Karlgren system. See general introduction.

– 24 –

1 Expand your heart-mind and release it.
  Relax your qi and allow it to extend.
  When your body is calm and unmoving,
  Guard the One and discard myriad disturbances.
5 You will see profit and not be enticed by it;
  You will see harm and not be frightened by it.
  Relaxed and unwound, and yet still caring,
  In solitude you will find joy in your own person.
  This is what we refer to as "circulating qi."
10 Your awareness and practice appear celestial.

Vocabulary

Nèiyè 內業 (adj./n.)	"Inward Training." Also translated as "Inner Cultivation/Work." Technically chapter 49 of the received *Guǎnzǐ* 管子 (Book of Master Guan). One of the so-called Xīnshù 心術 (Techniques of the Heart-mind) chapters, a.k.a. "Arts of the Heart"
xīn 心 (n.)	"heart-mind." Also translated as "heart" and/or "mind," but technically psychosomatic. May also mean "center." The psychospiritual center of human personhood. NY 14 tells us that there is an inner heart-mind within the ordinary heart-mind
qì 氣 (n.)	"qi." Also translated as "energy," "subtle/vital breath," and "pneuma" (Greek). May refer to both physical breath and a more subtle current/presence. The fundamental cosmic (non)material substance
xíng 形 (n.)	"form." Also translated as "shape." As associated with human personhood, the three-dimensional disposition or configuration of the human process. Technically speaking, *xíng*-form has a morphological rather than genetic or schematic nuance
shǒuyī 守一 (v./n.)	"guarding the One." One of the most well-known classical and foundational Daoist names for apophatic and quietistic (emptiness-/stillness-based) meditation. Here *yī* 一 (lit., "1") refers to the Dao (One), and the associated process (uniting) and state (union/unity) by extension. Also appears as *bàoyī* 抱一 ("embracing the One") and *zhíyī* 執一 ("grasping/holding the One"). Later becomes used as a general name for Daoist meditation (cf. *dǎzuò* 打坐 [lit., "undertake sitting"]). The appearance of *shǒuyī* in the *Nèiyè* is the earliest occurrence. See also LZ 10 & 22 and ZZ 11 & 23
rén 仁 (n.)	"care." More conventionally translated as "benevolence," "humaneness," or "kindness," and associated with classical Ruism ("Confucianism"). The character consists of *rén* 人/亻 ("person") and *èr* 二 ("two"). Human relationality
dú 獨 (adj.|n.)	"alone|aloneness." May also mean "solitary/solitude" and "independent/independence." Sometimes used in a Daoist technical sense designating solitary meditation and the associated contemplative state(s)

shēn 身 (n.)	"body|person|self." Probably a pictograph of the human physique/torso. Most frequently used to refer to one's entire psychosomatic process. In passages where *shēn* as "self" refers to the physical body, it is one's "lived body" viewed from within rather than "body as corpse" seen from without
yùnqì 運氣 (v./n.)	"circulate qi." Also translated as "circulate/revolve the breath." Later used synonymously with *xíngqì* 行氣 ("circulate qi") in the sense of related Yǎngshēng 養生 (Nourishing Life) practices
yì 意 (n.)	"awareness." May also mean "intention" and "thought." More technically, the spiritual faculty associated with the Earth phase, and the spleen by extension

Lesson 7

Dao-as-Mystery
From the Lǎozǐ 老子
(Book of Venerable Masters; DZ 664; ZH 553)

The *Lǎozǐ* 老子 (*Lǎo-tzǔ*; Book of Venerable Masters; abbrev. LZ), also known by its honorific title of *Dàodé jīng* 道德經 (*Tào-té chīng*; Scripture on the Dao and Inner Power; DZ 664; ZH 553; abbrev. DDJ) and colloquially as the *Wǔqián wén* 五千文 (Five Thousand [Character] Composition),[29] is a key work of the classical Daoist textual corpus. It also is one of the most widely translated, misinterpreted, and appropriated sacred texts in world literature (see Komjathy 2013b, 2020a, forthcoming). Briefly, although traditionally attributed to the legendary Lǎozǐ 老子 ("Master Lao"; trad. dat. 6th c. BCE), also known as Lǐ Ěr 李耳 and Lǎo Dān 老聃/儋 ("Elder/Venerable Dan"), the received *Lǎozǐ* actually is an anonymous multivocal anthology consisting of historical and textual layers dating from at least the fourth to the second century BCE. It contains the teachings and practices associated with various anonymous elders of the inner cultivation lineages of classical Daoism. Thus, the earliest title *Lǎozǐ* is better understood as the "Book of Venerable Masters" (plural), rather than the more conventional "Book of Master Lao" (singular). From a more radical perspective, we might consider

---

[29] In terms of Old Chinese based on the Baxter-Sagart system, the "Mandarin" *Lǎozǐ* and *Dàodé jīng* would have been pronounced something like *C.rˤuʔ-*tsəʔ (Karlgren: *Lôg-*tsi̯əg) and *Kə.lˤuʔ-*tˤək *k-lˤeŋ (Karlgren: *Dʼôg-*dʼi̯ək *kieng), respectively. Recalling the general introduction, I bring attention to this as a "tactic of resistance" and defamiliarization in translation, and to inhibit the nearly ubiquitous appropriation.

the text as the "Old Master" itself (see Komjathy forthcoming), that is, a collective wisdom text. Given our focus on translation, we should also note that *lǎo* 老 simply means "old," while *zǐ* 子 conventionally means "child." However, in context, the prefix *zǐ* means "adept/disciple," while as a suffix it means "elder/master/venerable." Thus, the *lǎo* of Lǎozǐ is not a name, and so-called "Laoism" is a modern fiction. The classical equivalent of the latter would be "Liism" or "Danism," which would make little sense to those engaging in modern appropriative constructions and agendas. In the "standard received edition," the redaction of the Xuánxué 玄學 (Profound Learning; so-called "Neo-Daoism" [sic]) representative Wáng Bì 王弼 (226–249 CE), the text consists of eighty-one untitled "verse-chapters," although there are actually at least three distinct formalistic structures. These include aphorisms/poetry/oral sayings, parallel prose (often rhymed), and prose (see Komjathy forthcoming). For present purposes, we will consider chapter one, which is one of the most influential passages in Daoist literature, both within and beyond the Daoist tradition. It provides a concise, albeit cryptic foundational discussion of Daoist theology (views of the sacred) and cosmology (underlying principles, patterns and structure of the universe), specifically centering on the Dào 道 (Tao/Way), pronounced something like *kə.lˤuʔ (Karlgren: *dʼôg) in Archaic/Old Chinese, as the sacred and ultimate concern of Daoists. In addition to (not) describing the Dao as Mystery (*xuán* 玄) (see Lesson #3), pronounced something like *ɢʷˤin (Karlgren: *gʼəg) in Archaic/Old Chinese, it brings our attention to the polyvalent connotations of 道 itself, which consists of *chuò* 辵/辶 ("walk/move") and *shǒu* 首 ("head"). The character may, in turn, mean "path/way," "walk," and even "speak." So, consider the opening line:

道	可	道	非	常	道
dào	kě	dào	fēi	cháng	dào
dao	can	dao	not	constant	dao

More literally, "dao that can be dao'ed is not the constant dao." The second *dào* is most often taken as meaning "to speak," but the original Chinese is more complex and interesting, especially from a Daoist theological ("Daological") perspective and connected to its "twofold mystery" (*chóngxuán* 重玄). The name "Dao," and any name for that matter (e.g., Mystery, One, Silence) cannot encompass that which is beyond name, concept, and comprehension. This is Dao-as-Mystery ("Reality"), or perhaps more accurately [   ] or]   [, or even   .
Like other classical discussions,[30] the chapter thus points towards the centrality of Daoist apophatic (negational/beyond) discourse, or non-discourse if you will. It may, in turn, be connected to other, parallel and more systematic discussions like those in chapters one and three of the mid-second century BCE *Huáinánzǐ* 淮南子 (Book of the Huainan Masters; DZ 1184; ZH 978; trl. Major et al. 2010) (see Lesson #10) and chapters one and nine of the early fourth-century CE *Bàopǔzǐ nèipiān* 抱朴子內篇 (Inner Chapters of Master Embracing Simplicity; DZ 1185; ZH 980) (see Lesson #3). As is the case with the *Lǎozǐ*, note that both *begin with Dao*. That is, like the ideal Daoist life and name of the tradition as such, this theological concern and sacred orientation frames each of the respective texts and associated communities. How can one make a translation informed by claims about untranslatability (chs. 56 and 71)? Here we may recognize that the text itself mentions the "teaching beyond/without words" (*bùyán zhī jiào* 不言之教) (chs. 2 and 43). Interestingly, in the later tradition, Daoists sometimes use Xuánfēng 玄風 (Mysterious Movement) and Xuánmén 玄門 (Mysterious Gate) to refer to "Daoism," with the latter being a direct allusion to the final two lines of the present chapter.

Considering grammar and vocabulary and as just indicated, DDJ 1 reveals the intricate interrelationship between Daoist views and technical terms. The chapter contains seven primary grammatical characters,

---

[30] Other key cosmological and theological LZ chapters include 1, 4, 5, 32, 34, 35, 37, 40, 42, and 43. Cf. ZZ 12–14.

namely, 非, 之, 故, 以, 其, 者, and 又. *Fēi* 非 ("not") (lines 1–2) indicates negation. It is related to the more common *bù* 不 ("not") and *wú* 無 ("without") (see Appendix #3), but *fēi* has a stronger sense of "it is not the case." With *shì* 是 ("to be"), it is sometimes used in the sense of "right and wrong" or "yes and no." *Zhī* 之 ("of") (lines 2–3, 8–10) indicates a possessive (e.g., 's), in a manner paralleling the modern Chinese *de* 的. Again, a challenge with classical Chinese is that one often reads "in reverse" from standard English practice. Thus, lines two and three are describing the "beginning of" (*zhī shǐ* 之始) and "mother of" (*zhī mǔ* 之母) something, respectively. In the present chapter, *gù* 故 ("thus") (line 5) functions as an adverb, although it may also mean "formerly" or "cause/reason." It is related to *shìyǐ* 是以 ("therefore") and *suǒyǐ* 所以 ("therefore") (see Appendix #3), with the former occurring fairly frequently in the received *Lǎozǐ*. As my lineation and larger translation-scholarship indicate, I believe that both structural elements are redaction or editorial interpolations inserted in an attempt to create greater textual cohesion. *Yǐ* 以 (lines 5–6) functions as a conjunction, in the sense of "by means of" or "in order to." In the lines in question, the preceding phrases (practices) frame the resultant experience, almost as a quasi-conditional. *Qí* 其 is a pronoun, usually indicating third-person possessive (his/her/its/their). Thus, it is sometimes translated as "one's." Here it refers to the Dao, so it is usually rendered as "its." However, in other chapters of the *Lǎozǐ* (e.g., 3, 4, 28, 52, and 56) and beyond, it is better thought of (and translated as) "the." *Zhě* 者 (line 7) may indicate topicalization ("as for"/"considering") and/or function as a suffix ("-er"/"-ist"/"one who"), in the sense of a person involved in something or a thing with a given set of characteristics. This sometimes makes composing fluid and elegant translation more challenging. For example, should *dàozhě* 道者 be taken as "considering the Dao," "one of/with the Dao," or "Daoist"? In the present chapter, it is used to topicalize "these two," so we may simply take the latter as the subject. *Yòu* 又 (line 9) may mean "also," "and," and "in addition." The appearance here as *zhī yòu* 之又 (lit., "of again") leads to a variety of possibilities. As the corresponding sentence structure only occurs in one other place (ch. 48) in the entire *Lǎozǐ*, it provides hints for translation-interpretation.

損之又損，以至於無為。

Decreasing and again decreasing,
One arrives at non-action.

玄之又玄，眾妙之門。

Mysterious and again more mysterious,
The gateway to all that is wondrous.

Under a contemplative reading of the text, it is twofold decreasing (*chóngsǔn* 重損) that leads to realizing the twofold mystery (*chóngxuán* 重玄) of the Dao. This reference to the Dao with the additional (non) descriptor as "Mystery" (*xuán* 玄) is germinal for the entire Daoist tradition (see Lessons #2 and #3). It in turn overlaps with other, parallel (non)designations, including Darkness (*mò* 默), Silence (*jì* 寂), Subtle (*wēi* 微), and Wondrous (*miào* 妙). Like "Dao," these are placeholders for that which transcends any and all names and conceptions. Finally, DDJ 1 also contains *ér* 而 (line 7), which we already explored in Lesson #6.

The *Lǎozǐ/Dàodé jīng* has been translated too many times to document, increasingly in versions and adaptations by individuals who do not know Chinese (e.g., Ursula LeGuin, Stephen Mitchell, Wayne Dyer). Such publications are not "translations," and are better understood as part of both the "Tao Te Ching Translation Industry" (TTCTI) and modern hybrid spirituality. My preferred translation obviously is my own (2008, v. 2 [partial]; forthcoming), with the latter being the first complete scholarly and literary annotated bilingual translation to locate the text in the inner cultivation lineages of classical Daoism and to focus on the contemplative and mystical layers as primary. Nonetheless, Stephen Addiss and Stanley Lombardo (1993) is a reliable literary translation;

Michael LaFargue (1992) a practical one; D.C. Lau 劉殿爵 (1921–2010) (1963/1989) a historical one; and Wú Yí 吳怡 (1989) a philological one. Both Lau and Wú are bilingual editions. I often recommend that people read these in concert. For more general guidance and critical discussions see Hardy 1998; LaFargue and Pas 1998; and Carmichael 2017. Interested individuals also may consult the "Self-Study Guide to the *Dàodé jīng*" circulated by the Daoist Foundation 道教基金會. We will return to the DDJ commentary tradition in Lessons #25–28.

Primary Text

一

1   　　　道可道非常道。
　　　　　名可名非常名。
　　　　　　　無名天地之始；*lə̥ʔ
　　　　　　　有名萬物之母。*məʔ
5   故　　　常無欲以觀其妙；*mewʔ-s
　　　　　　　常有欲以觀其徼。*kˤewʔ-s[31]
　　　　　此兩者、同出而異名。
　　　　　　　同謂之玄。
　　　　　　　玄之又玄，
10   　　　　眾妙之門。

---

[31] Again, these are Old Chinese phonetic reconstructions based on the simplified Baxter-Sagart system, which relies on the International Phonetic Alphabet (IPA) for pronunciation. I have only included these for rhymes. Observant readers also will note the recurrence of 名 (*C.meŋ) in lines 2 and 7 and of 玄 (*Gʷˤin) in lines 8 and 9. Many modern discussions rely on "Mandarin" (Běijīng dialect) pronunciations, which do not correspond to the context-specific rhyme patterns. See general introduction.

– 1 –

A way that can be spoken is not the constant Dao.
A name that can be named is not the constant Name.
   Nameless: The Beginning of the heavens and earth.
   Named: The Mother of the myriad beings.
Thus,   Constantly desireless, one may observe its subtlety.
   Constantly desiring, one may observe its boundaries.
These two emerge from sameness, but differ in name.
   This sameness is called mysterious.
   Mysterious and again more mysterious—
   The gateway to all that is wondrous.

Vocabulary

Lǎozǐ 老子 (adj./n.)	"Book of Venerable Masters." More conventionally understood as *Lǎozǐ* (name/suffix) and translated as "Book of Master Lao." Also referred to honorifically as *Dàodé zhēnjīng* 道德真經 (Perfect Scripture on the Dao and Inner Power), or *Dàodé jīng* for short
dào 道 (n.)	"Dao." Also appears as 衜/衟 and referred to as "Tao/Way." May also mean "path" and "to speak." The character consists of *chuò* 辵/辶 ("walk/move") and *shǒu* 首 ("head"). May refer to the Way (sacred/Reality) and a way, with the latter being a Daoist religious path here. As the former, the sacred and ultimate concern of Daoists
wànwù 萬物 (num./n.)	"myriad beings." More literally, "ten thousand beings/things." *Wù* 物 (lit., "animal"; cf. *shòu* 獸) contains the *niú* 牛/牜 ("ox") radical. *Wànwù* usually refers to everything in existence, including both animate/sentient beings and inanimate/nonsentient things
mǔ 母 (n.)	"Mother." Here another name for the Dao. Only loosely gendered. Thus, overlaps with other, parallel designations, including Ancestor (*zōng* 宗), Root (*běn* 本/*gēn* 根), and Source (*yuán* 元/原/源). That which births and nourishes all beings without distinction
guān 觀 (v.|n.)	"observe|observation." Daoist contemplative approach and practice. Later used to translate the Buddhist Pali *vipassanā* and Sanskrit *vipaśyanā* (insight meditation). As such, usually appears as *nèiguān* 內觀 ("inner observation")
miào 妙 (adj.|n.)	"subtle|subtlety." Also translated as "wondrous/wonder." One of the (non)descriptors of the Dao. Often used synonymously in the sense of the Wondrous
tóng 同 (adj.|n.)	"same|sameness." Also translated as "identical," "merge," and "unite." Often used in a Daoist technical sense of mystical identification, merging, and union

xuán 玄 (adj.|n.)	"mysterious|mystery." Also translated as "dark/darkness." One of the (non)descriptors of the Dao. Often used synonymously in the sense of the Mysterious/Mystery. Thus, overlaps with other, parallel designations, including Darkness (*mò* 默), Silence (*jì* 寂), Subtle (*wēi* 微), and Wondrous (*miào* 妙). Like "Dao," these are placeholders for that which transcends any and all names and conceptions. May also be connected to the Northern Darkness (*běimíng* 北冥) mentioned in ZZ 1 and 22

Lesson 8

Daoist Apophatic Meditation II
From the Zhuāngzǐ 莊子
(Book of Master Zhuang; DZ 670; ZH 616)

We have already explored basic background information on the *Zhuāngzǐ* 莊子 (Book of Master Zhuang; abbrev. ZZ), also known as the *Nánhuá zhēnjīng* 南華真經 (Perfect Scripture on Master Nanhua [Southern Florescence]; DZ 670; ZH 616), in Lesson #2.[32] Here we move into the actual text, specifically its contemplative core. These are the influential passages on *xīnzhāi* 心齋 ("fasting the heart-mind") and *zuòwàng* 坐忘 ("sitting-in-forgetfulness") as appearing in chapters four and six, respectively. As contained in the text, these are imaginary dialogic exchanges between Kǒngzǐ 孔子 (Master Kong; "Confucius"; ca. 551–ca. 479 BCE) and his favorite (and impoverished) student Yán Huí 顏回 (ca. 521–481 BCE), also known as Zǐyuān 子淵. In the first passage, Kǒngzǐ teaches Yán Huí, while Yán Huí surpasses Kǒngzǐ's own experience in the second. This reverses and potentially subverts the assumed, conventional teacher-student relationship. While the terms are roughly synonymous, with both referring to classical Daoist apophatic and quietistic (emptiness-/stillness-based) meditation in a manner paralleling *shǒuyī* 守一 ("guarding the One") (see Lesson #6), it also is possible to understand "heart-fasting" as a prerequisite and

---

[32] In terms of Old Chinese based on the Baxter-Sagart system, the "Mandarin" *Zhuāngzǐ* would have been pronounced something like *Tsraŋ-*tsəʔ (Karlgren: *Tṣi̯aŋ-*tsi̯əg). The honorific title of *Nánhuá jīng* was conferred much later.

foundation for "seated-forgetting," and to read the second passage as a more advanced variant exercise resulting in a deeper contemplative state. Under this reading, one moves from a more directed, intentional, and perhaps effortful initial approach to a more effortless form of disengagement. Along these lines, it is interesting that, at least textually speaking, one must have a variety of other experiences between the two sets of instructions, perhaps representing a specific training period in a manner paralleling other passages (e.g., chs. 6, 7, and 23). Here *wàng* 忘, sometimes mistranslated as "oblivion," is a contemplative and mystical state. Besides the obvious, the approximate equivalent of "forget/forgetting/forgetfulness" is preferable in terms of multiple linguistic expressions (try making "oblivion" into a verb) and drawing attention to the parallel contemplative states/traits of *jìng* 靜 ("stillness") and *xū* 虛 ("emptiness"). In fact, in addition to defining heart-fasting in terms of the latter, the second passage directs one towards a culminating (non) experience of absorption and union referred to as *dàtōng* 大通 ("great pervasion"). *Tōng*-pervasion, which is related to *tóng* 同 ("sameness") (see Lesson #7), later becomes incorporated into the phrase *língtōng* 靈通 ("numinous pervasion") and *shéntōng* 神通 ("spirit pervasion"), with the latter used to translate the Indian and Buddhist Sanskrit technical term *siddhi*. Of course, we must be careful with using later Daoist views and concepts to elucidate earlier ones, a common error of anachronistic interpretation. In any case, it is noteworthy that at the end of first passage, again in the larger context of the chapter, Yán Huí comments, "Before I heard this, I was certain that I was Huí. But now that I have heard it, there is no more Huí," which further connects to Zhuāng Zhōu's own disappearance into (not)being a butterfly (ch. 2) and a fish (ch. 17), and vice versa. That is, emptiness is further defined as a transpersonal (non)state, as no-self or egolessness (*wúwǒ* 無我; *wúwú* 無吾). These passages also connect to other ones that provide additional technical information on classical Daoist meditation, specifically chapters two, eleven, thirteen, twenty-three, twenty-eight, and thirty-three of the *Zhuāngzǐ* itself. In addition to the entirety of the

Nèiyè and the other *Xīnshù* chapters, they may be further connected to the seven "core contemplative chapters" of *Lǎozǐ*, namely, 10, 16, 20, 28, 37, 48, and 57 (see Komjathy forthcoming). When we combine these various materials, we also recognize an emerging and increasingly integrated, foundational Daoist "contemplative psychology" and "spiritual technology," which includes a subtle physiology. This includes three spiritual faculties and somatic constituents that would later become systematized as the internal Three Treasures (*sānbǎo* 三寶), namely, vital essence (*jīng* 精), subtle breath (*qì* 氣), and spirit (*shén* 神). Interestingly, LZ 3 directs us to "empty the heart-mind (*xū qí xīn* 虛其心) and fill the belly (*shí qí fù* 實其腹)." Combined with the present selection's emphasis on aspiration, heart-mind and qi, we have germinal views related to what would become the standard "Daoist body" (see Lessons #12 and #18). These materials open into a larger repertoire and lexicon of "heart" characters, including *qíng* 情 ("emotions/disposition"), *yì* 意 ("intent/awareness/thought"), *sī* 思 ("thinking/thought"), and *xìng* 性 ("innate nature").

Moving into the technical grammatical and lexigraphic elements, the passages selected here, like the *Nèiyè* and *Lǎozǐ* (see Lessons #6 and #7), once again reveal the intricate interrelationship between Daoist views and technical terms, with an additional technical praxis dimension. That is, as I have repeatedly (perhaps too repeatedly) emphasized, these classical Daoist works are about *contemplative practice and mystical being*, a specific mode of embodied being-in-the-world, rather than about disembodied ideas and thought. In any case, these passages contain three grammatical characters already encountered in Lesson #7, namely, *ér* 而 ("and/but"), *yǐ* ("by means of/in order to"), and *zhě* (topicalization) (see also Appendix #3). This will be the last time that I emphasize consulting the latter appendix. There are seven additional grammatical characters herein, namely, 將, 邪, 於, 唯, 也, 矣, and 謂. Here *jiāng* 將 indicates future verb tense ("will"). *Yé* 邪 (耶), pronounced *xié* with other meanings, is a sentence-final interrogative particle that functions as a question mark ("?"). It thus parallels the more common *hū* 乎. *Yú* 於

is a prepositional character variously indicating "at/by/in/on/through/to." It sometimes overlaps with *zài* 在, among others. Somewhat similar to *fú* 夫 ("now then"), *wéi* 唯 as a sentence-initial character means something like "only," but often is untranslated as indicating the introduction of a specific topic. Both *yě* 也 and *yǐ* 矣 are particles indicating completion and function as period marks (" 。"). There are similar to the modern Chinese use of *le* 了. Finally, *wèi* 謂, which also appears quite frequently in the *Lǎozǐ*, is a verb that indicates definitions. It may be translated as "call," "means," "name," and "tell." Sometimes I translate it more liberally as "I/we refer to this as □." Interestingly, both passages provide definitions, namely, heart-fasting as "emptiness" (*xū* 虛) and sitting-in-forgetfulness as "pervasion" (*tōng* 通), which is fairly rare in Daoist literature. Additional and important new vocabulary includes *zhì* 志 and *zhāi* 齋. The former is conventionally translated as "will" and "determination" by extension, but as a Daoist technical term it often refers to "aspiration." In the later tradition, it appears as *dàozhì* 道志 ("aspiration for the Dao"), which informs the Daoist etymological reading of the character as the heart-mind (*xīn* 心) of an adept (*shì* 士) (see Appendix #6). *Zhāi* 齋, here translated as "fast/fasting," may mean "purify/purification" and "retreat." Thus, from an applied, lived, and praxis-based Daoist perspective, "heart-fasting" involves "mind-retreat." Interestingly, in the larger passage on *xīnzhāi* the practice is referred to as *fāng* 方, which here parallels *fǎ* 法 in the sense of "method" and thus overlaps with *shù* 術 ("art/technique") (see Lesson #2).

Again, basic guidance on ZZ translations may be found in Lesson #2 above. Interestingly, the second passage explored herein became the basis for the late seventh- or early eighth-century *Zuòwàng lùn* 坐忘論 (Discourse on Sitting-in-Forgetfulness; DZ 1036; ZH 992), which we will explore in Lesson #18.

Primary Text

《人間世》

「齋!吾將語若。有而為之,其易邪?易之者,皞天不宜...若一志,無聽之以耳而聽之以心。無聽之以心而聽之以氣。聽止於耳,心止於符。氣也者,虛而待物者也。唯道集虛。虛者,心齋也。」

The Human World

"You must fast! I will tell you what that means. Do you think that it is easy to do anything while you have a heart-mind? If you do, the luminous heavens will not support you...Unify your aspirations! Don't listen with your ears; listen with your heart-mind. No, don't listen with your heart-mind; listen with qi.[33] Listening stops with the ears, the heart-mind stops with joining, but qi is empty and waits on all things. The Dao gathers in emptiness alone. Emptiness is the fasting of the heart-mind." (ch. 4)

---

[33] Note that Burton Watson (1968) in his highly influential and generally reliable rendering mistranslates *qì* 氣 as "spirit." This has led to widespread misinterpretation of the technical specifics of the associated practice on the part of non-specialist scholars and popularizers.

《大宗師》

「回益矣…回坐忘矣…墮肢體，黜聰明，離形去知，同於大通，此謂坐忘。」

The Great Ancestral Teacher

"I'm improving...I can sit and forget...I smash up my limbs and body, drive out perception and intellect, cast off form, do away with understanding, and make myself identical with Great Pervasion. This is what I mean by sitting-in-forgetfulness." (ch. 6)

Vocabulary

Zhuāngzǐ 莊子 (name/suffix)	"Book of Master Zhuang." Also referred to honorifically as *Nánhuá zhēnjīng* 南華眞經 (Perfect Scripture of Master Nanhua [Southern Florescence]), or *Nánhuá jīng* for short
zhāi 齋 (v.|n.)	"fast|fasting." Also translated as "purify/purification." Later used to refer to a specific form of Daoist ritual, also rendered as "retreat" and more technically "levée" (via French *lever* ["rise"]) in the sense of formal court audiences
zhì 志 (v.|n.)	"aspire|aspiration." Also translated as "will" and "determined/determination." More technically, the spiritual faculty associated with the Water phase, and the kidneys by extension. Later appears as *dàozhì* 道志 ("aspiration for the Dao")
xīn 心 (n.)	"heart-mind." Also translated as "heart" and/or "mind," but technically psychosomatic. May also mean "center." The psychospiritual center of human personhood
qì 氣 (n.)	"qi." Also translated as "energy," "subtle/vital breath," and "pneuma" (Greek). May refer to both physical breath and a more subtle current/presence. The fundamental cosmic (non)material substance
zhǐ 止 (v.)	"cease|stop." Key Daoist approach and practice. Later used to translate the Buddhist Pali *samatha* and Sanskrit *śamatha*, or calm abiding meditation
fú 符 (n.)	"talisman." Also translated as "agreement," "contract," and "tally." Here used as a verb in the sense of "join." Note that the character also appears in the title of ZZ 5
xū 虛 (adj.|v.|n.)	"empty|empty|emptiness." Often synonymous with *wú* 無 ("nonbeing/nothing") and *kōng* 空 ("emptiness"), but the latter also is later used to translate the Buddhist Sanskrit *śūnyatā* ("empty of own-being")

xīnzhāi 心齋 (n./v.)	"fasting of the heart-mind." Also translated as "heart-fasting" and "mind-retreat." One of the classical and foundational Daoist names for apophatic and quietistic (emptiness-/stillness-based) meditation. Points towards the possibility of "pure consciousness"

---

zōng 宗 (n.)	"Ancestor." Another name for the Dao 道. Thus, overlaps with other, parallel designations, including Mother (*mǔ* 母), Root (*běn* 本/*gēn* 根), and Source (*yuán* 元/原/源). That from which everything emerges and to which everything returns
Huí 回 (name)	Yán Huí 顏回 (ca. 521–481 BCE), also known as Zǐyuān 子淵. The favorite (and impoverished) student of Kǒngzǐ 孔子 (Master Kong; "Confucius"; 551–479 BCE). Here representing a classical Chinese example of illeism, that is, referring to oneself in the third-person, in place of a first-person pronoun (吾/我) in the present case
tǐ 體 (n.)	"body." Technically refers to "physical structure." Later said to be a "combination of twelve groups" or parts, including the scalp, face, chin, shoulders, spine, abdomen, upper arms, lower arms, hands, thighs, legs, and feet. Also used in the sense of "embody" (v.), as in the phrase *tǐdào* 體道 ("embodying the Dao")
xíng 形 (n.)	"form." Also translated as "shape." As associated with human personhood, the three-dimensional disposition or configuration of the human process. Technically, *xíng*-form has a morphological rather than genetic or schematic nuance
tóng 同 (adj.|n.)	"same|sameness." Also translated as "identical," "merge," and "unite." Often used in a Daoist technical sense of mystical identification, merging, and union

dàtōng 大通 (adj./n.)	"Great Pervasion." Also translated as "Great Throughfare." *Tōng* 通 may also mean "connection" and "throughness." Contains the *chuò* 辵/辶 ("walk/move") radical. May refer to both the Dao and an associated contemplative and mystical state, namely, meditative absorption and mystical union. Later used to translate the Sanskrit *siddhi* (numinous/paranormal/supernatural abilities/powers)
zuòwàng 坐忘 (v./v.)	"sitting-in-forgetfulness." More literally, "sit and forget." Problematically translated as "sitting in oblivion." Also referred to as "seated-forgetting" and "forgetful sitting." In technical Daoist usage, *wàng* 忘 ("forgetfulness") is a contemplative/mystical state basically synonymous with *jìng* 靜 ("stillness") and *xū* 虛 ("emptiness"). *Zuòwàng* is basically synonymous with the previous, associated *xīnzhāi* ("heart-fasting"), but the latter focuses on emptying the heart-mind, while the former emphasizes abiding in a contemplative state

Lesson 9

Primordial Nondifferentiation & Cosmic Emanation
From the *Huáinánzǐ* 淮南子
(Book of the Huainan Masters; DZ 1184; ZH 978)

The *Huáinánzǐ* 淮南子 (Book of the Huainan Masters; DZ 1184; ZH 978; abbrev. HNZ) is a collection of twenty-one essays edited in the second century BCE at the court and under the patronage of Liú Ān 劉安 (179–122 BCE), the Prince of *G^{ws}rij-*n^{ʕ}əm 淮南 (Huáinán; lit., "south of the Huái River" [present-day Ānhuī, Húběi, and Jiāngxī]). It was submitted to Hàn Emperor Wǔ 武 (r. 140–87 BCE) in 139 BCE. The anthology contains material from a variety of historical periods and diverse religio-cultural movements, including some that might be labeled "Daoist" or at least "Daoistic." The "Daoist question" is complex, but it may be that the collection represents a Syncretic Daoist ("Huáng-Lǎo 黃老") project. Although the HNZ completion date (139 BCE) is often used as a convenient end-date for classical Daoism as a whole, the latter feeds into the *Shǐjì* 史記 (Records of the Historian; dat. ca. 94 BCE) of the Sīmǎ 司馬 family, members of which may have been Syncretic Daoist adherents, or at least sympathizers, and into various Fāngshì 方士 (lit., "formula masters"; magico-religious practitioners) lineages, that, in turn, may have flowed into the early Daoist movements. This is what I refer to as "Daoism-between-Daoism" (ca. 140 BCE-ca. 140 CE), that is, the time between classical Daoism and early Daoism. This is a topic deserving deeper inquiry and further research. In any case, particularly noteworthy and influential with respect to the later moments of classical Daoism are chapter one, titled "Yuándào 原道" (Source-Dao/Dao-as-Source), the cosmologically-oriented chapter three, titled "Tiānwén 天文" (Celestial Patterns), and the more practical chapter seven, titled "Jīngshén 精神" (Concentrated Divinity/Quintessential Spirit). The *Huáinánzǐ* also includes chapter twelve, titled "Dàoyìng 道應" (Responding to the Dao), which is one of the earliest extant commentaries on the *Lǎozǐ* 老子 (Book of Venerable Masters). Here we explore the opening of chapters one and three, which provide insights into classical and foundational Daoist cosmogony (origins of the universe) and cosmology (patterns and principles of the universe), which specifically center on the emergence of the manifest universe through spontaneous transformation and emanation from primordial Nondifferentiation (*wújí* 無極), also referred to as Beginninglessness (*wúshǐ* 無始) and Formlessness (*wúxíng* 無形), to Differentiation based on yin-yang 陰陽 interaction (*tàijí* 太極). Interestingly, the second passage refers to this originary moment as Tàizhāo 太昭 (Great Inception), with the second character consisting of *rì* 日 ("sun") and *zhào* 召 ("decree"), which is probably a phonetic. This overlaps with other classical Daoist discussions in which the initial manifestation is referred to as Tàishǐ 太始 (Great Beginning) and Tàichū 太初 (Great Commencement). These eventually became systematized into the so-called Five Greats (*wǔtài* 五太) with corresponding degrees of differentiation: (1) Tàiyì 太易 (Great Purity); (2) Tàichū 太初 (Great Commencement) with *qì* 氣; (3) Tàishǐ 太始 (Great Beginning) with form (*xíng* 形); (4) Tàisù 太素 (Great Simplicity) with substance (*zhì* 質); and (5) Tàijí 太極 (Great Ultimate) with the appearance of myriad things (*wànwù* 萬物). The present chapter also brings our attention to the traditional Chinese and thus Daoist cosmological focus on the sky/heavens (*lˤin/tiān 天) and earth (*lˤej-s/dì 地), which also are referred to as Qián-heaven ☰ and Kūn-earth ☷. These correspond to pure yang and pure yin, respectively. The present HNZ chapter may, in turn, be connected to other classical Daoist accounts, including ZZ 12–14 (see Lessons #2 and #7), which are titled "Tiāndì 天地" (Heaven and Earth), "Tiāndào 天道" (Way of Heaven), and "Tiānyùn 天運" (Celestial Revolutions), respectively. The second phrase also appears in the *Lǎozǐ/Dàodé jīng* and in the *Huángdì nèijīng sùwèn* 黃帝內經素問 (Yellow Thearch's Inner Classic: Basic Questions; DZ 1018; ZH 884) (see Lessons #7 and #10).

On a more technical linguistic level and as was the case with Lessons #2–3 and #7–8, the text presents itself as part of the larger "masters literature" (*zǐshū* 子書). Here we may also apply our preliminarily work in Lessons #2–3, wherein we explored works with titled chapter divisions. The same is true with respect to *Huáinánzǐ*. Each and every chapter title includes *xùn* 訓, here rendered more technically as "treatise." Containing the *yán* 言 ("speech") radical, the character also may mean "explain," "instruct," "lecture," and so forth. It eventually has the connotation of more formal interpretation, or exegesis and hermeneutics in our terms. It may, in turn, be compared to Daoist employments of *lùn* 論 ("discourse/essay") and *piān* 篇 ("chapter/folios/treatise") (see Lessons #1–3, #8, #10, #18, #21, and #23). In terms of grammar, the passage contains a variety of previously-encountered characters, including *ér* 而 ("and/but"), *gǔ* 故 ("thus"), *zhě* 者 (topicalization), and *zhī* 之 ("of/it") (see Lesson #8). However, here *gǔ* 故 ("thus") appears in concert with *yuē* 曰 ("say"). The latter character functions as a definition, in the sense of "this was called/referred to as…" It thus has some parallels with *wèi* 謂 (see Lesson #8). One new grammatical character is *fú* 夫, which is a sentence-initial that means something like "now then." Like *wéi* 唯 ("only") (see Lesson #8), it usually introduces a given topic. With respect to vocabulary, the first passage is especially interesting for its use of various "water" (*shuǐ* 水/氵) characters, including *bó* 浡 ("gush"), *cè* 測 ("measure"), *chōng* 沖 ("empty/infuse"), *huá* 滑 ("surge"), *hùn* 混 ("mixed"), *liú* 流 ("drift/flow"), *qīng* 清 ("clear"), *quán* 泉 ("spring/well"), *shēn* 深 ("deep"), and *zhuó* 濁 ("turbid"). Here we also may recall the title of the chapter, with *yuán* 原 also appearing as *yuán* 源 ("source") and further connected to *yuān* 淵 ("abyss"). This might inspire us to consider this translation primer as a "sourcebook." For Daoists, the connection between the Dao and water also invokes various passages and chapters of the *Lǎozǐ* (see Lesson #7), with chapters eight, fifteen, and seventy-eight especially important for present purposes. Also noteworthy is the appearance of *chōng* 沖, which poses a further translation dilemma: It may mean "empty" and/or "infuse." It appears in the germinal LZ 42, wherein it is a quality associated with qi (see also ZZ 4; Lesson #8 herein). The character also appears in LZ 4 and 45, wherein, as in the current HNZ passage, it is paired with *yíng* 盈 ("full"). This cosmological framework centering on water sets a precedent for the early Daoist emphasis on the Three Bureaus (*sānguān* 三官), also translated as Three Offices/Officers, of heaven, earth, and water. The second passage from HNZ 3 is, in turn, helpful for engaging foundational cosmological terms, including (in order) *qì* 氣 ("subtle breath/energy"), *tiāndì* 天地 ("heaven and earth"), *yīnyáng* 陰陽 ("yin-yang"), and *wànwù* 萬物 ("myriad beings/things"). This will be the last reference to qi in the accompanying chapter vocabulary, so readers should consult Appendix #8 hereafter. More technically, the passage references *yǔzhòu* 宇宙, which is conventionally translated as "universe," but more technically as "space-time." There is an accompanying interpretive question: In terms of the cosmogonic emanationist account, *yǔzhòu* appears before *tiāndì*, and thus must be distinguished on some level and in certain respects. Also interesting is the connection of *yīnyáng* to the four seasons (*sìshí* 四時), which implicitly inspires us to consider the associations and applications. When combined, the four seasons are understood in the following solar cosmological terms: spring (minor yang), summer (major yang), autumn (minor yin), and winter (major yin) (see also Lesson #10).

The *Huáinánzǐ* is receiving increasing attention in Western language scholarship. *The Huainanzi and Textual Production in Early China* (2014) edited by Sarah Queen 桂思卓 and Michael Puett 普鳴 is representative, although the "Daoist question" remains underexplored. In addition to various translations and studies of individual chapters, there is a complete, partially annotated scholarly translation by John Major 馬絳

et al. (2010), which also was released in a selected edition (2012). Like Sinological translations of other texts (e.g., Rickett 1985/1998; Knoblock and Riegel 2000; Cook 2012; see general introduction herein), it often lacks literary elegance and readability. A list of the chapter titles of the *Huáinánzǐ* with English translations also is contained in Louis Komjathy's 康思奇 "Catalogue of Daoist Collectanea, Compendia, and Encyclopedias" (2022).

Primary Text

《原道訓》

夫道者，覆天載地，廓四方，柝八極，高不可際，深不可測，包裹天地，稟授無形；原流泉浡，沖而徐盈；混混滑滑，濁而徐清。

Treatise on the Source-Dao

Now then, the Dao shelters the heavens and covers the earth. It extends the four directions and expands the Eight Poles. So lofty, it cannot be reached; so deep, it cannot be measured. It envelops the heavens and earth, and it endows the formless. Flowing as source and gushing as springs, its emptiness gradually becomes full. Blended and mixed, surging and streaming, its turbidity gradually becomes clear. (ch. 1)

《天文訓》

天墬未形,馮馮翼翼,洞洞灟灟。故曰太昭。道始生虛廓。虛廓生宇宙。宇宙生氣。氣有涯垠。清陽者薄靡而為天；重濁者凝滯而為地。清妙之合專易,重濁之凝竭難。故天先成而地後定。天地之襲精為陰陽。陰陽之專精為四時。四時之散精為萬物。

Treatise on Celestial Patterns

When the heavens and earth were not yet formed, all was ascending and flying, diving and delving. This was called the Great Inception. The Dao originally produced the Nebulous Void. The Nebulous Void produced space-time; space-time produced [original] qi. A boundary divided this qi. The clear and light rose to become the heavens; the heavy and turbid sank to become the earth. It is easy for the clear and light to converge, but difficult for the heavy and turbid to coalesce. Thus, the heavens were completed first, while the earth was formed afterward. The conjoined essences of the heavens and earth produced yin and yang. The successive essences of yin and yang caused the four seasons. The scattered essences of the four seasons birthed the myriad beings. (ch. 3)

Vocabulary

Huáinán 淮南 (n./dir.)	"south of the Huái River." Here referring to the court of Liú Ān 劉安 (179–122 BCE), the Prince of *Gʷˤrij-*nˤəm (Huáinán; present-day Ānhuī, Húběi, and Jiāngxī)
yuándào 原道 (n./n. or adj./n.)	"Source-Dao." Also translated as "Dao-as-Source" and "tracing the Dao to its source." One explanation involves distinguishing the Dao (Way) as cosmological and theological term from the various human *daos* ("ways"). Also glossed as *yuán* 元, resulting in "original Dao." *Yuán* "source" also appears as 源 and connects to *yuán* 元 ("origin/source") and *yuān* 淵 ("abyss"). Here another name for the Dao 道. As such, should appear as "Source." Overlaps with other, parallel designations, including Ancestor (*zōng* 宗), Mother (*mǔ* 母), and Root (*běn* 本/*gēn* 根). That from which everything emerges and to which everything returns
bājí 八極 (num./n.)	"Eight Poles." Also translated as "Eight Limits." The four cardinal and four ordinal points
wúxíng 無形 (neg./n.)	"formless/formlessness." Lit., "without form." One of the primary (non)characteristics of the Dao. Related to parallel Daoist technical terms, including *wúmíng* 無名 ("namelessness"), *wúqíng* 無情 ("emotionlessness"), and *wúyù* 無欲 ("desirelessness"). Also said to be (non)characteristics of realized Daoists by extension
chōng 沖 (adj./n.)	"empty|emptiness." This character also may mean "infusing/infusion."
zhuó 濁 (adj./n.)	"turbid|turbidity." As a neutral cosmological quality, associated with earth and yin. Also used in contemplative and alchemical contexts in a negative sense, and contrasted with *qīng* 清 ("clarity")

qīng 清 (adj.|n.)	"clear|clarity." As a neutral cosmological quality, associated with heaven and yang. Also used in contemplative and alchemical contexts in a positive sense, and contrasted with zhuó 濁 ("turbidity")

tiānwén 天文 (adj./n.)	"celestial patterns." Also translated as "patterns of heaven." Connected to tiāndào 天道 ("Way of Heaven") as the cosmological process and human attunement by extension. From a Daoist perspective, relates to the Dao as "suchness" (zìrán 自然), manifesting in/as/through Nature. Later becomes used to refer to "celestial scripts" composed of/from primordial cosmic ethers
Tàizhāo 太昭 (adj./n.)	"Great Inception." Earliest cosmogonic moment and the beginning of emanation. Basically synonymous with Hùndùn 混沌/渾沌 (Primordial Chaos), Tàiyì 太易 (Great Purity), and Wújí 無極 (Nondifferentiation), which technically precedes the manifestation of qi
yǔzhòu 宇宙 (n./n.)	"space-time." Usually translated more generally as "cosmos/universe." Both characters contain the mián 宀 ("roof/cover") radical. Cf. tiāndì 天地 ("heavens and earth")
qì 氣 (n.)	"qi." Also translated as "energy," "subtle/vital breath," and "pneuma" (Greek). May refer to both physical breath and a more subtle current/presence. The fundamental cosmic (non)material substance
jīng 精 (n.)	"essence." Also translated as "vital essence" and "vitality." Generally discussed as the material substance of life. Some roughly contemporaneous Daoist sources understand it as concentrated qi

yīnyáng 陰陽 (n./n.)	"yin-yang." The two primary cosmic forces/principles, with various associations. The basis of emanation, differentiation, and interaction. Dynamic, interconnected, and interrelated. *Not* "polar opposites." Often misidentified as "Daoist," but part of a traditional Chinese worldview and traditional Chinese cosmology in particular, which also is utilized in classical Chinese medicine
sìshí 四時 (num./n.)	"four seasons." Spring (minor yang), summer (major yang), autumn (minor yin), winter (major yin)
wànwù 萬物 (num./n.)	"myriad beings." More literally, "ten thousand beings/things." *Wù* 物 (lit., "animal"; cf. *shòu* 獸) contains the *niú* 牛/牜 ("ox") radical. *Wànwù* usually refers to everything in existence, including both animate/sentient beings and inanimate/non-sentient things

FIGURE 13: *Wújí tú* 無極圖 (Diagram of Nondifferentiation)
SOURCE: *Yùqīng wújí zǒngzhēn Wénchāng dàdòng xiānjīng zhù*
玉清無極總真文昌大洞仙經註
(Commentary on the *Yuqing wuji zongzhen Wenchang dadong xianjing* [Immortal Scripture of Great Profundity by the Limitless and Completely Perfected Wenchang of Jade Clarity]), DZ 103, 1.9a (author's collection)

Lesson 10

Cosmological Attunement
From the *Huángdì nèijīng sùwèn* 黃帝內經素問
(Yellow Thearch's Inner Classic: Basic Questions; DZ 1018; ZH 884)

The *Huángdì nèijīng sùwèn* 黃帝內經素問 (Yellow Thearch's Inner Classic: Basic Questions; DZ 1018; ZH 884) is the most important and foundational work of classical Chinese medicine. Here we should note that, although commonly referred to as the *Nèijīng* and mistranslated as the "Yellow Emperor's Classic of Internal Medicine," *Sùwèn* (SW) is the more technically accurate abbreviation. This is because there are at least four known works that are part of the *Huángdì nèijīng* textual corpus, namely, *Língshū* 靈樞 (Numinous Pivot), *Míngtáng* 明堂 (Hall of Light), *Sùwèn* 素問 (Basic Questions), and *Tàisù* 太素 (Great Foundations), with the *Sùwèn* being most important and influential. In addition, *nèijīng* simply means "inner classic," so it suggests esoteric knowledge and may refer to any number of works. For Daoists, it may specifically invoke the nineteenth-century *Nèijīng tú* 內經圖 (Diagram of Internal Pathways) and related body-maps. In any case, it also is important to recognize that there are other contemporaneous works (e.g., *Huángdì sìjīng* 黃帝四經 [Yellow Thearch's Four Classics]) associated with the legendary Huángdì 黃帝 (Yellow Thearch/Yellow Emperor), who represents different things to different communities and traditions (see Lessons #1 and #16). For present purposes, the *Sùwèn* is generally understood as a more theoretical work, with a strong cosmological focus, while the *Língshū* is more technical in nature, including information on acupuncture and moxibustion (*zhēnjiǔ* 針灸), although the issues are more complex. The history of the received *Sùwèn* also is extremely complex. It contains material from at least the second century BCE to the second century CE. In addition, the standard redaction, which contains a preface dated to 762, is that of the Daoist scholar-physician Wáng Bīng 王冰 (Qǐxuán 啟玄 [Inspired Mystery]; fl. 760s). It is preserved in the received *Dàozàng* 道藏 (Daoist Canon; dat. 1445/1607). While not a "Daoist text" per se, there are many intriguing dimensions, which prove challenging due to the composite nature of the work and require further research. While some individuals may wish to deny the existence of distinct "traditions" like Daoism in the time in question, this does not hold up to critical analysis (see Lessons #2, #6–8; also general introduction). Here I will simply point out the opening framework centering on the Tiānshī 天師 (Celestial Master) (cf. ZZ 24), references to Dao 道 in a manner paralleling classical and foundational Daoist views (see Lesson #7), as well as the central importance of Wáng Bīng and the associated DZ edition in its preservation and transmission. In addition, there are some interesting overlaps and intersections with classical Daoist cosmological views (see Lessons #7 and #9), including seasonal attunement. Here we also should be aware of the increasing reference to and invocation of the neologism of so-called "Daoist medicine" (*dàojiào yīxué* 道教醫學) in the modern world. (For a critical discussion see Stanley-Baker 2019). Like other popular constructions of "Daoism," this often involves a conflation of traditional Chinese views with Daoism and/or various, often anachronistic reconstructions *à la* modern "Classical Chinese Medicine (CCM)," especially in TCM and East Asian medical schools. However, there are a number of mitigating factors that should temper wholesale dismissal and in fact inspire further investigation. These include the intersection of Chinese herbalists and physicians who also had some connection to the Daoist tradition, often formal affiliation. Some key figures include the semi-legendary

Huá Tuó 華佗 (Yuánhuà 元化 [Original Transformation]; ca. 140–208 CE); Gé Hóng 葛洪 (Bàopǔ 抱朴 [Embracing Simplicity]; 283–343); Táo Hóngjǐng 陶弘景 (Tōngmíng 通明 [Pervasive Illumination]; 456–536); Sūn Sīmiǎo 孫思邈 (581–682), who was later deified as the King of Medicine (*yàowáng* 藥王); and of course Wáng Bīng himself. We also need more work on the actual place and influence of the *Sùwèn* in the larger Daoist tradition.

Moving into the grammatical and linguistic elements, the received *Sùwèn* consists of eighty-one titled chapters, most of which include *lùn* 論 ("discourse"). As mentioned, this may mean "essay" and be compared to *piān* 篇 ("chapter/folios/treatise") and now *xùn* 訓 ("treatise") (see Lessons #1–3, #8–9, #18, #21, and #23). Here we should also note the Daoist ternary cosmology (9x9=81), which parallels the received *Dàodé jīng* (see Lessons #7, #25–28). In terms of grammar, the passages contain the following previously-discussed characters: *ér* 而 ("and/but"), *fú* 夫 ("now then"), *gǔ* 故 ("thus"), *qí* 其 ("its/the"), *wèi* 謂 ("means"), *yě* 也 (。), *yǐ* 以 ("by means of/in order to"), *yú* 於 ("at/by/in/on/through/to"), *zé* 則 ("then"), *zhě* 者 (topicalization), and *zhī* 之 ("of/it"). From this point forward, I will simply list previously-discussed grammatical characters and generally not comment on recurring ones. One new grammatical character is 與. Here *yǔ* 與 is a conjunction that may mean "and" and/or "with." The use of *dì* 帝 in the name Huángdì 黃帝 also deserves comment. While conventionally meaning and translated as "emperor," I prefer "thearch" (divine ruler) when referring to divine or quasi-divine beings, as is the case with the *Sùwèn*. For example, the received text opens as follows:

昔在黃帝 ... 成而登天。迺問於天師 [歧伯] 曰 ...

In ancient times, there was the Yellow Thearch...After he became completed, he ascended to the heavens. There he addressed the Celestial Master (*tiānshī* 天師) [Qí Bó 歧伯] saying... (SW 1)

Here we also note that the title of the chapter is "Shànggǔ tiānzhēn lùn 上古天眞論" (Celestial Perfection of High Antiquity). As we have seen and as we will rediscover shortly, *zhēn* 眞/真 ("perfect/perfected/ perfection") is a key Daoist term, although by no means only Daoist. Nonetheless, the title here recalls earlier and contemporaneous Daoist works. For example,

古之眞人，其寢不夢，其覺無憂，其食不甘，其息深深。
眞人之息以踵，眾人之息以喉。

Authentic people (*zhēnren* 眞人) of ancient times slept without dreaming and woke without cares; they ate without savoring and their breathing came from deep inside. Authentic people breathe with their heels; the masses breathe with their throats. (ZZ 6; adapted from Watson 1968, 77–78)

This may be further connected to other classical Daoist passages that discuss spiritual ideals:

故曰：至人無己，神人無功，聖人無名。

Thus it is said, "Utmost people (*zhiren* 至人) have no self; divine people (*shenren* 神人) have no merit; sages (*shengren* 聖人) have no fame." (ZZ 1; adapted from Watson 1968, 32)

Applying our basic religious literacy about Daoism, the *Sùwèn* presents itself as about inner cultivation, with specific attention to cosmological attunement, and spiritual realization. It involves a divine dialogue between Huángdì and the Celestial Master Qí Bó 歧伯 *in the heavens*. Thus, it is encountered as revealed, so perhaps *jīng* 經 should be translated as "scripture," rather than the more conventional and perhaps comfortable "classic" (see Lesson #1; general introduction herein). The present selection, taken from chapters one and two, also brings our attention to *jīng* 精 ("vital essence") as the basic material substance of life (*shēng* 生), which might be further connected to the *Nèiyè* 內業 (Inward Training) (see Lesson #6). The *Sùwèn*, in turn, emphasizes the importance of tending to one's heart-mind (*xīn* 心), spirit (*shén* 神), and overall wellness through basic non-dissipation, moderation, and dietetics. This involves awareness of and attunement with the yin-yang cycles of the four seasons, specifically connected to the solar cycles. These are clarified in the other parts of the chapters and in the larger text. Finally, the *Sùwèn* identifies 100 years as the natural lifespan (*mìng* 命) of those who follow its recommendations. Each of these views become normative in traditional Chinese and thus Daoist culture and society. Finally, and as expected, the text references *jí* 疾 ("ailments/disease/illness"), which also appears as *bìng* 病 in the larger text. However, perhaps most famously, the *Sùwèn* encourages us to embrace a proactive, rather than reactive or remedial approach: "Sages do not heal after illness occurs; they heal before illness" (*shèngrén búzhì yǐ bìng* 聖人不治已病; *zhì wèi bìng* 治未病) (SW 2). As we will explore in Lesson #26, *zhì* 治, apparently a socio-political character that conventionally means "govern" and "regulate" and "heal" by extension, also is a key technical term in the *Lǎozǐ* and the larger Daoist tradition. Thus, we might connect this SW insight to LZ 71: "To be sick of sickness is the end of sickness" (*fū wéi bìngbìng* 夫唯病病, *shìyǐ búbìng* 是以不病).

Very little reliable research has been published on the connection between classical Chinese medicine and Daoism. The standard Western language discussion of the history of Chinese medicine is *Medicine in China: A History of Ideas* (1985) by Paul Unschuld 文樹德. Unschuld also has published an independent interpretive study of the *Sùwèn* (2003), and, with Hermann Tessenow, a complete, annotated scholarly translation (2011). While extremely important for Chinese medicine, each of these works has issues with respect to Daoism. A translation of chapters one and two appears as Handbook #3 of Louis Komjathy's 康思奇 *Handbooks for Daoist Practice* 修道手冊 (2008), which is currently being revised in a Twentieth Anniversary Edition (TAE) with a tentative publication date of early 2023. A list of the chapter titles of the *Sùwèn* with English translations also is contained in Komjathy's "Catalogue of Daoist Collectanea, Compendia, and Encyclopedias" (2022).

Primary Text

《上古天眞論》

「上古之人，其知道者，法於陰陽，和於術數，食飲有節，起居有常，不妄作勞。故能形與神俱，而盡終其天年，度百歲乃去。今時之人不然也，以酒為漿，以妄為常，醉以入房，以欲竭其精，以耗散其眞，不知持滿，不時御神，務快其心，逆於生樂，起居無節，故半百而衰也。」

Discourse on Celestial Perfection of High Antiquity

"Human beings of ancient times understood the Dao. They patterned themselves on yin and yang and harmonized themselves through techniques and reckoning. Their eating and drinking had regulation. Their rising and retiring had constancy. They avoided being reckless and disorderly, and so did not become exhausted. Thus, their bodies and spirits were able to remain united. Reaching the culmination of the years allotted by the heavens, they departed at one hundred years of age.

"Human beings of today are not like this. They take alcohol as their drink of choice. They take recklessness as their constant. Intoxicated, they enter the bedchamber. Through desire, they drain their vital essence. Through dissipation, they scatter their perfection. They do not know how to preserve fullness. They do not know when to attend to spirit. Over-active, they strain their heart-minds. They go against the joy of living, and their rising and retiring lack regulation. Thus, at half of one hundred years of age, they decline." (ch. 1)

《四氣調神大論》

「夫四時陰陽者,萬物之根本也。所以聖人春夏養陽,秋冬養陰,以從其根,故與萬物沈浮於生長之門。逆其根,則伐其本,壞其眞矣。故陰陽四時者,萬物之終始也,死生之本也。逆之則災害生,從之則苛疾不起。是謂得道。」

Great Discourse on Harmonizing Spirit with the Four Qi

"Now then, the yin and yang of the four seasons are the root of the myriad beings. Because of this, sages nourish yang in the spring and summer, and nourish yin in the autumn and winter. Through this, they accord with the root. Thus, along with the myriad beings, sages immerse themselves and drift through the gateway to birth and development.

"Acting in opposition to the root severs the foundation and ruins one's perfection. Thus, yin and yang as well as the four seasons are the end and beginning of the myriad beings, the root of death and life. Acting in opposition to these is a calamity that injures life. According with these ensures that disease will not arise. We refer to this as realizing the Dao." (ch. 2)

Vocabulary

Huángdì 黃帝	"Yellow Thearch." A.k.a. Xuānyuán 軒轅. More conventionally referred to as "Yellow Emperor." A legendary Chinese ruler and culture-hero, with *dì*-thearch here indicating a divine ruler. Although traditionally considered the source of "Chinese civilization" more generally, Huángdì is a complex figure, often representing different things to different communities and traditions. Here he is the source-point, via other quasi-divine teachers, of Chinese medicine
Sùwèn 素問	"Basic Questions." Also translated as "Plain/Simple Questions." These are usually understood as "foundational inquiries"
yīnyáng 陰陽 (n./n.)	"yin-yang." The two primary cosmic forces/principles, with various associations. The basis of emanation, differentiation, and interaction. Dynamic, interconnected, and interrelated. *Not* "polar opposites." Often misidentified as "Daoist," but part of a traditional Chinese worldview and traditional Chinese cosmology in particular, which also is utilized in classical Chinese medicine
fǎ 法 (v.|n.)	"pattern|pattern." May also mean "emulate," "law," "method," "model," "norm," etc. Contains the *shuǐ* 水/氵 ("water") radical. Here recalls LZ 25: "Humans emulate the earth;/The earth emulates the heavens;/The heavens emulate the Dao;/The Dao emulates its own suchness (*zìrán* 自然)" (see also ch. 42)
shù 術 (n.)	"techniques." From a Daoist perspective, recalls both *dàoshù* 道術 ("techniques of the Dao") and *xīnshù* 心術 ("techniques of the heart-mind"), which are also translated as "arts of the Way" and "arts of the heart," respectively
jié 節 (n.)	"regulation." May also mean "joint," "node," "segment," etc. Includes the *zhú* 竹/⺮ ("bamboo") radical. Appears in the phrase *jiéqì* 節氣 (lit., "linking qi"), more liberally translated as "seasonal nodes" and "solar term." These are the six energetic divisions of the four seasons (6x4=24 nodes)

xíng 形 (n.)	"body." Also translated as "form." As associated with human personhood, the three-dimensional disposition or configuration of the human process. Technically speaking, *xíng*-form has a morphological rather than genetic or schematic nuance
shén 神 (n.)	"spirit." May refer to divinities (outer and inner), spiritual capacities, and consciousness in a more abstract sense. Also used as an adjective ("divine/spiritual"). Here used to refer to the spiritual faculty associated with the heart-mind (*xīn* 心)
jīng 精 (n.)	"vital essence." Also translated as "vitality." Generally discussed as the material substance of life. SW 1 discusses the *jīng*-cycles of ordinary human beings, centering on seven-year and eight-year periods for women and men, respectively, as well as ways to extend one's lifespan
zhēn 眞/真 (adj.|n.)	"perfect|perfection." Also translated as "authentic/authenticity," "real/reality," and "true/truth." Here associated with intact psychosomatic integrity
xīn 心 (n.)	"heart-mind." Also translated as "heart" and/or "mind," but technically psychosomatic. May also mean "center." The psychospiritual center of human personhood
nì 逆 (v.)	"go against." May also mean "disobey," "oppose," "rebel," and "reverse." The opposite and negative counterpart of *shùn* 順 ("accord with"). Has the sense of obstruction and disharmony. Contains the *chuò* 辵/辶 ("walk/move") radical

sìqì 四氣 (num./n.)	"Four Qi." Also translated as "Four Energies." The energetic signatures and patterns of the four seasons related to larger solar cycles
sìshí 四時 (num./n.)	"four seasons." Spring (minor yang), summer (major yang), autumn (minor yin), winter (major yin)
wànwù 萬物 (num./n.)	"myriad beings." More literally, "ten thousand beings/things." *Wù* 物 (lit., "animal"; cf. *shòu* 獸) contains the *niú* 牛/牜 ("ox") radical. *Wànwù* usually refers to everything in existence, including both animate/sentient beings and inanimate/nonsentient things

gēn 根 (n.)	"root." Here associated with preserving one's foundational vitality. Recalls LZ 16, which identifies "returning to the root" (*guīgēn* 歸根) as "stillness" (*jìng* 靜)
shèngrén 聖人 (adj./n.)	"sage." More literally, "sagely person." *Shèng* 聖 ("sage"), also used in the sense of "sacred," consists of *ěr* 耳 ("ear") + *kǒu* 口 ("mouth") + *rén* 壬 (great/north). *Shèngrén* was a pan-Chinese ideal in classical China, including among members of the inner cultivation lineages of classical Daoism. From a Daoist perspective, someone listening to the subtle sonorous patterns of the Dao. A person whose wisdom and insights are listened to by others
shēng 生 (n.)	"life." May also mean "aliveness," "birth," "produce," "vitality," etc. Both "being born" and "being alive." On a practice level, especially associated with *Yǎngshēng* 養生 (Nourishing Life), or health and longevity techniques
dédào 得道 (v./n.)	"realizing the Dao." More literally, "attain the Dao." Here used in the sense of following the Way of Heaven (*tiāndào* 天道), or cosmological/seasonal attunement. In the Daoist tradition, most often refers to spiritual realization, including mystical union with and abiding in the Dao

Lesson 11

Daoist Alchemical Symbology
From the Zhōuyì Cāntóng Qì 周易參同契
(Token for the Kinship of the Three According to the Changes of the Zhou Dynasty; DZ 999; ZH 665)

The *Zhōuyì Cāntóng Qì* 周易參同契 (Token for the Kinship of the Three According to the *Changes* of the Zhou Dynasty; DZ 999; ZH 665),[34] abbreviated as *Cāntóng qì* 參同契 (Token for the Kinship of the Three; CTQ), is a highly cryptic Daoist text of uncertain provenance. It is a foundational and influential work on external alchemy (*wàidān* 外丹), also referred to as "laboratory/operational alchemy," which is traditionally attributed to Wèi Bóyáng 魏伯陽 (151–221). However, the received version probably dates to the eighth century, with earlier layers possibly going back to the third and fourth centuries. Utilizing symbology derived from the ancient *Zhōuyì* 周易 (*Changes* of the Zhou Dynasty), more commonly known as the *Yìjīng* 易經 (Classic of Change), the *Cāntóng qì* is an obscure, metaphorical text that connects alchemical processes to cosmogonic and cosmological patterns. Here is at least one Daoist intersection point with that text (i.e., as symbology source), which is often misidentified as a "Daoist text." Also translated as "Seal of the Agreement/Unity of the Three," the text's title consists of three

---

[34] There are a wide variety of editions of the text. Here I use one of the more commonly cited ones from the *Dàozàng*.

individual Chinese characters that are especially important in the Daoist tradition. In the early bronze inscriptions (叄), *cān* 參 ("three"), which is a simplified form of 曑, consists of *jīng* 晶 ("stars"), *guāng* 光 ("light/brightness"), and *shān* 彡 ("light-rays"). More technically, it refers to the Shēn 參 (Three Stars) lunar lodge/mansion (*xiù* 宿). Here it invokes Daoist ternary numerology and cosmology (see also Lessons #7 and #10), especially yin-yang interaction as well as the Three Powers (*sāncái* 三才; lit., "three materials/talents") of heaven, earth, and humanity. Read symbolically from a Daoist perspective, it invokes 3x3=9 ("redoubled yang" [*chóngyáng* 重陽]), or complete alchemical transmutation (*liànhuà* 煉化) and perfection (*zhēn* 真) in the present case. *Tóng* 同, here translated as "kinship," but more often as "sameness" and "merge," is a classical Daoist term related to mystical union and abiding (see Lesson #7). *Qì* 契, here translated as "token," but also rendered as "contract," is often used synonymously with *fú* 符 ("talisman/tally") (see Lessons #2, #13, and #16). This technically refers to an object used for communication, contracts, direction, and so forth. Daoist talismans consist of two halves, one celestial/divine and one terrestrial/human, which, when rejoined, reveal original unity and result in efficacious power. The character also has been translated as "seal," but the latter more closely corresponds to *yìn* 印. Taken as a whole, the title suggests that it is a means of uniting with the cosmological and alchemical process, specifically through attentiveness to transformation informed by the *Yìjīng*. The present passages, which are the opening two stanzas, bring our attention to the use of trigrams as a map of yin-yang interaction applied to alchemical transmutation. These consist of "broken" or "yin-lines" (- -) and "solid" or "yang-lines" (—). While cosmologically neutral, in alchemical contexts they usually invoke negative and positive qualities, respectively. Thus, alchemical refinement is sometimes mapped as a movement from yang emerging in yin ䷗ (24), through yang in ascendence ䷊ (11), and eventually reaching pure yang ䷀ (1). There also are some potential, subtle connections to classical Daoism, which I document in the vocabulary. The text also helps to set a foundation for engagement with later internal alchemy (*nèidān* 內丹) literature, which sometimes follows the model of using *Yìjīng* symbology.

In terms of grammar and syntax, the *Cāntóng qì* has certain formalistic features that resemble the *Xíngqì yùpèi míng*, *Nèiyè*, and the *Lǎozǐ* to a lesser extent (see Lessons #5–7). That is, it presents itself as "poetry," or at least "aphorisms." Like those texts, it also may have required accompanying oral instruction (*kǒujué* 口訣), or commentaries (*zhù* 註) in our own historical moment. Two new grammar characters are 以為 and 在. Although we previously encountered *yǐ* 以 ("by means of/in order to"), here *yǐwéi* 以為, which often appears as *yǐ* 以...*wéi* 為, means "regard/take ☐ as ☐." In this way, it parallels some uses of *wéi* 為 as an independent character. Like the earlier *yú* 於, *zài* 在 is a prepositional character indicating "at/in," specifically with respect to location. The terminology itself is highly technical, so the chapter vocabulary is more necessary than normal. Here I just want to point out a historical connection that may not be obvious to the "non-Daoist" reader. This involves characters derived from or at least influenced by the *Lǎozǐ* (see Lesson #7), namely, *pìnmǔ* 牝牡 ("female and male [animals]") and *tuóyuè* 橐籥 ("bellows").

未知牝牡之合而全作；精之至也。

Not knowing the union of female and male, there is complete integration. This is the culmination of vital essence. (ch. 55; see also chs. 6, 10, 28, and 61)

天地之間，其猶橐籥乎？

The space between the heavens and earth, is it not like a bellows? (ch. 5)

The former primarily relates to yin-yang differentiation and interaction. *Tuóyuè*, which more literally means "bag and flute," is used in the technical sense of "bellows." It points towards the cosmological process, specifically with respect to "birth/growth" (*shēng* 生) and "development" (*zhǎng* 長), including aliveness/vitality, as the result of the interaction of the heavens and earth (see Lessons #9 and #10). From a Daoist perspective, this is analogous to the lungs and breathing by extension. Thus, the so-called "bellows analogy" is sometimes used to discuss abdominal breathing as a primary dimension of alchemical transmutation (see Lessons #19–21).

The *Cāntóng qì* has received a fair amount of scholarly attention, perhaps inordinately so due to its connection to "laboratory alchemy" as a form of supposed Chinese "proto-chemistry" and "pre-modern science." Fabrizio Pregadio 玄英 has published a complete translation with exegesis (2011), which falls somewhere between an annotated scholarly translation and a general-audience one. He also has included a second, supplemental volume (2012) on bibliographic studies.

Primary Text

一

1 乾坤者易之門戶,
  眾卦之父母。
  坎離匡廓,
  運轂正軸。
5 牝牡四卦,
  以為橐籥。

– 1 –

1   "Qián-heaven ☰ and Kūn-earth ☷ are the gateway of change";[35]
    They are the father and mother of all of the hexagrams.[36]
    Kǎn-water ☵ and Lí-fire ☲ are the framework;[37]
    They revolve the hub and align the axle.
5   Female and male, these four trigrams
    Are to be taken as the bellows.

---

[35] An allusion to the *Xìcí* 繫辭 (Appended Sayings) of the *Yìjīng*.

[36] An allusion to sec. 10 of the *Shuōguà* 說卦 (Explaining the Hexagrams) commentary on the *Yìjīng*: "Qián is heaven, and thus referred to as the father. Kūn is earth, and thus referred to as the mother."

[37] More literally, "inner wall" (*kuāng* 匡) and "outer wall" (*kuò* 廓), which refer to the lower line and upper line, respectively. The middle line corresponds to Qián (–) or Kūn (--).

二

1　　覆冒陰陽之道，
　　　尤工御者。
　　　準繩墨，
　　　執銜轡，
5　　正規距，
　　　隨軌轍，
　　　處中以制外，
　　　數在律曆紀。

– 2 –

1   Containing and emitting the Way of Yin-Yang
    Is like being an artisan or charioteer.
    One notes guidelines and markers;
    One takes hold of bit and bridle;
5   One aligns compass and square;
    One follows tracks and ruts.
    Abide in the Center to regulate the outside—
    The numerics reside in the system of pitch-pipes and calendrics.

Vocabulary

Zhōuyì 周易 (n./n.)	*"Changes* of the Zhou Dynasty." Another name for the *Yìjīng* 易經 (Classic of Change), an ancient Chinese (not Daoist) cosmological and divination text that consists of sixty-four hexagrams (*guà* 卦) and associated explanations. These usually are understood to consist of combinations of eight primary trigrams (*guà* 卦)
cān 參 (num.)	"three." In the early bronze inscriptions (𠫐) and the associated complex character (曑), consists of *jīng* 晶 ("stars"), *guāng* 光 ("light/brightness"), and *shān* 彡 ("light-rays"). More technically, refers to the Shēn 參 (Three Stars) lunar lodge/mansion (*xiù* 宿)
tóng 同 (n.)	"kinship." More commonly translated as "identical," "merge," "sameness," "unite," etc. Often used in a Daoist technical sense of mystical identification, merging, and union
qì 契 (n.)	"token." Also translated as "contract." Often used synonymously with *fú* 符 ("talisman/tally"). This technically refers to an object used for communication, contracts, direction, and so forth. Daoist talismans consist of two halves, one celestial/divine and one terrestrial/human, which, when rejoined, reveal original unity and result in efficacious power
qián 乾 (n.)	"Qián-heaven trigram" ☰. Consists of three solid or yang-lines. In addition to pure yang and the sky/cosmos, often refers to the head and spirit in Daoist practice
kūn 坤 (n.)	"Kūn-earth trigram" ☷. Consists of three broken or yin-lines. In addition to pure yin and the earth, often refers to the navel and qi in Daoist practice
guà 卦 (n.)	"trigram" and/or "hexagram. May refer to either the eight trigrams (three-line diagrams) or sixty-four hexagrams (six-line diagrams) of the *Yìjīng* 易經 (Classic of Change). The latter consist of eight combinations of the eight trigrams (8x8=64)
kǎn 坎 (n.)	"Kǎn-water trigram" ☵. Consists of one yang-line inside of two yin-lines. In addition to actual water, often refers to the kidneys and vital essence in Daoist practice. May also refer to clarity (*qīng* 清) inside of turbidity (*zhuó* 濁)

lí 離 (n.)	"Lí-fire trigram" ☲. Consists of one yin-line inside of two yang-lines. In addition to actual fire, often refers to the heart and spirit in Daoist practice. May also refer to stillness (*jìng* 靜) inside of agitation (*dòng* 動)
pìnmǔ 牝牡 (n./n.)	"female and male." Both characters contain the *niú* 牛/牜 ("ox") radical. *Not* human. Here corresponds to yin (*kūn/kǎn*) and yang (*qián/lí*), respectively. *Pìn* also is an important term in the *Dàodé jīng* 道德經 (Scripture on the Dao and Inner Power). See chs. 6, 10, 28, 55, and 61
tuóyuè 橐籥 (n./n.)	"bellows." Lit., "bag and flute." The *locus classicus* is LZ 5, wherein the phrase refers to the creative process of the universe

---

yīnyáng 陰陽 (n./n.)	"yin-yang." Also translated as "yin and yang." Both characters contain the *fù* 阜/阝 ("hillside") radical, accompanied by *yīn* 侌 ("shadows") and *yáng* 昜 ("sunlight"), respectively. The two primary cosmological principles and forces, with various associations. Complementary, interrelated, dynamic, and process-based. *Not* dualistic substances or polar opposites
zhōng 中 (n.)	"center." Often used as a name for the Dao. May also refer to the heart-mind (*xīn* 心) or the navel (*fù* 腹) region. One of the classical Daoist terms for apophatic and quietistic meditation is *shǒuzhōng* 守中 ("guarding the Center"). In the present context, has an astronomical and cosmological association. As such, sometimes designates Běijí 北極 (North Culmen; Polestar) as the "pivot" (*jī* 機/*shū* 樞) of the universe

Lesson 12

Daoist Subtle Anatomy & Physiology
From the *Tàishàng huángtíng wàijǐng yùjīng*
太上黃庭外景玉經
(Jade Scripture on the Outer View of the Yellow Court from the Most High; DZ 332; ZH 897)

Composed in heptasyllabic (seven-character) lines divided into three sections, the *Tàishàng huángtíng wàijǐng yùjīng* 太上黃庭外景玉經 (Jade Scripture on the Outer View of the Yellow Court from the Most High; DZ 332; ZH 897) is a major early medieval Daoist work on the "Daoist subtle body" and contains various esoteric names for corporeal locations. Abbreviated *Huángtíng wàijǐng jīng* 黃庭外景經 (Scripture on the Outer View of the Yellow Court), this is a shorter text related to the *Tàishàng huángtíng nèijǐng yùjīng* 太上黃庭內景玉經 (Jade Scripture on the Inner View of the Yellow Court from the Most High; DZ 331; ZH 896; abbrev. *Huángtíng nèijǐng jīng*). Like the abbreviation of the *Huángdì nèijīng sùwèn* 黃帝內經素問 (Yellow Thearch's Inner Classic: Basic Questions) as *Nèijīng* (see Lessons #1 and #10), the present text is sometimes referred to as the *Huángtíng jīng* 黃庭經 (Scripture on the Yellow Court ["Yellow Court Canon"]; HTJ), but that is technically inaccurate because there are two versions, potentially with different provenances. Although the relationship is complex, it appears that the "Outer View" version predates the Shàngqīng 上清 (Highest Clarity) movement, probably dating to the third century, and originates in a currently unidentified earlier regional Daoist community, while the "Inner View" is of actual Shàngqīng provenance and probably dates to the fourth century. Further research may reveal deeper connections between earlier Fāngshì 方士 (lit., "formula masters"; magico-religious practitioners) lineages and early medieval Daoism. Read in concert, the "Inner View" version may be understood as a more elaborate and detailed expression of the "Outer View" version. Both describe the subtle anatomy and physiology of the human body, including its inner divinities. In addition to being utilized in Shàngqīng visualization practice, the HTJ technical terminology became germinal in the later Daoist tradition in general and in internal alchemy (nèidān 內丹) in particular. Given its cryptic features, it is often read in combination with commentaries, with that by the court Daoist Bái Lǚzhōng 白履忠 (Liángqiū 梁丘 [Ridge Mound]; fl. 720s) (DZ 263, j. 58–60) being especially influential.

On a deeper language level, the text presents itself as a revelation from Tàishàng 太上 (Great High), which is probably an abbreviation of Tàishàng Lǎojūn 太上老君 (Great High Lord Lao) (see Lessons #1 and #4), the deified Lǎozǐ 老子 ("Master Lao"), high god of early Daoism, and personification of the Dao. It focuses on the "outer (i.e., non-Shàngqīng) view" (wàijǐng 外景) of the Daoist body and "inner pantheon." However, it is important to note that, in addition to "landscape" and "view," jǐng 景 also is often used in a technical Shàngqīng sense as "effulgences," specifically to refer to astral, lunar, and solar radiances that are ingested into one's body. This involves a rarefication and divinization process. Like the Nine Practices (see Lesson #4), the received "Outer View" version is divided into three sections, namely, shàng 上 ("upper"), zhōng 中 ("middle"), and xià 下 ("lower"), which are often used in the sense of "first/second/third." In terms of formalistic features, it again resembles poetry, with accompanying cryptic expressions (see Lessons #6–7 and #11). As such, and as the opening line itself tells us, the text is composed in heptasyllabic (seven-character) lines, in quasi-lǜshī 律詩 ("regulated verse"). It thus offers a different type of challenge in terms of grammar. Generally speaking, this type of poetry is usually composed and read with a slight pause after the fourth character, that is, as 4/3 rhythms and groupings (see also Lesson #21). The central concept of *huángtíng* 黃庭 ("Yellow Court") is an esoteric name for a subtle corporeal location and a placeholder for the somatological terminology more generally. Its actual correspondence is debatable. Although usually associated with the spleen, with yellow being the color associated with the Earth (*tǔ* 土) phase, it often is understood as a "non-location" between the navel and diaphragm or solar plexus that becomes activated through Daoist practice. A contextual reading seems to support the latter. Most of the other technical terms are elucidated in the vocabulary herein, but we should make a particular point of reference to the *dāntián* 丹田 ("Elixir Field"). Although later designating the Three Fields (*sāntián* 三田), and perhaps too familiar now, *dāntián* is a singular name in the HTJ texts corresponding to the navel region. In addition, it brings our attention to a view, influenced by and internalizing external alchemy (see Lessons #11 and #13), of the body as containing a subtle location ("field") wherein the "elixir" is produced. Here "elixir" translates *dān* 丹, which more literally corresponds to "cinnabar" (mercuric sulfide; HgS), a key ingredient in external alchemy. That is, the "elixir of immortality" is now being located *within* the human body, a shift that may be thought of as a key beginning of proto-*nèidān*. The HTJ reference is one of the earliest and most influential, although the phrase also appears in the *Lǎozǐ míng* 老子銘 (Inscription on Laozi; dat. 165 CE; trl. Csikszentmihalyi 2006, 105–12). Here we consider the opening six couplets, or first twelve lines (1ab).

Two early French studies by the late Kristofer Schipper 施舟人 (1934–2021) (1975) and Isabelle Robinet 賀碧來 (1932–2000) (1984) help with issues of dating and provenance with respect to the *Huángtíng jīng* texts. There are two complete translations (i.e., Huang 1987/1990, 2.221–29 and Carré 1999 [French]), neither of which is an annotated scholarly rendering. While Huang's English version is generally reliable, it lacks necessary contextualization and elucidation of technical terms and Daoist applications.

Primary Text

上

太上閑居作七言，解說身形及諸神。
上有黃庭下關元，後有幽闕前命門。
呼吸廬間入丹田，玉池清水灌靈根。
審能修之可長存，黃庭中人衣朱衣。
關元茂籥闔兩扉，幽闕俠之高巍巍。
丹田之中精氣微，玉池清水上生肥。

Upper Section

The Great High, dwelling in seclusion, composed these seven-character refrains
In order to explain clearly the human body and its various spirits.
Above there is the Yellow Court; below there is the Pass Origin.
Behind there are the Dark Towers; in front there is the Gate of Life.
Exhale and inhale into the Grass Hut so that the breath enters the Elixir Field.
The pure waters of the Jade Pond irrigate the Numinous Root.
Whoever can cultivate this will be able to attain long life.
In the center of the Yellow Court, there is a person dressed in vermilion robes.
Place the thatch key in the Pass Origin and close the two doors;
From the Dark Towers, the knight ascends to ever greater heights.
In the Elixir Field, vital essence and qi are subtle and rarefied.
The clear waters of the Jade Pond above are produced abundantly.

Vocabulary

Tàishàng 太上 (adj./adj.)	"Great High." Here most likely an abbreviation of Tàishàng Lǎojūn 太上老君 (Great High Lord Lao), the deified Lǎozǐ 老子 ("Master Lao"), high god of early Daoism, and personification of the Dao
huángtíng 黃庭 (adj./n.)	"Yellow Court." Also problematically translated as "Gold Pavilion" (jīntíng 金亭). Esoteric Daoist subtle corporeal location. Usually identified as somewhere between the heart and navel regions. Conventionally understood as the spleen (Earth/center/yellow)
wàijǐng 外景 (adj./n.)	"outer view." Jǐng 景 may also mean "landscape," "scenery," "circumstance," and most esoterically "effulgence/phosphor." In the present case, refers to the exoteric text and accompanying presentation/understanding
xián 閑 (adj.|n.)	"secluded|seclusion." May also mean "idleness" and "leisure." Often associated with eremitic withdrawal. Sometimes indicates solitary meditation
shēn 身 (n.)	"body|person|self." Probably a pictograph of the human physique/torso. Most frequently used to refer to one's entire psychosomatic process. In passages where shēn as "self" refers to the physical body, it is one's "lived body" seen from within rather than "body as corpse" seen from without
shén 神 (n.)	"spirit." May refer to divinities (outer and inner), spiritual capacities, and consciousness in a more abstract sense. Also used as an adjective ("divine/spiritual"). Here used to refer to Daoist body-gods
guānyuán 關元 (n./n.)	"Pass Origin." Also translated as "Original/Primordial Pass," but that would be yuánguān 元關. Usually interpreted as the perineum/coccyx region. In standardized Chinese medicine, corresponds to CV-4, which is three cùn below the navel
yōuquè 幽闕 (adj./n.)	"Dark Towers." Esoteric name for the kidneys
mìngmén 命門 (n./n.)	"Gate of Life." Also translated as "Door of Destiny." Usually refers to the point between the kidneys, but here suggests the navel region. The latter is more conventionally referred to as the Ocean of Qi (qìhǎi 氣海)

lú 廬 (n.)	"Grass Hut," or just "Hut." Context suggests an esoteric name for the nose
dāntián 丹田 (n./n.)	"Elixir Field." Also translated as "cinnabar field." May refer to various subtle corporeal locations. Without qualification usually designates the navel/lower abdominal region, as in the present case
yùchí 玉池 (adj./n.)	"Jade Pond." Esoteric name for the mouth
línggēn 靈根 (adj./n.)	"Numinous Root." Esoteric name for the tongue. Sometimes interpreted as the phallus, but an unlikely association in the HTJ
chángcún 長存 (adj./n. or adv./v.)	"long life." More literally, "perpetual preservation" or "constantly preserved." Also translated as "exist forever." Associated with extended longevity, often including immortality
jīng 精 (n.)	"vital essence." The most material of the vital corporeal substances, associated with foundational vitality and physicality. Often associated with semen in men and menstrual blood in women. Eventually identified as the first or lowest of the internal Three Treasures (*sānbǎo* 三寶)
shuǐ 水 (n.)	"water(s)." Here an esoteric referent for saliva and the vital fluids by extension. Associated with vital essence (*jīng* 精). More technically appears as Divine/Spirit Water (*shénshuǐ* 神水), Jade Fluids (*yùyè/yùyì* 玉液), and Sweet Dew (*gānlù* 甘露)

FIGURE 14: Illustration of Huàshān 華山 (Mount Hua)
SOURCE: *Gǔjīn túshū jíchéng* 古今圖書集成 (Complete Collection of Illustrations and Books of Antiquity and Today) (author's collection)

LESSON 13

Entering the Mountains & Making Elixirs
From the Bàopǔzǐ nèipiān 抱朴子內篇
(Inner Chapters of Master Embracing Simplicity; DZ 1185; ZH 980)

We have already explored basic background information on the *Bàopǔzǐ nèipiān* 抱朴子內篇 (Inner Chapters of Master Embracing Simplicity; DZ 1185; ZH 980) in Lesson #3. Here we move into the actual text, with a specific focus on the central importance of mountains and a representative example of elixir production. The first passage is taken from the opening (1a) of chapter seventeen, which is titled "Dēngshè 登涉" (Ascending and Fording). In addition to drawing attention to the varied associations of mountains in Daoism, including as preferred retreat and sacred site, here Gé Hóng invokes mountain travel and seclusion as analogous to the alchemical undertaking more generally. Both are difficult and perilous, with injury and even death as possible outcomes. Interestingly, Gé also invokes Huàshān 華山 (Mount Hua; near Huàyīn 華陰, Shǎnxī), the Western Marchmount (*xīyuè* 西嶽/西岳), which has a long, diverse, and celebrated history. For example, it is mentioned in chapter thirty-one of the ancient *Shàngshū* 尚書 (Esteemed Documents), also known as the *Shūjīng* 書經 (Classic of History/Book of Documents), and throughout the early first-century BCE *Shǐjì* 史記 (Records of the Historian) and early second-century CE *Hànshū* 漢書 (History of the

Han), all key works of traditional Chinese historiography. Given its rugged and relatively inaccessible pre-modern wilds, it is especially associated with eremitic withdrawal and ascetic pursuits in the Daoist tradition. The second passage is taken from section 10ab of chapter four, which is titled "Jīndān 金丹" (Golden Elixir). Also translatable more literally as "Gold and Cinnabar," Jīndān is often used as a Daoist name for "alchemy" in general. The present selection discusses the ingredients of the Tàiqīng dān 太清丹 (Great Clarity Elixir), the alchemical decoction of the namesake Tàiqīng 太清 (Great Clarity) movement.

Linguistically speaking and beginning with grammar, there are nine new characters, namely, 凡, 莫, 然, 曰, 雖, 乃, 耳, 若, and 即. As a sentence-initial character, *fán* 凡 means something like "generally speaking/in general." It may be compared to *fú* 夫 ("now then") and *wéi* 唯 ("only") as indicating the introduction of a specific topic (see Lessons #8 and #10). *Mò* 莫 functions as a quasi-pronoun, in the negative sense of "no one," "none," and/or "nothing." Here we encounter it followed by the negative *bù* 不 ("not"), thus leading to "no one not" (="everyone").[38] As double negatives are fairly common in classical Chinese, especially in Daoist texts, and as they are generally viewed disapprovingly in English composition, we once again face a translation dilemma. Gé Hóng has a slightly idiosyncratic use of *rán* 然 as "but/however," which more frequently appears as *dān* 但 or *rán'ér* 然而, and thus parallels the modern Chinese *kěshì* 可是. *Rán* also appears in the phrase *ránhòu* 然後 ("after/then"). Another new grammar character is the use of *yuē* 曰 ("say") to indicate a quotation (see also Lesson #9). *Suī* 雖 is an additional sentence-initial character meaning something like "although" or "even if." *Nǎi* 乃 may be an adverb or conjunction and means something like "hence" or "then," in the sense of temporal sequence. In this way, it often parallels *yúshì* 於是, and should be distinguished from *zé* 則 ("then") in if-then statements. Here *ěr* 耳 functions as phrase-final particle like a period mark (。) and

---

[38] Note that *bú* 不 is pronounced with the second/rising tone when followed by a character with the fourth/falling tone. For example, *búzài* 不在.

meaning something like "and that is all." It is sometimes glossed as *éryǐ* 而已. As a sentence-initial particle *ruò* 若, like *rú* 如, indicates a conditional ("if…"). It also may be used in the sense of "as if," "like/resembles," and/or "seems like." Finally, *jí* 即 (also 卽/既) may mean "although," "as soon as," "even if," and/or "then." Sometimes, as in the present case, it functions like *nǎi* 乃 ("then"). Moving into technical terminology, the first passage frames Daoist training in terms of *rùshān* 入山 ("entering the mountains"). While here referring to actual mountain seclusion as necessary for gathering elixir ingredients and undertaking elixir production, the phrase also is utilized in the larger Daoist tradition to refer to meditation and ritual, in the sense of "entering stillness" (*rùjìng* 入靜) and "ascending the altar" (*dēngtán* 登壇), respectively. We also note the reference to associated "methods" (*fǎ* 法), which in turn connects to the accompanying "Lǎojūn rùshān fú 老君入山符" (Lord Lao's Talismans for Entering the Mountains) (17.14a–15b).

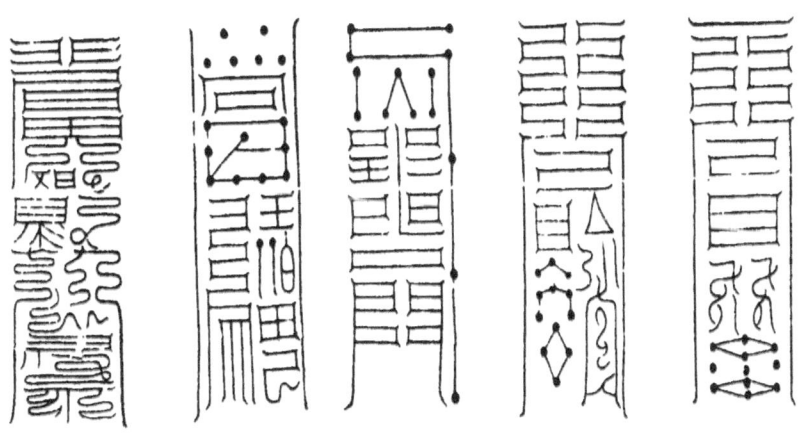

FIGURE 15: "Lǎojūn rùshān fú 老君入山符"
(Lord Lao's Talismans for Entering the Mountains)

In addition, there are methods for protecting oneself from potential dangers, including visualizing (*sī* 思; usually *cúnxiǎng* 存想 [lit., "maintain thought"]) oneself as a thirty-foot tall vermillion bird in the event of encountering a tiger (17.20b). The second passage provides a glimpse into the challenges of identifying and translating Chinese alchemical, herbological, and mineralogical terms. My identification of the elixir ingredients is tentative and largely indebted to Ware 1966 and consultation of the Chinese pharmacopeia, which also is referred to as the Chinese Materia Medica (see, e.g., Bensky et al. 2004). We should also note that these processes are often accompanied by additional purification and meditational methods as well as oral instructions (*kǒujué* 口訣) and ritual procedures. Although not contained in the current selection, the *Bàopǔzǐ nèipiān* (16.7a) also contains one of the most famous Daoist alchemist mottos and directives:

我命在我、不在天。

My fate is in me, not in the heavens.

This may be further connected to the Daoist emphasis on *xiānfēng dàogǔ* 仙風道骨 ("immortal currents and Way-bones"), which is an intra-Daoist debate about endowment versus actualization. Gé Hóng has clearly expressed the view that the "Way of Immortality" (*xiān zhī dào* 仙之道) "can be learned" (*kěxué* 可學) and that one can "attain immortality" (*déxiān* 得仙).

Again, basic guidance on BPZ studies and translations may be found in Lesson #3.

Primary Text

《登涉》

凡為道合藥,及避亂隱居者,莫不入山。然不知入山法者,多遇禍害。故諺有之曰,太華之下,白骨狼藉。皆謂偏知一事,不能博備,雖有求生之志,而反強死也。

Ascending and Fording

All of those seeking the Dao and preparing medicines, as well as those fleeing political disorders and living as hermits, go to the mountains. Many, however, meet with harm or even death because they do not know the method for entering mountains. Hence the saying, 'At the foot of the great Mount Hua, bleached bones lie scattered.' Everyone knows that someone may have special knowledge about one thing, but one cannot know everything about all things. Some people set on the search for life, drive themselves to their own deaths. (ch. 17)

《金丹》

作此太清丹，小為難合於九鼎，然是白日昇天之上法也。合之當先作華池赤鹽艮雪玄白飛符三五神水，乃可起火耳⋯九轉之丹，服之三日得仙。若取九轉之丹，內神鼎中，夏至之後，爆之鼎熱，內朱兒一斤於蓋下。伏伺之，候日精照之。須臾翕然俱起，煌煌煇煇，神光五色，即化為還丹。取而服之一刀圭，即白日昇天。又九轉之丹者，封塗之於土釜中，糠火，先文後武。

The Golden Elixir

Making the Elixir of Great Clarity is somewhat more difficult than the Elixir of the Nine Tripods,[39] but it is a superior method for mounting to the heavens in broad daylight. When you compound it, you should first prepare the Flowery Pond, red salt, Mountain Snow, Mysterious White, distilled binders, and Divine Water of the Three-and-Five. Only then can the fire be lit... Place the elixir of the ninth cycle in a divine tripod and expose it to the sun after summer solstice. When the tripod becomes hot, add one pound of the Vermilion Child beneath the lid and then retire, watching and waiting as the essence of the sun shines upon it. Suddenly, the five colors of divine radiance will appear together, glowing and sparkling, and the elixir of the ninth cycle will transmute itself into a reverted elixir. Ingest a knife-nick of it, and you will rise to the heavens in broad daylight. The elixir of nine cycles should be compounded in a sealed earthenware crucible and heated by a chaff fire, first gentle and then intense. (ch. 4)

---

[39] A description of this elixir appears in the preceding section of the text. Detailed instructions appear in the *Jiǔdǐng shéndān jīng jué* 九鼎神丹經訣 (Instructions on the Scripture on the Divine Elixirs of Nine Tripods; DZ 885,1.4a-5b), which is loosely translated by Ware (1966, 78–79).

Vocabulary

Bàopǔzǐ 抱朴子 (v./n./suffix)	"Master Embracing Simplicity." Conventionally and inelegantly translated as "The Master Who Embraces Simplicity." The Daoist sobriquet (*hào* 號) of Gé Hóng 葛洪 (283–343). *Pǔ* 樸/朴 ("unhewn simplicity"), also translated as "unadorned simplicity" and "uncarved block," refers to the pure and simple connection with the Dao inherent in all beings and in Being itself. Derives from LZ 19
yǐnjū 隱居 (adv./v.)	"live in seclusion." Eremitic withdrawal
rùshān 入山 (v./n.)	"enter the mountains." Mountain seclusion. May also refer to meditation and/or ritual
fǎ 法 (n.)	"methods." May also mean "teachings," "patterns," as well as "dharma" and "phenomena" (via Buddhism). As referring to practice, basically synonymous with *gōng* 功 ("exercise") and *shù* 術 ("technique")
Huàshān 華山 (n./n.)	"Mount Hua (Flower Mountain)." The Western Marchmount (*xīyuè* 西嶽) located near Huàyīn 華陰, Shǎnxī
zhì 志 (n.)	"will." Also translated as "determination" and "aspiration" in a Daoist sense. More technically, the spiritual faculty associated with the Water phase, and the kidneys by extension

---

Jīndān 金丹 (n./n. or adj./n.)	"Golden Elixir." More literally, "gold and cinnabar." Two key alchemical ingredients and substances, specifically associated with "elixirs" as such. In the technical sense of "Golden Elixir" refers to alchemy more generally
Tàiqīng 太清 (adj./n.)	"Great Clarity." Also translated as "Great Purity." Early medieval Daoist movement associated with the Gé 葛 family. Technically refers to a specific Daoist heaven and namesake elixir. Later the name of the lowest of the Three Heavens (*sāntiān* 三天)

dān 丹 (n.)	"cinnabar." Also translated as "elixir." Often shorthand for *dānshā* 丹砂 (lit., "cinnabar crystals/sand"; mercuric sulfide [HgS])
huáchí 華池 (adj./n.)	"Flowery Pond." Acetic acid/fortified vinegar [solvent] bath in which the ingredients are placed to prepare liquid solutions
chìyán 赤鹽 (adj./n.)	"red salt"
gěnxuě 艮雪 (adj./n.)	"Mountain Snow." Calomel (mercury[1] chloride [Hg_2Cl_2])
xuánbái 玄白 (adj./n.)	"Mysterious White." Extract from lead, gold, and mercury
fēifú 飛符 (v./n.)	"distilled binders." More literally, "flying talisman." Also translated as "Express Amulet." Most likely elixir-specific ingredients that facilitate compounding. In *wàidān* contexts, *fēi* 飛 may also mean "sublimate"
shénshuǐ 神水 (adj./n.)	"Divine Water." Brine
jiǔzhuǎn 九轉 (num./n.)	"nine cycles." Also translated as "nine-times reverted." Cyclic transmutation. *Zhuǎn* refers to the process of elixir refinement and formation. Here it is the most involved, resulting in pure yang (3x3=9)
zhū'ér 朱兒 (adj./n.)	"Vermillion Child." Cinnabar (mercuric sulfide [HgS])
huándān 還丹 (v./n.)	"reverted elixir." Original, essential, and pure state
dāoguī 刀圭 (n./n.)	"knife-nick." Technically, the tip or slice of a knife. More liberally translated as "dose" and "spatula." A specific measurement for elixirs. Somewhat analogous to "pinch," but that suggests a finger-measurement

Lesson 14

Principles of Yǎngshēng 養生 (Nourishing Life)
Bǎoshēng Míng 保生銘
(Inscription on Protecting Life; DZ 835; ZH 957)

With the present selection, we move from the cryptic terminology of Daoist external alchemy (Lessons #11 and #13) and somatology (Lesson #12) to Daoist Yǎngshēng 養生 (Nourishing Life). While the latter often refers to health and longevity techniques, especially movement practices, Yǎngshēng, which offers at least some precedents for modern Qìgōng 氣功 (Ch'ì-kūng; Energy Work/Qi Exercises), actually is a more all-encompassing existential and therapeutic approach. For example, according to the possibly sixth-century *Yǎngxìng yánmìng lù* 養性延命錄 (Record of Nourishing Innate Nature and Extending Life-destiny; DZ 838, 1.9b) (see Lesson #15), there are ten primary elements.

> (1) Strengthening spirit (sèshén 嗇神)
> (2) Cherishing qi (àiqì 愛氣)
> (3) Nourishing the body (yǎngxíng 養形)
> (4) Guided stretching (dǎoyǐn 導引)
> (5) Proper speech (yányǔ 言語)
> (6) Eating and drinking (yǐnshí 飲食)
> (7) Bedchamber arts/Sexual practices (fángshì 房室)
> (8) Rejecting the mundane (fǎnsú 反俗)
> (9) Herbal medicine (yīyào 醫藥)
> (10) Taboos and prohibitions (jìnjì 禁忌)

FIGURE 16: Ten Elements of Yǎngshēng 養生 (Nourishing Life)

For the uninitiated reader, #5, #8, and #10, which are related to virtue and conduct (see Lesson #4), may be surprising. However, virtue (dé 德) as a foundation of health, longevity, and wellness was already emphasized in the early Tiānshī 天師 (Celestial Masters) movement, wherein illness was often associated with immorality. From a larger Daoist perspective, emphasizing "cultivation and refinement" (xiūliàn 修煉), it is often discussed as "establishing the foundations" (zhújī 築基) in the sense of preliminary *and* essential. In any case, the place of Yǎngshēng in Daoism is complex, with different Daoist adherents, communities, and movements having different views. For example, in its Dǎoyǐn 導引 (Guided Stretching) form and perhaps engaging contemporaneous materials like the above-mentioned *Dǎoyǐn tú* 導引圖 (Illustrations of Guided Stretching; ca. 168 BCE) (Lesson #5), members of the inner cultivation lineages of classical Daoism rejected Yǎngshēng as an inferior form of practice. Specifically, those Daoists saw apophatic and quietistic meditation as not only necessary, but also sufficient (see Lessons #6 and #8). Nonetheless, later Daoists, by at least the early medieval period and growing dramatically from the late medieval period forward, began to incorporate Yǎngshēng into a more integrated and holistic approach to Daoist training. As we will explore in upcoming lessons, the "proper" understanding, application, and location of Yǎngshēng varies. The present selection is the complete text of the *Bǎoshēng míng* 保生銘 (Inscription on Protecting Life; DZ 835; ZH 957) (BSM), which is attributed to the famous Daoist physician and alchemist Sūn Sīmiǎo 孫思邈 (581–682). Formalistically speaking, it consists of twenty-four five-character couplets, or forty-eight total lines, with a concluding admonition couplet. The text is a brief exposition of basic Yǎngshēng principles, with a specific emphasis on moderation, regulated lifestyle, and virtuous attitudes. In this way, its views find some precedents in the *Huángdì nèijīng sùwèn* 黃帝內經素問 (Yellow Thearch's Inner Classic: Basic Questions; DZ 1018; ZH 884) (see Lesson #10), which contains many parallel principles. For example, chapter two, which is titled "Sìqì tiáoshén dàlùn 四氣調神大論" (Great Discourse on Harmonizing Spirit with the Four Qi), emphasizes adjusting one's sleep patterns in accordance with the changing solar patterns (dawn/dusk) in each season: spring (less), summer (least), fall (more), and winter (most). Interestingly, the *Bǎoshēng míng* is an inscription (*míng* 銘) originally engraved on the gate of an unknown person. Like the *Xíngqì yùpèi míng* 行氣玉佩銘 (Jade Ornament Inscription on Circulating Qi) (see Lesson #5), it thus brings our attention to the lived and living dimensions of Daoist practice, including as encountered through material culture and aesthetic experience. Consider engaging in Yǎngshēng practice surrounded and informed by the presence of this inscription in calligraphy.

On a deeper language level, the *Bǎoshēng míng*, like the previously-encountered Daoist aphoristic writing and poetry (see Lessons #6–7 and #11–12), lacks complex grammatical constructions, often due to the formalistic features of the poetic genre itself. Nonetheless, there are some grammar characters used in fairly simple ways. These include *yú* 於 ("at/by/in/on/through/to") (lines 1, 17, 18, 25), *bù* ("not") (lines 1, 2, 4, 13, 19), *le* 了 (perfective aspect/past tense) (line 3), *zé* ("then") (lines 6, 18), *nǎi* 乃 ("then") (line 6), *mò* 莫 ("do not") (line 7), *wú* 無 ("do not") (line 7), *dān* 但 ("merely/simply") (line 16), and *qí* 其 ("one's/the") (line 18), most of which we have encountered in earlier lessons. The text, in turn, assists us in developing a foundational Yǎngshēng lexicon, which is again mapped in the accompanying chapter vocabulary. In terms of practice as an all-pervading existential approach, including hygiene broadly understood, it is noteworthy that the *Bǎoshēng míng* mentions massage (*mó* 摩; lit., "rubbing") (line 3), sleeping (*shuì* 睡) (line 4), walking (*xíng* 行) (line 7), and eating (*shí* 食) (line 10). As readers are by now aware, I am especially interested in connections between diverse Daoist communities and movements and across different periods of Daoist history. Along these lines, we find the admonition to "decrease desires" (*shǎoyù* 少欲) (line 23), which recalls *Lǎozǐ* 19 (see Lessons #3 and #7). We also are encouraged to "study the Dao" (*xuédào* 學道) (line 24), which recalls *Lǎozǐ* 41, 48, 65, and 70 as well as *Zhuāngzǐ* 7, 15, 21, 22, and 33, among others.

Livia Kohn 柯恩 (2008) has published a systematic study of Dǎoyǐn, which includes information on the *Bǎoshēng míng* (132, 134–36, 140, 212). While reliable on pre-modern materials, the problematic invocation of modern Western postural yoga [sic] and discussion of modern practice (198–232) must be used with caution. Kohn also has published a sourcebook on Chinese health and longevity techniques (2012), which includes a complete translation of the *Bǎoshēng míng* (148). These may be supplemented by the earlier *Taoist Meditation and Longevity Techniques* (1989), also edited by her.

Primary Text

1 人若勞於形，百病不能成。
　飲酒忌大醉，諸疾自不生。
　食了行百步，數將手摩肚。
　睡不苦高枕，唾涕不遠顧。

5 寅丑日剪甲，理髮須百度。
　飽則立小便，飢乃坐漩溺。
　行坐莫當風，居處無小隙。
　向北大小便，一生昏羃羃。
　日月固然忌，水火仍畏避。

10 每夜洗腳臥，飽食終無益。
　忍辱為上乘，讒言斷親戚。
　思慮最傷神，喜怒傷和息。
　每去鼻中毛，常習不唾地。
　平明欲起時，下牀先左腳。

1. If people exercise their bodies, the hundred illnesses cannot occur.
   If they never drink to intoxication, various ailments will not emerge.
   Walk a hundred steps after eating and massage the belly a few times.
   For sleeping, avoid high pillows; when grieving, do not look backwards.[40]

5. Trim your nails on *yín* or *chǒu* days, and brush your hair a hundred times;
   When satiated, urinate standing up; when hungry, pass water sitting down.
   In walking and sitting, avoid the wind; in dwelling, avoid small spaces.
   Face north when relieving yourself, and remain obscure and hidden throughout life.
   Maintain the taboos of sun and moon, and avoid the perils of fire and water.

10. Wash your feet each night before sleeping, and do not eat beyond satiation.
    Forbearance is the highest vehicle; slander destroys familial relationships.
    Worry causes the greatest harm to spirit; and joy and anger injure the breath.
    Regularly remove the nasal hairs, and always refrain from spitting on the ground.
    Rise as soon as day breaks; when getting up, put the left foot first.

---

[40] The second line more literally reads, "when spitting (*tuò* 唾) and weeping (*tì* 涕), do not turn back." While this may point toward actual physiological actions, I take the characters as similes for resentment and lament.

15　一日免災咎，去邪兼辟惡。
　　但能七星步，令人常壽樂。
　　酸味傷於筋，辛味損正氣。
　　苦則損於心，甘則傷其志。
　　鹹多促人壽，不得偏耽嗜。

20　春夏任宣通，秋冬固陽事。
　　獨臥是守真，慎靜最為貴。
　　財帛生有分，知足將為利。
　　強知是大患，少欲終無累。
　　神氣自然存，學道須終始。

25　書於壁戶間，將用傳君子。

15 Avoid calamities throughout the day, and get rid of deviance and depravity.
Simply perform Pacing the Seven Stars, and encourage others towards abiding joy.
Sour flavors harm the sinews, while pungent flavors injure the aligned qi;
Bitter flavors injure the heart, while sweet flavors harm aspiration;
Excessive salt diminishes longevity—do not indulge in cravings for these.

20 In spring and summer, go with ease; in autumn and winter, strengthen yang.
Sleep alone and guard perfection; remaining careful and tranquil is best.
Wealth and finery have their allotments—knowing sufficiency is [true] profit.
Coercing knowledge is a great affliction; decreasing desires ensures vitality.
Then spirit and qi remain naturally preserved, and studying the Dao is complete.

25 *Write this on walls and doors, and transmit it to worthy disciples*

Vocabulary

xíng 形 (n.)	"body." More technically translated as "form." As associated with human personhood, the three-dimensional disposition or configuration of the human process. Technically speaking, xíng-form has a morphological rather than genetic or schematic nuance
bìng 病 (n.)	"illness." Also translated as "ailment" and "disease." Technically refers to actual diseases, but may designate any major discomfort or enduring disharmony. There are various classical Chinese medical categories
xíngbù 行步 (v./n.)	"walk." Literally, "take steps." Xíng 行 may also mean "move," "travel," and most technically "practice." Bù 步 ("step") may also mean "pace," "stroll," and "walk." Also used more technically for "stage" and related to "making progress" (jìnbù 進步; lit., "advance steps")
mó 摩 (v.)	"massage." May also mean "grind" and "rub." Often appears as ànmó 按摩 (lit., "press and rub"), which refers to massage, including Daoist self-massage
yín 寅 (n.)	"yín." The third of the twelve terrestrial branches (dìzhī 地支). Here refers to various branch-suffix days in the sexagenary cycle (3, 15, 27, 39, 51)
chǒu 丑 (n.)	"chǒu." The second of the terrestrial branches (dìzhī 地支). Here refers to various branch-suffix days in the sexagenary cycle (2, 14, 26, 38, 50)
shàngchéng/shàngshèng 上乘 (adj./n.)	"highest vehicle." Technically refers to Mahāyāna (Greater Vehicle) Buddhism. Use here possibly suggests a polemical subtext advancing Daoist Yǎngshēng 養生 (Nourishing Life) as actually superior
xī 息 (v.|n.|n.)	"breathe/breath/breathing." Also appears as bíxī 鼻息 (lit., "nose breathing"). Basically synonymous with hūxī 呼吸 (lit., "exhale and inhale")

qīxīng bù 七星步 (num./n./n.)	"Pacing the Seven Stars." Most likely a reference to the Yǔbù 禹步 (Pace/Steps of Yu), a.k.a. Bùxū 步虛 (Pacing the Void). Tracing the nine (seven visible and two invisible) stars of the Northern Dipper, especially in Daoist ritual. Associated with fate (mìng 命) in Daoism. Apparently a specific Daoist walking method here
lè 樂 (n.)	"joy." Often appears as zhēnlè 真樂 ("perfect/real/true joy)." Sometimes contrasted with xǐ 喜 as object-directed and ephemeral happiness. Note the alternative pronunciation of 樂 as yuè for "music"
zhèngqì 正氣 (adj./n.)	"aligned qi." Also translated as "correct/upright energy." Key concept in classical Chinese medicine. Qi flowing in its proper direction, exerting a harmonious, ordering, and regulating influence. Often contrasted with nìqì 逆氣 ("rebellious/counterflowing qi") and/or xiéqì 邪氣 ("aberrant/deviant qi"). The latter is basically synonymous with External Pathogenic Factors/Influences (EPFs/EPIs)
zhì 志 (n.)	"aspiration." Also translated as "will" and "determination." More technically, the spiritual faculty associated with the Water phase, and the kidneys by extension
shǒuzhēn 守真 (v./n.)	"guarding perfection." Zhēn 真/真 also is translated as "authentic/real/true." Here associated with conserving vitality and energetic integrity
jìng 靜 (adj.|v.|n.)	"still|still|stillness." Also translated as "tranquil/tranquility." Usually associated with Daoist silent meditation and the associated contemplative state(s)
zhīzú 知足 (v./n.)	"knowing sufficiency." Zú 足 also may mean "enough," "content/contentment," and even "abundance/affluence." The phrase zhīzú first appears in LZ 33, 44, and 46. Also appears as Practice #8 in the Nine Practices

shǎoyù 少欲 (v./n.)	"lessen desires." As the alternate guǎyù 寡欲, this Daoist admonition and practice first appears in LZ 19, wherein it also is associated with "embracing simplicity" (bàopǔ 抱樸)
zìrán 自然 (n./suffix)	"suchness." Literally, "self-so." Also translated as "naturalness," "spontaneity," and even "Nature." As-is-ness. Being-so-of-itself
xuédào 學道 (v./n.)	"studying the Dao." Daoist study-practice and practice-realization. According to LZ 48 involves "redoubled/twofold decreasing" (chóngsǔn 重損)
jūnzǐ 君子 (n./suffix)	"worthy disciple." Literally, "son of a lord." Also translated as "superior person," and earlier as "gentleman." Originally an aristocratic designation indicating nobility by birth, used in classical Ruism ("Confucianism") for its ideal of individuals distinguished by cultural refinement and moral cultivation. Individuals aspiring to become "sages" (shèngrén 聖人). Here designates individuals dedicated to following the prescribed Yǎngshēng path

LESSON 15

DIETARY GUIDELINES
FROM THE *YǍNGXÌNG YÁNMÌNG LÙ*
養性延命錄
(RECORD OF NOURISHING INNATE NATURE AND
EXTENDING LIFE-DESTINY; DZ 838; ZH 952)

AS WE SAW IN THE previous lesson, Daoist Yǎngshēng 養生 (Nourishing Life) practice includes dietetics, which specifically relates to drinking and eating (*yǐnshí* 飲食). As articulated in the "Ten Elements of Yǎngshēng" cited in Lesson #14, dietetics corresponds to the sixth element, with some connection to the tenth element (taboos and prohibitions) as well. The latter includes various principles, including prescriptions and proscriptions, related to consumption and behavior patterns. Here we consider a longer explication of Daoist dietetics from chapter two (1.11b-12a), which is titled "Shíjiè 食戒" (Dietary Prescriptions), of the *Yǎngxìng yánmìng lù* 養性延命錄 (Record of Nourishing Innate Nature and Extending Life-Destiny; DZ 838; ZH 952). This is one of the more influential early medieval sources on Yǎngshēng. It covers various aspects of Yǎngshēng, including dietetics, prohibitions, qi-ingestion, massage, and gymnastics. It is most often attributed to Táo Hóngjǐng 陶弘景 (Tōngmíng 通明 [Pervasive Illumination]; 456–536), a renowned Daoist alchemist and herbalist and the Ninth Patriarch of Shàngqīng 上清 (Highest Clarity) Daoism (see general introduction), who also is associated with a commentary on and supplement to the foundational *Shénnóng běncǎo jīng* 神農本草經 (Divine Husbandman's Classic of Herbology). Taking the traditional attribution as received, it points to this key Daoist as someone interested in the full spectrum of humanistic concerns, from health and longevity to therapeutics and even immortality. Along these lines, one thinks of Táo's eventual position as a leading figure in the Daoist community of Máoshān 茅山 (Mount Mao; Jùróng 句容, Jiāngsū), which included diverse individuals with varied aspirations. Interestingly, Táo's Daoist dietetical concerns, with their emphasis on moderation and regulation, already find a Daoist precedent in the mid-fourth century BCE *Nèiyè* 內業 (Inward Training) (see Lesson #6), again acknowledging the complexity of the "Daoist question." There we are told,

凡食之道：
大充氣傷
而形弗。
大攝骨枯
而血洰。
充攝之間，
此謂和成。

Consider the Way of Eating (*shí zhī dào* 食之道):
If you over-indulge, your qi will be injured;
This will cause your body to deteriorate.
If you over-restrict, your bones will be weakened;
This will cause your blood to congeal.
The place between over-indulgence and over-restriction,
We call this "harmonious completion" (*héchéng* 和成).
(ch. 23)

This further connects with the *Huángdì nèijīng sùwèn* 黃帝內經素問 (Yellow Thearch's Inner Classic: Basic Questions; DZ 1018; ZH 884) (see Lesson #10).

In terms of developing greater Daoist classical Chinese language facility, the passage includes the following grammar characters, all of which we have already encountered: *bù* 不 ("not"), *dān* 但 ("but/merely/simply"), *ér* 而 ("and/but"), *ěr* 耳 (｡), *gù* 故 ("thus"), *suī* 雖 ("although/even if"), *yě* 也 (｡), *yuē* 曰 ("say/speak"), and *zhī* 之 ("of/it"). There are two new ones and one new grammatical construction: 亦, 皆, and 所…為. *Yì* 亦 may mean "also/too," "only," and/or "indeed." As the latter, it is usually employed for emphasis. *Jiē* 皆 generally means "all" and/or "every"; it is sometimes used as a plural marker. *Suǒ* 所…*yǐ* 以 functions like "that which," with some resemblance to *yǐ* 以…*wéi* 為 ("take ___ as ___"). With respect to developing our larger Daoist lexigraphy, the present text is one of the earliest occurrences of *xìng* 性 ("innate nature") and *mìng* 命 ("life-destiny") in combination. While these are roughly synonymous in classical Daoism (see Lessons #2, #6–8), corresponding to one's endowed life-potential or "life-path," including as constitutional embodiment, they eventually become utilized as distinct aspects of personhood. *Xìng* is associated with the heart-mind and spirit, while *mìng* is associated with the kidneys and vital essence. In a late medieval and larger Daoist framework, they often further relate to meditation and Yǎngshēng practices, or mind-cultivation and body-cultivation, respectively. These are referred to as "stillness practice" (*jìnggōng* 靜功) and "movement practice" (*dònggōng* 動功), respectively, and generally relate to spirit and qi in Daoist terms. In the case of the *Yǎngxìng yánmìng lù*, *xìngmìng* ("nature/life") practice may be thought of as emphasizing something like mind-body holism, although we must remember the associated qi-based views. In addition, while it may initially seem counter-intuitive to "nourish innate nature," given the latter's association with one's original and inherent connection to the Dao, there is a classical Daoist precedent in the title of chapter sixteen of the *Zhuāngzǐ* 莊子 (Book of Master Zhuang), which is titled "Shànxìng 繕性" (Mending Innate Nature). That is, although *xìng* and *mìng*, or *xìngmìng*, are given on some level, they may be supplemented, cultivated, and actualized. As was the case in the *Nèiyè* chapter just cited, the *Yǎngxìng yánmìng lù* uses *dào* in the sense of a way, that is, a specific approach to self-cultivation and a distinct way of life. Here it is Yǎngshēng as the "Way of Nourishing Innate Nature," which also recalls other, parallel Daoist usages like Daoism as the "Way of Antiquity" (*gǔ zhī dào* 古之道) and "Way of Sages" (*shèngrén zhī dào* 聖人之道). *Dào* also becomes used in this manner to refer to distinct Daoist movements and sub-traditions, like Tiānshī dào 天師道 (Way of the Celestial Masters). The text further brings our attention to the central importance of walking (*xíng* 行) and of the belly (*fù* 腹) in Daoist practice, and life more generally. As is the case with classical Daoism, perhaps most famously documented in chapters three and twelve of the *Dàodé jīng* 道德經 (Scripture on the Dao and Inner Power), *fù*-belly may refer to the stomach, including the spleen-stomach (Earth) network and digestion, and/or to the navel region as the core of the body and the primary storehouse of qi. In the latter sense, it later becomes identified as the "Elixir Field" (*dāntián* 丹田) (see Lesson #12). In the present selection, walking and rubbing the belly assist digestion and ensure the free flow of qi throughout the body. Finally, the passage contains one of the most famous Yǎngsheng mottos, directives, and principles:

流水不腐，戶樞不蠹。

Flowing water does not mold; a door hinge does not rot.

The *Yǎngxìng yánmìng lù* has yet to receive a comprehensive scholarly study. Selections are translated in Livia Kohn's 柯恩 *A Source Book in Chinese Longevity* (2012, 165–76, 182–203), already mentioned in Lesson #14.

Primary Text

《食戒》

真人曰：雖常服藥物，而不知養性之術，亦難以長生也。養性之道，不欲飽食便臥及終日久坐。皆損壽也。人欲小勞，但莫至疲及強所不能堪勝耳。人食畢，當行步躊躇，有所修為為快也。故流水不腐，戶樞不蠹。以其勞動數故也。

故人不要夜食；食畢但當行中庭，如數里可佳。飽食即臥生百病，不消成積聚也。食欲少而數，不欲頓多難銷。常如飽中飢、飢中飽。故養性者，先飢乃食，先渴而飲。恐覺飢乃食，食必多；盛渴乃飲，飲必過。食畢當行，行畢使人以粉摩腹數百過，大益也。

Dietary Prescriptions

The Perfected have said: Though one may regularly take medicinal supplements, without knowing the arts of nourishing innate nature, it is difficult to actually attain longevity. The Way of Nourishing Innate Nature is to avoid eating to satiation, followed by avoiding lying down or extended sitting day after day. Each of these actions diminishes longevity. Rather, one should exert the body somewhat, but not to the point of fatigue or by forcing oneself to do what is utterly unattainable. After eating, go for a walk or leisurely stroll—that will assist cultivation. Thus it is said that flowing water does not mold; that a door hinge does not rot. This is because they move and exert themselves constantly.

On another note, it is better not to eat a lot at night; if you do, make sure to take a walk in the courtyard for several *lĭ*. This is most excellent. Eating to satiation and then lying down causes the hundred illnesses, including indigestion, stagnation, and obstructions. Eat little but often, never a lot all at once. Always feel a little hungry even when full, a little full even when hungry. Thus, for nourishing innate nature, make sure to eat before you get really hungry and to drink before you get really thirsty. The concern is that once you notice you are hungry, you will be tempted to eat too much; once you notice you are thirsty, you will drink too much. After a meal, go for a walk. After the walk, take some rice flour and rub it on your belly, massaging it several hundred times. This will be of great benefit.

Vocabulary

xìng 性 (n.)	"innate nature." From a Daoist perspective, one's original and inherent connection to the Dao. Associated with the heart (*xīn* 心) and spirit (*shén* 神). Primarily cultivated through stillness practice, meditation in particular
mìng 命 (n.)	"life-destiny." Also translated as "fate." From a Daoist perspective, one's allotment of vitality and constitution. Associated with the kidneys (*shèn* 腎) and vital essence (*jīng* 精), including physicality. Usually cultivated through movement practices, especially health and longevity techniques
jiè 戒 (n.)	"precept." The most general Daoist term for rules and regulations. Conduct principles and guidelines
zhēnrén 眞人/真人 (adj./n.)	"Perfected." Also translated as "authentic/real/true being/person." One of the primary ideals of later Daoism
yào 藥 (n.)	"medicine." Also translated as "herbs," but technically includes minerals and even animal substances. Includes the *cǎo* 艸/艹 ("grass") radical. Often used synonymously with *běncǎo* 本草 (lit., "roots and grasses"; a.k.a. *materia medica*), herbology and pharmacology
yǎngxìng 養性 (v./n.)	"nourishing innate nature." Here used synonymously with *Yǎngshēng* 養生 (Nourishing Life), which technically refers to health and longevity techniques
shù 術 (n.)	"arts." Also translated more technically as "technique." As referring to practice, basically synonymous with *fǎ* 法 ("method") and *gōng* 功 ("exercise")
chángshēng 長生 (adj./n.)	"long life/longevity." More literally, "perpetual life" or even "continually born." Basically synonymous with *shòu* 壽 ("longevity"). One of the ideals of Yǎngshēng

xíngbù 行步 (v./n.)	"walk." More literally, "take steps." *Xíng* 行 also may mean "move," "travel," and most technically "practice." *Bù* 步 ("step") may also mean "pace," "stroll," and "walk." Also used more technically for "stage" and related to "making progress" (*jìnbù* 進步; lit., "advance steps")
xiū 修 (v.)	"cultivate." More conventionally means "build," "mend," "prune," and "regulate." Appears in key Daoist phrases, including *xiūdào* 修道 ("cultivating the Dao"), *xiūliàn* 修煉 ("cultivation and refinement"), and *xiūzhēn* 修真 ("cultivating perfection")
lǐ 里 (n.)	"*lǐ*." A unit of distance with varying lengths depending on historical period. Approximately half a kilometer. Several *lǐ* thus equals about 1.5 kilometers or 1 English mile
fù 腹 (n.)	"belly." Also translated as "abdomen" and "navel." May refer to the stomach, as the locus of material sustenance via digestion, and to the navel region, as the core of the body and primary storehouse of qi. A classical Daoist precedent appears in LZ 3 and 12. Eventually identified as the "Elixir Field" (*dāntián* 丹田)
mó 摩 (v.)	"massage." May also mean "grind" and "rub." Often appears as *ànmó* 按摩 (lit., "press and rub"), which refers to massage, including Daoist self-massage

LESSON 16

THE WAY OF HEAVEN
FROM THE *HUÁNGDÌ YĪNFÚ JĪNG* 黃帝陰符經
(YELLOW THEARCH'S SCRIPTURE ON THE HIDDEN TALISMAN; DZ 31; ZH 642)

THE *HUÁNGDÌ YĪNFÚ JĪNG* 黃帝陰符經 (Yellow Thearch's Scripture on the Hidden Talisman; DZ 31; ZH 642) is an obscure, anonymous text of uncertain provenance, but probably dates to the sixth century CE. Although earlier discussed as a "military treatise" and sometimes attributed to Lǐ Quán 李筌 (fl. 713–741), such characterizations fail to recognize the esoteric Daoist encryption. Abbreviated as *Yīnfú jīng* 陰符經 (Scripture on the Hidden Talisman) (YFJ), the text is primarily composed in four- and five-character combinations, and there are two extant versions. The shorter version consists of approximately 300 characters (323 in total), while the longer version contains approximately 400 characters (437 in total). It has been conjectured that the shorter text is the older edition. If one drops the final/additional 113 characters, the versions are almost identical. In either case and in terms of formalistic features and translation dilemmas, the *Yīnfú jīng*, like DZ texts as a whole, is received as single blocks of text, so we must decide both how to punctuate it and possibly how to lineate it. I have chosen the latter, but it could also be presented in paragraph form. In terms of the title, the *Yīnfú jīng* presents itself as a revelation from the legendary and now deified Huángdì 黃帝 (Yellow Thearch) (see Lessons #1 and

#10). *Yīnfú* is translated here as "hidden talisman," but *fú* has also been rendered variously as "agreement/contract/convergence/tally." *Yīn* 陰, in the sense of yin-yang and related to the homonym *yǐn* 隱 ("hidden"), invokes darkness, secrecy, and open receptivity. From a Daoist perspective, it connects to other "yin categories," with the Mysterious Female (*xuánpìn* 玄牝) and Valley Spirit (*gǔshén* 谷神) (LZ 6) as well as "guarding the feminine" (*shǒucí* 守雌) (LZ 10 and 28) being especially important and influential. *Fú* 符, which contains the *zhú* 竹/⺮ ("bamboo") radical, refers to Daoist talismans (see Lessons #3, #8, #11, and #13). As expressed in the text itself, the "hidden talisman" is an esoteric designation for the heart-mind (*xīn* 心), specifically the purified heart-mind, characterized by stillness (*jìng* 靜) and associated with original spirit (*yuánshén* 元神), as one's quasi-divine capacity to connect with the Dao:

心生於物，死於物。機在目。

The heart-mind is born from things;
The heart-mind dies from things.
The pivot [of the heart-mind] is in the eyes.
(1b)

The text consists of three section headings, divided into *shàng* 上 ("upper/first"), *zhōng* 中 ("middle/second"), and *xià* 下 ("lower/third") (see Lessons #4 and #12).

---

(1) "Shénxiān bàoyī yǎndào 神仙抱一演道"
    (Extensive Way of Spirit Immortality and Embracing the One)
(2) "Fùguó ānmín yǎnfǎ 富國安民演法"
    (Extensive Method for Enriching the Country and Pacifying the People)
(3) "Qiángbīng zhànshèng yǎnshù 強兵戰勝演術"
    (Extensive Technique for Strengthening the Troops and Preparing for Battle)

FIGURE 17: Section Titles of the *Yīnfú jīng* 陰符經
(Scripture on the Hidden Talisman)

What is rarely recognized is that these titles, with the exception of the phrase *shénxiān*, are allusions to and probably derived from the *Dàodé jīng* 道德經 (Scripture on the Dao and Inner Power), specifically chapters ten, twenty-two, thirty, fifty-seven, sixty-eight, and seventy-six. Here chapter ten is especially noteworthy, as it is one of the most technical chapters on classical Daoist apophatic and quietistic meditation, referred to therein as *bàoyī* 抱一 ("embracing the One") (see Lessons #6 and #8). Like the *Dàodé jīng* and some of its commentary traditions (see Lessons #25–28), the *Yīnfú jīng* uses political and military terms as analogies for Daoist inner cultivation, especially meditation. It contains a Daoist encryption. The *Yīnfú jīng* in turn became canonical in internal alchemy (*nèidān* 內丹) circles during the Sòng dynasty (960–1279), including in the Quánzhēn 全真 (Complete Perfection) movement. In fact, it became one of the three core Quánzhēn scriptures (*sānjīng* 三經), with the other two being the *Dàodé jīng* (see Lesson #7) and the eighth-century *Qīngjìng jīng* 清靜經 (Scripture on Clarity and Stillness; DZ 620; ZH 350) (see Lesson #17). These are pre-Quánzhēn works that were incorporated into that Daoist sub-tradition. They remain a central focus in the contemporary movement as well.

On a deeper language level, the *Yīnfú jīng*, like other cryptic Daoist compositions, including aphorisms and poetry (see Lessons #5, #6–7, #11–12), is extremely concise and often lacks fuller grammatical constructions. The current passage (1a), which is the opening of the text, contains the following relevant characters: *yě* 也 (。), *yǐ* 以 ("by means of/in order to"), *yǐ* 矣 (。), *yú* 於 ("at/by/in/on/through/to"), *zài* 在 ("at/in/on"), *zhě* 者 ("as for/one who"), and *zhī* 之 ("of"). There also are two new grammar characters, namely, 盡 and 乎. *Jìn* 盡, which may mean "end," "exhaust," "finish," and "entire," is here used in the sense of "and that is all." I have translated it more liberally as "until complete fulfillment," with the connotation of necessary and sufficient. We previously encountered *hū* 乎 as a sentence-final interrogative particle functioning like a question mark (?), but here it is used as preposition in the sense of "at/in/on/with" and paralleling *yú* 於. In terms of vocabulary, the previously cited section headings emphasize following a particular "way" (dào 道) and utilizing specific "methods" (fǎ 法) and "techniques" (shù 術), specifically quietistic meditation in concert with energetic listening and cosmological attunement. Along the latter lines, aspiring Daoist adepts are encouraged to follow the "Way of Heaven" (tiāndào 天道; tiān zhī dào 天之道). This phrase also appears in the classical Daoist textual corpus, including chapters nine, seventy-three, seventy-seven, and eighty-one of the Dàodé jīng and as the title of chapter thirteen of the Zhuāngzǐ 莊子 (Book of Master Zhuang) (see Lessons #2, #7, and #8). It also occurs throughout the Huángdì nèijīng sùwèn 黃帝內經素問 (Yellow Thearch's Inner Classic: Basic Questions; DZ 1018; ZH 884) (see Lesson #10). Another noteworthy feature of this passage involves recognizing and cultivating the heart-mind (xīn 心) as the "pivot" (jī 機), which also is translated as "mechanism" and even "workings." Often used synonymously with shū 樞 ("pivot"), the character, which contains the mù 木 ("wood") radical, originally designated various mechanisms, including crossbow triggers, which date to at least as early as the early Warring States period (480–222 BCE) in China. The text further links realization of the original or pure heart-mind, associated spirit (shén 神), with the necessity of disengaging sense perception (Five Thieves [wǔzéi 五賊]), thus connecting to classical and foundational Daoist "contemplative psychology" (see Lessons #6 and #8).

A complete translation of the Yīnfú jīng has been published by Louis Komjathy 康思奇 as Handbook #7 of his Handbooks for Daoist Practice (2008 [2003]). This includes a scholarly introduction that discusses historical and interpretive issues, including technical terminology. Komjathy's translation has, in turn, been widely circulated on the internet and become the basis of various plagiarized versions, most often by individuals who do not know Chinese. In his The Way of Complete Perfection (2013, 186–208), Komjathy also included a complete annotated translation of the Huángdì yīnfú jīng zhù 黃帝陰符經註 (Commentary on the Huángdì yīnfú jīng; DZ 122; ZH 658) by Liú Chǔxuán 劉處玄 (Chángshēng 長生 [Perpetual Life]; 1147–1203), one of the members of the so-called

Seven Perfected (*qīzhēn* 七眞) of early Quánzhēn 全眞 (Complete Perfection) Daoism. Thomas Cleary (1949–2021) (1991, 220–38) has published a popular and often unreliable translation of the *Yīnfú jīng zhù* 陰符經注 (Commentary on the *Yīnfú jīng*; ZW 255) by Liú Yīmíng 劉一明 (Wùyuán 悟元 [Awakening-to-the-Origin]; 1734–1821), an influential eleventh-generation Lóngmén 龍門 (Dragon Gate) monk. Here we also should note that the *Historical Companion to the Daozang* (Schipper and Verellen 2004, 319–21) miscategorizes the text as "philosophy," with the associated entry also containing a variety of other problematic information. The *Yīnfú jīng* is better understood as a "contemplative work." It provides a map of contemplative practice and contemplative experience, including the associated contemplative psychology.

Primary Text

《神仙抱一演道章上》

觀天之道，執天之行，盡矣。
天有五賊，見之者昌。
五賊在心，施行於天。
宇宙在乎手，萬物生乎身。
天性人也；人心機也。
立天之道，以定人也。

Upper Section:
Extensive Way of Spirit Immortality and Embracing the One

Observe the Way of Heaven,
Attend to the activities of heaven,
Until complete fulfillment.
Heaven has Five Thieves;
One who perceives this prospers.
The Five Thieves are in the heart-mind.
They extend to and even affect heaven.
The canopy of space-time is in your hands.
Ten thousand things arise from your body.
The innate nature of heaven is humanity.
The human heart-mind is the pivot.
Establishing the Way of Heaven
Enables the settling of humanity.[41]

---

[41] Following the grammar more closely, these lines also might be rendered as an admonition: "Establish the Way of Heaven in order to settle humanity."

Vocabulary

Huángdì 黄帝	"Yellow Thearch." A.k.a. Xuānyuán 軒轅. More conventionally referred to as "Yellow Emperor." A legendary Chinese ruler and culture-hero, with *dì*-thearch here indicating a divine ruler. Although traditionally considered the source of "Chinese civilization" more generally, Huángdì is a complex figure, often representing different things to different communities and traditions. Here he is the revelatory source-point of the present scripture
yīnfú 陰符 (adj./n.)	"hidden talisman." Also translated as "hidden agreement/contract/convergence/tally." *Fú* 符 ("talisman") technically refers to an object used for communication, contracts, direction, and so forth. Daoist talismans consist of two halves, one celestial/divine (*líng* 靈) and one terrestrial/human (*bǎo* 寶), that, when rejoined, reveal original unity and result in efficacious power. There are many types and functions (e.g., exorcism, protection). Here the "hidden talisman" is the heart-mind as innate nature/spirit as Dao
shénxiān 神仙 (adj./n.)	"spirit immortality." Also translated as "divine transcendence." Often identified as the highest form of Daoist immortality, characterized by the creation of a yang-spirit (*yángshén* 陽神) capable of transcending physical death and entering the Daoist sacred realms
bàoyī 抱一 (v./n.)	"embracing the One." A classical Daoist technical term for apophatic and quietistic (emptiness-/stillness-based) meditation. Here *yī* 一 (lit., "1") refers to the Dao (One), and to the associated process (uniting) and outcome/state (union/unity) by extension. Also appears as *shǒuyī* 守一 ("guarding the One") and *zhíyī* 執一 ("grasping/holding the One"). The phrase *bàoyī* first appears in LZ 10. See also NY 24 and ZZ 11 & 23
guān 觀 (v.|n.)	"observe|observation." Daoist contemplative approach and practice. Also used to translate the Buddhist Pali *vipassanā* and Sanskrit *vipaśyanā* (insight meditation)

tiāndào 天道 (n./n.)	"Way of Heaven." Both the universe as transformative process (zàohuà 造化) based on yin-yang differentiation and interaction as well as associated human cosmological attunement. See also LZ 9, 47, 73, 77, 79, and 81; ZZ 12–14; and SW 2
wǔzéi 五賊 (num./n.)	"Five Thieves." Usually understood as the five primary sense organs and associated modes of perception. Also referred to as the Five Doors/Gates (wǔmén 五門). Contemplatively viewed as potential sources of dissipation, at least when employed excessively
xīn 心 (n.)	"heart-mind." Also translated as "heart" and/or "mind," but technically psychosomatic. May also mean "center." The psychospiritual center of human personhood. Associated with innate nature (xìng 性) and spirit (shén 神)
yǔzhōu 宇宙 (n./n.)	"space-time." Also translated as "cosmos/universe." Cf. tiāndì 天地 ("heavens and earth"). See also HNZ 3
wànwù 萬物 (num./n.)	"ten thousand things." Also translated as "myriad beings/things." Wù 物 (lit., "animal"; cf. shòu 獸) contains the niú 牛/⺧ ("ox") radical. Wànwù usually refers to everything in existence, including both animate/sentient beings and inanimate/nonsentient things
xìng 性 (n.)	"innate nature." One's inherent and original connection to the Dao. Associated with the heart-mind (xīn 心) and spirit (shén 神). Primarily cultivated through stillness practice, meditation in particular
jī 機 (n.)	"pivot." More literally, "trigger," and "mechanism" by extension. Often used synonymously with shū 樞 ("pivot"). Here identified as the heart-mind
dìng 定 (v.)	"settle." Also translated as "concentration," "stability," and most technically "absorption." Also used to translate the Indian and Buddhist Sanskrit samādhi (meditative absorption/yogic stasis)

Lesson 17

Returning to the Dao
From the Tàishàng Lǎojūn shuō cháng qīngjìng miàojīng 太上老君說常清靜妙經
(Wondrous Scripture on Constant Clarity and Stillness, as Spoken by the Great High Lord Lao; DZ 620; ZH 350)

The Tàishàng Lǎojūn shuō cháng qīngjìng miàojīng 太上老君說常清靜妙經 (Wondrous Scripture on Constant Clarity and Stillness, as Spoken by the Great High Lord Lao; DZ 620; ZH 350) is another anonymous text of uncertain provenance that probably dates to the eighth century CE. Abbreviated as Qīngjìng jīng 清靜經 (Scripture on Clarity and Stillness) (QJJ), the text is part of a larger corpus of Táng-dynasty (618–960) texts that may be labelled "Clarity-and-Stillness Literature." This formally begins with the earlier, also anonymous seventh-century Tàishàng shèngxuán xiāozāi hùmìng miàojīng 太上昇玄消災護命妙經 (Great High's Wondrous Scripture on Ascending to the Mysterious, Dispersing Calamities, and Protecting Life-destiny; DZ 19; ZH 368; abbrev. Hùmìng jīng 護命經 or Shèngxuán hùmìng jīng 昇玄護命經; trl. Komjathy 2019). This is a Daoist adaptation of the Mahāyāna (Greater Vehicle) Buddhist Bōrě bōluómìduō xīnjīng 般若波羅蜜多心經 (Prajñāpāramitā-hridaya sutrā [Heart Sutra on the Perfection of Wisdom]; T.250–257), with the latter also abbreviated with the alternative Romanization of Pánruò xīnjīng or just referred to as Heart Sutra in English. The latter is a condensed version of the "perfection of wisdom" (*prajñā-pāramitā*) sutras that was probably composed in China in the early seventh century. Both Buddhist and Daoist texts focus on *kōng* 空 (Skt.: *śūnyatā*), or "emptiness" and associated views of interdependence. The *Shèngxuán hùmìng jīng* in turn fed into the *Tàishàng Lǎojūn qīngjìng xīnjīng* 太上老君清靜心經 (Great High Lord Lao's Heart Scripture on Clarity and Stillness; DZ 1169; ZH 358; abbrev. *Qīngjìng xīnjīng*) and culminated with the *Qīngjìng jīng* itself. It is composed of verses in four- and five-character combinations (391 characters in total). Thus, like the *Yīnfú jīng* and in terms of formalistic features and translation dilemmas, the *Qīngjìng jīng* is received as single blocks of text, so we must decide both how to punctuate it and possibly how to lineate it. I have chosen the latter, but it could also be presented in paragraph form (see Komjathy 2019). The *Qīngjìng jīng* in turn combines the worldview of the *Dàodé jīng* 道德經 (Scripture on the Dao and Inner Power) with the structure (as well as some content) of the *Bōrě xīnjīng*. On a text-critical level, the received edition includes an epilogue, which discusses the text's supposed transmission, attributed to Gé Xuán 葛玄 (164–244), the paternal grand-uncle of Gé Hóng 葛洪 (Bàopǔ 抱朴 [Embracing Simplicity]; 283–343) and key figure in the formation of the Tàiqīng 太清 (Great Clarity) movement (see Lessons #3 and #13). However, this appears to be a later addition, perhaps in order to create greater cultural capital. As the title indicates, the *Qīngjìng jīng* presents itself as a revelation from Lǎojūn 老君 (Lord Lao), the deified Lǎozǐ 老子 ("Master Lao"), high god of early Daoism, and personification of the Dao (see Lessons #1, #4, #12, and #13). By the late medieval period, Lǎojūn was increasingly recognized as Dàodé tiānzūn 道德天尊 (Celestial Worthy of the Dao and Inner Power) in the Sānqīng 三清 (Three Purities), the highest "gods" of the standardized Daoist pantheon and anthropomorphized representations of three primordial cosmic ethers. The *qīngjìng* 清靜 ("clarity and stillness") of the title, which also appears as the variant 清淨 and is translated as "purity and tranquility," refers to an important Daoist contemplative state (temporary psychological condition) and trait (enduring character quality) and is a key connective strand throughout the Daoist tradition. For example, it appears as a paired phrase in chapters fifteen and forty-five of the *Dàodé jīng* and as Practice #5 of the Nine Practices (see Lesson #4). Like the *Yīnfú jīng*, the *Qīngjìng jīng* became canonical in internal alchemy (*nèidān* 內丹) circles during the Sòng dynasty (960–1279), including in the Quánzhēn 全真 (Complete Perfection) movement. In fact, it became one of the three core Quánzhēn scriptures (*sānjīng* 三經), with the other two being the *Dàodé jīng* (see Lesson #7) and the sixth-century *Yīnfú jīng* 陰符經 (Scripture on the Hidden Talisman; DZ 31; ZH 642) (see Lesson #16). These are pre-Quánzhēn works that were incorporated into that Daoist sub-tradition. They remain a central focus in the contemporary movement as well. As expressed in section 1b,

常能遣其欲而心自靜；
常能澄其心而神自清。

If you can constantly banish desires,
Then the heart-mind will become still naturally.
If you can constantly settle the heart-mind,
Then spirit will become clear naturally.

Interestingly, these lines have some resemblance to LZ 15:

孰能濁以靜之徐清？
孰能安以動之徐生？

Who can, through stillness, gradually bring clarity to turbidity?
Who can, through movement, gradually bring vitality to calmness?

Grammatically speaking, the current passage (1ab), which is the opening of the text, contains the following relevant characters: *ér* 而 ("and/but"), *fú* 夫 ("now then"), *jiē* 皆 ("all/every"), *yuē* 曰 ("say/speak"), *zhě* 者 ("as for/one who"), and *zhī* 之 ("of"). With respect to Daoist lexigraphy, in addition to its near-standard discussion of *qīngjìng*, we should note the use of *cháng* 常 ("constant") in the title and culminating in the final line (2a). This is a key quality in the *Dàodé jīng*. The *Qīngjìng jīng* in turn does not just emphasize clarity and stillness, but rather *constancy* in/of these. In technical Daoist contemplative terminology, this is *dìng* 定 ("absorption"), which also is used translate the Indian and Buddhist Sanskrit *samādhi*. The use of *wú* 無, literally "without," but more technically "beyond/non-," also connects to classical Daoism, as do the various cosmological terms (see Lessons #9 and #10). Interestingly, the opening three lines speak of three "non-states," thus again invoking Daoist ternary cosmology and numerology (see Lessons #4, #7, #10–12, and #16).

The *Qīngjìng jīng* has been translated a number of times. A complete translation appears as Handbook #4 of Louis Komjathy's 康思奇 *Handbooks for Daoist Practice* (2008 [2003]). This includes a scholarly introduction that discusses historical and interpretive issues, including technical terminology. Komjathy's translation has, in turn, been widely circulated on the internet and become the basis of various plagiarized versions, most often by individuals who do not know Chinese. In his *The Way of Complete Perfection* (2013, 176–86)), Komjathy also included a complete annotated translation of the *Tàishàng Lǎojūn shuō cháng qīngjìng jīng sòngzhù* 太上老君說常清靜經頌註 (Recitational Commentary on the *Tàishàng Lǎojūn shuō cháng qīngjìng jīng*; DZ 974; ZH 354; abbrev. *Qīngjìng jīng zhù*) by Liú Tōngwēi 劉通微 (Mòrán 默然 [Silent Suchness]; d. 1196), one of the less well-known senior members of the early Quánzhēn community. Here we also should note that the *Historical Companion to the Daozang* (Schipper and Verellen 2004, 562) miscategorizes the work as a Língbǎo 靈寶 (Numinous Treasure) text, apparently because of the epilogue. Again, the purpose of this epilogue it is unclear, but there may have been an as-yet-unidentified local lineage that constructed itself along these lines. In any case, this deviates from the primary revelatory source, and, in the larger parameters of the *Dàozàng*, the *Qīngjìng jīng* is better thought of as part of "contemplative literature" in general and the "Clarity-and-Stillness Literature" in particular. For a more recent discussion, which also includes a complete translation of the *Shèngxuán hùmìng jīng*, see Komjathy 2019.

Primary Text

老君曰：

大道無形，生育天地；
大道無情，運行日月；
大道無名，長養萬物。

吾不知其名，強名曰道。

夫道者、
有清有濁，有動有靜；
天清地濁，天動地靜...

清者濁之源，動者靜之基。

人能常清靜，天地悉皆歸。

人神好清，而心擾之；
人心好靜，而慾牽之。

常能遣其欲而心自靜；
常能澄其心而神自清。

Lord Lao spoke:

The great Dao is without form:
It brings forth and nurtures heaven and earth.
The great Dao is without feelings:
It regulates the course of the sun and moon.
The great Dao is without name:
It raises and nourishes the ten thousand beings.

I do not know its name;
Compelled to name it, I call it "Dao."

Within the Dao,
There is clarity and turbidity;
There is movement and stillness.
Heaven is clarity, and earth is turbidity.
Heaven is movement, and earth is stillness...

Clarity is the source of turbidity.
Movement is the root of stillness.

If humans can be constantly clear and still,
Heaven and earth completely return.

The human spirit is fond of clarity,
But the heart-mind disturbs it.
The human heart-mind is fond of stillness,
But desires meddle with it.

If you can constantly banish desires,
Then the heart-mind will become still naturally.
If you can constantly settle the heart-mind,
Then spirit will become clear naturally.

Vocabulary

Lǎojūn 老君 (name/title)	"Lord Lao." The deified Lǎozǐ 老子 ("Master Lao"), high god of early Daoism, and personification of the Dao. From the late medieval period forward, increasingly recognized as Dàodé tiānzūn 道德天尊 (Celestial Worthy of the Dao and Inner Power) in the Sānqīng 三清 (Three Purities), the highest "gods" of the standardized Daoist pantheon and anthropomorphized representations of three primordial cosmic ethers
qīngjìng 清靜 (n./n.)	"clarity and stillness." May also appear and be used as adjectives: "clear and still." Also translated as "clear stillness" and "purity and tranquility." Interrelated and interdependent contemplative states/traits. Thus better thought of as "clarity-and-stillness." Also used in ascetic and monastic contexts to refer to celibacy (no sex), whether temporary or permanent
dào 道 (n.)	"way." Also appears as 衜/衟. May also mean "path" and "to speak." The character consists of *chuò* 辵/辶 ("walk/move") and *shǒu* 首 ("head"). The sacred and ultimate concern of Daoists. An early precedent for the additional demarcation of *dà* 大 ("great"; read: *zhēn* 眞 ["real/true"]) appears in LZ 25. See also chs. 18, 34, 41, 53, & 67
wúxíng 無形 (neg./n.)	"formlessness." Lit., "without form." The Dao as fundamentally and essentially beyond materiality and substance. Subtle
wúqíng 無情 (neg./n.)	"emotionlessness." Lit., "without emotion/feeling." The Dao as fundamentally beyond attachment, concern, preference, and the like. Impersonal
wúmíng 無名 (neg./n.)	"namelessness." Lit., "without name." *Míng* 名 technically refers to one's personal given name. It also refers to "fame" and "reputation," and social identity by extension. The Dao as fundamentally beyond conception, language, separate identity, and the like. Undifferentiated

qiáng 強 (v.)	"compel." Also translated as "force" and "strength." As a negative quality and approach, often contrasted with *ruò* 弱 ("weakness"). Here suggests reluctance to speak about the Dao. Finds a precedent in LZ 4, 15, 25, 56, and 71, with the current QJJ passage representing the Daoist culmination of ch. 25
zhuó 濁 (adj.|n.)	"turbid|turbidity." Alchemically speaking, the negative/harmful ("yin") counterpart of "clarity" (*qīng* 清). Also used in a more neutral cosmological sense and associated with the earth. See, e.g., HNZ 3
dòng 動 (adj.|n.)	"moving|movement." Also rendered more technically as "agitated/agitation." Alchemically speaking, the negative/harmful ("yin") counterpart of "stillness" (*jìng* 靜). Also used in a more neutral cosmological sense and associated with the heavens. See, e.g., HNZ 3. May also refer to the movement of qi, specifically as circulating (*yùn* 運) in the cosmos and one's body
shén 神 (n.)	"spirit." Also earlier translated as "daemon" (Greek). May refer to actual deities, spiritual capacities, and consciousness in a more abstract sense. The most subtle of the vital (non)substances. Also identified as the third or highest of the internal Three Treasures (*sānbǎo* 三寶)
xīn 心 (n.)	"heart-mind." Also translated as "heart" and/or "mind," but technically psychosomatic. May also mean "center." The psychospiritual center of human personhood. Associated with innate nature (*xìng* 性) and spirit (*shén* 神) within the larger Daoist tradition
chéng/dèng 澄 (v.)	"settle." May also mean "clear," "purify/pure," "precipitate," and "strain." Contains the *shuǐ* 水/氵 ("water") radical

Lesson 18

Emptiness & Forgetfulness
From the "Zuòwàng piān 坐忘篇"

(Treatise on Sitting-in-Forgetfulness; DZ 1017, 2.1a–8b)

The "Zuòwàng piān 坐忘篇" (Treatise on Sitting-in-Forgetfulness) is a meditation manual preserved in the *Dàoshū* 道樞 (Pivot of the Dao; DZ 1017; ZH 949; abbrev. DS). The latter is a large textual compendium that was probably compiled around 1150 by the Chinese court scholar-official and bibliophile Zēng Zào 曾慥 (a.k.a. Zēng Cào; Zhìyóu 至遊 [Utmost Wanderer]; 1091–1155). The present "Zuòwàng piān" is closely connected to the more well-known *Zuòwàng lùn* 坐忘論 (Discourse on Sitting-in-Forgetfulness; DZ 1036; ZH 992; trl. Kohn 1987; Kohn 2010) and the associated *Zuòwàng míng* 坐忘銘 (Inscription on Sitting-in-Forgetfulness; see Wú 1981; Kohn 1987, 113–17, 172–76). The former is a key late medieval meditation manual composed by Sīmǎ Chéngzhēn 司馬承禎 (Zhēnyī 貞一 [Pure Unity]; 647–735), the Twelfth Patriarch of Shàngqīng 上清 (Highest Clarity) and thus connected to the later articulation of that sub-tradition (see also Lesson #15). In the Táng dynasty (618–907), Shàngqīng became the highest ordination rank in the standardized monastic system. Dating to 829, the *Zuòwàng míng* is an inscription (*míng* 銘) derived from a stone stele (*shíbēi* 石碑) engraved on Mount Wángwū 王屋 (near Jìyuán 濟源, Hénán) in 829. It supposedly derives from an earlier oral transmission brought from Mount Tóngbó/Tóngbǎi 桐柏 (Paulownias-and-Cedars; Tiāntái 天台, Zhèjiāng) by an otherwise unknown "Master Xú 徐." It thus again brings our attention to the lived experience of place-specific Daoist being and community, including as expressed and encountered in Daoist material culture such as steles and inscriptions (see Lessons #5 and #14). Section 7a-8a of our present "Zuòwàng piān" closely resembles said inscription. All of these three related "texts" are connected to the Táng dynasty "insight meditation" literature, with the latter usually referred to as *nèiguān* 內觀 ("inner observation") under the influence of earlier Indian and then Chinese Buddhist *vipassana/vipaśyanā*. As expressed in the *Zuòwàng lùn*, which is one of the most systematic Daoist meditation manuals, there are seven primary steps or stages.

---

(1) Reverence and Trust (*jìngxìn* 敬信)

(2) Interrupting Karma (*duànyuán* 斷緣)

(3) Gathering the Heart-mind (*shōuxīn* 收心)

(4) Detachment from Affairs (*jiǎnshì* 簡事)

(5) Perfect Observation (*zhēnguān* 眞觀)

(6) Major Concentration (*tàidìng* 泰定)

(7) Realizing the Dao (*dédào* 得道)

FIGURE 18: Seven Steps to the Dao

These late medieval Daoist meditation manuals develop classical Daoist apophatic and quietistic meditation informed by Buddhist insight meditation. Here we find not only a connection to and modification of the germinal discussion in chapter six of the *Zhuāngzǐ* 莊子 (Book of Master Zhuang) (see Lesson #8), but also explicit citation of the latter. This reveals both continuities and departures within the Daoist tradition, including in the development of a unique Táng-dynasty contemplative literature that discusses the technical specifics of meditation. As documented in the present selection (7a) from the "Zuòwàng piān," these may also be understood as quasi-commentaries on the earlier ZZ passage. As received, the "Zuòwàng piān" consists of three sections, divided into *shàng* 上 ("upper"/first), *zhōng* 中 ("middle"/second), and *xià* 下 ("lower"/third) (see Lessons #4, #12, and #16). Here we focus on a passage from the latter.

Considering grammatical characters, there are the following previously-explored ones: *ér* 而 ("and/but"), *fú* 夫 ("now then"), *gù* 故 ("thus"), *jí* 即 ("then"), *qí* 其 ("its/the"), *yě* 也 (。), *yǐ* 以 ("by means of/in order to"), *yòu* 又 ("also/and"), *yú* 於 ("at/by/in/on/through/to"), *yǔ* 與 ("and/with"), *zé* 則 ("then"), *yuē* 曰 ("say/speak"), *zhě* 者 ("as for/one who"), and *zhī* 之 ("of"). There are four new such characters, namely, 豈, 云, 相, and 焉. Often used in conjunction with the sentence-final *hū* 乎 (?), *qǐ* 豈 usually appears as a sentence-initial particle indicating a question and translated as "how." *Yún* 云 ("say") usually indicates a quotations, which proves helpful in both translation and text-critical work. Although paralleling *yuē* 曰 in certain respects, more technically the former refers to written citation, while the latter indicates orality. Here *xiāng* 相 functions as an adverb in the sense of "together/with." It also indicates mutuality and reciprocity. Finally, *yān* 焉 is a sentence-final particle that functions like a question mark (?). It is variously translated as "how," "why," "where," or "when." It is sometimes used as a contraction of *yú* 於 + *zhī* 之 ("from this"). In terms of vocabulary, we find continued use of the earlier, classical Daoist meditation lexicon (see Lessons #6 and #8), now combined with emerging proto-inner alchemy (*nèidān* 內丹) vocabulary and immortal aspirations. The latter includes *liàn* 煉/鍊 ("refine/refinement") and *zhēn* 眞/真 ("perfect/perfected/perfection"), with a specific focus on qi 氣 and spirit (*shén* 神). In addition, the text brings our attention to more Daoist-specific meanings of technical terms, here under Buddhist influence. Especially noteworthy is the appearance of *jìng* 境 ("border/area/condition") as "mental projection." The text further assists us in developing an ability to identify and read intertextual citations.

The primary *Zuòwàng lùn* has been translated by Livia Kohn 柯恩 (1987, 77–111; 2010, 137–58), who problematically renders *zuòwàng* (lit., "sit and forget") as "sitting in oblivion." While *wàng* 忘 does consist of wáng 亡 ("lose/perish") and xīn 心 ("heart-mind"), "oblivion" has the connotation of annihilation and even obliviousness, neither of which is the context-specific meaning. It also obscures the parallelism of the contemplative state of "forgetful*ness*" with "empti*ness*" (xū 虛) and "still*ness*" (jìng 靜). Kohn's publications also include translations of other, related texts, including the Zuòwàng míng (1987, 113–17; 2010, 159–62), and provide important background information on these meditation manuals. There also are two popular translations (Cleary 2000, 81–105; Wu 2015), which should be used with caution.

Primary Text

　余聞之先師曰,「坐忘者,長生之基也。」故招眞以煉形;形清則合於氣。含道以煉氣;氣清則合於神。體與道冥,謂之得道。道固無極,仙豈有窮?

　夫眞者、道之元也。故澄神以契眞。《莊子》云、「墮肢體,黜聰明,離形去知,同於大通。」即此意也。又曰:「智與恬交相養;和理出其恬性。」是也。又曰:「宇泰定發乎天光。」宇者、心也;天光者、慧照也。先定其心,則慧照內發。照見萬境,虛忘而融心于寂寥。是之謂坐忘焉。

I heard my late teacher say, "Sitting-in-forgetfulness is the foundation of perpetual life." Thus, we focus on perfection to refine form; if form is pure, then it may unite with qi. We cherish the Dao to refine qi; if qi is pure, then it may unite with spirit. When the body joins with the Dao in silence, we refer to this as "realizing the Dao." As the Dao is undoubtedly undifferentiated, how could immortals ever perish?

Now then, Perfection is the origin of the Dao. Thus, we purify spirit to join with Perfection. As the *Zhuāngzǐ* 莊子 (Book of Master Zhuang) [ch. 6] tells us, "I smash up my limbs and body, drive out perception and intellect, cast off form, do away with understanding, and make myself identical with Great Pervasion." This is exactly it. The text [ch. 16] also says, "Wisdom and serenity nourish each other; harmony and order emerge from serene innate nature." This is it. It [ch. 23] also says, "Abiding in great stability manifests as celestial radiance." "Abiding" refers to the heart-mind, while "celestial radiance" refers to the illumination of insight. First settle the heart-mind, and then the illumination of insight will manifest internally. With this illumination, you can perceive the myriad mental projections. In emptiness and forgetfulness, you blend the heart-mind with solitude and tranquility. This is what is meant by "sitting-in-forgetfulness."

Vocabulary

zuòwàng 坐忘 (v./v.)	"sitting-in-forgetfulness." More literally, "sit and forget." Problematically translated as "sitting in oblivion." In technical Daoist usage, *wàng* 忘 is a contemplative/mystical state basically synonymous with *jìng* 靜 ("stillness") and *xū* 虛 ("emptiness")
chángshēng 長生 (adj./n.)	"perpetual life." Also translated as "long life," "longevity," and "live forever." Here associated with immortality
liàn 煉/鍊 (v.|n.)	"refine|refinement." Forging, fusing, smelting, and the like. Usually refers to alchemical transmutation. Appears in key Daoist phrases, including *liàndān* 煉丹 ("refining the elixir") and *xiūliàn* 修煉 ("cultivation and refinement")
xíng 形 (n.)	"form." Also translated as "shape." As associated with human personhood, the three-dimensional disposition or configuration of the human process. Technically, *xíng*-form has a morphological rather than genetic or schematic nuance
tǐ 體 (n.)	"body." Technically refers to "physical structure." Said to be a "combination of twelve groups" or parts, including the scalp, face, chin, shoulders, spine, abdomen, upper arms, lower arms, hands, thighs, legs, and feet. Also used in the sense of "embody" (v.), as in the phrase "embodying the Dao" (*tǐdào* 體道)
míng 冥 (adj.|n.)	"silent|silence." May also mean "dark," "deep," and "profound." Part of a whole repertoire of Daoist contemplative/mystical vocabulary. Often used synonymously with *mò* 默 ("silence/serenity"). May refer to the Dao-as-Silence
wújí 無極 (neg./n.)	"Wuji/Nondifferentiation." Also translated as "Limitlessness" and "Non-Ultimate." A state of primordial chaos and mystical (non)union. Technically absent of yin-yang differentiation (*jí* 極)

xiān 仙 (n.)	"immortal." Also translated as "ascendent" and "transcendent." Usually appears as *xiānrén* 仙人 or related terms. Technically human beings (*rén* 人/亻) living in the mountains (*shān* 山). Also appears as 僊, which points towards flight (*qiān* 羉). One of the ideals of later Daoism, usually associated with alchemical transmutation and personal post-mortem survival/existence
zhēn 眞/真 (adj.|n.)	"perfect|perfection." Also translated as "true/truth" and "real/reality." Sometimes refers to the original unity of the Dao ("Perfection/Reality"). The character depicts a reaction vessel, consisting of *bǐ* 匕 ("spoon") and *dǐng* 鼎 ("tripod"). Alchemically speaking, the resultant state of complete refinement and transmutation. Appears in key Daoist phrases, including *xiūzhēn* 修眞 ("cultivating perfection") and *zhēnrén* 眞人 ("Perfected")
yuán 元 (adj.|n.)	"original|origin." Also translated as "prime," "primordial," and "source." Often used synonymously with *yuán* 原/源 ("source") and *yuān* 淵 ("abyss"). May refer to the Dao-as-Source. For example, HNZ 1 is titled "Yuándào 原道" (Source-Dao/Dao-as-Source)
chéng/dèng 澄 (v.)	"purify." May also mean "precipitate," "settle," and "strain." Contains the *shuǐ* 水/氵 ("water") radical
qì 契 (v.)	"join." More literally, "contract," "tally," and "token." Most famously used in the title of the *Cāntóng qì* 參同契 (Token for the Kinship of the Three), which also is translated as "Seal of the Agreement/Unity of the Three"
lǐ 理 (v.|n.)	"order|order." Also translated as "regulate." Sometimes used in a more technical, cosmological sense of "Principle"
dìng 定 (adj.|n.)	"stable|stability." Also translated as "concentration" and most technically "absorption." Also used to translate the Indian and Buddhist Sanskrit *samādhi* (meditative absorption/yogic stasis)

xìng 性 (n.)	"innate nature." One's inherent and original connection to the Dao. Associated with the heart-mind (*xīn* 心) and spirit (*shén* 神). Primarily cultivated through stillness practice, meditation in particular
tiānguāng 天光 (adj./n.)	"celestial radiance." Also translated as "light of heaven." Often used synonymously with *shénguāng* 神光 ("divine/spirit radiance") and *shénmíng* 神明 ("divine/spirit illumination"). The numinous and luminous presence, often actual white and/or golden light, that emerges in the context of committed and prolonged practice
huì 慧 (n.)	"insight." Also translated as "intelligence" and "wisdom." Here has the Buddhist connotation of liberating/liberated insight, especially as seeing through phenomenal appearances (*fǎ* 法) into the true (non)nature of existence (impermanence)
zhào 照 (v.|adj.|n.)	"illuminate|illuminated|illumination." Related to a whole repertoire of "light" characters, including *guāng* 光 ("radiance") and *míng* 明 ("brightness/illumination"). Often associated with divinity and spirit in Daoism
jìng 境 (n.)	"mental projection" (Buddhism). More literally, "landscape" and "region." Also used in the sense of "condition/situation." Here suggests a Buddhist mind-only view of the phenomenal world (*fǎ* 法) as illusory on some level, dependent on one's own psychospiritual condition
xū 虛 (adj.|v.|n.)	"empty|empty|emptiness." Often synonymous with *wú* 無 ("nonbeing/nothing") and *kōng* 空 ("emptiness"), but the latter also is used to translate the Buddhist Sanskrit *śūnyatā* ("empty of own-being"). Here *xū* includes the latter technical connotation
róng 融 (v.)	"blend." May also mean "fuse," "harmonize," "melt," and "merge/unite" by extension
jì 寂 (adj.|n.)	"solitary|solitude." May also mean "quiet/quiescence" and "tranquil/tranquility." May refer to the Dao-as-Silence

liáo 寥 (adj.|n.)	"tranquil|tranquility." May also mean "silent/silence" and "alone/aloneness." May refer to the Dao-as-Alone

FIGURE 19: *Mèngxiān cǎotáng tú* 夢仙草堂圖 (Dreaming of Immortality in a Thatched Hut) by Táng Yín 唐寅 (1470–1523)
SOURCE: Freer Gallery of Art, Smithsonian Institution, Washington, D.C.: Purchase—Charles Lang Freer Endowment, F1939.60

Lesson 19

Alchemical Transmutation
Lǚzǔ Bǎizì Bēi 呂祖百字碑
(Ancestor Lü's Hundred Character Stele; ZW 216, 3.12b-13a [111–12])

The *Lǚzǔ bǎizì bēi* 呂祖百字碑 (Ancestor Lü's Hundred Character Stele), also known as the *Lǚ xiānwēng bǎizì bēi* 呂仙翁百字碑 (Immortal Elder Lü's Hundred Character Stele), is an anonymous inscription of unclear provenance.[42] It is preserved in the third scroll (*juǎn* 卷) of the *Lǚzǔ quánshū* 呂祖全書 (Complete Works of Ancestor Lü), as contained in the *Zàngwài dàoshū* 藏外道書 (Daoist Books Outside the Canon; dat. 1992/1994; 991 texts; abbrev. ZW) (ZW 216, 3.12b-13a [7.111–12]).[43] The complete history of the *Lǚzǔ quánshū* is unclear, but, as the title indicates, it collects a variety of texts from various historical periods attributed to Lǚ Dòngbīn 呂洞賓 (Chúnyáng 純陽 [Pure Yang]; b. 796?), one of the most famous Daoist immortals in Chinese history and patriarch of internal alchemy (*nèidān* 內丹) more generally. Historically speaking, Lǚ is especially important for his association with the so-called Zhōng-Lǚ textual tradition of internal alchemy, which dates to the late ninth and

---

[42] Not to be confused with the text of the same name preserved at Yǒnglè gōng 永樂宮 (Palace of Eternal Peace; Ruìchéng 芮城, Shānxī). The latter is translated in Paul Katz, *Images of the Immortal* (1999, 120).

[43] The first number is the traditional woodblock page number, while the second is the ZW volume and page number.

early tenth centuries and represents the earliest systemization. In terms of the *Lǚzǔ quánshū*, some of the texts are pseudonymous, while others are presented as revealed. The *Lǚzǔ bǎizì bēi* itself appears to date to the late imperial period, possibly the 1400s. There are early commentaries by Lù Xīxīng 陸西星 (Qiánxū 潛虛 [Hidden-in-Emptiness]; 1520–1606), the reputed founder of the so-called Dōngpài 東派 (Eastern Branch) of internal alchemy, and Liú Yīmíng 劉一明 (Wùyuán 悟元 [Awakening-to-the-Origin]; 1734–1821), a major eleventh-generation Lóngmén 龍門 (Dragon Gate) monk (see Lessons #16 and #28). Paralleling earlier Daoist material culture (see Lessons #5, #14, and #18), it presents itself as derived from a stone stele (*shíbēi* 石碑), again with the location unidentified. The "text" has been influential in late imperial and modern *nèidān* circles, and it is widely disseminated among modern Daoists as a "primer in internal alchemy," specifically containing foundational concerns and approaches. Although lacking detailed information on the technical specifics of *nèidān* practice, especially methods related to stage-based training, it approximates the standardized, simplified tripartite framework:

> (1) Refining vital essence to become qi
> (*liànjīng huàqì* 煉精化氣)
> (2) Refining qi to become spirit
> (*liànqì huàshén* 煉氣化神)
> (3) Refining spirit and returning to the Void
> (*liànshén huánxū* 煉神還虛)

FIGURE 20: Three Stages of Internal Alchemy

In terms of formalistic features, the *Lǚzǔ bǎizì bēi* consists of ten five-character couplets, or twenty lines amounting to 100 characters. On a language level, the text reveals the ways in which earlier Daoist literature became foundational for and integrated into later materials (see Lessons #11 and #12), with the technical *nèidān* lexicon documented in the chapter vocabulary herein. It again brings our attention to Daoist anthropology, including views of human being and personhood in general and Daoist subtle anatomy and physiology, with accompanying esoteric somatic terminology, in particular (see Lessons #8, #10, #12, and #14). The text also mentions various meditative experiences (lines 12–14, 17), often referred to as "fruits of the Dao" (*dàoguǒ* 道果) and "experiential confirmation/verification/signs of proof" (*zhèngyàn* 證驗). Especially interesting is the reference to "stringless music" (*wúxián qū* 無弦曲), which refers to the Dao's numinous presence, here especially associated with qi circulation through the practitioner's body in meditation. It thus recalls the energetic listening emphasized in other Daoist texts (see Lessons #7–10), including Daoism as the "Teaching beyond/without Words" (*bùyán zhī jiào* 不言之教) (LZ 2 and 43).

Grammatically speaking, the *Lǚzǔ bǎizì bēi* contains three unfamiliar characters, which also reveal a transition to more vernacular and even "modern Chinese." These are *xū* 須 ("must"), *shuí/shéi* 誰 ("who"), and *dōu* 都 ("all"). In terms of vocabulary, and paralleling the use of the *Bǎoshēng míng* in relationship to *Yǎngshēng* (see Lesson #14), the *Lǚzǔ bǎizì bēi* may be engaged as a "primer in *nèidān* terminology," although we must again be careful with respect to potential anachronistic applications.

The definitive Western-language study of Lǚ Dòngbīn is Paul Katz's *Images of the Immortal: The Cult of Lü Dongbin at the Palace of Eternal Joy* (1999). A popular translation of the *Lǚzǔ bǎizì bēi* has been published by Thomas Cleary (1949–2021) (1991, 185–91), which includes a commentary attributed to the Daoist immortal Zhāng Sānfēng 張三丰 (d. 1457?), an obscure, perhaps legendary Daoist hermit who became associated with Wǔdāng shān 武當山 (Mount Wudang; Shíyàn 十堰, Húběi) and seen as the mythological founder of so-called "Wǔdāng martial arts" (see Seidel 1970; Wong 1982; Lagerwey 1992; De Bruyn 2004, 2010; Shahar 2008; Hausen and Tsaur 2021). The contemporary situation of Daoist affiliation on Wǔdāng is complex and sometimes factional.

Primary Text

養氣忘言守，降心為不為。
動靜知宗祖，無事更尋誰。
真常須應物，應物要不迷。
不迷性自住，性住炁自回。
炁回丹自結，壺中配坎離。
陰陽生返復，普化一聲雷。
白雲朝頂上，甘露灑須彌。
自飲長生酒，逍遙誰得知。
坐聽無弦曲，明通造化機。
都來二十句，端的上天梯。

Nourish qi and forget words in meditation;
Sublimate the heart-mind and do not-doing.
In movement and stillness, know the Ancestor;
Beyond affairs, whom is there to seek?
Perfect constancy must respond to things;
Responding to things, it is essential not to be confused.
When unconfused, innate nature naturally abides;
When innate nature abides, qi naturally returns.
When qi returns, the elixir naturally coalesces—
Inside the vessel, match Kǎn-water ☵ and Lí-fire ☲.
Yin and yang emerge through reversal;
Everything transforms through a single thunderclap.
White Clouds assemble on the summit;
Sweet Dew bathes Mount Sumeru.
Spontaneously imbibe the wine of long life;
In carefree ease, who can know you?
You sit and listen to the stringless music;
You clearly connect with the pivot of transformation.
The whole of these twenty phrases
Offers a ladder straight to heaven.

Vocabulary

Lǚzǔ 呂祖 (name/title)	"Ancestor Lü." Honorific title for Lǚ Dòngbīn 呂洞賓 (Chúnyáng 純陽 [Pure Yang]; b. 796?). *Zǔ* is often used as an abbreviation of *zǔshī* 祖師 ("patriarch")
yǎngqì 養氣 (v./n.)	"nourishing qi." Here most likely focusing on the lower elixir field (*dāntián* 丹田), the navel region
wàngyán 忘言 (v./n.)	"forgetting words." *Yán* 言 technically refers to speech. Connects to the Daoist emphasis on "namelessness" (*wúmíng* 無名) and the "teaching beyond/without words" (*bùyán zhī jiào* 不言之教). See, e.g., LZ 2 and 43; also 56, 70, and 73. Also recalls the practice of "sitting-in-forgetfulness" (*zuòwàng* 坐忘) in ZZ 6
shǒu 守 (v.)	"guard." Here translated more liberally as "meditation." Most famously appears in the phrase *shǒuyī* 守一 ("guarding the One"). See NY 24 and ZZ 11. Later used as a general term for Daoist meditation. Cf. *dú* 獨 ("solitude") and *dǎzuò* 打坐 ("undertake sitting")
jiàngxīn 降心 (v./n.)	"sublimate the heart-mind." Also translated as "control/subdue the mind." *Jiàng* 降 more literally means "descend/lower." "Jiàngxīn" is the title of Discourse 8 in Wáng Zhé's *Lìjiào shíwǔ lùn* 立教十五論 (Fifteen Discourses to Establish the Teachings)
bùwéi 不為 (neg./v.)	"not-doing." Or, "not-acting." Basically synonymous with *wúwéi* 無為 ("non-action"), or effortlessness. However, *bù* has a stronger action connotation, while *wú* is beyond. The text invokes LZ 38 and 48: "Through non-action, nothing is left undone"
zōngzǔ 宗祖 (n./n.)	"Ancestor." Also translated as "ancestral." Refers first and foremost to the Dao-as-Source. See, e.g., ZZ 6. Somatically, may refer to the kidneys, navel, heart, and/or head region
wúshì 無事 (neg./n.)	"beyond/without affairs." More technically translated as "non-concern" and "uninvolvement." Disengaged from and untangled in mundane matters, preoccupations, pursuits, and so forth

cháng 常 (adj.|n.)	"constant|constancy." Also translated as "enduring" and "eternal." Here suggests psychospiritual stability in the midst of unending change
mí 迷 (adj.|n.)	"confused/confusion." Contains the *chuò* 辵/辶 ("walk/move") radical. Often used synonymously with *huò* 惑 ("deluded") and *luàn* 亂 ("chaotic")
qì 炁 (n.)	"qi." Often appears as *dàoqì* 道炁 ("qi of the Dao") and *zhēnqì* 眞炁 ("perfect qi") when referring to primordial, sacred and numinous presence. Esoteric Daoist character variant of 氣. Also translated as "energy," "subtle/vital breath," and "pneuma" (Greek). May refer to both physical breath and a more subtle current/presence. The fundamental cosmic (non)material substance. Identified as the second or middle of the internal Three Treasures (*sānbǎo* 三寶)
dān 丹 (n.)	"elixir." More literally, "cinnabar" (mercuric sulfide [HgS]). The psychosomatic, energetic and spiritual integrity and wholeness that results from alchemical training and transformation. May also refer to "alchemy" in general
hú 壺 (n.)	"vessel." More literally, "jar," "pot," "vase," and so forth. Also translated as "calabash/gourd," but that more technically renders *hú* 葫 and *hù* 瓠
kǎn 坎 (n.)	"Kǎn-water." The trigram ☵, which consists of one yang-line inside of two yin-lines. Associated with the kidneys and vital essence (*jīng* 精) in internal alchemy. Sometimes read as qi moving within stillness
lí 離 (n.)	"Lí-fire." The trigram ☲, which consists of one yin-line inside of two yang-lines. Associated with the heart and spirit in internal alchemy. Sometimes read as fluids settling within movement
fǎnfù 返復 (v./v.)	"reversal." Both characters mean "return." Also translated as "inversion." In internal alchemy, generally refers to reversing ordinary patterns of dissipation, especially vital essence (*jīng* 精). Famously referred to as "reverting vital essence to repair/replenish the brain" (*huánjīng bǔnǎo* 還精補腦) and the associated state of "non-dissipation" (*wúlòu* 無漏; lit., "without leakage")

léi 雷 (n.)	"thunder." Internal rumbling, usually in the lower elixir field, identified as a sign of experiential confirmation (*zhèngyàn* 證驗). Also invokes the Zhèn-thunder ☳ trigram
báiyún 白雲 (adj./n.)	"White Clouds." Here a symbolic referent to qi gathering in the head region ("summit")
gānlù 甘露 (adj./n.)	"Sweet Dew." Symbolic name for saliva. Also referred to as Divine/Spirit Water (*shénshuǐ* 神水) and Jade Fluids (*yùyè/yùyì* 玉液)
Xūmí 須彌 (transliteration)	"Sumeru." Mount Sumeru. Also referred to as Mount Meru. A mythic mountain of traditional Indian cosmology identified as the *axis mundi*. Here used microcosmically to refer to the head region. Parallels Kūnlún 崑崙 in other texts/contexts
chángshēng 長生 (adj./n.)	"long life/longevity." More literally, "perpetual life" or even "continually born." Basically synonymous with *shòu* 壽 ("longevity"). One of the ideals of Yǎngshēng 養生 (Nourishing Life). Here used in the alchemical sense of immortality
xiāoyáo 逍遙 (adj./n.)	"carefree ease." Also translated as "being carefree" and "free and easy." Contains the *chuò* 辵/辶 ("walk/move") radical. Derives from the title of ZZ 1. Used in the larger Daoist tradition to refer to one of the "fruits of the Dao" (*dàoguǒ* 道果), higher-level contemplative states of spiritual realization
tōng 通 (v.|n.)	"connect|connection." May also mean "through/throughness" and "pervade/pervasion." Contains the *chuò* 辵/辶 ("walk/move") radical
zàohuà 造化 (v./v.)	"transformation." More technically translated as "transformative process." Mistranslated as "creation" and most problematically "Creator"
jī 機 (n.)	"pivot." More literally, "trigger," and "mechanism" by extension. Often used synonymously with *shū* 樞 ("pivot"). In Daoist contemplative practice associated with the heart-mind

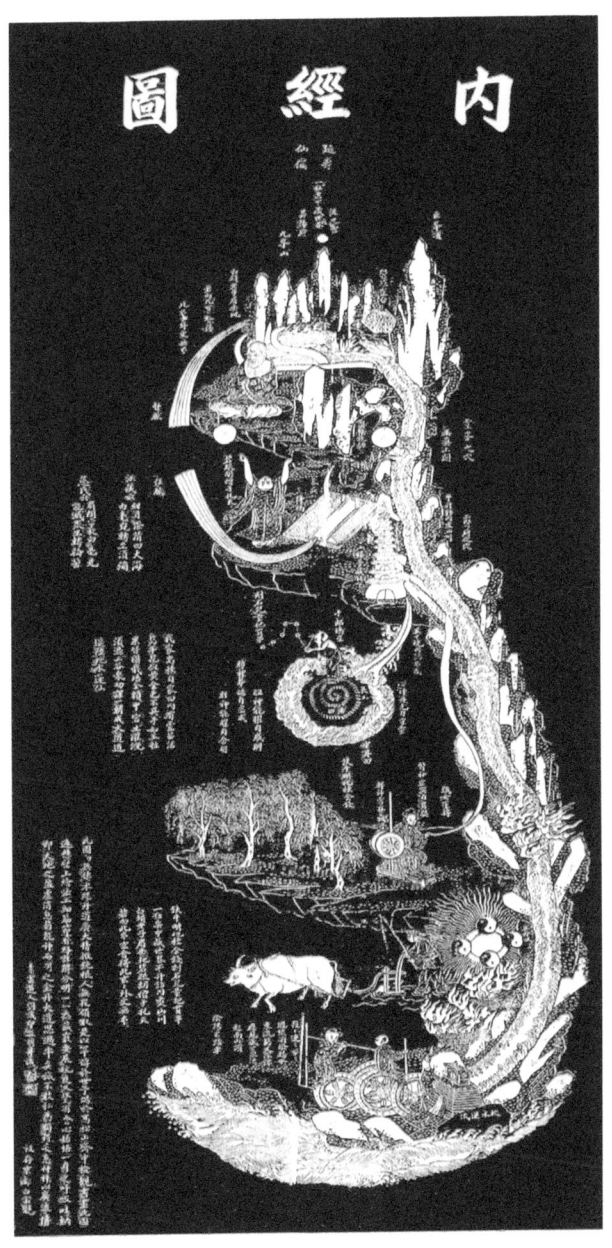

FIGURE 21: *Nèijīng tú* 內經圖 (Diagram of Internal Pathways)
SOURCE: Author's collection

Lesson 20

Activating the Daoist Alchemical Body
From the Zhōng-Lǚ chuándào jí
鍾呂傳道集
(Anthology of the Transmission of the Dao from Zhong to Lü; DZ 263, J. 14–16)

With the present selection we move back to the formative moments of internal alchemy (*nèidān* 內丹) as a holistic and integrated system for complete psychosomatic transformation, or "immortality" in Daoist terms. Along with the *Bìchuán Zhèngyáng zhēnrén língbǎo bìfǎ* 秘傳正陽眞人靈寶畢法 (Perfected Zhengyang's Secret Transmission of the Final Methods of Numinous Treasure; DZ 1191; ZH 810; abbrev. *Língbǎo bìfǎ*; trl. Baldrian-Hussein 1984 [French]; Kohn 2020),[44] the *Zhōng-Lǚ chuándào jí* 鍾呂傳道集 (Anthology of the Transmission of the Dao from Zhong to Lü; DZ 263, j. 14–16) is one of the most important texts of the so-called Zhōng-Lǚ 鍾呂 lineage or "school," which primarily refers to a specific corpus. Both texts most likely date to the tenth century, that is, the end of the Táng dynasty (618–907). As the name indicates, these texts present themselves as dialogic exchanges between the immortals Zhōnglí Quán 鍾離權 (Zhèng**yáng** 正陽 [Aligned Yang]; 168?–256?) and

---

[44] In Daoist Studies, the character 秘/祕 ("esoteric/secret") is usually pronounced *bì*, rather than *mì*. One of the most famous examples is *Wúshàng bìyào* 無上秘要 (Esoteric Essentials of the Limitless; DZ 1138; ZH 1076), a major sixth-century Daoist encyclopedia. See Komjathy 2022c. Although both are acceptable, in addition to precedent, *bì* helps distinguish this character from *mì* 密 (also "secret"), which occur together in the modern phrase *mìmì* 秘密.

Lǚ Dòngbīn 呂洞賓 (Chúnyáng 純陽 [Pure Yang]; b. 796?). Our present text is contained in the *Xiūzhēn shíshū* 修真十書 (Ten Books on Cultivating Perfection; DZ 263, j. 14–16; abbrev. XZSS; cf. DZ 1017, j. 39–41), with the latter being an anonymous textual collection that dates to around 1300. Abbreviated as *Chuándào jí* 傳道集 (Anthology on the Transmission of the Dao) (CDJ), the text consists of eighteen titled chapters on a wide variety of *nèidān*-related topics, including technical specifics and methods of associated training regimens. Here we examine a passage (15.20a-21a) from chapter twelve, which is titled "Héchē" 河車 (Waterwheel). The latter, also referred to as the Celestial Cycle (*zhōutiān* 周天/週天; a.k.a. "Microcosmic Orbit"), usually involves circulating qi up the Governing Channel (*dūmài* 督脈; centerline of the spine) and down the Conception Channel (*rènmài* 任脈; front centerline of the torso). These relate to a larger series of subtle corporeal locations, with the three elixir fields (*dāntián* 丹田) being especially important, and a network of energy channels, with the so-called Eight Extraordinary Channels/Vessels (*qíjīng bāmài* 奇經八脈) being primary here. Of these, Daoist "embryogenesis" generally recognizes the Governing and Conception Channels as earliest and more essential.

Considering grammar characters, the following appear herein: *ér* ("and/but"), *nǎi* ("then"), *yě* 也 (。), *yì* 亦 ("also/and/indeed"), *yǐ* 矣 (。), *yú* 於 ("at/by/in/on/through/to"), *zé* 則 ("then"), *zhě* ("as for/one who"), and *zhī* ("of/it"). There also are three unfamiliar ones, namely, 且, 蓋, and 甚. Here *qiě* 且 is used to indicate future tense ("will"), in a manner paralleling *jiāng* 將. However, the character also appears in classical Chinese in the sense of "if" and "moreover," and in the construction 且 囗且囗 ("both ___ and ___"). *Gài* 蓋 is used as a sentence-initial particle meaning something like "generally speaking," which again parallels *fán* 凡. Here *shèn* 甚 is used as an adjective/adverb for "very." It is thus similar to the modern Chinese *hěn* 很. The passage also uses the grammatical construction 或囗或囗 ("either ___ or ___"). Finally, *rú* 如, which we previously encountered in the sense of "if/assuming," is used in the sense of "for example." With respect to technical terms, the text again allows us to explore additional Daoist *nèidān* vocabulary. We may note the continuing macrocosmic/microcosmic correspondences, including the internalization of immortal realms like Mount Kūnlún 崑崙 (see Lessons #12, #17, and #19), and use of the trigrams as a symbol system of alchemical transmutation (see Lessons #11 and #19). Taken as a whole, the *Chuándào jí* provides a fuller glimpse into the "Daoist alchemical body," the subtle, even mystical body activated and actualized through dedicated and prolonged *nèidān* training.

A foundational discussion of the Zhōng-Lǚ textual corpus appears in Judith Boltz's 鮑菊隱 (1947–2013) *A Survey of Taoist Literature* (1987, 139–43), which, although still pioneering, has been largely replaced by the entries in the *Historical Companion to the Daozang* (Schipper and Verellen 2004). A complete popular translation has been published by Eva Wong. This must be used with caution as it lacks the necessary historical contextualization and often resembles a paraphrase, rather than translation per se. A more recent complete translation has been published by Livia Kohn 柯恩 (2020). Like most of Kohn's more recent translation work, this falls somewhere between an annotated scholarly translation and a popular one. It is intended for a general audience. A list of the chapter titles of the *Chuándào jí* with English translations is contained in Louis Komjathy's "Catalogue of Daoist Collectanea, Compendia, and Encyclopedias" (2022).

Primary Text

《河車》

高道之士，取喻於車，且車行於地而轉於陸。今於河車，亦有說矣。蓋人身之中，陽少陰多，言水之處甚眾。車則取意於搬運，河乃主象於多陰。故此河車、不行於地而行於水。自上而下，或前或後，駕載於八瓊之內，驅馳於四海之中。升天，則上入崑崙。既濟，則下奔鳳闕。運載元陽，直入於離宮；搬負眞氣，曲歸於壽府。往來九州，而無暫停；巡歷三田，而無休息⋯

　河車者，起於北方正水之中。腎藏眞氣，眞氣之所生之正氣。乃曰河車。河車作用，今古罕聞，眞仙秘而不說者也。如乾再索於坤而生坎。坎本水也；水為陰之精。陽既索於陰，陽返負陰而還位，所過者艮、震、巽。以陽索陰，因陰取陰。搬運入離，承陽而生，是此河車。搬陰入於陽宮。

The Waterwheel

Practitioners of the exalted Dao chose the metaphor of a wheel because the associated cart travels across the land and turns over soil. We may accordingly discuss the Waterwheel. Generally speaking, in the human body, because there is less yang and more yin, we speak of the numerous places in terms of water. The "wheel" in turn refers to transportation and transference, while "water" is used as a symbol for the voluminous yin. Thus, this Waterwheel does not travel across the land, but rather moves through water. Moving up and down, forward or backward, it circulates inside the Eight Rarities and penetrates into the Four Oceans. Ascending, it enters Kūnlún. After it crosses through there, it quickly descends to Phoenix Tower. Circulating and transporting the original yang, it directly enters the Palace of Lí-fire ☲. Carrying and transferring the perfect qi, it meanderingly returns to the Storehouse of Longevity. It moves through the Nine Realms without ever pausing; it circulates through the Three Fields without ever resting...

The Waterwheel arises from the correct waters of the northern direction. The kidneys store perfect qi. The perfect qi is what is produced from the upright qi. This, then, refers to the Waterwheel. From ancient times to the present, the [procedure for] activating and employing the Waterwheel rarely has been heard. This is because perfected immortals were secretive and did not speak about it. For example, when Qián-heaven ☰ seeks out Kūn-earth ☷, it produces Kǎn-water ☵. Kǎn-water refers to the root-water; this water corresponds to the essence of yin. When yang encounters yin, yang reverses and carries yin, and then returns to its [original] position. As it moves through, it becomes Gèn-mountain ☶, Zhèn-thunder ☳, and Xùn-wind ☴. Yang attracts yin, and yin accordingly gathers yin. When transported to Lí-fire ☲, it connects with yang and generates. This is the Waterwheel. It transports yin to the Palace of Yang.

Vocabulary

héchē 河車 (n./n.)	"Waterwheel." More literally, "River Cart." Literally a mechanical device for moving water, often in a watermill. Here refers to a specific Daoist inner alchemical technique for activating the subtle body and circulating qi through the body meridians. Often used synonymously with the Celestial Cycle (*zhōutiān* 周天), which usually is referred to in English as the "Microcosmic Orbit." The practice sometimes is charted according to the Three Carts (*sānchē* 三車), namely, Ram Cart (Tailbone Gate; coccyx), Deer Cart (Narrow Ridge; mid-spine), and Ox Cart (Jade Pillow; occiput)
chuándào 傳道 (v./n.)	"transmitting the Dao." Usually associated with oral instructions (*kǒujué* 口訣) from a Daoist master-father (*shīfu* 師父) to one or more disciples. Here centers on Zhōnglí Quán 鍾離權 (Zhèngyáng 正陽 [Aligned Yang]; 168?–256? CE) and Lǚ Dòngbīn 呂洞賓 (Chúnyáng 純陽 [Pure Yang]; b. 796?).
shì 士 (n.)	"practitioner." Also translated as "adept." More conventionally means "knight" and "scholar-official." Originally the lowest aristocratic rung of the Chinese feudal order, amounting to something like "retainer." Used in classical Daoism and the larger tradition to refer to Daoist adherents and practitioners. More technically appears as *dàoshi* 道士 (lit., "adept of the Dao"), which refers to ordained Daoist priests and monastics
yīn 陰 (n.)	"yin." Here associated with "water." In terms of internal alchemy, associated with vital fluids in general and vital essence (*jīng* 精) in particular. May also refer to qì 氣, which also is connected to "wind" (*fēng* 風)
xiàng 象 (n.)	"symbol." Technically "elephant." Also translated as "appearance," "emblem," "image," "representation," and "shape." Used most technically to refer to the images of the hexagrams (six-line diagrams) of the *Yìjīng* 易經 (Classic of Change) as well as Daoist statuary and other devotional objects that serve as conduits for divine presences

bāqióng 八瓊 (num./n.)	"Eight Rarities." In external alchemy (*wàidān* 外丹) refers to cinnabar, realgar, azurite, sulfur, mica, crystal salt, saltpeter, and orpiment. Appears in the *Huángtíng nèijǐng jīng* 黃庭內景經 (Scripture on the Inner View of the Yellow Court), without elucidation. Here most likely refers to the Eight Extraordinary Vessels (*qíjīng bāmài* 奇經八脈)
sìhǎi 四海 (num./n.)	"Four Oceans." The sources and storehouses of marrow, blood, qi, and fluids in the body
Kūnlún 崑崙 (n./n.)	"Kūnlún." A Daoist terrestrial paradise. More technically the immortal mountain residence of Xīwángmǔ 西王母 (Queen Mother of the West), where the peaches of immortality (*xiāntáo* 仙桃) grow. Here used in the Daoist microcosmic sense and as an esoteric designation for the head
fèngquè 鳳闕 (n./n.)	"Phoenix Tower." *Què* 闕 may also mean "gateway/portal" and "palace." An obscure esoteric subtle somatic location. Based on context, appears to designate the tongue or trachea
yuányáng 元陽 (adj./n.)	"original yang." Also translated as "primal/primordial yang." The pure, sacred and numinous presence of the Dao in the body. Associated with movement. Often used synonymously with the "dose" (*dāoguī* 刀圭 [lit., "knife-nick"]) and "spark (*yīdiǎn* 一點 [lit., "a bit"])
lígōng 離宮 (n./n.)	"Palace of Lí-fire." Lí-fire refers to the trigram ☲. Esoteric name for the heart
zhēnqì 眞氣 (adj./n.)	"perfect qi." Also translated as "real/true energy." The term has various meanings in Daoist practice. More often refers to the pure, refined and transformed qi activated, cultivated, and circulated in alchemical training. Paralleling classical Chinese medicine, also may designate the more "physiological" qi associated with and circulating through the organ-meridian system

shòufǔ 壽府 (n./n.)	"Palace of Longevity." *Fǔ* 府/腑 also is translated as "depot" and "repository." As used more technically in Chinese medicine, it refers to the yang-organs. Here the "Palace of Longevity" is an obscure esoteric name apparently designating the navel region. The latter is more commonly referred to as the "Ocean of Energy" (*qìhǎi* 氣海)
jiǔzhōu 九州 (num./n.)	"Nine Realms." Also translated as "Nine Continents." Literally the nine known inhabited lands or provinces in ancient China. Here used in the Daoist microcosmic sense to refer to the various regions of the human body
sāntián 三田 (num./n.)	"Three Fields." The three primary subtle corporeal locations. Also referred to as "three elixir fields" (*sān dāntián* 三丹田). Usually designates the navel (lower), heart (middle), and head (upper)
zhèngshuǐ 正水 (adj./n.)	"correct waters." *Zhèng* 正 also is translated as "aligned," "upright," and even "orthodox." Here the "correct waters" refer to vital essence (*jīng* 精), associated with the kidneys (Water), including in its transformed form of qi
běi 北 (n.)	"north." As a somatic direction, may refer to the kidneys/back (horizontal) and/or to the perineum/lower torso (vertical). Thus, when moving qi up the spine, one is technically "travelling south"
zhèngqì 正氣 (adj./n.)	"upright qi." Also translated as "aligned/correct energy." Technically refers to qi moving in the correct direction. In classical Chinese medicine, as in the present context, often thought of in terms of a somatic warp/weft, with *zhèngqì* related to vertical energetic connection between the heavens and earth
zhēnxiān 真仙 (adj./n.)	"perfected immortals." As shorthand for *zhēnrén* 真人/真人 and *xiānrén* 仙人, also translated as "Perfected and immortals." Technically individuals who have completed the process of alchemical transmutation and ensured personal postmortem survival and existence
bì/mì 秘 (adj.)	"secret." Also appears as 祕. Often synonymous with *mì* 密, as in the phrase *mìmì* 秘密. Frequently associated with oral instructions (*kǒujué* 口訣) in Daoism

bāguà 八卦 (num./n.)	"eight trigrams." The eight three-line diagrams viewed as the essential components of the sixty-four hexagrams (six-line diagrams) (8x8=64) of the *Yìjīng* 易經 (Classic of Change). Consist of one or more broken/yin-lines (- -) or solid/yang-lines (—)
kǎn 坎 (n.)	"Kǎn-water." The trigram ☵, which consists of one yang-line inside of two yin-lines. Associated with the kidneys and vital essence (*jīng* 精) in internal alchemy
lí 離 (n.)	"Lí-fire." The trigram ☲, which consists of one yin-line inside of two yang-lines. Associated with the heart and spirit (*shén* 神) in internal alchemy
yánggōng 陽宮 (n./n.)	"Palace of Yang." An obscure esoteric name apparently designating the head region. As associated with "yang," both the trigram Qián-heaven ☰ (pure yang [3]) and hexagram Qián-heaven ䷀ (redoubled yang [3x3=9]). The upper elixir field of the head is more commonly referred to as the Hall of Light (*míngtáng* 明堂) or Ancestral Cavity (*zǔqiào* 祖竅), although it actually consists of many mystical cranial locations

LESSON 21

STUDYING IMMORTALITY
FROM THE WÙZHĒN PIĀN 悟眞篇
(TREATISE ON AWAKENING TO PERFECTION; DZ 263, J. 26–30)

IF THE *LǙZǓ BǍIZÌ BĒI* 呂祖百字碑 (Ancestor Lü's Hundred Character Stele) (Lesson #19) is a basic *nèidān* text and the *Chuándào jí* 傳道集 (Anthology on the Transmission of the Dao) (Lesson #20) an intermediate one, the *Wùzhēn piān* 悟眞篇 (Treatise on Awakening to Perfection; DZ 263, j. 26–30; abbrev. WZP) represents one of the most complex works. It is a highly esoteric, cryptic and symbolic work written in "regulated verse" (*lǜshī* 律詩), here in the form of eight seven-character lines (cf. Lessons #5–7, #11–12, and #14). These are usually composed and read with a slight pause after the fourth character, that is, as 4/3 rhythms and groupings. Written around 1075, the *Wùzhēn piān* is a seminal and highly influential inner alchemical text composed by Zhāng Bóduān 張伯端 (Zǐ**yáng** 紫陽 [Purple Yang]; d. 1082), a central figure in so-called Nánzōng 南宗 (Southern School). As his Daoist name indicates, there is some connection to the precursor Zhōng-Lǚ 鍾呂 sub-tradition as associated with the immortals Zhèng**yáng** 正陽 (Aligned Yang) and Chún**yáng** 純陽 (Pure Yang) (see Lesson #20). Formalistically speaking and as a poetry cycle, the *Wùzhēn piān* is divided into sets of sixteen, sixty-four and twelve verses describing the stages of alchemical practice. Like the *Chuándào jí*, it is contained in the anonymous early fourteenth-century *Xiūzhēn shíshū* 修眞十書 (Ten Books on Cultivating Perfection; DZ 263, j. 26–30; abbrev. XZSS), which includes an accompanying commentary. Here we focus on poem #3 (26.9a-11b). The *Wùzhēn piān* is further connected to another key text attributed to Zhāng Bóduān, namely, the *Jīndān sìbǎizì* 金丹四百字 (Four Hundred Characters on the Golden Elixir; DZ 1081; ZH 848; also DZ 263, j. 4; trl. Cleary 1986). In terms of the title, the text frames the inner alchemical path as "awakening to perfection" (*wùzhēn* 悟真), or "awakened perfection." As we have seen, *zhēn* 眞/真 also is translated as "authenticity," "reality," and "truth" depending on context. Here emphasis is placed on alchemical refinement and transmutation, so "perfection" is more accurate and appropriate. *Piān* 篇 is interesting as well. It technically refers to "folios" and "chapters" by extension, but it also is used in the sense of "treatise" (see Lessons #2, #3, #9–10, and #18).

Outside the poetic structure and accompanying compositional requirements, there is little grammar in the present poem. The following characters stand out: *shǐ* 使 ("apply/cause/use"), *suì* 遂 ("follow/then"), *wéi* 惟 ("only"), *xū* 須 ("must"), and *zhǐ* ("just/only"). The technical terminology is again elucidated in the chapter vocabulary herein, but two more general terms deserve note. First, continuing earlier alchemical discussions, the text utilizes *Jīndān* 金丹 (Golden Elixir) as a general name for "alchemy" (see Lessons #3 and #13), here referring to internal alchemy. Second, Zhāng Bóduān encourages aspiring adepts to focus on "celestial immortality" (*tiānxiān* 天仙). While often synonymous with "spirit immortality" (*shénxiān* 神仙) (see Lesson #16), other systems identify the latter as the penultimate level and celestial immortality as the highest. This is the case in the tripartite discussion in the *Bàopǔzǐ nèipiān* (2.11a) and in the quintipartite discussion in the *Chuándào jí* (14.2b–5b [ch. 1]). Given the high degree of symbolic encryption, the *Wùzhēn piān* also points towards the importance, perhaps necessity of oral instruction (*kǒujué* 口訣) and/or commentaries (*zhù* 註/注) (see Lessons #16 and #17; also below). It also is noteworthy that the text continues the mainstream, perhaps near-normative Daoist view that "immortality can be learned" (*kěxué* 可學) and thus "can be attained" (*kědé* 可得). In addition to the texts already mentioned, one of the most renowned precedents is the essay titled "Shénxiān kěxué lùn 神仙可學論" (On Divine Immortality Being Learnable; DZ 1051, 9b-16a) by Wú Yún 吳筠 (Zōngxuán 宗玄 [Ancestral Mystery]; d. 778) (see De Meyer 2006), a Daoist poet-recluse with connections to the Shàngqīng 上清 (Highest Clarity) movement.

Thomas Cleary (1949–2021) (1987) has published a popular translation of the *Wùzhēn piān*, which again must be used with caution because it often more closely resembles paraphrase than translation as such. The book is actually a translation of the *Wùzhēn zhízhǐ* 悟眞直指 (Direct Pointers to the *Wùzhēn piān*; ZW 253), which is a commentary by Liú Yīmíng 劉一明 (Wùyuán 悟元 [Awakening-to-the-Origin]; 1734–1821), an influential eleventh-generation Lóngmén 龍門 (Dragon Gate) monk (see Lessons #16 and #28). The text is contained in his *Dàoshū shíèr zhǒng* 道書十二種 (Twelve Daoist Texts). More recently, Fabrizio Pregadio 玄英 has published a complete translation with some notes and exegesis (2009), which falls somewhere between an annotated scholarly translation and a general-audience one.

Primary Text

三

學仙須是學天仙，惟有金丹最的端。
二物會時情性合，五行全處龍虎蟠。
本因戊己為媒娉，遂使夫妻鎮合歡。
只候功成朝北闕，九霞光裏駕祥鸞。

– 3 –

When studying immortality, you should study celestial immortality;
This alone is the most superior matter of the Golden Elixir.
When the two things meet,[45] disposition and innate nature unite;
When the Five Phases completely settle, Dragon and Tiger entwine.
From the beginning, *wùjĭ* is taken as the matchmaker;
This causes husband and wife to be protected in commingled bliss.
Simply wait until accomplishment is complete by attending to the
    Northern Tower;
Amidst the illumination of nine vapors, you mount an auspicious
    phoenix.

---

[45] Possibly yin-yang. See Lesson #11.

Vocabulary

wùzhēn 悟真 (v./n.)	"awakening to perfection." Also translated as "awakening to reality/truth." *Wù* 悟 ("awaken") is related to a whole repertoire of characters used by Daoists to refer to spiritual realization, including *dé* 得, *jué* 覺, and *liǎo* 了. Here *zhēn* 眞/真 ("perfection") refers to the resultant state of complete alchemical refinement and transmutation
xuéxiān 學仙 (v./n.)	"studying immortality." Practicing alchemy, specifically with the aspiration to become an immortal (*xiānrén* 仙人). *Xiān* 仙 consists of *rén* 人/亻 ("person") and *shān* 山 ("mountain")
tiānxiān 天仙 (adj./n.)	"celestial immortality." Also translated as "heavenly transcendence." Technically the highest form, level, or rank of immortality. Specifically involves entrance to and eternal life in the Daoist sacred realms
jīndān 金丹 (adj./n.)	"Golden Elixir." One of the general names for Chinese "alchemy." May refer to either external alchemy (*wàidān* 外丹) or internal alchemy (*nèidān* 內丹)
qíng 情 (n.)	"disposition." More conventionally translated as "emotions/feelings." As a positive term, refers to one's general tendencies and temperament. Also appears as *dàoqíng* 道情 ("disposition of the Dao") for the qualities and presence characteristic of committed Daoists
wǔxíng 五行 (num./n.)	"Five Phases." Also translated as "Five Agents/Elements." The five foundational substances and processes associated with traditional Chinese cosmology. Wood, Fire, Earth, Metal, Water. Here primarily associated with the five yin-organs (liver, heart, spleen, lungs, kidneys) and associated spiritual faculties (ethereal soul, spirit, thought, corporeal soul, will)
lóng 龍 (n.)	"Dragon." As used symbolically in internal alchemy and as paired with the Tiger, usually associated with spirit (*shén* 神), innate nature (*xìng* 性), lead (*qiān* 鉛), and so forth. Depending on teacher, community, and lineage, sometimes the correspondences are reversed

hǔ 虎 (n.)	"Tiger." As used symbolically in internal alchemy and as paired with the Dragon, usually associated with subtle breath (*qì* 氣), life-destiny (*mìng* 命), mercury (*hōng* 汞), and so forth. Depending on teacher, community, and lineage, sometimes the correspondences are reversed
wùjǐ 戊己 (n./n.)	"*wùjǐ*." The fifth and sixth celestial stems (*tiāngān* 天干), respectively. Correspond to Earth and the center. In internal alchemy, usually associated with the lower elixir field (*dāntián* 丹田), the navel region. Not to be confused with the homophone *wújí* 無極 ("nondifferentiation")
gōng 功 (n.)	"accomplishment." More technically "exercise(s)," and "practice" by extension. Also translated as "merit" and "result." As related to Daoist practice, basically synonymous with *fǎ* 法 ("method") and *shù* 術 ("technique")
cháo 朝 (v.)	"attend to." May also mean and be translated as "assemble," "audience," "court," "face," "gather," "pay homage," and so forth. Often used in Daoist contemplative practice to indicate awareness, concentration, or focus as in the phrase *cháoyuán* 朝元 ("attending to the Origin")
běiquè 北闕 (adj./n.)	"Northern Tower." *Què* 闕 may also mean "gateway/portal" and "palace." An obscure esoteric subtle somatic location. Based on context, appears to designate the kidneys or perineum

Lesson 22

Dǎoyǐn 導引 (Guided Stretching) & Ànmó 按摩 (Self-Massage)
From Zázhù jiéjìng 雜著捷徑
(Shortcuts from Various Authors; DZ 263, j. 17–25 [19])

As we discovered in Lesson #14, Dǎoyǐn 導引 (Guided Stretching), variously referred to as "calisthenics," "gymnastics," and inaccurately "Chinese yoga," is a key dimension of holistic and integrated Daoist training, albeit with a complex history and relationship to Daoism. In the larger tradition, it is most often identified as a specific element of Yǎngshēng 養生 (Nourishing Life), or health and longevity practice. It also is viewed as a supplement to intensive meditation. As such, Dǎoyǐn includes Ànmó 按摩 (lit., "press and rub"), which here refers to self-massage. One of the most famous sets is the Seated Bāduàn jǐn 八段錦 (Eight Brocades), with *duàn* being a measure word for length in general and *jǐn* ("silk brocade") in the present case. The current selection comes from section 19.4a-5b of the *Zázhù jiéjìng* 雜著捷徑 (Shortcuts from Various Authors), a compendium of miscellaneous materials of unclear provenance. The received edition is contained in the anonymous early fourteenth-century *Xiūzhēn shíshū* 修眞十書 (Ten Books on Cultivating Perfection; DZ 263, j. 17–25) (see Lessons #20 and #21). Given the increasing interest in stretching and breathwork in the modern world (so-called "yoga"), including in contemporary constructions like so-called "Tao/Taoist Yoga" and so-called "Yin Yoga,"[46] two qualifications need to be made. First, considered from a more comprehensive perspective, meditation and ritual are the two primary and foundational, perhaps normative Daoist practices. There is only one independent work on guided stretching in the entire received *Dàozàng* 道藏 (Daoist Canon; dat. 1445/1607), namely, the *Dǎoyǐn jīng* 導引經 (DZ 818; ZH 934). Second, although frequently conflated, the Seated Eight Brocades is only nominally related to the later Standing Eight Brocades. The latter appears to be a Buddhist set, most likely of Shàolín 少林 (Dēngfēng 登封, Hénán) provenance and possibly dating to the late nineteenth century (see Shahar 2008, 160; Kohn 2008, 190–92). One clue is that the standard illustrations depict a bare-chested Buddhist monk with shaven head. In any case, the entire relevant section of the *Xiūzhēn shíshū* (19.1a-5b) attributes the set to the famous Daoist immortal Zhōnglí Quán 鍾離權 (Zhèngyáng 正陽 [Aligned Yang]; 168?-256?) (see Lesson #20) and describes an opening meditation (*míngxīn zuò* 冥心坐) practice. The larger text and later commentaries connect this to "burning the body" (*fénshēn* 焚身), a purificatory practice used in internal alchemy to eliminate ailments, defilements, and other negative influences. Here we focus on the illustrated instructions of the Seated Eight Brocades proper. These incorporate earlier Daoist Yǎngshēng practices like "tapping the teeth" (*kòuchǐ* 叩齒), which is often mistranslated as "clacking/gnashing/grinding the teeth." In fact, this involves lightly tapping the teeth. It is usually done in combination with "swallowing saliva" (*yànjīn* 嚥津). In addition to strengthening the teeth, these practices conserve fluids, associated with vital essence (*jīng* 精), and strengthen the kidneys by extension. The Seated Eight Brocades, in turn, became germinal and fairly standard in later Daoist self-massage regimens.

Beyond a bilingual engagement with the Dǎoyǐn set itself, the primary formalistic feature to note centers on the use of *dì* 第 as a ordinal

---

[46] Both so-called "Taoist Yoga" and so-called "Yin Yoga" are forms of hybrid spirituality, as "Tao/Taoist/Yin" derive from indigenous Chinese terms, while "Yoga" refers to indigenous Indian disciplines.

prefix, that is, *dìyī* 第一 ("first"), *dì'èr* 第二 ("second"), and so forth. This construction also appears in the complete chapter titles of the *Chuándào jí* 傳道集 (Anthology on the Transmission of the Dao) (see Lesson #20).

Foundational information on Daoist Dǎoyǐn may be gleaned from consulting *Taoist Meditation and Longevity Techniques* (Kohn 1989) and Livia Kohn's 柯恩 independent book-length study (2008), which includes a translation of the present section of the *Zázhù jiéjìng* (180–83). It also is translated in her supplemental sourcebook (2012, 255–59). A list of the individual works collected in the *Xiūzhēn shíshū* with English translations is contained in Louis Komjathy's "Catalogue of Daoist Collectanea, Compendia, and Encyclopedias" (2022).

Primary Text

《八段錦》

第一段
叩齒集神三十六,兩手抱崑崙,雙手擊天鼓二十四。

第二段
左右搖天柱,各二十四。

第三段
左右舌攪上齶三十六,漱三十六,分作三口如硬物嚥之,然後方得行火。

第四段
兩手磨腎堂三十六,以數多更妙。

第五段
左右單關轆轤,各三十六。

第六段
雙關轆轤三十六。

第七段
兩手相搓當呵五呵,後又手托天按頂,各三或九次。

第八段
以兩手如鉤,向前攀雙腳心,十二,再收足端坐。

FIGURE 22: Seated Eight Brocades Dǎoyǐn 導引 (Guided Stretching)

Eight Brocades

1. Tap the teeth and gather spirit thirty-six times. Place both hands on Kūnlún and beat the Celestial Drum twenty-four times.

2. Rotate the Celestial Pillar to the right and the left twenty-four times each.

3. Move the tongue around the mouth right and left, reaching upward to the gums. Repeat thirty-six times. Swallow the saliva in three gulps like a hard object. After that you may activate the fire.

4. Massage the Kidney Hall with both hands. Rub the kidneys thirty-six times. The more you do this, the more marvelous the results will be.

5. Rotate the torso at the single pass like an axle to the right and left. Repeat this thirty-six times.

6. Rotate the torso at the double pass like a pulley to the right and left. Repeat this thirty-six times.

7. Rub the hands together and exhale with *hē*. Repeat five times. Then interlock the fingers, palms facing outward, and raise the arms above the head to support the heavens. Then press the hands against the top of the head. Repeat nine times.

8. With both hands formed into hooks, bend forward and press the soles of the feet. Repeat this twelve times. Then pull the legs in and sit upright with the back straight.

Vocabulary

kòuchǐ 叩齒 (v./n.)	"tap the teeth." Mistranslated as "clack/gnash/grind the teeth." Key Daoist Yǎngshēng 養生 (Nourishing Life) practice. In addition to strengthening the teeth, and the kidneys/vital essence by extension, opens the head region and expands consciousness
jíshén 集神 (v./n.)	"gather spirit." Also translated as "assemble the spirits." May be understood as concentrating on the center of the head (consciousness) and/or awakening the various "body-gods" (e.g., of the teeth and brain)
Kūnlún 崑崙 (n./n.)	"Kunlun." A Daoist terrestrial paradise. More technically the immortal mountain residence of Xīwángmǔ 西王母 (Queen Mother of the West), where the peaches of immortality (xiāntáo 仙桃) grow. Here used in the Daoist microcosmic sense and as an esoteric designation for the head
jī tiāngǔ 擊天鼓 (v./adj./n.)	"beating the Celestial Drum." Placing the palms over the ears and flicking the index finger over the middle finger on the occiput. The latter is usually referred to as the Jade Pillow (yùzhěn 玉枕), which corresponds to the upper of the Three Passes (sānguān 三關). The method thus helps to open the Governing Vessel in general and the head in particular. Also awakens the "brain-gods"
tiānzhù 天柱 (adj./n.)	"Celestial Pillar." Daoist esoteric name for the neck
yànjīn 嚥津 (v./n.)	"swallow saliva." Key Daoist Yǎngshēng 養生 (Nourishing Life) practice. Conserves fluids, associated with vital essence (jīng 精) and the kidneys by extension. Also considered a key "ingredient" in elixir formation
xínghuǒ 行火 (v./n.)	"activating the fire." May refer to various specific methods, but an active mode usually involving circulating qi (xíngqì 行氣/ yùnqì 運氣) with intentionality (yì 意). Also appears as "advancing the fire" (jìnhuǒ 進火)
dānguān 單關 (adj./n.)	"single pass." The waist
shuāngguān 雙關 (adj./n.)	"double pass." The shoulders

hē 呵 (n.)	"hē." Literally, "expel breath." Here a specific sound vocalized while exhaling. The sound of the heart in the Six Character Instruction (*liùzì jué* 六字訣), a.k.a. Six Healing Sounds. Expels toxins, purifies the heart, and activates the associated meridian
duānzuò 端坐 (adj./n.)	"upright sitting/sit upright." Usually synonymous with *zhèngzuò* 正坐 (Jpn.: *seiza*), which also is translated as "aligned/correct/standard sitting." As such, involves sitting on the heels. Sometimes refers to cross-legged sitting (*jiāfū zuò* 跏趺坐), which most technically designates full-lotus posture

LESSON 23

DAOIST LIVING &
SPIRITUAL COMPANIONSHIP
FROM THE *CHÓNGYÁNG LÌJIÀO SHÍWǓ LÙN*
重陽立教十五論
(REDOUBLED YANG'S FIFTEEN DISCOURSES TO ESTABLISH THE TEACHINGS; DZ 1233; ZH 1010)

AMONG THE MANY DIMENSIONS OF Daoist being and living, residences and companionship are important considerations. In the present selection, we explore two sections of the *Chóngyáng lìjiào shíwǔ lùn* 重陽立教十五論 (Redoubled Yang's Fifteen Discourses to Establish the Teachings; DZ 1233; ZH 1010) (see Lesson #1), namely, (1) "Zhù'ān 住庵" (Living in Hermitages) (1a), and (6) "Hé dàobàn 合道伴" (Joining with Companions of the Dao) (3a). The *Chóngyáng lìjiào shíwǔ lùn*, variously abbreviated as *Chóngyáng shíwǔ lùn* 重陽十五論 (Chongyang's Fifteen Discourses), *Lìjiào shíwǔ lùn* 立教十五論 (Fifteen Discourses to Establish the Teachings), or simply *Shíwǔ lùn* 十五論 (Fifteen Discourses), is a key work of the early Quánzhēn 全眞 (Complete Perfection) movement (see Lessons #16 and #17). It is attributed to the founder Wáng Zhé 王嚞 (Chóng**yáng** 重陽 [Redoubled Yang]; 1113–1170), whose Daoist name again links him to the immortals Zhèng**yáng** 正陽 (Aligned Yang) and Chún**yáng** 純陽 (Pure Yang) (see Lessons #20 and #21). However, few specialists accept the viability of this attribution. The most generous critical analysis suggests that the text may be a systematization of earlier teachings associated with Wáng, possibly composed by one or more first-generation Quánzhēn adherents. It may be understood as a primer in early Quánzhēn lifeways and praxis, probably intended for committed community members associated with the various regional Daoist associations (*dàohuì* 道會) and/or ascetics and formal members of the emerging early Quánzhēn monastic system. As the title indicates, the *Chóngyáng shíwǔ lùn* consists of fifteen "discourses" (*lùn* 論), here in the form of individual essays and short chapters, on wide-ranging topics. The titles are as follows:[47]

(1) Zhù'ān 住庵 (Living in Hermitages)

(2) Yúnyóu 雲遊 (Cloud Wandering)

(3) Xuéshū 學書 (Studying Texts)

(4) Héyào 合藥 (Preparing Medicinal Herbs)

(5) Gàizào 蓋造 (On Construction)

(6) Hé dàobàn 合道伴 (Joining with Companions of the Dao)

(7) Dǎzuò 打坐 (Seated Meditation)

(8) Jiàngxīn 降心 (Controlling the Heart-mind)

(9) Liànxìng 錬性 (Refining Innate Nature)

(10) Pīpèi wǔqì 匹配五氣 (Matching the Five Qi)

(11) Hùn xìngmìng 混性命 (Merging Innate Nature and Life-destiny)

(12) Shèngdào 聖道 (The Way of Sages)

(13) Chāo sānjiè 超三界 (Going Beyond the Three Realms)

(14) Yǎngshēn zhī fǎ 養身之法 (Methods for Nourishing the Body)

(15) Lí fánshì 離凡世 (Leaving the Mundane World)

FIGURE 23: Section Titles of the *Chóngyáng shíwǔ lùn* 重陽十五論 (Redoubled Yang's Fifteen Discourses)

---

[47] Interestingly, Discourses #7, 8, 9 and 13 appear in the fourteenth-century *Qúnxiān yàoyǔ zuǎnjí* 群仙要語纂集 (Collection of Essential Sayings from Various Immortals; DZ 1257; ZH 1074) as a concise guide to Daoist meditation.

Here the first selection follows the early Quánzhēn emphasis on meditative seclusion in a separate hut or hermitage (*ān* 庵/菴/庵), with the most famous one being Wáng's own Quánzhēn ān 全眞庵 (Hermitage of Complete Perfection). This was partly inspired by the discussion of "four-walled rooms" (*huándǔ* 環堵) in chapters twenty-three and twenty-eight of the *Zhuāngzǐ* 莊子 (Book of Master Zhuang) (cf. *Lǐjì* 禮記, ch. 41), and also connected to earlier Daoist uses of "pure chambers" (*jìngshì* 淨室), which originally were small detached, wooden huts with minimal furnishings. The second selection focuses on ideal Daoist spiritual companions, here referred to as *dàobàn* 道伴, but more commonly as *dàoyǒu* 道友. The earliest, classical discussion appears in chapter six of the *Zhuāngzǐ*, wherein friendship is again framed in terms of being a "death-doula" and involves "not having any obstruction in the heart-mind" (*mò nì yú xīn* 莫逆於心). That is, there are shared affinities, aspirations, commitments, orientations, and so forth. A parallel view is expressed in the *Dānyáng zhēnrén yǔlù* 丹陽眞人語錄 (Discourse Record of Perfected Danyang (Elixir Yang); DZ 1057; ZH 1016; abbrev. *Dānyáng yǔlù*; trl. Komjathy 2013, 106–11), which is associated with Mǎ Yù 馬鈺 (Dān**yáng** 丹陽 [Elixir Yang]; 1123–1183), one of the so-called Seven Perfected (*qīzhēn* 七眞) and the Second Patriarch of the early Quánzhēn movement.

昇平快活莫過於閒。道人若住庵稍倦，結一兩人作伴。掛搭腋袋，拖條挂杖。且歌且遊，撞著好山好水。且為盤桓，不可貪程途。

"To attain peace and a joyous life, nothing is better than seclusion. If Daoists are able to reside in a hermitage, they can decrease their level of fatigue by joining with one or two people as companions. Together they can gather fur in order to make padded jackets and find treefall to make walking sticks. Moreover, they can sing and travel together, encountering amazing mountains and streams along the way. They can also admire Soapberry trees together and ensure that each other avoid the path to avarice." (3a)

Drawing upon the classical Daoist emphasis on "appearing plain" (*xiànsù* 見素) and "embracing simplicity" (*bàopǔ* 抱樸), here we find a model of Daoist minimalism, self-sufficiency, and voluntary poverty, including using "found materials."

With this lesson, we move back into more robust classical Chinese grammar. The passages include the following relevant characters: *fán* 凡 ("generally speaking"), *qí* 其 ("its/the"), *wéi* 唯 ("only"), *yě* 也 (。), *yǐ* 矣 (。), *zé* 則 ("then"), *zhě* 者 ("as for/one who"), *zhī* 之 ("of/it"). One new phrase for us is *ránhòu* 然後 ("after"). Formalistically speaking, each chapter title also contains the ordinal prefix *dì* 第 (see Lesson #22). The Daoist lexicon is again elucidated in the chapter vocabulary, but one phrase deserves particular mention. This is *chūjiā* 出家, which literally means "leave the family." In early Quánzhēn, it refers to formal renunciants, while in the monastic order it refers to monastics (monks and nuns). As a monastic category, it specifically assumes voluntary celibacy and the accompanying rejection of biological and social reproduction. It contrasts with "householders" (*zàijiā* 在家 [lit., "in the family"]), which is also referred to as "fire-dwelling" (*huǒjū* 火居). This includes both "non-monastic" Daoist ordinands (e.g., Zhèngyī 正一 [Orthodox Unity]) and lay disciples. In the fully development Quánzhēn monastic order, "leaving the family" involves three core commitments and vows, namely, celibacy (no sex), sobriety (no intoxicants), and vegetarianism (no meat). Given the issues in modern Chinese and global Daoism, we probably should emphasize the need for an accompanying commitment to "abandon the mundane" (*chúsú* 除俗; cf. *huánsú* 還俗).

The definitive Western-language study of early Quánzhēn Daoism is Louis Komjathy's 康思奇 *Cultivating Perfection: Mysticism and Self-transformation in Early Quanzhen Daoism* (2007), which includes a comprehensive discussion of the associated textual corpus. The *Chóngyáng shíwǔ lùn* itself has been translated multiple times, probably too many times, often with accompanying mischaracterizations of the text as the "authoritative" or "definitive Quánzhēn text." A more general-audience translation, but with attention to historical context and technical terminology, appears as Handbook #8 of Komjathy's *Handbooks for Daoist Practice* (2008 [2003]), which has been widely circulated on the internet and become the basis of various plagiarized versions, most often by individuals who do not know Chinese. A complete annotated scholarly translation also appears in Komjathy's *The Way of Complete Perfection* (2013, 108–14), which is a comprehensive sourcebook that more accurately locates the *Chóngyáng shíwǔ lùn* in the larger Quánzhēn textual corpus. A list of the section titles of the text with English translations also is contained in Louis Komjathy's "Catalogue of Daoist Collectanea, Compendia, and Encyclopedias" (2022).

Primary Text

《第一論住庵》

凡出家者、先須投庵。庵者舍也，一身依倚。身有依倚，心漸得安，氣神和暢，入眞道矣。凡有動作，不可過勞，過勞則損氣。不可不動，不動則氣血凝滯。須要動靜得其中，然後可以守常安分，此是住安之法。

Discourse 1: Living in Hermitages

All renunciants must first retreat to a hermitage. A hermitage is an enclosure, a place where the body may be attuned and entrusted. When the body is attuned and entrusted, the heart-mind gradually realizes serenity. Qi and spirit become harmonious and expansive. Then you may enter the Way of Perfection.

Now, when movement and activity become necessary, you must not overdo things and exhaust yourself. If you overdo things and become exhausted, you will dissipate your qi. And yet, you cannot remain entirely inactive either. If you do not move, your qi and blood will become obstructed and weakened.

You should, therefore, find a middle way between movement and stillness. Only then can you guard constancy and be at peace with your endowments. This is the method of residing in serenity.

《第六論合道伴》

道人合伴，本欲疾病相扶。你死我埋，我死你埋。然先擇人而後合伴，不可先合伴而後擇人。不可相戀，相戀則繫其心，不可不戀，不戀則情相離。戀欲不戀，得其中道可矣。有三合三不合：明心，有慧，有志，此三合也。不明著外境，無智慧、性愚濁，無志氣、乾打鬨，此三不合也。立身之本在叢林，全憑心志，不可順人情，不可取相貌，唯擇高明者，是上法也。

Discourse 6: Joining with Companions of the Dao

Daoists join together as companions because they can assist each other in sickness and disease. "If you die, I'll bury you; if I die, you'll bury me."

Therefore, you must first choose the right person and only then join with that person as a companion. Do not join with someone first and then consider them as a person.

Once this is accomplished, do not become overly attached to each other. Attachment between people ensnares the heart-mind.

At the same time, do not remain completely without attachment. A complete lack of attachment will cause your feelings to diverge. You should find a middle way between attachment and non-attachment.

There are three kinds of people with whom you should join and three whom you should avoid. Join those with an illuminated heart-mind, wisdom, or strong determination. Avoid those who are ignorant concerning external projections of the heart-mind, who lack wisdom and are turbid in innate nature, or who lack determination and are inclined to quarrel.

When establishing yourself in a monastery, completely accord with your own heart-mind and aspirations. Do not just follow your emotions or trust the outer appearance of others. Only choose the elevated and illumined. This is the supreme method.

Vocabulary

jiào 教 (v.|n.)	"teach|teachings." Also translated as "doctrine." Often shorthand for *dàojiào* 道教 (lit., "Teachings of the Dao"; Daoism)
ān 庵 (n.)	"hermitage." More literally, "hut." Also appears as 菴/厂. Often used to designate a small Buddhist temple, including nunneries
chūjiā 出家 (v./n.)	"renunciant." Literally, "leave the family." Also translated as "monastic." In early Quánzhēn 全眞 (Complete Perfection) Daoism, involves celibacy (no sex) and sobriety (no intoxicants), and later vegetarianism (no meat). These are the three core vows/commitments
zhēndào 眞道 (adj./n.)	"Way of Perfection." May also be translated as "perfect/real/true Dao/Way." Here probably used in both senses, but especially to designate Quánzhēn 全眞 (Complete Perfection) as the true path to the Dao
shǒucháng 守常 (v./n.)	"guarding constancy." *Shǒu* 守 ("guard") is a Daoist technical term for "meditation," while *cháng* 常 ("constancy") here refers to psychospiritual integrity and stability. In early Quánzhēn related to "clarity-and-stillness" (*qīngjìng* 清靜), which most technically refers to celibacy (no sex) and the conservation of vital essence (*jīng* 精) by extension
fèn 分 (n.)	"endowment." May also mean "divide," "portion/share," and "lot." Also translated as "allotment." As a Daoist technical term, refers to "fate" (*mìng* 命) as endowed by the cosmos and manifested as one's constitution and tendencies. Also appears in the phrase *yuánfèn* 緣分 ("pre-destined affinities")

---

dàobàn 道伴 (n./n.)	"Companions of the Dao." More commonly appears as *dàoyǒu* 道友. Daoist spiritual companions
liàn 戀 (n.)	"attachment." May also mean "craving." Contains the *xīn* 心 ("heart") radical

xì 繫 (v.|n.)	"ensnare|ensnarement." May also mean "bind/bindings" and "entangle/entanglement." Contains the *mì* 糸 ("silk") radical
huì 慧 (n.)	"wisdom." Also translated as "intelligence" and "insight." Here has the Buddhist connotation of liberating/liberated insight, especially as seeing through phenomenal appears (*fǎ* 法) into the true (non) nature of existence (impermanence)
zhì 志 (adj.|n.)	"determined|determination." Also translated as "aspire/aspiration" and "will." More technically, the spiritual faculty associated with the Water phase, and the kidneys by extension. Also appears as *dàozhì* 道志 ("aspiration for the Dao")
jìng 境 (n.)	"mental projection" (Buddhism). More literally, "landscape" and "region." Also used in the sense of "condition/situation." Here suggests a Buddhist mind-only view of the phenomenal world (*fǎ* 法) as illusory on some level, dependent on one's own psychospiritual condition
cónglín 叢林 (n./n.)	"monastery." Literally, "clustered forest." Usually refers to a Buddhist monastery, especially a Chán 禪 (Zen) one. Cf. *guàn* 觀

LESSON 24

ETHICAL CULTIVATION &
MONASTIC PROTOCOL
FROM THE *CHŪZHĒN JIÈ* 初真戒
(PRECEPTS OF INITIAL PERFECTION; JY 292; ZW 404)

WITH THIS FINAL SELECTION BEFORE we turn to some examples from Daoist commentary literature, we move beyond the received *Dàozàng* 道藏 (Daoist Canon; dat. 1445/1607) and its *terminus ante quem* in the Míng dynasty (1368–1644) and the accompanying bias in mainstream Daoist Studies. Here we focus on the *Chūzhēn jiè* 初真戒 (Precepts of Initial Perfection; JY 292; ZW 404), a Daoist precept text and monastic manual dating to the early seventeenth-century, that is, the beginning of the Qīng dynasty (1644–1912). In addition to independently circulated manuscripts and woodblock printings, it is preserved in the *Dàozàng jíyào* 道藏輯要 (Collected Essentials of the Daoist Canon; dat. 1700/1906; 315 texts; abbrev. JY) and *Zàngwài dàoshū* 藏外道書 (Daoist Books Outside the Canon; dat. 1992/1994; 991 texts; abbrev. ZW) (see also Lesson #19).[48] The *Chūzhēn jiè* was compiled by Wáng Chángyuè 王常月 (Kūnyáng 崑陽

---

[48] Again, the primary index, which establishes standardized numbering systems, is Louis Komjathy's 康思奇 *Title Index to Daoist Collections* (TIDC; 2002). There also is a recent Chinese catalogue edited by Lai Chi-tim 黎志添 (2021), which is modelled on the *Historical Companion of the Daozang* (Schipper and Verellen 2004) and continues the earlier work of Monica Esposito 莫尼卡 (1962–2011). However, the JY companion has a wide variety of deficiencies and must be supplemented with additional specialist knowledge.

[Paradisiacal Yang]; 1622?-1680),[49] the first Qīng-dynasty abbot of Báiyún guàn 白雲觀 (White Cloud Monastery; Běijīng) and the founder of the official Lóngmén 龍門 (Dragon Gate) lineage. It is a collection of Lóngmén precepts (jiè 戒) and monastic codes (see also Lesson #4). The namesake Ten Precepts of Initial Perfection (chūzhēn shíjiè 初眞十戒) (9ab [12.18]),[50] our focus here, parallel those found in the early eighth-century Chūzhēn shíjiè wén 初眞十戒文 (Ten Precepts of Initial Perfection; DZ 180; ZH 1316). The text is transmitted to ordinands of the first level of the Lóngmén lineage of the Quánzhēn 全眞 (Complete Perfection) monastic order and represents the order's most fundamental guidelines and practical precepts. It is further located within three ordination ranks with associated texts.

Ordination Rank	Precept Text	Ritual Vestment
Wondrous Practice/ Initial Perfection	Chūzhēn jiè 初眞戒 (Precepts of Initial Perfection)	Devotion Robe of Initial Perfection
Wondrous Virtue/ Medium Ultimate	Zhōngjí jiè 中極戒 (Precepts of Medium Ultimate)	Pure Robe of Lightened Dust
Wondrous Dao/ Celestial Immortality	Tiānxiān jiè 天仙戒 (Precepts of Celestial Immortality)	Mist Robe of Celestial Immortality

FIGURE 24: Three Lóngmén 龍門 (Dragon Gate) Ordination Ranks

As outlined in the Chūzhēn jiè, Lóngmén aspirants and novitiates begin by taking the Three Refuges (sān guīyī 三皈依) (Dao, scriptures,

---

[49] Wáng Chángyuè's Daoist name is somewhat complex and probably should be left untranslated as "Kunyang." Kūn 崑 technically refers to Mount Kūnlún 崑崙, the western Daoist terrestrial immortal paradise, specifically associated with Xīwángmǔ 西王母 (Queen Mother of the West). I thus render kūn more liberally as "paradisiacal" in order to provide an actual English translation.

[50] The first number is the traditional woodblock page number, while the second is the ZW volume and page number.

teachers), followed by study and application of the Five Precepts and the *Tàishàng gǎnyìng piān* 太上感應篇 (Treatise on Resonance and Response According to the Great High [Lord Lao]; DZ 1167; ZH 1321; abbrev. *Gǎnyìng piān*; trl. Suzuki and Carus 1973 [1906]; Wong 1994), an anonymous and influential twelfth-century popular morality book (*shànshū* 善書). Following this, formal ordinands receive and focus on the Ten Precepts of Initial Perfection.[51] The next ordination ranks focus on the Three Hundred Precepts of Medium Ultimate and then the Ten Virtues of Celestial Immortality and the Twenty-Seven Virtuous Activities of Celestial Immortality, respectively. This means that there are 352 total guidelines and qualities for fully ordained and observant Lóngmén Daoists.

Grammatically speaking, this section of the *Chūzhēn jiè*, which is a list of precepts, is quite simple. Each entry includes *dì* 第 (ordinal prefix) and *zhě* 者 (topicalization), followed by *bù* 不 ("do not") and then *dāng* 當 ("ought/should"). The former represents the primary proscription, accompanied by a prescriptive admonition. Somewhat like the Nine Practices (see Lesson #4), there is a question concerning relationship. That is, should we take these as complimentary and/or sequential, with the proscription clarifying the prescription? The Daoist technical terminology is again documented in the chapter vocabulary.

The definitive Western-language studies of the Lóngmén lineage are two posthumously-released book-length publications by Monica Esposito 莫尼卡 (1962–2011) (2013, 2014). A more comprehensive discussion of Daoist precepts is Livia Kohn's 柯恩 *Cosmos and Community: The Ethical Dimension of Daoism* (2004). A complete annotated scholarly translation is included in Louis Komjathy's 康思奇 *The Way of Complete Perfection* (2013, 326–60), which is the only such translation of a traditional Lóngmén text.

---

[51] The *Chūzhēn jiè* also includes conduct guidelines for women titled the *Nǚzhēn jiǔjiè* 女眞九戒 (Nine Precepts for Female Perfected).

Primary Text

《初真十戒》

第一戒者，不得不忠不孝，不仁信，當盡節君親，推誠萬物。
第二戒者，不得陰賊潛謀，害物利己，當行陰德，廣濟群生。
第三戒者，不得殺害含生，以充滋味，當行慈惠，以及昆蟲。
第四戒者，不得淫邪敗真，穢慢靈氣，當守貞操，使無缺犯。
第五戒者，不得敗人成功，離人骨肉，當以道助物，
　　令九族雍和。
第六戒者，不得讒毀賢良，露才揚己，當稱人之美善，
　　不自伐其功能。
第七戒者，不得飲酒食肉，犯律違禁，當調和氣性，專務清虛。
第八戒者，不得貪求無厭，積財不散，當行節儉，惠卹貧窮。
第九戒者，不得交遊非賢，居處穢雜，當慕勝己，棲集清虛。
第十戒者，不得輕忽言笑，舉動非真，當持重寡辭，
　　以道德為務。

Ten Precepts of Initial Perfection

1. Do not be disloyal, unfilial, inhumane, or dishonest. Always exhaust your allegiance to your lord and family, and be sincere when relating to the myriad beings.
2. Do not secretly steal things, harbor hidden plots, or harm other beings in order to profit yourself. Always practice hidden virtue and widely aid the host of living beings.
3. Do not kill or harm anything that lives in order to satisfy your own appetites. Always act with compassion and kindness to all, even insects and worms.
4. Do not be debased or deviant, squander your perfection, or defile your numinous qi. Always guard purity and integrity, and remain without deficiencies or transgressions.
5. Do not ruin others to create gain for yourself or leave your own flesh and bones. Always use the Dao to help other beings and make sure that the nine clan members all live in harmony.
6. Do not slander or defame the worthy and good or exhibit your talents and elevate yourself. Always praise the beauty and goodness of others and never be contentious about your own accomplishments and abilities.
7. Do not drink alcohol or eat meat in violation of the prohibitions. Always harmonize qi and innate nature, remaining attentive to clarity and emptiness.
8. Do not be greedy and acquisitive without ever being satisfied or accumulate wealth without giving some away. Always practice moderation in all things and show kindness and sympathy to the poor and destitute.
9. Do not have any relations or exchange with the unworthy or live among the confused and defiled. Always strive to control yourself, becoming perched and composed in clarity and emptiness.
10. Do not speak or laugh lightly or carelessly, increasing agitation and denigrating perfection. Always maintain seriousness and speak humble words, so that the Dao and inner power remain your primary concern.

Vocabulary

chūzhēn 初眞 (adj./n.)	"Initial Perfection." The first ordination level of the traditional tripartite Lóngmén 龍門 (Dragon Gate) lineage ranks of the Quánzhēn 全眞 (Complete Perfection) monastic order. Also referred to as "Wondrous Practice" (*miàoxíng* 妙行).
jiè 戒 (n.)	"precept." Also translated as "admonishment." The most general Daoist term for rules and regulations. Contains the *gē* 戈 ("halberd") radical. Conduct principles and guidelines. Here primarily refers to the Ten Precepts of Initial Perfection, but for full and observant Lóngmén ordinands designates 352 total guidelines and qualities
xìn 信 (adj.|n.)	"honest|honesty." Also translated as "sincere/sincerity" and "trustworthy/trust." The character consists of *rén* 人/亻 ("person") and *yán* 言 ("speech"). A person standing by words
wànwù 萬物 (num./n.)	"myriad beings." More literally, "ten thousand beings/things." *Wù* 物 (lit., "animal"; cf. *shòu* 獸) contains the *niú* 牛/牜 ("ox") radical. *Wànwù* usually refers to everything in existence, including both animate/sentient beings and inanimate/nonsentient things
yīndé 陰德 (adj./n.)	"hidden virtue." Also appears as *yǐndé* 隱德 and related to *yīngōng* 陰功 ("hidden merit"). Refers to performing "good deeds" without recognition or recompense
chóng 蟲 (n.)	"insect." Consists of three *chóng* 虫 ("insect") characters. Here indicates concern and compassion that extends to all beings, even the infinitesimal and (apparently) "insignificant"
zhēn 眞/真 (adj.|n.)	"perfect|perfection." Also translated as "authentic/real/true." Sometimes refers to the original unity of the Dao ("Perfection/Reality"). The character, consisting of *bǐ* 匕 ("spoon") and *dǐng* 鼎 ("tripod"), depicts a reaction vessel. Alchemically speaking, the resultant state of complete refinement and transmutation. Appears in key Daoist phrases, including Quánzhēn 全眞 ("Complete Perfection"), *xiūzhēn* 修眞 ("cultivating perfection"), and *zhēnrén* 眞人 ("Perfected")

língqì 靈氣 (adj./n.)	"numinous qi." The Dao manifesting as subtle presence and influence in the world and being. Often used synonymously with *dàoqì* 道炁 ("qi of the Dao") and *zhēnqì* 眞炁 ("perfect/true qi")
jìn 禁 (n.)	"prohibition." Also translated as "proscription." Here refers to Daoist monastic rules and mandated behavior patterns
qīng 清 (adj.|n.)	"clear|clarity." Also translated as "pure/purity." Here refers to moral purity, sexual propriety, and psycho-spiritual stability. Often appears in the paired phrase *qīngjìng* 清靜 ("clarity-and-stillness"), which may more technically refer to celibacy (no sex)
xū 虛 (adj.|v.|n.)	"empty|empty|emptiness." Often synonymous with *wú* 無 ("nonbeing/nothing") and *kōng* 空 ("emptiness"), but the latter also is used to translate the Buddhist Sanskrit *śūnyatā* ("empty of own-being"). Here *xū* includes the latter technical connotation
jiǎn 儉 (adj.|n.)	"moderate|moderation." Also translated as "frugality" and "modesty." One of the classical Daoist Three Treasures (*sānbǎo* 三寶) mentioned in LZ 67
dào 道 (n.)	"Dao." Also appears as 衜/衟 and referred to as "Tao/Way." The character consists of *chuò* 辵/辶 ("walk/move") and *shǒu* 首 ("head"). The sacred and ultimate concern of Daoists
dé 德 (n.)	"Inner power." Also appears as 悳. Also translated as "integrity," "potency," and "virtue." The way in which the Dao manifests in/as/through embodied human activity and being in the world, especially beneficial and transformative presence, behavior and influence

吾言甚易知甚易行

天下莫能知莫能行

Lesson 25

Titles of Chapters 1–18 of the Lǎozǐ zhāngjù 老子章句
(Chapter-and-Verse Commentary on the Laozi; DZ 682; LZ* 8; ZH 556)

With these culminating four lessons we move from reading and translating Daoist anthologies/collections (*jí* 集) (Lessons #20 and #22), discourses (*lùn* 論) (Lesson #23), inscriptions (*míng* 銘) (Lessons #14 and #19), masters literature (*zǐshū* 子書) (Lessons #7–9, #13),[52] precepts (*jiè* 戒) (Lessons #4 and #24), records (*lù* 錄) (Lesson #15), scriptures (*jīng* 經) (Lessons #12, #16–17,), and treatises (*piān* 篇) (Lessons #18 and #21) into a different genre of Daoist literature, namely, "commentaries" (*zhù* 註/注). These works bring our attention to not only another type of Daoist literature, beyond primary compositions, but also Daoist approaches to reading, study, and interpretation. Specifically, we will explore commentaries on the *Lǎozǐ* 老子 (Book of Venerable Masters), which is also known honorifically as the *Dàodéjīng* 道德經 (Scripture on the Dao and Inner Power) (see Lessons #1, #4, and #7). By at least one count (see Komjathy 2022h), there are over 260 pre-modern ones. Given the primary text's fathomlessness, inexhaustibility, and profundity, how could there

---

[52] As discussed in the corresponding lessons, the *Lǎozǐ* 老子 (Book of Venerable Masters) became canonized as the *Dàodéjīng* 道德經 (Scripture on the Dao and Inner Power) and the *Zhuāngzǐ* 莊子 (Book of Master Zhuang) as the *Nánhuájīng* 南華經 (Scripture of Nanhua [Southern Florescence]). That is, as preserved, transmitted, and received, these are Daoist scriptures.

not be? Given the emphasis on "non-knowing" (*wúzhī* 無知) in the "Old Master" and among the "old masters," should we really be unsurprised that so many have felt inspired, even obliged to interpret and explain?

夫唯不可識，
故強為之容。

It is only because they could not be recognized
That we feel compelled to describe them.
(ch. 15)

吾不知其名，字之曰道。
強為之名曰大。

I do not know its name; I style it "Dao."
Compelled to name it further, I call it "great."
(ch. 25)

知者不言；
言者不知。

One who knows does not speak;
One who speaks does not know.
(ch. 56)

吾言甚易知、甚易行。
天下莫能知、莫能行。

My words are very easy to understand and very easy to practice;
But no one in the world understands them and no one practices them.
(ch. 70)

知不知上；
不知知病。

To know that you do not know is best;
Not to know that you are knowing is sickness.
(ch. 71)

This is not to mention various cryptic phrases and obscure statements. As briefly mentioned in Lesson #7, this is partially because the received *Dàodé jīng* is an anonymous multi-vocal anthology consisting of historical and textual material dating from the fourth to second centuries BCE and containing the teachings and practices of various anonymous elders of the inner cultivation lineages of classical Daoism. Daoist commentaries in turn assist us in not only deciphering the text, but also understanding the ways in which *Daoists* have read and interpreted it. This includes from applied, committed, and lived perspectives rooted in Daoist practice-realization. If the *Dàodé jīng* is a Daoist scripture, should we not be interested in how earlier *Daoists and Daoist communities* have understood and interpreted it? Commentary composition may, in turn, be understood as a form of "Daoist hermeneutics" and "Daoist scholasticism." As discussed in the general introduction, it represents at least one tradition-based model for being a Daoist scholar-practitioner.

With this installment, we return to our earlier skillset (Lessons #2 and #3), in which we explored chapter titles. In the present case, we explore the first eighteen chapter titles of the Héshàng gōng (HSG) commentary. There are a number of reasons to reengage such a preliminary and foundational reading and translation methodology. First, we may apply and gauge our progress in gaining the necessary language facility in classical Chinese. Second, it reveals the way in which a text that is perhaps both too familiar and too unfamiliar was altered and adapted in later, but here still early Daoist history. The HSG is the first commentary to supply chapter titles, and these became germinal for the larger Daoist tradition and are still engaged to this day. For example and in terms of global Daoism, they are used as part of scripture study focusing on the *Dàodé jīng* in the Daoist Foundation 道教基金會. Third and related, they evidence a deep engagement with the primary text, and thus provide guidance on major themes, which we will return to momentarily. They thus may inform scholarship and ideally annotation. For example, chapter one is here titled "Tǐdào 體道" (Embodying the Dao). Given the chapter's emphasis on the Dao as a Daoist cosmological and theological "concept" (reality), and the frequent (mis)interpretation as "philosophy," it is noteworthy that the title emphasizes *embodiment* (*tǐ* 體), rather than some imagined concern like "thought" (*sīxiǎng* 思想).

Also later referred to as the *Dàodé zhēnjīng zhù* 道德真經註 (Commentary on the Perfect Scripture on the Dao and Inner Power),[53] the *Lǎozǐ zhāngjù* 老子章句 (Chapter-and-Verse Commentary on the *Laozi*; DZ 682; LZ* 8; ZH 556)[54] is one of the most influential early commentaries on the key classical Daoist text. The commentary is better known by the name of its author, Héshàng gōng 河上公 (Elder Dwelling-by-the-River; fl. 160s CE?) (HSG), concerning whom scant reliable historical information exists. He most likely was a Daoist recluse and Yǎngshēng 養生 (Nourishing Life) practitioner (see Lessons #14 and #15). While legend identifies Héshàng gōng as a teacher of the Hàn Emperor Wén 文 (r. 179–157 BCE), the namesake commentary probably dates to the second century CE, although some would date it as late as the sixth century. If the former is accurate, the *Lǎozǐ zhāngjù* would be the fourth oldest of the six earliest extant commentaries on the *Lǎozǐ*. It interprets the *Dàodé jīng* especially in terms of Yǎngshēng practice and Hàn political concerns, specifically those of the so-called "Huáng-Lǎo 黃老 school" (Syncretic Daoism). It has been especially influential and

---

[53] This also is the title of the equally influential commentary (DZ 690; LZ* 12; ZH 560) by Wáng Bì 王弼 (226–249 CE), a major Daoist scholar-practitioner and member of the Daoist quasi-salon and hermeneutic movement known as Xuánxué 玄學 (Profound Learning). The latter is referred to as so-called "Neo-Daoism" [sic] in outdated and inaccurate Orientalist accounts.

[54] The abbreviation LZ*, with an asterisk to distinguish it from the primary text itself, refers to the *Lǎozǐ jíchéng* 老子集成 (Collection on the *Laozi*; dat. 2011; 267 titles). It has been indexed with a standardized numbering system in Louis Komjathy's 康思奇 recent "Supplements to *Title Index to Daoist Collections*" (STIDC; 2022-). See general introduction and bibliography herein.

even considered definitive in Daoist circles. For present purposes, it is important for a variety of reasons. First, it most likely represents the base-edition/redaction for the standard, received text of the *Dàodé jīng*, albeit via Wáng Bì 王弼 (226–249 CE). Second, it is the earliest known edition to divide that work into eighty-one numbered chapters (9x9=81). For example and in contrast, traditional sources report that some versions were divided into 64, 68, 72, or 77 chapters, and some did not have chapter divisions at all (see Komjathy forthcoming). Third, tracing the legend surrounding Héshàng gōng and the associated commentary reveals important connective strands through the Daoist tradition, including from classical Daoism through various Hàn-dynasty Fāngshī 方士 (lit., "formula masters"; magico-religious practitioners) lineages into the Tàiqīng 太清 (Great Clarity) movement. Finally, and as explored herein, it is the primary commentary to supply *titles* to each *Dàodé jīng* chapter, which became largely definitive in later periods of Daoist history and even into the modern period. As such, it provides not only deep insights into each chapter's primary thematic concerns, but also serves as a guide to the primary text as a whole. Here a major issue related to translation methodology arises: Should we retranslate the primary text each time through the filter of the given commentary?

As we are dealing with the chapter titles themselves, there is no grammar as such. However, like some of the earlier texts explored herein, the numbered chapter titles include the ordinal prefix *dì* 第 (see Lessons #22–24). In terms of vocabulary, the chapter titles largely mirror the internal contents of the *Dàodé jīng* itself and overlap with much of our foundational "Daoist classical Chinese lexigraphy" already acquired. Some key terms/concepts include the following: *chéng* 成 ("complete"), *guī* 歸 ("return"), *tāo* 韜 ("hide"), *tǐ* 體 ("embody"), *xiǎn* 顯 ("manifest"), *yǎng* 養 ("nourish"), and *yùn* 運 ("circulate"). It is interesting that these are verbs and may thus serve as admonitions and apparently direct us towards *embodied activity in the world*. So, perhaps this is the manifestation of *wúwéi* 無為 ("non-action") and further connected to *dé* 德 ("inner power"), *jìng* 靜 ("stillness"), *pǔ* 樸 ("unhewn simplicity"), and *xìng* 性

("innate nature"). For example, in the larger classical Daoist textual corpus and specifically in the *Zhuāngzǐ*, we are told,

正則靜, (*tsʿreŋ)
靜則明, (*mraŋ)
明則虛, (*qʰra)
虛則無為 (*Gʷraj)
而無不為。(*Gʷraj)

Alignment results in stillness;
Stillness results in illumination;
Illumination results in emptiness;
Emptiness results in non-action.
Then nothing is left undone.
(ch. 23)

Recalling the HSG commentary's connection with the Daoist Yǎngshēng tradition, *yǎng* and *yùn* are especially noteworthy, as they may invoke *yǎngshēng* 養生 ("nourishing life") and *yùnqì* 運氣 ("circulate qi"). Again, on a deeper level, this might be thought of as yet another "primer in Daoist practice vocabulary," and thus inform Daoist training and lifeways. Moreover, as we did in Lessons #2 and #3, we may engage the Héshàng gōng chapter titles as a contemplative inquiry as such. If we nourish self (2), pacify the people (3), hide the radiance (7), and restrict desires (12), perhaps we will come to embody the Dao (1), discover the Source of Nonbeing (4), and circulate the subtle (9). Perhaps then we will see beyond mundane approaches (18) and eventually reach redoubled yang (9x9=81), which is characterized by non-contention (*wúzhēng* 無爭).

To date, Isabelle Robinet 賀碧來 (1932–2000) has been the Western scholar to devote the most attention to Daoist commentaries on the *Dàodé jīng*. She has published a comprehensive, two-volume French overview (1977) as well as two article-length overviews (1998; 1999). Alan K.L. Chan 陳金樑 has published a book-length comparison of the Héshàng gōng and Wáng Bì commentaries (1991) as well as an article-length distillation (1998). There also is an outdated and deficient early translation (1950) by Eduard Erkes 何可思 (1891–1958). There also is a popular self-published translation by Dan Reid (2015/2019). I have not examined the latter in detail as I consider it derivative. In addition to lack of engagement with Daoist Studies as such, the author's association with various adherents of Popular Western Taoism (PWT) and "Daoist" popularizers gives sufficient pause. The HSG commentary is currently being retranslated by Louis Komjathy 康思奇 in a more comprehensive project focusing on Daoist commentaries on the *Dàodé jīng*. Komjathy's "Title Index to the *Lǎozǐ jíchéng* 老子集成 (Collection on the *Laozi*)" (2022), which is part of the "Supplements to *Title Index to Daoist Collections*" (STIDC) series, is helpful for providing a catalogue of pre-modern commentaries.

Primary Text

Chapter #	Title	Translation
1	Tǐdào 體道	Embodying the Dao
2	Yǎngshēn 養身	Nourishing Self
3	Ānmín 安民	Pacifying the People
4	Wúyuán 無源	Source of Nonbeing
5	Xūyòng 虛用	Application of Emptiness
6	Chéngxiàng 成象	Completing Appearance
7	Tāoguāng 韜光	Hiding the Radiance
8	Yìxìng 易性	Altering Innate Nature
9	Yùnyí 運夷	Circulating the Subtle
10	Néngwéi 能為	Being Able to Act
11	Wúyòng 無用	Application of Nonbeing
12	Jiǎnyù 檢慾	Restricting Desires
13	Yànchǐ 厭恥	Distaining Shame
14	Zànxuán 贊玄	Admiring the Mystery
15	Xiǎndé 顯德	Manifesting Inner Power
16	Guīgēn 歸根	Returning to the Root
17	Chúnfēng 淳風	Pure Influence
18	Súbó 俗薄	Mundane Approaches

Vocabulary

tǐdào 體道 (v./n.)	"embodying the Dao." Tǐ 體 is one of a number of Chinese characters related to "body" (cf. *shēn* 身; *xíng* 形). Technically refers to "physical structure." Said to be a "combination of twelve groups" or parts, including the scalp, face, chin, shoulders, spine, abdomen, upper arms, lower arms, hands, thighs, legs, and feet. Here used in the sense of "embody" (v.). From a Daoist perspective, one element of the Three Expressions (*sānxiàn* 三現), namely, cultivation (*xiū* 修), embodiment (*tǐ* 體), and transmission (*chuán* 傳). The character 體 does not appear in the LZ, but there are other "body/embodiment" characters
yǎng 養 (v.)	"nourish." In a technical sense, invokes Daoist Yǎngshēng 養生 (Nourishing Life), or health and longevity practice. The character appears in LZ 34 and 51. There also are various other "tending/nourishment" characters, with an assumed agricultural and/or animal husbandry analogy. For example, *xiū* 修 ("cultivate") appears in LZ 54, while *xù* 畜 ("tend") appears in LZ 10, 51, and 61
shēn 身 (n.)	"body|person|self." Probably a pictograph of the human physique/torso. Most frequently used to refer to one's entire psychosomatic process. In passages where *shēn* as "self" refers to the physical body, it is one's "lived body" viewed from within rather than "body as corpse" seen from without. The character appears throughout the LZ, with chs. 13 and 54 being especially important for present purposes
yuán 源 (n.)	"Source." Also appears as *yuán* 原 and related to *yuán* 元 ("origin/source") and *yuān* 淵 ("abyss"). Also translated as "headwaters" and "origin." Here another name for the Dao 道. Thus, overlaps with other, parallel designations, including Ancestor (*zōng* 宗), Mother (*mǔ* 母), and Root (*běn* 本/ *gēn* 根). That from which everything emerges and to which everything returns. The character does not appear in the LZ, but 淵 occurs in chs. 4, 8, and 36. There also are a wide variety of other "abyss" and "depth" characters

xū 虛 (n.)	"emptiness." Also used as an adjective ("empty") and verb ("empty"). One of the (non)qualities of the Dao and existence more generally. Cf. *kōng* 空 ("emptiness"; Skt.: *śūnyatā*) and *wú* 無 ("nonbeing/nothingness"). The character 虛 appears in LZ 3, 5, 16, 22, and 53; see also ch. 11
xiàng 象 (n.)	"appearance." Technically "elephant." Also translated as "emblem," "image," "representation," "shape," and "symbol." Used most technically to refer to the images of the hexagrams (six-line diagrams) of the *Yìjīng* 易經 (Classic of Change) as well as Daoist statuary and other devotional objects that serve as conduits for divine presences. The character 象 appears in LZ 4, 14, 21, 35, and 41
tāoguāng 韜光 (v./n.)	"hiding the radiance." Also connected to *cángguāng* 藏光 ("storing the radiance") and *shénmíng* 神明 ("divine illumination/luminosity"). The character 韜 does not appear in the LZ, but it is related to a variety of "hidden/storing" characters. 光 appears in LZ 4, 52, 56, and 58
wú 無 (n.)	"Nonbeing." Also translated as "nothingness." Lit., "without," and conventionally used as negation. In more Daoist technical usages, indicates "absent of/free from," including various "beyond/non-states." Cf. *kōng* 空 ("emptiness"; Skt.: *śūnyatā*) and *xū* 虛 ("emptiness"). The character 無 appears throughout the LZ. As related to the present sense, which more technically appears as *wúyǒu* 無有, see especially chs. 11, 14, 32, 37, 39, 40, 41, and 43
jiǎn 檢 (v.)	"restrict." May also mean "examine," "inspect," "measure," and "restrain." The character does not appear in the LZ, but connects to various other "decreasing" characters, including *guǎ* 寡 ("decrease"), *shǎo* 少 ("lessen"), and *sǔn* 損 ("decrease"). May also be connected to *jiǎn* 儉 ("frugality"), which is identified as one of the Three Treasures (*sānbǎo* 三寶) in LZ 67

xuán 玄 (n.)	"Mystery." Also used as an adjective ("mysterious"). Also translated as "dark/darkness." Here used as a Daoist (non) name for the Dao 道. Thus, overlaps with other, parallel designations, including Darkness (*mò* 默), Silence (*jì* 寂), Subtle (*wēi* 微), and Wondrous (*miào* 妙). Like "Dao," these are placeholders for that which transcends any and all names and conceptions. The character 玄 appears in LZ 1, 6, 10, 15, 51, 56, 65, with the *locus classicus* in the present sense being ch. 1
dé 德 (n.)	"inner power." Also appears as 惪. Also translated as "integrity," "potency," and "virtue." The way in which the Dao manifests in/as/through embodied human activity and being in the world, especially beneficial and transformative presence, behavior and influence. The character appears throughout the LZ, with chapters 38–81 conventionally referred to as the so-called *déjīng* 德經 ("inner power section")
guīgēn 歸根 (v./n.)	"returning to the root." Key Daoist contemplative practice often designating apophatic and quietistic (emptiness-/stillness-based) meditation. Here "Root" refers, first and foremost, to the Dao 道, and thus connects to other related characters, including Ancestor (*zōng* 宗), Mother (*mǔ* 母), and Source (*yuán* 元/原/源). "Root" also may be used in more technical Daoist practice contexts to designate the navel, perineum, phallus, or tongue. The phrase 歸根 appears in LZ 16, wherein it is defined as stillness (*jìng* 靜). Independently, 歸 appears in chs. 14, 20, 22, 28, 34, 52, and 60. It also relates to other "return" characters, including *fǎn* 反/返 ("revert") and *fù* 复/復 ("return"). 根 appears independently in chs. 6, 26, and 59. It is related to the cognate *běn* 本 ("root"), which appears in chs. 26 and 39

LESSON 26

GOVERNING THE COUNTRY, REGULATING THE SELF
FROM THE *LǍOZǏ ZHĀNGJÙ* 老子章句
(CHAPTER-AND-VERSE COMMENTARY ON THE *LAOZI*; DZ 682; LZ* 8; ZH 556)

WE HAVE ALREADY EXPLORED BASIC background information on the *Lǎozǐ zhāngjù* 老子章句 (Chapter-and-Verse Commentary on the *Laozi*; DZ 682; LZ* 8; ZH 556), more commonly referred to as the Héshàng gōng 河上公 (Elder Dwelling-by-the-River) (HSG) commentary, in Lesson #25. Here we move into the actual text, specifically the representative chapter fifty-nine. Titled "Shǒudào 守道" (Guarding the Dao), this is one of the most influential passages, revealing the HSG emphasis on microcosmic/macrocosmic correspondences, including cultivational and interiorized interpretations of socio-political references. We also should note that, assuming the revisionist dating (2nd c. CE) is accurate, the Héshàng gōng commentary is roughly contemporaneous with the formative moments of the Tàiqīng 太清 (Great Clarity), Tiānshī 天師 (Celestial Masters), and Xuánxué 玄學 (Profound Learning; so-called "Neo-Daoism" [sic]) movements, thus revealing intra-Daoist diversity. Parallelling classical Daoist concerns and approaches (see Lessons #6–9), the *Lǎozǐ zhāngjù* emphasizes inner cultivation and spiritual realization, here with particular attention to Yǎngshēng 養生 (Nourishing Life; health and longevity techniques) and cosmological attunement. The text specifically focuses on the "inner power" (*dé* 德), one's connection with the Dao manifesting as embodied being-in-the-world, as rooted in the conservation of vital essence (*jīng* 精) and qi 氣.

In terms of grammar, the passage contains the following relevant characters: *wèi* 謂 ("means"), *yě* 也 (。), *yǐ* 以 ("by means of/in order to"), *yú* 於 ("at/by/in/on/through/to"), *zé* 則 ("then") and *zhě* (topicalization). On a deeper language level, *shǒu* 守 ("guarding") recalls the seminal *shǒuyī* 守一 ("guarding the One") as a classical Daoist technical term for apophatic and quietistic meditation (see Lessons #6 and #8). The chapter in turn opens directing aspiring adepts to follow the Way of Heaven (*tiāndào* 天道), that is, cosmological and seasonal attunement (see Lessons #9, #10, and #16). By far the most influential and pivotal line is the following: "The country is the body" (*guó shēn tóng yě* 國身同也). This further connects to understanding *zhìguó* 治國 ("governing the country") as *zhìshēn* 治身 ("regulating the self") (see LZ 3, 10, 11, 16, 26, 28, 29, 35, 36, 41, 43, 44, 46, 51, 60, 64, 65, and 74). The latter may also mean "healing the body," thus revealing the multidimensional meanings of *zhì* and its potentially varied Daoist applications. With these apparently simple glosses, the "River-Elder commentary" reframes the entire *Dàodé jīng*, including its supposed socio-political elements, as about self-cultivation. One is encouraged to see self-as-world, and perhaps world-as-self. While often viewed by conventional scholars as a "departure" from the "original meaning" of the source-text, it is possible that the present Daoist commentary actually continues the views of the inner cultivation lineages of classical Daoism documented in the *Dàodé jīng* itself. Under this reading, the latter's references to *bīng* 兵 ("army/troops"), *guó* 國 ("country"), *jūn* 君 ("ruler"), *mín* 民 ("the people"), *tiānxià* 天下 (lit., "under-sky"; "world"), *wáng* 王 ("king"), and the like direct one to various dimensions of Daoist praxis. If, following the HSG commentary, the country is the body and the world is the self, each and every "political" and "military" reference provides insights into one's own training, one's own lived, embodied experience (see Komjathy forthcoming). Along these lines and interestingly, in the present chapter, the *Lǎozǐ zhāngjù* directs our attention to the "Five Spirits" (*wǔshén* 五神), which are sometimes synonymous with the "Five Qi" (*wǔqì* 五氣). Utilizing traditional Chinese Five Phase (*wǔxíng* 五行) cosmology, these are the energetic presences and spiritual faculties associated with the five yin-organs (*zàng* 藏/臟): Wood/liver/ethereal soul (*hún* 魂), Fire/heart/spirit (*shén* 神), Earth/spleen/thought (*yì* 意), Metal/lungs/corporeal soul (*pò* 魄), and Water/kidneys/will (*zhì* 志) (see Lessons #6 and #8). Although here focusing on Yǎngshēng practice (see Lessons #14 and #15), this also connects to related, contemporaneous Daoist visualization (*cúnxiǎng* 存想) methods (see Lesson #12), specifically centering on the yin-organs as orbs or body-gods of corresponding colors (green, red, yellow, white, and black [purple]), and later inner alchemical (*nèidān*) techniques (see Lessons #19–21), specifically the "Wǔqì cháoyuán 五氣朝元" (Five Qi Attending to the Origin).

Again, basic guidance on studies and translations of the *Lǎozǐ zhāngjù* may be found in Lesson #25. Note that this lesson and the following two use a distinctive format in which the primary text appears in standard font size, while the commentary appears using smaller font size. The English also uses italics for the primary text. See also Komjathy 2013a.

Primary Text

守道第五十九

治人，
謂人君治理人民。

事天，
事，用也。當用天道，順四時。

莫若嗇。
嗇，愛惜也。治國者當愛民財，不為奢泰。身者當愛精氣，不為放逸。

夫為嗇，是謂早服。
早，先也。服，得也。夫獨愛民財，愛精氣，則能先得天道也。

早服謂之重積德。
先得天道，是謂重積德於己也。

重積德則無不剋，
剋，勝也。重積德於己，則無不勝。

– 59 –
Guarding the Dao

In governing people
This means that the ruler wants to govern the people.

and serving the heavens,
"To serve" (shì 事) means "to apply" (yòng 用). You must apply the Way of Heaven and accord with the four seasons.

Nothing is better than frugality.
"To be frugal" (sè 嗇) means "to cherish" (àixī 愛惜). For governing the country, you must cherish the prosperity of people. Do not be extravagant. For regulating the self, you must cherish vital essence and qi. Do not allow them to become dissipated.

Abiding solely in frugality is called early submission.
"Early" (zǎo 早) means "first" (xiān 先). "To submit" (fú 服) means "to realize" (dé 得). Now, by solely cherishing the prosperity of the people, which is cherishing vital essence and qi, one can first realize the Way of Heaven.

To submit early is called fully gathered inner power.
To first realize the Way of Heaven means to fortify and amass inner power within oneself.

When inner power is fully gathered, there is nothing that is not overcome.
"To overcome" (kè 剋) means "to bear" (shèng 勝). When inner power is amassed within oneself, anything may be overcome.

無不剋則莫知其極,
無不剋勝,則莫知有知己德之窮極也。

莫知其極可以有國。
莫知己德者有極,則可以有社稷,為民致福。

有國之母,可以長久。
國身同也。母,道也。人能保身中之道,使精氣不勞,五神不苦,則可以長久。

是謂深根固蒂,
人能以氣為根,以精為蒂,如樹根不深則拔,蒂不堅則落。言當深藏其氣,固守其精,使無漏泄。

長生久視之道。
深根固蒂者,乃長生久視之道。

When there is nothing that is not overcome, one's boundaries are beyond knowing.
When everything is overcome, one realizes that there is no limit to inner power.

When boundaries are beyond knowing, one may possess the country.
When inner power is limitless, one may possess the earth-shrines and ensure that the people are blessed and prosperous.

When one possesses the mother of the country, one can become long-lasting.
The country is the body. The mother is the Dao. When we protect the Dao within the body, vital essence and qi remain unlabored and the Five Spirits are free from vexation. Then one attains longevity.

This is called being "deeply rooted and firmly stalked."
Humans should regard qi as the root and vital essence as the stalk. When a tree's roots are not deep, it may be uprooted. When a plant's stalks are not strong, it may fall. This means that we should keep qi stored deeply and guard vital essence firmly. Do not let them become dissipated!

It is the way of longevity and enduring vision.
"Deep roots" and "firm stalks" are thus the way of longevity and enduring vision.

Vocabulary

shǒudào 守道 (v./n.)	"guarding the Dao." *Shǒu* 守 ("guard") is a Daoist technical term for meditation, as in the phrase *shǒuyī* 守一 ("guarding the One"). *Shǒudào* refers to both formal meditation and an all-encompassing Daoist existential approach
jūn 君 (n.)	"ruler." More literally, "lord." In the HSG commentary, frequently refers to the heart-mind (*xīn* 心)
tiāndào 天道 (n./n.)	"Way of Heaven." Both the universe as transformative process (*zàohuà* 造化) based on yin-yang differentiation and interaction as well as associated human cosmological attunement. Here associated with seasonal awareness. See also LZ 9, 47, 73, 77, 79, and 81; ZZ 12–14; and SW 2
sè 嗇 (n.)	"frugality." May also mean "cherish" and "conserve." The meaning is straightforward, but connects with *jiǎn* 儉 ("frugality") in LZ 67, which identifies it as one of the "Three Treasures" (*sānbǎo* 三寶)
zhìshēn 治身 (v./n.)	"regulate the self." May also mean "heal the body." *Shēn* 身 ("body|person|self"), probably a pictograph of the human physique/torso, most frequently refers to one's entire psychosomatic process. In passages where *shēn* as "self" refers to the physical body, it is one's "lived body" seen from within rather than "body as corpse" seen from without. Here one's body/self is identified as "the country" (*guó* 國) and its various constituents as "the people" (*mín* 民)
dú 獨 (adj.|n.)	"alone|aloneness." May also mean "solitary|solitude" and "independent|independence." Sometimes used in a Daoist technical sense designating solitary meditation and the associated contemplative state(s)
shèjì 社稷 (n./n.)	"earth-shrine." More literally, "[gods of] soil and grain [harvest]." Here suggesting regional demarcation of land, with the associated geo-political and ritual administration

mǔ 母 (n.)	"mother." Here another name for the Dao 道, so technically should appear as the upper-case "Mother." Only loosely gendered. Thus, overlaps with other, parallel designations, including Ancestor (*zōng* 宗), Root (*běn* 本/*gēn* 根), and Source (*yuán* 元/原/源). That from which everything emerges and to which everything returns. That which births and nourishes all beings without distinction
wǔshén 五神 (num./n.)	"Five Spirits." The energetic presences and spiritual faculties associated with the Five Phases/five yin-organs: Wood/liver/ethereal soul (*hún* 魂), Fire/heart/spirit (*shén* 神), Earth/spleen/thought (*yì* 意), Metal/lungs/corporeal soul (*pò* 魄), and Water/kidneys/will (*zhì* 志)
chángjiǔ 長久 (adj./n.)	"long-lasting/longevity." Basically synonymous with *chángshēng* 長生 (lit., "perpetual life"). In the context of the HSG's emphasis on Yǎngshēng 養生 (Nourishing Life), extended health and longevity
lòuxiè 漏泄 (v./v.)	"dissipate." Literally, "leak and leak." Double leakage. Often associated with vital essence (*jīng* 精). Both characters contain the *shuǐ* 水/氵 ("water") radical. One ideal in Daoism is attaining the state of "non-dissipation" (*wúlòu* 無漏; Skt.: *anāsrava*)
jiǔshì 久視 (adj./n. or adv./v.)	"enduring vision." An obscure phrase in the LZ. As it appears in concert with *chángshēng* 長生 (lit., "perpetual life"), suggests longevity. However, given the primary text's emphasis on (not)attaining a transpersonal contemplative and mystical (non)state of abiding in the Dao, perhaps some other alteration of perception and consciousness as well as a transformed mode of being/experiencing. May then be connected to "mysterious perception" (*xuánlǎn* 玄覽) and mysterious inner power (*xuándé* 玄德)

LESSON 27

PRECEPT STUDY & APPLICATION
FROM THE *LǍOZǏ XIǍNG'ĚR ZHÙ* 老子想爾注
(COMMENTARY THINKING THROUGH THE *LAOZI*;
DH 55; LZ* 9; S.6825; TK 56; ZH 557)

THE *LǍOZǏ XIǍNG'ĚR ZHÙ* 老子想爾注 (Commentary Thinking through the *Laozi*; DH 55; LZ* 9; S.6825; TK 56; ZH 557; abbrev. XE)[55] is another early Daoist commentary on the *Lǎozǐ* 老子 (Book of Venerable Masters). It has been dated by some to the second century CE and by others to the fifth century. Accepting an earlier date of composition, the text is associated with the early Tiānshī 天師 (Celestial Masters) movement and is attributed to Zhāng Lǔ 張魯 (d. 216 CE), the paternal grandson of the founder Zhāng Líng 張陵 (a.k.a. Zhāng Dàolíng 張道陵; fl. 140s CE) and the third Celestial Master. As such, the present text is the fifth oldest of the six earliest extant commentaries on the *Dàodé jīng*. The title is best understood as "thinking through," with *ěr* 爾 being a grammatical cognate of *ěr* 耳 (而已) ("merely/just") and/or *rán* 然 ("so/in this manner"). Stephen Bokenkamp 柏夷, following Ōfuchi Ninji 大淵忍爾 (1912–2003), renders it as "Thinking of You," taking it as suggesting that the commentary may have been intended for geographically remote

---

[55] "DH," "S," and "TK" are abbreviations for the following: *Dūnhuáng dàozàng*; Stein manuscripts; and *Tonkō dōkei*, respectively. Observant readers will note that "TK" now replaces my earlier use of "DH" for the latter in my *Title Index to Daoist Collections* (2002). The *Dūnhuáng dàozàng* has been indexed with a standardized numbering system in my recent "Supplements to *Title Index to Daoist Collections*" (STIDC; 2022-) series. See general introduction and bibliography herein.

members of the Tiānshī religious community. The text was lost until the early twentieth century, when it was discovered among the cache of manuscripts, primarily Buddhist, in the archaeological site of Dūnhuáng 敦煌 in Gānsù province. The manuscript itself probably dates to around the fifth century, and only chapters 3–37 are extant. It was collected by the Hungarian-born British archaeologist Aurel Stein 史坦因 (1862–1943) and is currently housed in the Stein collection (abbrev. "S.") in the British Library (London). Like other, associated Daoist manuscripts, the text has been reproduced in the *Dūnhuáng dàozàng* 敦煌道藏 (Dunhuang Daoist Canon; dat. 1999; 138 texts; abbrev. DH) and *Tonkō dōkei* 敦煌道經 (Dunhuang Daoist Scriptures; dat. 1978–1979; 100 texts; abbrev. TK). It also was included in the *Zhōnghuá dàozàng* 中華道藏 (Chinese Daoist Canon; dat. 2003; 1,524 texts; abbrev. ZH). The commentary interprets the *Lǎozǐ* in terms of early Celestial Masters' concerns. It also is associated with the so-called "Xiǎng'ěr Precepts," a set of twenty-seven conduct guidelines. In the present selection, we explore chapter fifteen, which focuses on precept (*jiè* 戒) study and application. As the text does not mention specific precepts, it is difficult to know which ones Zhāng Lǔ intended, but it may have been the Nine Practices (see Lesson #4). Although beyond our present concerns, the XE redaction of the *Lǎozǐ* contains a variety of interesting character variants (see Komjathy forthcoming). Here I translate the source-text through the commentary.

On a grammatical level, the passage contains the following grammar characters: *fú* 夫 ("now then"), *gù* 故 ("thus"), *nǎi* 乃 ("then"), *xiāng* 相 ("together/with"), *yě* 也 (。), *yǐ* 以 ("by means of/in order to"), *yǔ* 與 ("with"), and *zhī* 之 ("of/it"). The Daoist technical terms are again explored in the chapter vocabulary. However, in terms of deepening our translation facility with respect to Daoist literature, it is interesting that Daoist precepts are here referred to as *dàojiè* 道誡 (lit., "precepts of the Dao"), which parallels Daoist uses of phrases like *dàojiào* 道教 (lit., "teachings of the Dao"; Daoism), *dàojīng* 道經 (lit., "scriptures of the Dao"; Daoist scriptures), and *dàoshù* 道術 (lit., "techniques of the

Dao"; Daoist techniques). That is, there are precepts, scriptures, teachings, techniques, and the like that are "not Daoist." Thus, while Dao first and foremost refers to the sacred and ultimate concern of Daoists, it also becomes used as a prefix meaning something like "Daoist," in the sense of associated with Daoists, Daoist communities, and the larger Daoist tradition. The same is obviously true of 道 as a Daoist cosmological and theological category (see general introduction). The *Lǎozǐ xiǎng'ěr zhù* in turn links precept study and application as the means to avoid "contravening the Dao" (*fàndào* 犯道). *Fàn* may also mean "attack," "encroach," "violate," and so forth. It further relates to other "divergent/obstructing/oppositional" patterns and states, including *nì* 逆 and *xié* 邪, which may be further associated with "chaos" (*luàn* 亂) and "confusion" (*huò* 惑), whether internal or external. Such conditions may be contrasted with the positive counterparts of *hé* 和 ("harmony"), *shùn* 順 ("accordance"), and *zhèng* 正 ("alignment").

There are a number of specialist Western-language studies of the early Tiānshī 天師 (Celestial Masters) movement (Kleeman 1998, 2016; Bokenkamp 1997; Raz 2012; Goossaert 2022). While important "micro-histories," these works, which utilize a truncated and Strickmannian view, overemphasize the significance of that movement and often advance deficient interpretations of the Daoist tradition as a whole. Bokenkamp's *Early Daoist Scriptures* (1997, 78–148) includes a complete, annotated scholarly translation of the *Lǎozǐ xiǎng'ěr zhù*.

Primary Text

十五

古之善為士者，微妙玄通。
玄，天也。古之仙士，能守信微妙，與天相通。

深不可識。
人行道奉誡，微氣歸之，為氣淵淵深也，故不可識也。

夫唯不可識，故強為之容。
唯，獨也。容，形狀也。獨行道，德備淵深。不知當名之云何，強名之善為士者，道美大之也 …

安以動之徐生。
人欲舉事，先孝之道誡。安思其義，不犯道，乃徐施之，生道不去。

– 15 –

In ancient times, those who excelled at being practitioners were subtle and wondrous, able to communicate with the Mysterious.
"Mysterious" (*xuán* 玄) refers to the heavens (*tiān* 天). Immortal practitioners of ancient times were able to maintain trust in the subtle and wonderous and were in communication with the heavens.

Their depths were unknowable.
When people practice the Dao and honor the precepts, subtle qi returns to them. These emanations enter the innermost depths [of their bodies] and are therefore unrecognizable.

Precisely because they are unknowable, we are compelled to fashion an appearance for them.
"Precisely" (*wéi* 唯) means "solely" (*dú* 獨). "Appearance" (*róng* 容) means "form" (*xíngzhuàng* 形狀). Only through practicing the Dao is this store of inner power deeply implanted [in them]. Since we do not know what to call such people, we are compelled to call them "excelling practitioners." It is the Dao that beautifies and ennobles them…

When you use serenity to move, [your actions] will gradually produce life.
Whenever human beings wish to undertake some action, they should first gauge it against the precepts of the Dao, considering it calmly to determine that the principles of their action do not contravene the Dao. Only then should they gradually pursue it, so that the way of life does not depart from them.

Vocabulary

shàn 善 (adj.|v.|n.)	"excelling|excel|excellent." More literally means "good/goodness," "be good at," and "skilled." Also used in a technical Daoist sense of "adept|aptitude"
shì 士 (n.)	"practitioner." Also translated as "adept." More conventionally means "knight" and "scholar-official." Originally the lowest aristocratic rung of the Chinese feudal order, amounting to something like "retainer." Used in classical Daoism and the larger tradition to refer to Daoist adherents and practitioners. More technically appears as *dàoshi* 道士 (lit., "adept of the Dao"), which contextually refers to ordained Daoist priests
miào 妙 (adj.|n.)	"wondrous|wonder." Also translated as "subtle|subtlety." One of the (non)descriptors of the Dao 道. Often used synonymously in the sense of the Wondrous. The *locus classicus* is LZ 1
xuán 玄 (adj.|n.)	"mysterious|mystery." Also translated as "dark|darkness." One of the (non)descriptors of the Dao 道. Often used synonymously in the sense of the Mystery/Mysterious. The *locus classicus* is LZ 1
tōng 通 (v.|n.)	"connect|connection." May also mean "through/throughness" and "pervade|pervasion." Contains the *chuò* 辵/辶 ("walk/move") radical
xiān 仙 (n.)	"immortal." Also translated as "ascendent" and "transcendent." Usually appears as *xiānrén* 仙人 or related terms. Technically human beings (*rén* 人/亻) living in the mountains (*shān* 山). Also appears as 僊, which points towards flight (*qiān* 䙴). One of the ideals of later Daoism, usually associated with alchemical transmutation and personal post-mortem survival/existence
xíng 行 (v.)	"practice." More literally means "walk/move/travel." Also later used in the Buddhist-influenced sense of "good deeds"

jiè 誡 (n.)	"precept." Also appears as 戒. Also translated as "admonishment." The most general Daoist term for rules and regulations. The standard character contains the *gē* 戈 ("halberd") radical, while the present one adds *yán* 言 ("speech"). Conduct principles and guidelines. Here may refer to the "Nine Practices" (*jiǔxíng* 九行) and possibly to the associated and derivative "Twenty-seven Xiǎng'ěr Precepts"
yuān 淵 (adj.|n.)	"deep|abyss." Often used synonymously with *yuán* 元 ("origin") and *yuán* 原/源 ("source"). Contains the *shuǐ* 水/氵 ("water") radical. Often designates the Dao-as-Abyss and the associated Daoist contemplative/mystical state(s). See, e.g., ZZ 7
dú 獨 (adj.|n.)	"alone|aloneness." Here translated as "solely." May also mean "solitary|solitude" and "independent|independence." Sometimes used in a Daoist technical sense designating solitary meditation and the associated contemplative state(s)
ān 安 (adj.|n.)	"serene|serenity." Also translated as "calm/calmness" and "peaceful/peace." Related to a larger repertoire of Daoist characters related to serenity, including *jì* 寂 ("silence"), *jìng* 靜 ("stillness"), *níng* 寧 ("tranquility"), *tián* 恬 ("quiescence"), and so forth
fàndào 犯道 (v./n.)	"contravene the Dao." *Fàn* may also mean "attack," "encroach," "violate," etc. It contains the *quǎn* 犬/犭 ("dog") radical. Further relates to other "divergent/obstructing/oppositional" patterns and states, including *nì* 逆 and *xié* 邪. This may be contrasted with the positive counterparts of *hé* 和 ("harmonized"), *shùn* 順 ("accordance"), and *zhèng* 正 ("alignment")
shēng 生 (n.)	"life." May also mean "be born," "birth," "generate," "produce," and so forth. Usually used in the sense of personal aliveness and vitality. Occurs in such important phrases as Yǎngshēng 養生 ("Nourishing Life") and *chángshēng* 長生 ("perpetual life"; longevity). May also be thought of along ecological lines as life as a whole, both individual and collective. Here suggests enlivening presence

Lesson 28

Reflections from Dragon Gate
From the *Dàodé jīng huìyì* 道德經會義
(Assembled Meaning of the Scripture on the Dao and Inner Power; LZ* 163)

This final selection reveals the enduring relevance of and engagement with the *Dàodé jīng* in the later Daoist tradition, including cultivational continuities with earlier Daoist concerns and interpretive tendencies. Dating to 1803, the *Dàodé jīng huìyì* 道德經會義 (Assembled Meaning of the Scripture on the Dao and Inner Power; LZ* 163) is a late imperial commentary composed by Liú Yīmíng 劉一明 (Wùyuán 悟元 [Awakening-to-the-Origin]; 1734–1821), an influential eleventh-generation Lóngmén 龍門 (Dragon Gate) monk (see Lessons #16, #21, and #24). This precision of authorship and date of composition contrasts with most of the other works that we have examined. The commentary also stands in contrast to the previous ones. Rather than providing line-by-line exegesis, the *Dàodé jīng huìyì* cites each DDJ chapter in full, followed by a quasi-paraphrase paragraph. Liú is, in turn, most well-known for his *Dàoshū shíèr zhǒng* 道書十二種 (Twelve Daoist Texts; ZW 254–271), the original edition (dat. 1801) of which includes said number of texts, while the later, received edition (dat. 1819) adds seven more titles, for a total of nineteen individual works. This key late imperial collection includes both commentaries on earlier Daoist texts as well as original compositions. Somewhat surprisingly, the *Dàodé jīng huìyì*, and its more concise version titled *Dàodé jīng yàoyì* 道德經要義 (Essential Meaning of the Scripture on the Dao and Inner Power; LZ* 164; dat. 1803), is not included and remains largely unknown outside of Lóngmén circles. It is, however, contained in the more recent "extra-canonical" and "supplemental" Daoist textual collection titled *Lǎozǐ jíchéng* 老子集成 (Collection on the *Laozi*; dat. 2011; 267 titles; abbrev. LZ*), which has been indexed in Louis Komjathy's 康思奇 recent "Supplements to *Title Index to Daoist Collections*" (STIDC; 2022–) series.

Formalistically speaking, the present complete translation of chapter six of the *Dàodé jīng huìyì* takes us full circle, and back to the classical Chinese grammatical construction using *zé* 則 (see Lesson #5; also Lesson #10). I chose this particular chapter because it has been an ongoing source of fascination and perplexity for commentators and interpreters, with diverse explanations and applications of the associated technical terms. Liú Yīmíng follows earlier Daoist *nèidān* commentators in taking the Mysterious Female (*xuánpìn* 玄牝)/Valley Spirit (*gǔshén* 谷神) as referring to the mystical space, sometimes referred to as the Square Inch (*fāngcùn* 方寸) (see Lesson #12), in the heart, but also interpreted as the numinous presence contained in a mystical cranial location. Although Liú does not explicitly mention it, his base-edition has Original Female (*yuánpìn* 元牝), rather than the standard Mysterious Female. In addition to the obvious engagement with a key classical Daoist text, the *Dàodé jīng huìyì* evidences some influence from the Táng-dynasty Clarity-and-Stillness Literature (see Lesson #17), including the accompanying emphasis on "emptiness" (*xū* 虛) via the Mahāyāna (Greater Vehicle) Buddhist concept of *śūnyatā* (absence of own-being) from the Perfection of Wisdom (*prajñā-pāramitā*) sutras. Interestingly, Liú Yīmíng emphasizes the importance of finding an authentic teacher to provide deeper guidance, a theme that overlaps with the texts in Lessons #7, #8, #10, #13, #18, #20, #23, and #24. On a deeper language level, I again document the technical terminology in the accompanying vocabulary. However, it is noteworthy that the commentary incorporates additional allusions to chapters one and twenty-one of the *Dàodé jīng* (see Lesson #7). The latter reads as follows:

> 孔德之容，
> 唯道是從。
> 道之為物，
> 唯恍唯惚。
> 惚兮恍兮，
> 其中有象。
> 恍兮惚兮，
> 其中有物。
> 窈兮冥兮，
> 其中有精。
> 其精甚真，
> 其中有信。
> 自古及今，
> 其名不去。
> 以閱眾甫。
> 吾何以知眾甫之狀哉？以此。

> The quality of broad inner power
> Is that only the Dao is followed.
> The Dao considered as a thing—
> It is only vague and indistinct.
> Indistinct! Vague!
> Its center contains appearances (*xiàng* 象).
> Vague! Indistinct!
> Its center contains beings (*wù* 物).
> Deep! Dark!
> Its center contains essences (*jīng* 精).
> Vital essence is fundamentally real;
> The Center contains something trustworthy.
> From ancient times to the present,
> Its name has not been abandoned.

Through it, we may observe all beginnings.
How can I know the shape (zhuàng 狀) of every beginning?
Through this.

The *Dàodé jīng huìyì* also allows us to draw upon and apply our earlier explorations of Daoist proto-*nèidān* and *nèidān* proper (see Lessons #12 and #19–21). Finally, Liú's commentary includes two related illustrations (cf. DZ 263, 9.3a), which add support for my translation and offer yet another installment of Daoist aesthetics and material culture (see Lessons #5, #13, #14, #18, #19, and #22). This is sometimes referred to as "Daoist culture" (*dàojiào wénhuà* 道教文化). Here we might once again recall all of the nameless artisans, bibliophiles, calligraphers, scholars, scribes, students, teachers, and so forth who enabled the texts explored in this primer to be preserved and transmitted throughout history. These are the classical Chinese texts, now in bilingual form, held in your hands in this particular time-place.

Again, for reliable Western-language discussions of the Lóngmén lineage, see Esposito 2013, 2014 and Komjathy 2013a. Liú Yīmíng's writings are most well-known in the West through various popular translations by Thomas Cleary (1949–2021), which again must be used with caution. Nonetheless, Cleary did translate Liú Yīmíng's commentaries on the *Huángdì yīnfú jīng* (Cleary 1991, 220–38) (see Lesson #16), on the *Jīndān sìbǎizì* (Cleary 1986) and *Wùzhēn piān* (Cleary 1987) (see Lesson #21), and on the *Yìjīng* (Cleary 1986) (see Lessons #11 and #20), any or all of which may be profitably compared to the *Dàodé jīng huìyì*. Liú Yīmíng's *Dàoshū shíèr zhǒng* has also been indexed in Louis Komjathy's 康思奇 "Catalogue of Daoist Collectanea, Compendia, and Encyclopedias" (2022).

Primary Text

六

谷神不死，
是謂元牝。
元牝之門，
是謂天地根。
綿綿若存，
用之不勤。

上章言多言不如守中。中即虛也。虛則靈，靈則神。試觀山中。兩山壁列，其中一谷。人呼則應。謂無則有聲，謂有則無形。不有不無，以其至虛至靈。故謂谷神。人能虛中，其中有神。亦猶是也。故以谷神喻之。是谷神也，真空而藏妙有，妙有而含真空。寂然不動，感而遂通。動之靜之，動靜相需，互為其根。是謂谷神不死。不死者、因能動靜而不死，因其不死而有動靜。是謂陽元陰牝出入之門。谷神既為陰陽出入之門，則谷神即能生天地。故又謂天地根。谷即是門，亦即是母，即是徼。神即是根，亦即是始，即是妙。天地即元牝，亦即陰陽。人能抱此一谷，養此一神，不即不離，綿綿用功，勿忘勿助，則恍惚有物，窈冥有精。谷神若常存而不死矣。谷神常存，則母徼元牝之門，開闔隨時，始妙天地之根，動靜自然。信步早去，頭頭是道。順手採來，俱是命寶。左之右之，無不宜之。用之何待勤勞而勉強呼？旦谷神最難識認。須求真師點破，方能知之。若不遇真師，妄猜私議，而欲谷神不死難矣。後附二圖以備參考。

– 6 –

The Valley Spirit does not die;
It is called the Original Female.
The gateway to the Original Female
Is called the root of heaven and earth.
Continuous and uninterrupted, it seems to exist.
Applying this does not require effort.

The various words of this chapter are not equal to guarding the Center. The Center is emptiness. Emptiness leads to numinosity; numinosity leads to divinity. Observe the center of the mountain. In the center of the partition between the paired peaks, there is a single valley. When people exhale, it responds. Considered as absence, there is sound; considered as presence, there is formlessness. Without either Being or Nonbeing, there is utmost emptiness and utmost numinosity. This is referred to as the "Valley Spirit."

If people can empty the Center, the center will contain spirit. It is indeed like this. Thus, the Valley Spirit is a metaphor. The Valley Spirit, in perfect emptiness, stores subtle presence; in subtle presence, it contains perfect emptiness. Silently unmoving, it responds and becomes pervaded. Moving it and stilling it, movement and stillness are both necessary. This mutuality becomes the root, which is referred to as the "Valley Spirit not dying." Not dying involves being able to move or rest while remaining undying. According with this undying in movement and stillness is called the gateway for the exit and entrance of the yang-prime and yin-female.

The Valley Spirit then becomes the gateway of the exit and entrance of yin-yang. Then the Valley Spirit can produce the heavens and earth. Thus, it also is referred to as the "root of heaven and earth." The valley is the gateway. It also is the Mother and the boundaries. Spirit is the root. It also is the Beginning and the Wondrous. Heaven and earth are the Origin and the Female, which also are yang and yin. If people can embrace the singular valley and nourish unified spirit, without haste or separation, continuously applying effort, without forgetting or assistance, then there will be being in indistinctness and essence in obscurity. The Valley Spirit will be constantly preserved and remain undying.

If the Valley Spirit is constantly preserved, then the gateway of the Mother and boundaries and of the Origin and Female will open and close according to the times. The root of the Beginning and the Wondrous and of heaven and earth move and rest naturally. Progress leisurely, with the Dao as the lead; make your way effortlessly, accompanied by the treasure of life-destiny. Holding it on both sides, there is nothing that is not suitable. Employing it, what need is there for diligence or force? However, the Valley Spirit is extremely difficult to recognize. You must find an authentic teacher to reveal the subtle points, and then you will know it. If you do not meet an authentic teacher, [relying on] your own mistaken assumptions and personal opinions, longing for the Valley Spirit that does not die will be difficult.

I am attaching the following two illustrations for consultation.[56]

---

[56] I leave the illustrations untranslated as a culminating translation exercise for readers.

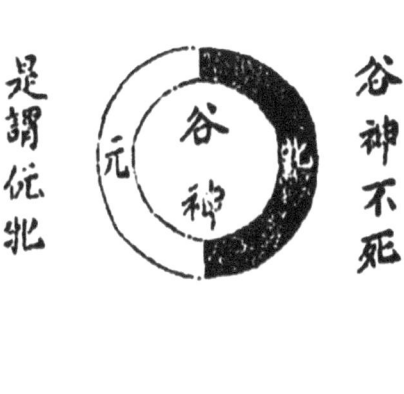

FIGURE 25: Illustrations of the Valley Spirit and Original Female

Vocabulary

shǒuzhōng 守中 (v./n.)	"guarding the Center." Classical Daoist technical term for apophatic and quietistic meditation. First appears in LZ 5. "Center" is often used as a name for the Dao, but also may refer to the heart-mind (*xīn* 心) or the navel (*fù* 腹) region. Here refers to the center of the head, the Ancestral Cavity (*zǔqiào* 祖竅), as the storehouse of original spirit (*yuánshén* 元神)
xū 虛 (adj./v./n.)	"empty|empty|emptiness." Often synonymous with *wú* 無 ("nonbeing/nothing") and *kōng* 空 ("emptiness"), but the latter also is used to translate the Buddhist Sanskrit *śūnyatā* ("empty of own-being"). Here *xū* includes the latter technical connotation
líng 靈 (adj./n./n.)	"numinous|numinosity|numen." Sacred presence and connection. Sometimes used synonymously with *shén* 神 ("spirit"), but also may have a more technical sense
shén 神 (n.)	"divinity." Later translated as "spirit" herein. May refer to actual deities, spiritual capacities, and consciousness in a more abstract sense. The most subtle of the vital (non)substances. Associated with the Fire phase, housed in the heart (*xīn* 心), and connected to innate nature (*xìng* 性). The third or highest of the internal Three Treasures (*sānbǎo* 三寶)
guān 觀 (v./n.)	"observe|observation." Daoist contemplative approach and practice. Also used to translate the Buddhist Pali *vipassanā* and Sanskrit *vipaśyanā* (insight meditation). As such, usually appears as *nèiguān* 內觀 ("inner observation")
liǎngshān 兩山	"paired peaks." Here most likely referring to the breasts, directing one's observation to the center-point and the heart by extension. May also refer to the eyebrows and thus to the "third-eye" by extension
wú 無 (n.)	"Nonbeing." Also translated as "nothingness." Lit., "without," and conventionally used as negation. In more Daoist technical usages, indicates "absent of/free from," including various "beyond/non-states"

yǒu 有 (n.)	"Being." Also translated as "somethingness." May also mean "have," "possess," etc.
wúxíng 無形 (neg./n.)	"formlessness." Lit., "without form." The Dao as fundamentally and essentially beyond materiality and substance. Subtle
tōng 通 (v.|n.)	"pervade|pervasion." May also mean "connect/connection" and "through/throughness." Contains the *chuò* 辵/辶 ("walk/ move") radical
dòngjìng 動靜 (n./n.)	"movement and stillness." Also "activity and rest." Two fundamental qualities of heaven/yang and earth/yin, respectively. Also used in a contemplative sense as "agitation and stillness," which further relate to "clarity and turbidity" (*qīngzhuó* 清濁)
yángyuán 陽元 (adj./ n.)	"yang-prime." Here used to designate primordial yang (*yuányáng* 元陽), associated with heaven/head/spirit
yīnpìn 陰牝 (adj./n.)	"yin-female." Invokes the opening "Mysterious Female" (*xuánpìn* 玄牝). Here used to designate primordial yin (*yuányīn* 元陰), associated with earth/navel/qi
mǔ 母 (n.)	"Mother." Another name for the Dao, especially as an only loosely-gendered concept. The Source that births and nourishes all beings without distinction. Here an allusion to LZ 1
jiǎo 徼 (n.)	"boundaries." Here an allusion to LZ 1, wherein it designates the physical manifestations and spatio-temporal limits of the Dao. In the present context, related to phenomenal appearances (*fǎ* 法)
yuánpìn 元牝 (n./n.)	"Origin and Female." Here used as distinct, but related concepts designating heaven and earth, respectively. This is a common technical *nèidān* reading. However, read more straightforwardly, "Original Female"
bào 抱 (v.)	"embrace." As related to the *Dàodé jīng*, invokes *bàoyī* 抱一 ("embracing the One") (chs. 10 and 22), which is a classical Daoist technical term for apophatic and quietistic meditation

yònggōng 用功 (v./n.)	"apply effort." *Gōng* 功 may also mean "accomplishment," "exercises," "merit," "result," etc.
shǐ 始 (n.)	"Beginning." Another name for the Dao as Source. Again, here an allusion to LZ 1
miào 妙 (n.)	"Wondrous." Another name for the Dao as Mystery (*xuán* 玄). Again, here an allusion to LZ 1
mìng 命 (n.)	"life-destiny." Also translated as "fate." Here appears to designate one's entire psychosomatic being, including vital essence (*jīng* 精), qi 氣, and spirit (*shén* 神). Also related to a sense of meaning and purpose. Lifeway
zhēnshī 真師/真師 (adj./n.)	"authentic teacher." The meaning is obvious, but read contextually refers to a formal master-disciple relationship, specifically a lineage-based (*pài* 派) "master-father" (*shīfu* 師父). This usually includes spiritual direction (*zhǐshén* 指神) and oral instruction (*kǒujué* 口訣)

Appendices

Appendix 1

Chinese Character Radicals

This appendix consists of the standard Chinese Kāngxī 康熙 character radicals (bùshǒu 部首; lit., "section headers"), with the name derived from Kāngxī zìdiǎn 康熙字典 (Kangxi Dictionary; dat. 1716) and alluding to the Kāngxī reign period (1661–1722) of the Kāngxī Emperor (r. 1661–1722), the third emperor of the Qīng dynasty (1644–1912). Also known as the Zìhuì 字彙 (Character Collection) radicals, after its namesake Chinese dictionary (dat. 1615), this system consists of 214 character radicals organized according to radical-and-stroke sorting method (see, e.g., Wilkinson 2018; also Yong and Peng 2008).

```
1    一丨丶丿乙亅
2    二亠人儿入八冂冖冫几凵刀力勹匕匚匸十卜卩厂厶又
3    口囗土士夂夊夕大女子宀寸小尢尸屮山巛工己巾干幺广廴廾弋弓彐彡彳
4    心戈戶手支攴文斗斤方无日曰月木欠止歹殳毋比毛氏气水火爪父爻爿片牙牛犬
5    玄玉瓜瓦甘生用田疋疒癶白皮皿目矛矢石示禸禾穴立
6    竹米糸缶网羊羽老而耒耳聿肉臣自至臼舌舛舟艮色艸虍虫血行衣襾
7    見角言谷豆豕豸貝赤走足身車辛辰辵邑酉釆里
8    金長門阜隶隹雨青非
9    面革韋韭音頁風飛食首香
10...  馬骨高髟鬥鬯鬲鬼  魚鳥鹵鹿麥麻  黃黍黑黹  黽鼎鼓鼠  鼻齊  齒  龍龜  龠
```

FIGURE 26: List of the 214 Kāngxī 康熙 Character Radicals

This system replaced earlier ones like that contained in the Shuōwén jiězì 說文解字 (Discussing Writing and Explaining Characters; dat. 100/121 CE), which consists of 540 radicals (bù 部; lit., "categories"). I recommend that individuals begin memorizing some commonly occurring radicals, including number of strokes. Recall that this is based on calligraphy. Consider the following as a starting point: 一 (1 stroke; radical 1), 人 (2 strokes; radical 9), 口 (3 strokes; radical 30), 土 (3 strokes; radical 32), 彳 (3 strokes; radical 60), 心 (4 strokes; radical 61), 手 (4 strokes; radical 64), 日 (4 strokes; radical 72), 木 (4 strokes; radical 75), 水 (4 strokes; radical 85), 火 (4 strokes; radical 86), 目 (5 strokes; radical 109), 示 (5 strokes; radical 113), 糸 (6 strokes; radical 120), 艸 (6 strokes; radical 140), 言 (7 strokes; radical 149), 辵 (7 strokes; radical 162), 金 (8 strokes; radical 167), 門 (8 strokes; radical 169), and 馬 (10 strokes; radical 187). This will expedite the consultation of traditional Chinese dictionaries, including by facilitating some general orientation points with respect to other radicals with parallel stroke counts.

Appendix 1: Chinese Character Radicals

No.	Radical	Variants	Simplified Radical	Pinyin	English Name	Stroke Count
1	一			yī	one	1
2	丨			gǔn	line	1
3	丶			zhǔ	dot	1
4	丿	fú ㇏/yí ㇏		piě	slash	1
5	乙	乚/乁		yì	second	1
6	亅			jué	hook	1
7	二			èr	two	2
8	亠			tóu	lid	2
9	人	亻		rén	person	2
10	儿			ér	legs	2
11	入			rù	enter	2
12	八	丷		bā	eight	2
13	冂			jiǒng	down box	2
14	冖			mì	over	2
15	冫			bīng	ice	2
16	几			jī	table	2
17	凵			qiǎn	open box	2
18	刀	刂		dāo	knife	2
19	力			lì	power	2
20	勹			bāo	wrap	2
21	匕			bǐ	spoon	2
22	匚			fāng	right open box	2
23	匸			xǐ	hiding enclosure	2
24	十			shí	ten	2
25	卜			bǔ	divine	2
26	卩			jié	seal	2
27	厂			hǎn (chǎng)	cliff	2
28	厶			sī	private	2
29	又			yòu	again	2
30	口			kǒu	mouth	3
31	囗			wéi	enclosure	3
32	土			tǔ	earth	3
33	士			shì	scholar	3
34	夂			zhǐ (top)	go	3
35	夊			suī (bottom)	go slowly	3
36	夕			xī	evening	3

No.	Radical	Variants	Simplified Radical	Pinyin	English Name	Stroke Count
37	大			dà	big	3
38	女			nǚ	woman	3
39	子			zǐ	child	3
40	宀			mián	roof	3
41	寸			cùn	inch	3
42	小			xiǎo	small	3
43	尢	兀		wāng	lame	3
44	尸			shī	corpse	3
45	屮			chè	sprout	3
46	山			shān	mountain	3
47	川	巛/guì巜		chuān	river	3
48	工			gōng	work	3
49	己			jǐ	oneself	3
50	巾			jīn	kerchief	3
51	干			gān	dry	3
52	幺			yāo	short thread	3
53	广			guǎn	dotted cliff	3
54	廴			yǐn	long stride	3
55	廾			gǒng	two hands	3
56	弋			yì	shoot	3
57	弓			gōng	bow	3
58	彐	彑		jì	snout	3
59	彡			shān	bristle	3
60	彳			chì	step	3
61	心	忄		xīn	heart	4
62	戈			gē	halberd	4
63	戶			hù	door	4
64	手	扌		shǒu	hand	4
65	支			zhī	branch	4
66	攴	攵		pū	rap	4
67	文			wén	script	4
68	斗			dǒu	dipper	4
69	斤			jīn	axe	4
70	方			fāng	square	4
71	无			wú	not	4
72	日			rì	sun	4

Appendix 1: Chinese Character Radicals

No.	Radical	Variants	Simplified Radical	Pinyin	English Name	Stroke Count
73	曰			yuē	say	4
74	月			yuè	moon	4
75	木			mù	tree	4
76	欠			qiàn	lack	4
77	止			zhǐ	stop	4
78	歹			dǎi	death	4
79	殳			shū	weapon	4
80	毋			wú	do not	4
81	比			bǐ	compare	4
82	毛			máo	fur	4
83	氏			shì	clan	4
84	气			qì	steam	4
85	水	氵		shuǐ	water	4
86	火	灬		huǒ	fire	4
87	爪	爫		zhǎo	claw	4
88	父			fù	father	4
89	爻			yáo	double x	4
90	爿	丬		pán/qiáng	half tree trunk	4
91	片			piàn	slice	4
92	牙			yá	fang	4
93	牛	牜		niú	ox	4
94	犬	犭		quǎn	dog	4
95	玄			xuán	profound	5
96	玉		王	yù	jade	5
97	瓜			guā	melon	5
98	瓦			wǎ	tile	5
99	甘			gān	sweet	5
100	生			shēng	life	5
101	用			yòng	use	5
102	田			tián	field	5
103	疋			pǐ	bolt of cloth	5
104	疒			chuáng	sickness	5
105	癶			bò	dotted tent	5
106	白			bái	white	5
107	皮			pí	skin	5
108	皿			mǐn	dish	5

No.	Radical	Variants	Simplified Radical	Pinyin	English Name	Stroke Count
109	目			mù	eye	5
110	矛			máo	spear	5
111	矢			shǐ	arrow	5
112	石			shí	stone	5
113	示	礻		shì	omen	5
114	禸			rǒu	track	5
115	禾			hé	grain	5
116	穴			xuè	cave	5
117	立			lì	stand	5
118	竹	⺮		zhú	bamboo	6
119	米			mǐ	rice	6
120	糸	糹	纟	mì (sī)	silk	6
121	缶			fǒu	jar	6
122	网	⺲		wǎng	net	6
123	羊			yáng	sheep	6
124	羽			yǔ	feather	6
125	老			lǎo	old	6
126	而			ér	and	6
127	耒			lěi	plow	6
128	耳			ěr	ear	6
129	聿			yù	brush	6
130	肉			ròu	meat	6
131	臣			chén	minister	6
132	自			zì	self	6
133	至			zhì	arrive	6
134	臼			jiù	mortar	6
135	舌			shé	tongue	6
136	舛			chuǎn	oppose	6
137	舟			zhōu	boat	6
138	艮			gèn	stopping	6
139	色			sè	color	6
140	艸	艹		cǎo	grass	6
141	虍			hū	tiger	6
142	虫			chóng	insect	6
143	血			xuě	blood	6
144	行			xíng	walk/move	6

APPENDIX 1: CHINESE CHARACTER RADICALS

No.	Radical	Variants	Simplified Radical	Pinyin	English Name	Stroke Count
145	衣	衤		yī	clothes	6
146	西	覀		yà	west	6
147	見		见	jiàn	see	7
148	角			jué	horn	7
149	言		讠	yán	speech	7
150	谷			gǔ	valley	7
151	豆			dòu	bean	7
152	豕			shǐ	pig	7
153	豸			zhì	badger	7
154	貝		贝	bèi	shell	7
155	赤			chì	red	7
156	走			zǒu	run	7
157	足		𧾷	zú	foot	7
158	身			shēn	body	7
159	車		车	chē	cart	7
160	辛			xīn	bitter	7
161	辰			chén	morning	7
162	辵	辶		chuò	walk/move	7
163	邑	阝(right)		yì	city	7
164	酉			yǒu	alcohol	7
165	釆			biàn	distinguish	7
166	里			lǐ	village	7
167	金			jīn	metal	8
168	長		长	cháng	long	8
169	門		门	mén	door/gate	8
170	阜	阝(left)		fù	mound	8
171	隶			dài	slave	8
172	隹			zhuī	short-tailed bird	8
173	雨			yǔ	rain	8
174	青			qīng	green	8
175	非			fēi	wrong	8
176	面			miàn	face	9
177	革			gé	leather	9
178	韋		韦	wéi	tanned leather	9
179	韭			jiǔ	leek	9
180	音			yīn	sound	9

No.	Radical	Variants	Simplified Radical	Pinyin	English Name	Stroke Count
181	頁		页	yè	leaf	9
182	風		风	fēng	wind	9
183	飛		飞	fēi	fly	9
184	食	飠	饣	shí	eat	9
185	首			shǒu	head	9
186	香			xiāng	fragrant	9
187	馬		马	mǎ	horse	10
188	骨			gǔ	bone	10
189	高			gāo	tall	10
190	髟			biāo	hair	10
191	鬥			dòu	fight	10
192	鬯			chàng	sacrificial wine	10
193	鬲			lì	cauldron	10
194	鬼			guǐ	ghost	10
195	魚		鱼	yú	fish	11
196	鳥		鸟	niǎo	bird	11
197	鹵			lǔ	salt	11
198	鹿			lù	deer	11
199	麥		麦	mài	wheat	11
200	麻			má	hemp	11
201	黃			huáng	yellow	12
202	黍			shǔ	millet	12
203	黑			hēi	black	12
204	黹			zhǐ	embroidery	12
205	黽		黾	měng (mǐn)	frog	13
206	鼎			dǐng	tripod	13
207	鼓			gǔ	drum	13
208	鼠		鼡	shǔ	rat	13
209	鼻			bí	nose	14
210	齊		齐	qí	even	14
211	齒		齿	chǐ	tooth	15
212	龍		龙	lóng	dragon	16
213	龜		龟	guī	turtle	16
214	龠			yuè	flute	17

APPENDIX 2

Important Chinese Character Radicals for Daoist Studies

This appendix draws attention to important Chinese character radicals from a Daoist perspective, including Daoist associations. The latter often deviate from more common and conventional views. Nonetheless, they inspire deeper engagement with radicals from an applied and lived perspective, ideally including a contemplative approach.

Appendix 2: Important Chinese Character Radicals

No.	Radical	Pinyin	English Name	Daoist Associations
1	一	yī	one	One/oneness. Above=heaven; below=earth
2	丨	gǔn	line	vertical connection
9	人/亻	rén	person	human being
11	入	rù	enter	access/interiority
21	匕	bǐ	spoon	alchemy
25	卜	bǔ	divine	divination/omen
30	口	kǒu	mouth	orality/transmission
32	土	tǔ	earth	ground/center/place
33	士	shì	scholar	adept/practitioner
46	山	shān	mountain	stillness/meditation
60	彳	chì	step	movement/practice
61	心/忄	xīn	heart	psychology/spirituality
64	手/扌	shǒu	hand	activity
71	无 (無)	wú	not	absence/freedom/nonbeing
84	气	qì	steam	qi 氣/炁
85	水/氵	shuǐ	water	kidneys/vital essence
86	火/灬	huǒ	fire	heart/spirit
96	玉	yù	jade	treasure
102	田	tián	field	cultivation/subtle locale
113	示	shì	omen	revelation/manifestation
120	糸	mì	silk	thread/connection
144	行	xíng	walk/move	movement/practice
158	身	shēn	body	embodiment/physicality
162	辵/辶	chuò	walk/move	movement/practice
167	金	jīn	metal	gold/alchemy
169	門	mén	door/gate	portal/affiliation
183	飛	fēi	fly	immortals/immortality
206	鼎	dǐng	tripod	crucible/alchemy

Appendix 3

Foundational Classical Chinese Grammar

This appendix lists common classical/literary Chinese grammatical characters. It is intended as a "pocket guide" to said grammar, including "punctuation" characters (e.g., 也 [。], 乎 [?], 哉 [!]). For additional, foundational guidance see Pulleyblank 1996; Fuller 2004; Rouzer 2007; Kroll 2017; Van Norden 2019.

bèi 被: indicates passive verb tense
bǐ 比: compare/compared to/contrast
bǐ 彼: that/those
bù 不: not
bùrú 不如: not as good as
céng 曾: still/not yet
cǐ 此: this/these
cóng 從: from
ěr 耳 (而已): just/merely/that's all/period mark (。)
ér 而: and/and yet/but. Sometimes "under the condition of" (utc)
ěr 爾: then. Also used as a grammatical cognate of *ěr* 耳 (而已) ("merely/just") and/or *rán* 然 ("so/in this manner")
fēi 非: it is not/unless/it is not the case that...
fú 夫: now then

gèng 更: more/even more
gù 故: therefore/thus
hé 何: how?/what?/where?/why?
hé 盍: how?/why?
hū 乎: question mark (?)
jí 及: and
jí 即: although/as soon as/even if/then
jì 既: already/since/then
jiāng 將: will
jiē 皆: all/every
kuàng: compare/how much more
mò 末: no/no one/not. *Distinguish from* 未
mò 莫: no one/none/nothing/do not
nǎi 乃: then
qí 其: her/his/its/their. Sometimes functions as "the"
qǐ 豈: how?
qiě 且: and/both/if/in addition/moreover
què 卻: but/yet
rán 然: so
rú 如: as if/for example/if/like/more than
rú 如…**zé** 則…: if…then…
ruò 若: as if/if/like/seem
shèn 甚: very/what?
shǐ 使: cause/supposing/use
shìyǐ 是以: therefore/thus
shú 孰: who?/what?/which?
suī 雖: although/even if
suǒ 所…**yǐ** 以: that which
suǒyǐ 所以: therefore

wèi 未: not/have not/not yet. *Distinguish from* 末

wèi 為: because of

wú 無/无: without/non-/-less

wú 毋: do not. Sometimes used as alternative for *wú* 無 ("without")

wù 勿: do not/not

xī 兮: exclamation point (!). Sometimes used in poetry as an untranslatable placeholder. Unifying rhythmic device sometimes acting as point of punctuation

yān 焉: how?/why?/where?/when? Sometimes used as a contraction of 於 + 之 ("from this")

yě 也: also/and/too/period mark (。)

yǐ 已: already/finish/that is all

yì 亦: also/indeed/too

yī 衣: according to

yǐ 矣: period mark (。)

yǐ 以: by/by means of/in order to/through

yǐ 以...**wèi** 為: take ____ as ____

yǐ 以...**zhī gù** 之故: the reason why...is because...

yīn 因: according to/because/thus

yòu 又: again/also/both

yóu 猶: be like/resemble/still

yú 於: at/by/for/in/on/than

yǔ 與: and/with

yù 喻: analogy/example/metaphor

yù 愈: more/even more

yuē 曰: be called/say/speak

zài 在: at/in/on. May also indicate in the process of (...ing)

zāi 哉: exclamation point (!)

zé 則: then

zhě 者: nominalization/topicalization: as for.../considering.../one who... (-er/-or/-ist)

zhī 之: of. Classical equivalent of *de* 的. Also used as third-person pronoun/object (him/her/it/them)

zhū 諸: all/every/many/various

zì 自: from/naturally/personally/since

Appendix 4

Pinyin to Wade-Giles Romanization Conversion Chart

Wade-Giles 威翟式拼音 refers to an early Romanization/transcription system for approximating Chinese character pronunciations in "Mandarin" dialect using Roman (Latin) alphabetic script. It was originally created by the British diplomat Thomas Francis Wade 威妥瑪 (1818–1895) and completed by his fellow British diplomat Herbert Allen Giles 翟理思 (1845–1935) in 1892. It is characterized by the use of apostrophes (') for different sounds (e.g., ch/ch', k/k', p/p', t/t', tz/tz') and hyphens (-) to separate individual characters in paired phrases (e.g., *ch'uán-tào*). It conventionally includes tone indications in superscript (e.g., *tao*[4]). It became the standard early Romanization system, especially in English-language publications. Pīnyīn 拼音 (lit., "spelled sound") refers to a more recent Romanization/transcription system. It was created in the 1950s by a group of Chinese linguists under the supervision of the Chinese Communist government. It was originally published in 1958, with subsequent revisions, and represents the only "indigenous" Chinese system. It is characterized by the use of "strange" letters (e.g., q, x, z, zh). Pinyin is the official Romanization system of the People's Republic of China and became adopted as the international standard (1982), by the United Nations (1986), and finally by Taiwan (2019). Previous generations often resisted its adoption and utilization on political grounds, including support for the Republic of China. Although most Western-language publications now use Pinyin, it is helpful to have conversion charts in order to facilitate "translation" between older and newer scholarship, especially for individuals unfamiliar with one or the other system. The present appendix moves from Pinyin to Wade-Giles.

PY	W-G	PY	W-G	PY	W-G
a	a	chuan	ch'uan	fo	fo
ai	ai	chuang	ch'uang	fou	fou
an	an	chui	ch'ui	fu	fu
ang	ang	chun	ch'un	ga	ka
ao	ao	chuo	ch'o	gai	kai
ba	pa	ci	tz'u	gan	kan
bai	pai	cong	ts'ung	gang	kang
ban	pan	cou	ts'ou	gao	kao
bang	pang	cu	ts'u	ge	ko
bao	pao	cuan	ts'uan	gen	ken
bei	pei	cui	ts'ui	geng	keng
ben	pen	cun	ts'un	gong	kung
beng	peng	cuo	ts'o	gou	ko
bi	pi	da	ta	gu	ku
bian	pien	dai	tai	gua	kua
biao	piao	dan	tan	guai	kuai
bie	pieh	dang	tang	guan	kuan
bin	pin	dao	tao	guang	kuang
bing	ping	de	te	gui	kuei
bo	po	deng	teng	gun	kun
bu	pu	di	ti	guo	kuo
ca	ts'a	dian	tien	ha	ha
cai	ts'ai	diao	tiao	hai	hai
can	ts'an	die	tieh	han	han
cang	ts'ang	ding	ting	hang	hang
cao	ts'ao	diu	tiu	hao	hao
ce	ts'e	dong	tung	he	ho
cen	ts'en	dou	tou	hei	hei
ceng	ts'eng	du	tu	hen	hen
cha	ch'a	duan	tuan	heng	heng
chai	ch'ai	dui	tui	hong	hung
chan	ch'an	dun	tun	hou	hou
chang	ch'ang	duo	to	hu	hu
chao	ch'ao	e	o	hua	hua
che	ch'e	en	en	huai	huai
chen	ch'en	er	erh	huan	huan
cheng	ch'eng	fa	fa	huang	huang
chi	ch'ih	fan	fan	hui	hui
chong	ch'ung	fang	fang	hun	hun
chou	ch'ou	fei	fei	huo	huo
chu	ch'u	fen	fen	ji	chi
chuai	ch'uai	feng	feng	jia	chia

PY	W-G	PY	W-G	PY	W-G
jian	chien	liu	liu	nou	nou
jiang	chiang	long	lung	nu	nu
jiao	chiao	lou	lou	nuan	nuan
jie	chieh	lu	lu	nüe	nüeh
jin	chin	luan	luan	nuo	no
jing	ching	luan	lüan	nü	nü
jiong	chiung	lüe	lüeh	ou	ou
jiu	chiu	lun	lun	pa	p'a
ju	chü	luo	lo	pai	p'ai
juan	chüan	lü	lü	pan	p'an
jue	chüeh	ma	ma	pang	p'ang
jun	chün	mai	mai	pao	p'ao
ka	k'a	man	man	pei	p'ei
kai	k'ai	mang	mang	pen	p'en
kan	k'an	mao	mao	peng	p'eng
kang	k'ang	mei	mei	pi	p'i
kao	k'ao	men	men	pian	p'ien
ke	k'o	meng	meng	piao	p'iao
ken	k'en	mi	mi	pie	p'ieh
keng	k'eng	mian	mien	pin	p'in
kong	k'ung	miao	miao	ping	p'ing
kou	k'ou	mie	mieh	po	p'o
ku	k'u	min	min	pou	p'ou
kua	k'ua	ming	ming	pu	p'u
kuai	k'uai	miu	miu	qi	ch'i
kuan	k'uan	mo	mo	qia	ch'ia
kuang	k'uang	mou	mou	qian	ch'ien
kui	k'uei	mu	mu	qiang	ch'iang
kun	k'un	na	na	qiao	ch'iao
kuo	k'uo	nai	nai	qie	ch'ieh
la	la	nan	nan	qin	ch'in
lai	lai	nang	nang	qing	ch'ing
lan	lan	nao	nao	qiong	ch'iung
lang	lang	nei	nei	qiu	ch'iu
lao	lao	nen	nen	qu	ch'ü
le	le	neng	neng	quan	ch'üan
lei	lei	ni	ni	que	ch'üeh
leng	leng	nian	nien	qun	ch'ün
li	li	niang	niang	ran	jan
lian	lien	niao	niao	rang	jang
liang	liang	nie	nieh	rao	jao
liao	liao	nin	nin	re	je
lie	lieh	ning	ning	ren	jen
lin	lin	niu	niu	reng	jeng
ling	ling	nong	nung	ri	jih

Appendix 4: Pinyin to Wade-Giles

PY	W-G	PY	W-G	PY	W-G
rong	jung	tao	t'ao	yin	yin
rou	jou	te	t'e	ying	ying
ru	ju	teng	t'eng	yo	yo
ruan	juan	ti	t'i	yong	yung
rui	jui	tian	t'ien	you	yu
run	jun	tiao	t'iao	yu	yü
ruo	jo	tie	t'ieh	yuan	yüan
sa	sa	ting	t'ing	yue	yüeh
sai	sai	tong	t'ung	yun	yün
san	san	tou	t'ou	za	tsa
sang	sang	tu	t'u	zai	tsai
sao	sao	tuan	t'uan	zan	tsan
se	se	tui	t'ui	zang	tsang
sen	sen	tun	t'un	zao	tsao
seng	seng	tuo	t'o	ze	tse
sha	sha	wa	wa	zei	tsei
shai	shai	wai	wai	zen	tsen
shan	shan	wan	wan	zeng	tseng
shang	shang	wang	wang	zha	cha
shao	shao	wei	wei	zhai	chai
she	she	wen	wen	zhan	chan
shen	shen	weng	weng	zhang	chang
sheng	sheng	wo	wo	zhao	chao
shi	shih	wu	wu	zhe	che
shou	shou	xi	hsi	zhen	chen
shu	shu	xia	hsia	zheng	cheng
shua	shua	xian	hsien	zhi	chih
shuai	shuai	xiang	hsiang	zhong	chung
shuan	shuan	xiao	hsiao	zhou	chou
shuang	shuang	xie	hsieh	zhu	chu
shui	shui	xin	hsin	zhua	chua
shun	shun	xing	hsing	zhuai	chuai
shuo	shuo	xiong	hsiung	zhuan	chuan
si	ssu	xiu	hsiu	zhuang	chuang
song	sung	xu	hsü	zhui	chui
sou	sou	xuan	hsüan	zhun	chun
su	su	xue	hsüeh	zhuo	chuo
suan	suan	xun	hsün	zi	tzu
sui	sui	ya	ya	zong	tsung
sun	sun	yai	yai	zou	tsou
suo	so	yan	yen	zu	tsu
ta	t'a	yang	yang	zuan	tsuan
tai	t'ai	yao	yao	zui	tsui
tan	t'an	ye	yeh	zun	tsun
tang	t'ang	yi	i	zuo	tso

Appendix 5

Wade-Giles to Pinyin Romanization Conversion Chart

As discussed in Appendix #4, Wade-Giles is the earlier, standard Romanization system, while Pinyin is a more recent and now standard one. The present appendix moves from Wade-Giles to Pinyin.

W-G	PY	W-G	PY	W-G	PY
a	a	ch'iung	qiong	hang	hang
ai	ai	cho	zhuo	hao	hao
an	an	ch'o	chuo	hei	hei
ang	ang	chou	zhou	hen	hen
ao	ao	ch'ou	chou	heng	heng
cha	zha	chu	zhu	ho	he
ch'a	cha	ch'u	chu	hou	hou
chai	zhai	chü	ju	hsi	xi
ch'ai	chai	ch'ü	qu	hsia	xia
chan	zhan	chua	zhua	hsiang	xiang
ch'an	chan	chuai	zhuai	hsiao	xiao
ch'ang	chang	chuan	zhuan	hsien	xian
chao	zhao	ch'uan	chuan	hsin	xin
ch'ao	chao	chüan	juan	hsing	xing
che	zhe	ch'üan	quaheartn	hsiu	xiu
ch'e	che	chuang	zhuang	hsiung	xiong
chen	zhen	ch'uang	chuang	hsü	xu
ch'en	chen	chüeh	jue	hsüan	xuan
cheng	zheng	ch'üeh	que	hsüeh	xue
ch'eng	cheng	chui	zhui	hsün	xun
chi	ji	ch'ui	chui	hu	hu
ch'i	qi	chun	zhun	hua	hua
chia	jia	ch'un	chun	huai	huai
ch'ia	qia	chün	jun	huan	huan
chiang	jiang	ch'ün	qun	huang	huang
ch'iang	qiang	chung	zhong	hui	hui
chiao	jiao	ch'ung	chong	hun	hun
ch'iao	qiao	en	en	hung	hong
chieh	jie	erh	er	huo	huo
ch'ieh	qie	fa	fa	i	yi
chien	jian	fan	fan	jan	ran
ch'ien	qian	fang	fang	jang	rang
chih	zhi	fei	fei	jao	rao
ch'ih	chi	fen	fen	je	re
chin	jin	feng	feng	jen	ren
ch'in	qin	fo	fo	jeng	reng
ching	jing	fou	fou	jih	ri
ch'ing	qing	fu	fu	jo	ruo
chiu	jiu	ha	ha	jou	rou
ch'iu	qiu	hai	hai	ju	ru
chiung	jiong	han	han	juan	ruan

Appendix 5: Wade-Giles to Pinyin

W-G	PY	W-G	PY	W-G	PY
jui	rui	lei	lei	ni	ni
jun	run	leng	leng	niang	niang
jung	rong	li	li	niao	niao
ka	ga	liang	liang	nieh	nie
k'a	ka	liao	liao	nien	nian
kai	gai	lieh	lie	nin	nin
k'ai	kai	lien	lian	ning	ning
kan	gan	lin	lin	niu	niu
k'an	kan	ling	ling	no	nuo
kang	gang	liu	liu	nou	nou
k'ang	kang	lo	luo	nu	nu
kao	gao	lou	lou	nü	nü
k'ao	kao	lu	lu	nuan	nuan
ken	gen	lü	lü	nüeh	nüe
k'en	ken	luan	luan	nung	nong
keng	geng	lüan	luan	o	e
k'eng	keng	lüeh	lüe	ou	ou
ko	ge	lun	lun	pa	ba
k'o	ke	lung	long	p'a	pa
kou	gou	ma	ma	pai	bai
k'ou	kou	mai	mai	p'ai	pai
ku	gu	man	man	pan	ban
k'u	ku	mang	mang	p'an	pan
kua	gua	mao	mao	pang	bang
k'ua	kua	mei	mei	p'ang	pang
kuai	guai	men	men	pao	bao
k'uai	kuai	meng	meng	p'ao	pao
kuan	guan	mi	mi	pei	bei
k'uan	kuan	miao	miao	p'ei	pei
kuang	guang	mieh	mie	pen	ben
k'uang	kuang	mien	mian	p'en	pen
kuei	gui	min	min	peng	beng
k'uei	kui	ming	ming	p'eng	peng
kun	gun	miu	miu	pi	bi
k'un	kun	mo	mo	p'i	pi
kung	gong	mou	mou	piao	biao
k'ung	kong	mu	mu	p'iao	piao
kuo	guo	na	na	pieh	bie
k'uo	kuo	nai	nai	p'ieh	pie
la	la	nan	nan	pien	bian
lai	lai	nang	nang	p'ien	pian
lan	lan	nao	nao	pin	bin
lang	lang	nei	nei	p'in	pin
lao	lao	nen	nen	ping	bing
le	le	neng	neng	p'ing	ping

W-G	PY	W-G	PY	W-G	PY
po	bo	tang	dang	tsei	zei
p'o	po	t'ang	tang	tsen	zen
p'ou	pou	tao	dao	ts'en	cen
pu	bu	t'ao	tao	tseng	zeng
p'u	pu	te	de	ts'eng	ceng
sa	sa	t'e	te	tso	zuo
sai	sai	teng	deng	ts'o	cuo
san	san	t'eng	teng	tsou	zou
sang	sang	ti	di	ts'ou	cou
sao	sao	t'i	ti	tsu	zu
se	se	tiao	diao	ts'u	cu
sen	sen	t'iao	tiao	tsuan	zuan
seng	seng	tieh	die	ts'uan	cuan
sha	sha	t'ieh	tie	tsui	zui
shai	shai	tien	dian	ts'ui	cui
shan	shan	t'ien	tian	tsun	zun
shang	shang	ting	ding	ts'un	cun
shao	shao	t'ing	ting	tsung	zong
she	she	tiu	diu	ts'ung	cong
shen	shen	to	duo	tzu	zi
sheng	sheng	t'o	tuo	tz'u	ci
shih	shi	tou	dou	wa	wa
shou	shou	t'ou	tou	wai	wai
shu	shu	tu	du	wan	wan
shua	shua	t'u	tu	wang	wang
shuan	shuan	t'uan	tuan	wen	wen
shuang	shuang	tui	dui	weng	weng
shui	shui	t'ui	tui	wo	wo
shun	shun	tun	dun	wu	wu
shuo	shuo	t'un	tun	ya	ya
so	suo	tung	dong	yai	yai
sou	sou	t'ung	tong	yang	yang
ssu	si	tsa	za	yao	yao
su	su	ts'a	ca	yeh	ye
suan	suan	tsai	zai	yen	yan
sui	sui	ts'ai	cai	yin	yin
sun	sun	tsan	zan	ying	ying
sung	song	ts'an	can	yo	yo
ta	da	tsang	zang	yu	you
t'a	ta	ts'ang	cang	yü	yu
tai	dai	tsao	zao	yüan	yuan
t'ai	tai	ts'ao	cao	yüeh	yue
tan	dan	tse	ze	yün	yun
t'an	tan	ts'e	ce	yung	yong

Appendix 6

Daoist Character Etymology

99The present appendix explores Chinese character etymology from an applied, experiential, and lived Daoist perspective. As such, it is probably the most controversial dimension of this primer. "Daoist etymology" (*dàojiào cíyuán* 道教詞源) often differs from common and conventional Sinological and philological accounts, which at times claim, occasionally absurdly, that the pictographic (*xiàngxíng* 象形) and ideogrammatic (*zhǐshì* 指事) elements of Chinese written language are largely anomalous and/or fictitious. This includes resistance to attendant etymological discussions (cf. Wieger 1965 [1927]; Wu 2015). Let me be clear: I am not claiming that etymology is straightforward and unproblematic, and I recognize that etymological discussions can easily descend into fabrication and fantasy, especially in unsound popular imaginings without a philological root. However, deeper etymological inquiry often is enlightening and creates additional insights with respect to technical terminology. This installment is informed by traditional Chinese philology, including ancient oracle bone and bronze inscriptions, as well as my own Daoist participant-observation ethnographic work and contemplative inquiry. The latter involves exploring Chinese character composition as informed by and informing Daoist practice-realization, often in ways that transcend conventional human modes and that controvert mandated academic approaches. Here we might pause and consider the possibility of at least some characters being *xiàng* 象/像, not simply in the sense of "images" or "symbols," but also as "appearances" and "containers." This might be further connected to classical and foundational Daoist "vessel (*qì* 器) theory," in which communication and expression involve a series of transmissions analogous to fluids being transferred from one vessel to another.

APPENDIX 6: DAOIST CHARACTER ETYMOLOGY

Character	Translation	Components	Daoist Explanation
ān 菴	hut/hermitage	艹 (grass) + 广 (cliff) + 奄 (cover)	Grass-thatched shelters. Residing among living grasses
bǎo 寶	treasure	宀 (roof) + 玉 (jade) + 貝 (shell [currency])	Precious substances, especially one's own vital substances. Assumes guarding (守) and storing (藏)
bìng 病	ailment/disease/illness	疒 (sickness) + 丙 ([stem]), with the latter consisting of 一 (one/cover) + 冂 (enclosure) + 人 (person)	Illness as constraint and confinement, including stagnation (滯). May require convalescence (床)
chén 塵	dirt/dust	鹿 (deer) + 土 (earth)	Psychospiritual defilements, comparable to a dust cloud formed by deer running. Also a backcountry road in summer
chī 痴	ignorance	疒 (illness) + 知 (know)	The illness of knowing; knowing as illness. Open receptivity as remedy
chōng 沖	empty/infusing	氵(water) + 中 (center)	The Center (Dao) infused with and infusing water (qi). Also the heavens and earth (二) and four directions (口), including fields (田), joined through water (丨). In practice, the torso (中), specifically connected (丨) through the Thrusting Channel (工), infused with qi
chuán 傳	transmit	亻(person) + 專 (special), with the latter consisting of 叀 (spindle) + 寸 (hand)	Gnosis and insight passed between individuals, specifically elders/teachers (子/公/師) and students (士/子). 人←→人. Embodied (體) community (家/會)
cí 雌	female (bird)	此 (this) + 隹 (sparrow)	Small female bird hidden in ravines and shadows. Familiar with secret places
cùn 寸	inch	彐 [pictograph]. Hand, specifically pulse of radial artery	Often used in Daoism as "Square Inch" (方寸), an esoteric name for the heart

Character	Translation	Components	Daoist Explanation
dān 丹	elixir	丹 [pictograph]	Technically cinnabar (mercuric sulfide [HgS]). Elixir of immortality
dào 道	Dao (Tao; Way)	辶 (walk) + 首 (head). From a Daoist perspective, the latter consists of yin-yang (丷) joined in oneness (一) within oneself (自)	Way moving through everything. Walking on the path towards the Way
dào 衜	Dao (Tao; Way)	彳 (left step) + 首 (head) + 亍 (right step). Alternatively, 行 (crossroads/walk) + 首 (head)	Walking with the Way within and between one's steps. Ever-present
dé 德	inner power/virtue	彳 (left step) + 直 (direct) + 心 (heart). Connected to listening (聽 [耳 (ear) + 直 (direct) + 心 (heart)])	An aligned heart-mind manifesting as embodied activity (行) in the world (世)
diǎn 點	bit/drop/point	黑 (black) + 占 (divine)	A spark. Divining the darkness. Dark illumination
dìng 定	absorption/settle	宀 (roof) + 疋 (foot). The latter is also glossed as 止 and read as containing 人 (person). Also interpreted as 正 (aligned)	Pausing to rest. Also complete alignment in one's being, especially below the crown-point (宀). Also samādhī (meditative absorption/yogic stasis)
dìng 鼎	tripod	鼎 [pictograph]	Crucible and cauldron. Alchemical refinement (煉) and transformation (化)
dòng 洞	cave/grotto	氵 (water) + 同 (meet)	Access-points (口) in the mountains (山) and portals (門) into the sacred (聖). Sometimes associated with mystical cranial cavities (竅) and palaces (宮)

Appendix 6: Daoist Character Etymology

Character	Translation	Components	Daoist Explanation
fù 腹	belly/abdomen/navel	月 (flesh) + 复 (return). Alternatively 月 (moon) + 复 (return)	The location to which qi 氣 returns and the point on which one focuses during meditation. Alternatively, the storehouse of lunar light. The Ocean of Qi (氣海)
guān 觀	observe/observation	雚 (egret) + 見 (see)	Listening (聽) to barely visible and subtle presences and patterns. Also *vipassanā/vipaśyanā* (insight meditation)
guàn 觀	temple/monastery	雚 (egret) + 見 (see)	Literally, "observatory." A dark and secluded place where one may observe the sun, moon, and stars. Also an observation-site for exploring the inner landscape (境/景/經) of the body (身)
gǔn ǀ	(vertical stroke)	ǀ. Through	Alignment (正) and connection (通), especially through the torso (中) and Thrusting Channel (工)
huò 惑	delusion	或 (either/or) + 心 (heart)	Confusion as a mind clouded by doubt and rumination
jí 極	ridgepole/polarity	木 (tree) + 一 (heaven) + 口 (mouth) + 又 (hand) + ǀ (connect) + 一 (earth)	Yin-yang differentiation (二) as that which occurs through the interaction of the heavens and earth. Analogous to speaking and working
jiā 家	family/home	宀 (shelter) + 豕 (pig)	Traditional co-habitation with animals. Perhaps tradition as centering on shared animality
jīng 精	vital essence	米 (rice) + 青 (green/pure/young)	Vitality as analogous to grains of rice (substance)
jìng 靜	stillness	青 (pure) + 爭 (contend)	Stillness as non-contention (無爭)
jīng 經	meridian	糸 (silk/thread) + 巠 (underground stream)	Somatic energy channels as watercourses (川)
jīng 經	scripture	糸 (silk/thread) + 巠 (underground stream)	Scriptures as threads and watercourses (川) forming and reforming networks of connection (ǀ)

Character	Translation	Components	Daoist Explanation
kōng 空	emptiness	穴 ("cave") + 工 (work)	The body, especially the heart-mind (穴), connecting heaven and earth (工). The heart-mind as cave offering space and dwelling for spirit. Also śūnyatā
liàn 煉	refine	火 (fire) + 柬 (select). Also 金 (metal) + 柬 (select)	Forging, fusing, smelting. Alchemical transmutation (化)
líng 靈	numinous	雨 (rain) + 口 (mouth) + 巫 (medium). The latter consists of 一 (heaven) + 人 (person) + 丨 (connect) + 一 (earth)	Two humans singing and dancing to bring rain. Connection, power, and efficacy
mén 門	gate	門 [pictograph]	Traditional Chinese homes as having lower openings for pigs to come and go. Also invokes sensory engagement
míng 明	illumination	日 (sun) + 月 (moon)	The combined radiance of sun and moon. Invokes the left and right eye, respectively
mìng 命	fate/life-destiny	亼 (three sides/gather) + 叩 (tap/bow), with the latter consisting of 口 (mouth) and 卩 (kneel). Alternatively, 口 (mouth) + 令 (order)	The two kidneys (叩) beneath the lower back ribcage (亼). Also 脊. A decree from the cosmos manifesting as one's body and constitution. Associated with vital essence (精)
niàn 念	recollect	今 (now) + 心 (heart)	Re-collection. Present to/in the moment. Here-and-now. Attentiveness. Also sati (mindfulness)
pài 派	lineage	氵(water) + 辰 (tributary)	Lineages as branches flowing out of and into the larger streams (流) of movements and the river (河) of tradition, eventually returning to the ocean (海) of the Dao

Appendix 6: Daoist Character Etymology

Character	Translation	Components	Daoist Explanation
péng 蓬	bramble	艹 (grass) + 逢 (meet), with the latter including 辶 (move)	Habituated consciousness and ordinary mind comparable to wild brambles, including relational entanglement (紛/結)
pìn 牝	female (animal)	牛 (ox) + 匕 (spoon)	Female animal hidden in ravines and shadows. Possibly a doe (鹿) as model of Daoist living and being
pǔ 樸	unhewn simplicity	木 (tree) + 業 (thicket)	Gnarled, twisted and commingled trees unable to be felled and carpentered. Associated with innate nature (性) and suchness (自然)
qì 氣	qi	气 (steam) + 米 (rice)	Energy comparable to vapor produced from cooking rice (vital essence)
qì 炁	qi	灬 (fire) + 旡 (collect/full)	The fire (火) of Nonbeing (无) connected/connecting (丨) to the Dao-as-One (一). Daoist qi as a subtle corporeal heat
qì 器	vessel	口 (container) + 工 (table)	Implements used for making offerings at an altar (壇) during rituals (禮/儀). Vessels holding and transferring fluids (水). Associated with the body (身) and Daoist being/identity more generally
qīng 青	azure/pure/young	青 [pictograph]. Consists of 生 (life) + 丹 (cinnabar)	Greening-power. Life as emerging from seeds (種) and manifesting as sprouts (芽). Primarily connected to plants (艹/木), but also water (水). Related to soil (土) and blood (血 [紅]). The elixir which is life
qíng 情	disposition/emotions	忄 (heart) + 青 (pure)	A disposition of the Dao (道情) based on ordinary emotionality becoming stilled (靜) and stabilized (定)
qīng 清	clarity	氵 (water) + 青 (pure)	Pure consciousness as comparable to clear water. A clear pond out of which a lotus flower (蓮) grows

Character	Translation	Components	Daoist Explanation
sān 三	three	三. Three strokes, so three 一 (one)	The primary yang number. Associated with yin-yang (二) interaction (三), with the latter often including qi and/or Principle (理). Invokes various Daoist ternary associations, including heaven (upper 一), earth (lower 一), and water or humans (middle 一). Also represented as 工. Also the Three-in-One (三一)
shān 山	mountain	山 [pictograph]. Also trigram ☶	Actual mountains, mountain seclusion, contemplative silence, and altars. Associated with stillness (靜)
shēn 身	body/person/self	身 [pictograph]. Sometimes understood as a pregnant woman	Human torso viewed from the side. Physical embodiment
shèn 腎	kidneys	臤 (firm/stable) + 月 (flesh). The former is sometimes glossed as 叩 (tap/bow) =kidneys	The actual kidneys as the storehouse of vital essence (精), one's foundational vitality. Also connected to the spine (脊) and life-destiny (命)
shén 神	spirit	礻 (omen/manifest) + 申 (extend)	Quasi-divine capacity to connect (｜) with unseen influences and subtle presences. Associated with the heart (心) and the heavens (天). The One (一) in the center (中). Alternatively, the heart region (田) with the Thrusting Channel (｜) activated
shēng 生	birth/life	生 [pictograph]. Consists of 屮 (bud) + 土 (earth/ground)	Both aliveness and life as connected (｜) to the earth. Growth and development. Associated with greening-power (青)
shèng 聖	sage	耳 (ear) + 口 (mouth) + 壬 (great/north)	Someone listening (聽) to the subtle sonorous patterns (文/法) of the Dao. A person whose wisdom and insights are listened to by others

APPENDIX 6: DAOIST CHARACTER ETYMOLOGY

Character	Translation	Components	Daoist Explanation
shì 士	adept/practitioner	市 [pictograph]. An axe-like tool, and "warrior" by extension	Individuals who remember the ground (一) and tend to the heart as center (中) and axis (+). For Daoists, includes renouncing a warrior mentality and associated violence, ultimately resulting in non-contention (無爭)
shǒu 守	guard [meditate]	宀 (roof) + 寸 (hand/inch)	Protecting one's primary abode (室/身). Also tending to the heart-mind (心) as Center (中) and Square Inch (方寸)
shū 樞	pivot	木 (tree) + 區 (district/dwelling), with the latter consisting of 匚 (container) + 口 (mouth/container). Also 機 (木 [tree] + 幾 [trigger])	Invokes the Polestar (北極) and Northern Dipper (北斗), connected with fate (命). Also the heart-mind (心) as center (中) and axis (+)
shuǐ 水	water	氵 [pictograph]. Connected to 川 (river/stream)	Actual water as the basis of life. Also a model for Daoist being and living characterized by flexibility and yielding, softness and weakness. Flow. Associated with both vital fluids (津/液/血) and qi in the body
shùn 順	accord/follow	順 [ideogram]. 川 (stream) + 頁 (head)	Following the currents and the Dao's subtle flow by extension
sī 思	thought/worry	田 (field) + 心 (heart)	Thought as the activity and content occurring in the field of the heart-mind. Comparable to plants (艹) and weeds (草/萇) filling space (囗). Also the heart as the space of consciousness
tán 壇	altar	土 (earth) + 亶 (plenty), with the latter consisting of 㐭 (granary) + 旦 (dawn) (日 [sun] + 一 [horizon])	Altars as storehouses of divine light. Originally outside. Associated with mountains (山)

Character	Translation	Components	Daoist Explanation
tán 檀	sandalwood	木 (tree) + 亶 (plenty), with the latter consisting of 㐭 (granary) + 旦 (dawn) (日 [sun] + 一 [horizon])	One of the primary types of incense (香) used in Daoist ritual (禮/儀). Invokes altars (壇), a parallel character containing 土 (earth/ground). Incense sticks as the trees (木) planted in the ground of the altar (土)
tǐ 體	body/embody	骨 (bones) + 豊 (abundant), with the latter consisting of 鼓 (drum) and 玨 (paired jade)	Physical structure as connection (丨) and perhaps invocation (咒)
tián 田	field	⊕ [pictograph]	Both the quadrants of a farm and the four primary cardinal directions. Also the axis (+) that connects (丨) these. The latter points towards the heart-mind (心) as center (中)
tōng 通	connect/pervade	辶 (move) + 甬 (bell-handle/partition-screen)	Connection (丨) that moves through the body (月/身). Associated with both alignment (正) and numinous presence (靈)
tǔ 土	earth/ground	土 [pictograph]. Possibly a lump of clay on a potter's wheel. Alternatively, a boundary marker (+)	The actual ground on which one stands (立/止). Also associated with the navel region (腹)
wàng 忘	forget/forgetfulness	亡 (perish) + 心 (heart)	Extinguishing the false fire (火) of the heart-mind. Referred to as "dead ashes" (sǐhuī 死灰). Enables divine illumination (光/明) to emerge and shine forth
wù 物	animal/thing	牛 (ox) + 勿 (blood). The latter also means "without" and may be read as a phonetic	Animals as beings with their own lives and aspirations, beyond thinghood and human exploitation. Also 獸 and/or 螘

Appendix 6: Daoist Character Etymology

Character	Translation	Components	Daoist Explanation
wú 無	without	🔣 [pictograph]. Possibly a person dancing with a pole in their hands. Alternatively people (人) among a canopy (一) of trees (木) and forests (林)	Ten people in a forest. Disappearing in space and darkness. The bioregion and watershed that encompasses human being and activity. Being and beings inside of Nonbeing
wù 悟	awakening	忄 (heart) + 吾 (I/me)	Spiritual realization attained through personal effort and accomplishment. Self-reliance as pre-requisite
xiān 仙	immortal	亻 (person) + 山 (mountain). Also 仚	A person living in the mountains. Immortality as being-mountain and mountain-being
xiān 僊	immortal	亻 (person) + 䙴 (fly)	Soaring (飛) above and beyond mundane concerns (事)
xián 閑	leisure/seclusion	門 (gate) + 木 (tree). Alternatively 門 (gate) + 月 (moon)	A forest sanctuary with a fenced perimeter (forest within gates) and a gated hermitage surrounded by a forest. The moonlight shining through secluded gates and shut doors of one in retirement from the ordinary world (塵). Enclosure and interiority (内)
xīn 心	heart-mind	🔣 [pictograph]	Psychospiritual center (中) of human personhood (身). Associated with innate nature (性) and spirit (神)
xìn 信	honesty/sincerity/trust	亻 (person) + 言 (speech)	A person standing by words
xìng 性	innate nature	忄 (heart) + 生 (birth/life)	The heart-mind one was born with. Associated with spirit (神)
xíng 行	act/go/move	🔣 [pictograph]. Eventually divided into 彳 (left step) + 亍 (right step)	Crossroads. More technically, practice. Moving step-by-step. Making progress

Character	Translation	Components	Daoist Explanation
xiū 修	cultivate/cultivation	攸 (place) + 彡 (feathers/hair-strands). 攸 includes 亻 (person) and 攴 (tap), with the latter comprised of 卜 (divine) and 又 (hand)	Animal husbandry and/or ancient divination practices used to determine the auspiciousness of a given undertaking. From a Daoist perspective, involves connecting (丨) with the extending and expansive reality of the Dao in its myriad threefold expressions (彡 = 三)
xù 畜	nurture/tend	畜 [pictograph]	Feedbag. Animal husbandry, specifically tending to the nourishment of animals, as care
xuán 玄	dark/mystery/profound	玄 [pictograph]. Sometimes glossed as related to 糸 (系)(silk/thread)	A skein of silk dipped in indigo dye (藍). The (non)color of the Dao. The Darkness that pervades and connects (通) everything (萬)
yáng 陽	yang	阝 (mound) + 昜 (sunlight), with the latter composed of 旦 (dawn) (日 [sun] + 一 [horizon]) + 勿 (rays). The simplified character 阳 consists of 阝 (mound) + 日 (sun), with the latter referred to as "Great Yang"	Sunlight on a hillside. The light-counterpart of yin 陰. Specific qualities and patterns occurring in same place (丨) at different times (一). Understood as dynamic and interrelated patterns (文/法) of interaction (極)
yǎng 養	nourish	羊 (goat/sheep) + 食 (feed). Related to xù 畜 (tend), which consists of 玄 (rope) and 田 (feed-bag)	Animal husbandry. Feeding (not eating) sheep. Taking care of oneself *in relationship* with other beings. Working in the fields (田)
yī 一	one	一 (horizontal stroke). Numeral 1	A circle (O) on its side. Both the Dao (One) and all individual things (ones)
yì 意	awareness/intention/thought	音 (sound) + 心 (heart)	The sound of the heart. Also concentration

APPENDIX 6: DAOIST CHARACTER ETYMOLOGY

Character	Translation	Components	Daoist Explanation
yīn 陰	yin	阝(mound) + 侌 (shadows), with the latter consisting of 今 (now) + 云 (clouds). The simplified character 阴 consists of 阝(mound) + 月 (moon), with the latter referred to as "Great Yin"	Shadows on a hillside. The dark-counterpart of yang 陽. Specific qualities and patterns occurring in same place (丨) at different times (一). Understood as dynamic and interrelated patterns (文/法) of interaction (極)
yǐn 隱	hidden	阝(mound) + 㥯 (cautious), with the latter including 工 (heaven-earth connection) and 心 (heart)	Retirement and seclusion as being hidden among mountains and shadows. Includes hidden adepts (士), immortals (仙), residence (居), virtue (德), and so forth
zhāi 齋	fast/retreat	齊 (grain field/uniform height) + 示 (omen)	A field for revelation. Leveling one's being as the ground for sacred connection. Also used in a technical sense for *zhāi*-purification rites, which are also referred to as "levée" (via French *lever* ["rise"]) in the sense of formal court audiences
zhēn 真	perfect	匕 (spoon) + 鼎 (tripod)	Reaction vessel and alchemical crucible. Both Reality and actualization attained through alchemical refinement (煉) and transformation (化). Includes cultivation (修) completed (全) by human beings (人)
zhèng 正	align/aligned	一 (heaven) + 止 (foot/stop)	Postural alignment (丨) of the body (體) as well as connection (通) with the Dao. Also applies to the heart-mind (心) as the center (中) and axis (+). Manifests as illumination (明) and numinosity (靈)
zhǐ 止	pause/stop/cessation	ᐩ/止 [pictograph]. Foot/Footprint	Pausing with attentiveness, awareness, and presence. Also *samatha/śamatha* (calm abiding meditation)

Character	Translation	Components	Daoist Explanation
zhì 治	govern/regulate	氵 (water) + 台 (platform/station), with the latter consisting of 厶 (private) + 口 (mouth/container)	Governing the state (治國) as regulating the self (治身), and vice versa. Also "healing the body." Governing, regulating, healing
zhì 志	aspiration/will	士 (adept/practitioner) + 心 (heart)	The heart-mind of an adept characterized by an aspiration for the Dao (道志). Also alignment (正), embodiment (體), listening (聽), resonance (感), trust (信), virtue (德), and the like
zhōng 中	center	𠁩 / 𠁦 / 中. Originally probably a flagpole and a drum, indicating territorial center	The Dao. In practice, primarily identified as the heart-mind (心) as the center of the chest (□). Also the connection (│) of the Thrusting Channel (工)
zōng 宗	ancestor	宀 (roof) + 示 (omen/manifest)	The Dao. Also an ancestral shrine or temple where divine presences manifest
zuò 坐	sit [meditation]	人 (person) + 土 (ground)	Traditionally sitting on the heels with postural alignment (正). Usually solitary (獨), but may involve two or more companions (人/人) and even a multitude (眾). Centered (中), guarded (守), and still (靜). Also sometimes utilizes cushions (座蒲) and mats (座布団)

Appendix 7

Principles of Daoist Translation

The following guidelines were composed by the Daoist Translation Committee 道教翻譯學會, a collaborative collective being organized by the Daoist Foundation 道教基金會 and under the general editorship of Louis Komjathy 康思奇. The principles are intended to inspire deeper reflection on the possibility of "Daoist translation" and to inform such translation projects. In addition to providing guidance for our own work, they represent a "living document" for inquiry, reflection, discussion, application, and revision. They are one of the foundations for our collaborative translation work.

~ Daoist translation is, first and foremost, translation that is **Daoist-informed and ideally Daoist-inspired and Daoist-infused**. As such, it is rooted in a **Daoist scholar-practitioner approach** (SPA), or at least a **Daoist study-practice model** (SPM).

~ Daoist translation is *translation*, the "**carrying over**" from source-text to target-text, here referring to Chinese Daoist literature and English translation, respectively. It is the degree to which the connection is honored and maintained that the resultant translation is translation as such. Some **defining characteristics and core commitments of translation** include accessibility, accuracy, fluency, readability, and reliability. Our own approach centers on composing complete, annotated scholarly and literary translations through deep attentiveness to language and context, including what might be understood as **"Daoist linguistics"** and "Daoist etymology."

~ More specifically, Daoist translation is translation work **informed by and ideally expressing foundational Daoist commitments, principles, qualities, and values**. Some of these include alignment, attunement, clarity, connection, cultivation, honesty, refinement, simplicity, stillness, and trustworthiness. Daoist translation should be infused with a "Daoist spirit" and "Daoist flavor," if you will.

~ For us, Daoist translation is rooted in Daoist practice. It is **study informing practice, and practice informing study**. Specifically, it involves having direct experiential understanding of the insights, perspectives, views, and actual practices documented in the texts being translated. While ours is an **inner cultivation model**, we recognize the value and importance of lived ritual literacy for translating liturgical literature. For "non-Daoist" translators, a Daoist approach to translation may be approximated through formal consultation and dialogic exchange with knowledgeable Daoists, or at least "thinking through" the literature in question.

~ **Daoist translation *is* Daoist practice**. Daoist translation may be understood as a form of both **scripture study and close reading**. It also connects to meditation and Yǎngshēng 養生 (Nourishing Life). This is translation as a way of life. Here we recall that "scriptures" (*jīng* 經) are one of the external Three Treasures (*sānbǎo* 三寶) of Daoism, with the others being the Dao 道 and the teachers (*shī* 師). In this way, Daoist translation is theological, in the sense of being orientated towards something larger and something more. Like the composition of commentaries based on original sources, scholarly annotation involves deep engagement and familiarity with the given text. By undertaking Daoist translation, we thus participate in the larger Daoist scholastic and hermeneutical sub-tradition.

~ Daoist translation involves **contemplative reading**. This is a mode of reading and interpretation informed by Daoist meditation, specifically as characterized by interiority, presence, and silence. "Contemplative reading" is, in turn, attentive, careful, intentional, reflective, and the like. We allow the primary text to inform our lives and to infuse our being.

~ Daoist translation is **community-oriented**. Daoist translators recognize the need for access to traditional Daoist literature by individuals who do not read Chinese. The associated translation work is undertaken with the aspiration to assist not just ourselves, but also others in deepening their understanding, practice, and realization. Daoist translations are **reverential gestures and offerings from and to the Daoist tradition**.

~ The resultant Daoist translations are **documentations of affiliation and lines of transmission**. They reveal Daoism as a **lived/living community, expression, and tradition** with contemporary relevance, manifesting in new forms and new places. Beyond texts as historical artifacts, Daoist translations provide opportunities for engagement, reflection, and application in/as/through **Daoist being, presence, and participation**.

~ **ESSENTIAL PRINCIPLES OF DAOIST TRANSLATION** ~

Daoist-Infused
Values-Informed
Practice-Based
Community-Oriented
Applied, Committed, Lived

Appendix 8

Towards a Dictionary of Daoist Classical Chinese

This appendix builds on my earlier work (Komjathy 2007, 2013a, 2017) to develop a Daoist-specific lexigraphy and lexicography. This may be thought of as "Daoist classical Chinese" (*dàojiào gǔwén* 道教古文). In addition to developing a bilingual Daoist engagement with Daoism, the present glossary also includes common and recurring characters appearing throughout the literature engaged in this primer. These may be thought of as foundational Daoist vocabulary and technical terminology. "DTC" indicates the preferred choice of the Daoist Translation Committee 道教翻譯學會, a collaborative collective being organized by the Daoist Foundation 道教基金會 and under the general editorship of Louis Komjathy 康思奇.

ān 庵/蓭: hut/hermitage. Sometimes used to designate a small temple, often a Buddhist one.

bìgǔ 辟穀: abstention from grains. Also appears as *duàngǔ* 斷穀/*juégǔ* 絕穀/*quègǔ* 卻穀. Also translated as "grain avoidance" and "abandonment of cereals." Key Daoist ascetic and dietetical practice. Sometimes refers to complete fasting.

chànhuǐ 懺悔: atonement. Also translated as "repentance." Daoist ritual involving moral purification and rectification, often with a Buddhist dimension centering on karma. DTC preferred translation: "atonement" (at-one-ment).

chángshēng 長生: perpetual life. Also translated as "longevity." May also be understood as "recurring birth." Born again in and to each moment. Sometimes refers to "immortality."

cúnshén 存神: preserve spirit. As such, refers to a conservation approach and method. Also used in the technical sense of "visualize gods/spirits."

cúnxiǎng 存想: visualization. Lit., "maintain thought." Sometimes appears or glossed as *cúnxiàng* 存象 (lit., "maintain image"), with some connection to *xiǎngxiàng* 想像 ("imagine"). One of the five major types of Daoist meditation.

dàkuài 大塊: Great Clod. A Daoist name for the earth. Recalls the Daoist emphasis on "merging with dust" (*tóngchén* 同塵).

dàtōng 大通: great pervasion. Also problematically translated as "Great Pervader." Contemplative and mystical state of complete alignment and connection with the Dao. Basically synonymous with meditative absorption.

dǎzuò 打坐: meditation. Lit., "engage in/undertake sitting." General name for Daoist seated meditation.

dān 丹: elixir/pill. Technically refers to "cinnabar" (mercuric sulfide [HgS]). Often appears as shorthand for *dānshā* 丹砂. Also translated more liberally as "alchemy."

dāndào 丹道: Way of the Elixir. Also rendered as "alchemical path." May refer to external alchemy or internal alchemy.

dāntián 丹田: elixir field(s). Also occasionally translated as "cinnabar field(s)." Subtle corporeal locations. Without qualification usually refers to the navel region.

dào 道: Dao/Tao/Way. Sacred and ultimate concern of Daoists. DTC preferred translation: "Dao."

dàoguǒ 道果: fruits of the Dao. Also referred to as "Way-Fruits" or just "fruition" for short. More refined or realized states/traits resulting from dedicated Daoist practice. Some examples include *shénxiān* 神仙 ("spirit immortality"), *wúlòu* 無漏 ("non-dissipation"), *wúwéi* 無為 ("non-action"), and *xiāoyáo* 逍遙 ("carefree ease").

dàohào 道號: Daoist name. Also referred to as "Daoist sobriquet." Sometimes synonymous with a Daoist's religious name (*fǎmíng* 法名). Usually a formal initiation/ordination/institutional name bestowed by one's primary teacher (*shīfu* 師父).

dàohuì 道會: Daoist association. Lit., "meeting of the Dao."

dàojiā 道家: Family of the Dao. One of the indigenous names for "Daoism." Referred to as so-called ~~philosophical Daoism~~ in outdated and inaccurate Orientalist constructions of Daoism (avoid). May be approximated in English as "classical Daoism."

dàojiào 道教: Teachings of the Dao. One of the indigenous names for "Daoism." Referred to as so-called ~~religious Daoism~~ in outdated and inaccurate Orientalist constructions of Daoism (avoid). May be approximated in English as "organized Daoism."

dàojiè 道戒: Daoist precepts. Daoist conduct guidelines, principles, rules, and so forth.

dàojīng 道經: Daoist scriptures. Most important, influential and revered Daoist literary genre.

dàoqì 道炁: qi of the Dao. Also referred to as "Way-Energy" for short. The specific type of qi associated with the Dao (numinous/sacred presence) and with realized Daoists and the Daoist community by extension. Connected with the view of Daoism as the "teaching beyond/without words" (*bùyán zhī jiào* 不言之教) and "Mysterious Movement" (*xuánfēng* 玄風).

dàoshì 道士: Daoist priest. Lit., "adept of the Dao." Technically refers to ordained Daoist priests and monastics. Most common form of honorific address for Daoist affiliates. DTC preferred translation: "Daoist priest."

dàoshù 道術: techniques of the Dao. Also translated as "arts of the Way" and referred to as "Way-Arts" for short. Daoist methods for cultivating and realizing the Dao. DTC preferred translation: "techniques of the Dao."

dàoxìng 道性: Dao-nature. Synonymous with "original nature" (*běnxìng* 本性), one's original and inherent connection to and expression of the Dao.

dǎoyǐn 導引: Daoyin (Guided Stretching). Lit., "guiding and pulling." Also referred to as "calisthenics," "gymnastics," and most problematically "healing exercises." Not so-called "Daoist/Taoist Yoga." Daoist stretching and breathwork, often including self-massage (*ànmó* 按摩 ["pressing and rubbing"]). DTC preferred translation: "Daoyin."

dàozàng 道藏: Daoist Canon. Lit., "storehouse of the Dao." Also referred to as "Daoist collectanea." Received edition dates to 1445, with a 1607 supplement. Contains 1,487 individual titles. DTC preferred translation: "Daoist Canon."

dàozhǎng 道長: Daoist elder. Also referred to as "Way-Elder" for short. Honorific term for ordained Daoist priests and monastics.

dé 德: inner power. Also translated as "integrity," "potency," and "virtue." The Dao manifesting as embodied activity in the world, activity that exerts a beneficial and transformational influence. DTC preferred translation: "inner power," with "virtue" sometimes more appropriate and accurate.

dédào 得道: realizing the Dao. Also translated as "attaining the Dao," which is slightly problematic because of the Daoist emphasis on "non-grasping."

dìng 定: absorption. Also translated as "concentration" and "stability." Also the Chinese translation of the Indian and Buddhist Sanskrit *samādhi*. Contemplative state and trait. In terms of the latter, DTC preferred translation: "absorption."

dònggōng 動功: movement practice. Usually refers to Yǎngshēng practice. May be understood as "body-training," remembering the informing Daoist energetic view.

dú 獨: alone/aloneness. Sometimes used as a Daoist technical term for solitary meditation, including the resultant state of detachment, imperviousness, and spiritual independence.

fǎ 法: method. May also mean "dharma," "pattern," "phenomena," and "teaching."

fúqì 服氣: ingesting qi. Also referred to as "qi-ingestion." Key Yǎngshēng practice. Also one of the five primary types of Daoist meditation.

gǎnyìng 感應: resonance. Also translated as "response and retribution." May also mean "induction" and even "telepathy." Most basically refers to sacred alignment and cosmological attunement (at-tune-ment), including appropriate responsiveness. Sometimes has a Buddhist influence emphasizing karma.

gāogōng 高功: head officiant. Lit., "lofty accomplishment/merit." The head priest who performs a given Daoist ritual.

gōng 公: elder. In ancient usage, refers to "dukes."

APPENDIX 8: TOWARDS A DICTIONARY OF DAOIST CLASSICAL CHINESE 405

gōng 功: exercise. May also mean "accomplishment" and "merit."

gōng 宮: palace. In Daoist usage, designates a Daoist temple. Technically indicates imperial recognition, so ends in 1911. DTC preferred translation: "palace."

gōngkè 功課: liturgy. More literally refers to "homework/schoolwork." Key liturgical texts chanted in Daoist ritual.

guān 觀: observe/observation. Sometimes translated as "contemplation." Key Daoist principle, practice, and quality. Also the Chinese translation of the Indian Buddhist Pali *vipassanā*/Sanskrit *vipaśyanā* ("insight meditation"). DTC preferred translation: "observation."

guàn 觀: monastery. Also translated as "abbey/belvedere/observatory/temple." Note the fourth tone when indicating a Daoist temple. In a modern context, technically designates a monastery.

hòutiān 後天: Later Heaven. Also translated as "deuterocosmic/Posterior Heaven/postnatal." Generally understood as the cosmogonic moment(s) associated with the appearance of the manifest universe. Corresponds to energy derived from breath and food after birth ("postnatal qi") in human existence.

huì 會: association. Also translated as "congregation" and "meeting-hall." Often referred to as *dàohuì* 道會 ("Daoist associations") in order to distinguish Daoist places/spaces from other types of meetings.

Hùndùn 混沌/渾沌: Primordial Chaos. Refers to early, often earliest cosmogonic moment characterized by Oneness and Nondifferentiation.

Hùnyuán 混元: Chaos Prime. Also translated as "Primordial Origin/Source." Often used synonymously with Hùndùn. Also appears as the honorific name for Lǎozǐ 老子 ("Master Lao") and Lǎojūn 老君 (Lord Lao).

jī 機: pivot. Also translated as "mechanism," "trigger," and even "workings." May designate an actual machine or refer to opportunity. Often used synonymously with *shū* 樞 ("center/hub/pivot"). In Daoist technical usage, often refers to the primary source of a given pattern or experience (e.g., Dao and the heart-mind).

jí 極: ridgepole. The crossbeam rafter in an architectural structure. May also mean "apex," "extreme," "pole," and "ultimate." In Daoist technical usage, often refers to cosmological processes and deeper, primary influences/movements, specifically yin-yang differentiation and interaction.

jiào 醮: offering. Also referred to as the "rite of cosmic renewal." One of the two major forms of large-scale Daoist public ritual.

jiè 戒: precepts. Usually refers to moral guidelines and religious rules. Often referred to as *dàojiè* 道戒 ("Daoist precepts") in order to distinguish Daoist principles and values from those of other traditions (e.g., Buddhism).

jīndān 金丹: golden elixir. May refer to the final outcome and culmination of external alchemy or internal alchemy. Sometimes used in the sense of Golden Elixir as the name for alchemical movements as a whole.

jīng 精: vital essence. One's foundational vitality. Associated with the kidneys, physicality, sexuality, and procreation. Generally considered finite in quantity, dissipating and eventually becoming exhausted with age. Associated with semen in men and menstrual blood in women. The first, lowest, and most material of the internal Three Treasures.

jǐng 景: effulgence(s). Also translated as "phosphors," "scenery," and "view." In Daoist visualization practices, refers to luminous and numinous energies related to the sun, moon, and stars. Sometimes used in a Buddhist technical sense of phenomenal appearances.

jīng 經: scripture. Daoist sacred texts. Most important, influential and revered Daoist literary genre. Usually anonymous and considered revealed and/or inspired. The second of the external Three Treasures. Often referred to as *dàojīng* 道經 ("Daoist scriptures") in order to distinguish Daoist sacred texts from those of other traditions (e.g., Ruism ["Confucianism"] and Buddhism). The term may thus also be rendered as "classic" and even "sutra." DTC preferred translation: "scripture."

jīng 經: meridians. Energy channels and pathways in the body.

jìng 靜: still/stillness. Also translated as "tranquil/tranquility." Key Daoist approach, value, principle, practice, quality, and state/trait. DTC preferred translation: "stillness."

jìnggōng 靜功: stillness practice. Usually refers to meditation practice. May be understood as "mind-training," remembering the informing Daoist energetic view.

jìngshì 淨室: pure chamber. Also appearing as *jìngshì* 靜室, *qīngshě* 清舍, or some variant, and also translated as "quiet chamber," "room of quiescence," and more occasionally "oratory." Originally small detached, wooden huts with minimal furnishings. Usually used for purification and religious practice. Later may designate a meditation studio or room. DTC preferred translation: "pure chamber."

jìngzuò 靜坐: Quiet Sitting. Also translated as "sitting-in-stillness" and "tranquil sitting." Emphasis placed on entering and abiding in the state of stillness (*jìng* 靜). Most common modern Daoist technical term for Daoist apophatic and quietistic meditation. DTC preferred translation: "Quiet Sitting."

Lǎojūn 老君: Lord Lao. The deified Lǎozǐ 老子 ("Master Lao"), high god of early Daoism, and personification of the Dao. Appears as Dàodé tiānzūn 道德天尊 (Celestial Worthy of Dao and Inner Power) in the Sānqīng 三清 (Three Purities).

liàndān 煉丹: refining the elixir. One of the names for Daoist alchemical practice and transmutation, whether external or internal.

Língbǎo 靈寶: Numinous Treasure. Key early medieval Daoist movement emphasizing ritual and universal salvation.

Lóngmén 龍門: Dragon Gate. Largest lineage of Quánzhēn 全眞 (Complete Perfection) Daoism emphasizing precept study and application (ethics).

lùndào 論道: discourse on the Dao. Also translated as "discussing the Dao" and referred to as "Way-Discourse" for short. Daoist conversations, discussions and lectures about the Dao, Daoism, and/or Daoist practice-realization.

mìng 命: life-destiny. May also refer to "fate." In the larger Daoist tradition, associated with the kidneys and vital essence (*jīng* 精). One's foundational vitality and physicality. Usually cultivated through movement practice (e.g., Yǎngshēng).

nèidān 內丹: internal alchemy. Also translated as "inner elixir/pill." Also referred to as "physiological alchemy." Usually refers to stage-based Daoist training regimens aimed at complete psychosomatic transformation, or "immortality" in Daoist terms.

nèigōng 內功: inner work. Also translated as "internal exercises/practice." Usually refers to meditation.

nèiguān 內觀: inner observation. One of five major types of Daoist meditation. May involve non-discriminating awareness of all phenomena and/or exploration of the Daoist body as an inner landscape.

niàn 念: recollection. May also mean "chant," "think," "read," and "reflect." Also the Chinese translation of the Indian Buddhist Pali *sati* ("mindfulness").

niànjīng 念經: chant scriptures. Also translated as "recitation."

pài 派: lineage. Lit., "tributary." Various branches within Daoist movements and sub-traditions. The most specific and narrowest form of Daoist religious identity, affiliation, and location.

pǔ 樸/朴: unhewn simplicity. Also translated as "unadorned simplicity" and "uncarved block." Key Daoist value, principle, practice, quality, and state/trait. DTC preferred translation: "unhewn simplicity" or just "simplicity."

qì 氣/炁: qi. Variously translated as "subtle/vital breath," "energy," and even "pneuma" (Greek). The latter often indicates affiliation with the Schafer (actually Strickmann) school. Qi may refer to both physical breath and a more subtle current/presence. The fundamental cosmic (non)material substance. The second of the internal Three Treasures. DTC preferred translation: "qi."

qīngjìng 清靜: clarity and stillness. Also translated as "purity and tranquility." Key Daoist value, principle, practice, quality, and state/trait. Usually associated with Daoist apophatic and quietistic meditation. One of the main connective strands throughout the entire Daoist tradition. DTC preferred translation: "clarity and stillness" or "clear stillness."

Qīngjìng wúwéi dào 清靜無為道: Way of Clear Stillness and Nonaction. One of the indigenous Chinese Daoist names for "Daoism."

Quánzhēn 全眞/全真: Complete Perfection. Also translated as "Complete Authenticity/Reality/Realization" and obfuscatingly as "Completion of Authenticity." Most influential late medieval Daoist movement and one of two forms of institutional Daoism surviving into the modern world. Emphasis placed on alchemy, asceticism, and mysticism. As a monastic order, technically involves the three core commitments and vows, namely, celibacy (no sex), sobriety (no intoxicants), and vegetarianism (no meat). DTC preferred translation: "Complete Perfection."

rìyòng 日用: daily application. Also translated as "daily practice."

rùjìng 入靜: entering stillness. Daoist term for meditation. Points towards innate nature-as-stillness, which is the Dao-as-Stillness.

rùshān 入山: entering the mountains. May refer to actual mountain seclusion, eremitic withdrawal, meditation, and/or ritual. Draws attention to the central importance of actual mountains, their symbolic associations, and one's lived experience thereof in Daoism.

sānbǎo 三寶: Three Treasures. May refer to the internal Three Treasures of vital essence, qi, and spirit or the external Three Treasures of the Dao, scriptures, and teachers.

sāncái 三才: Three Powers. Lit., "three materials/talents." Three primary consists of the universe. Heaven, earth, and humanity. Sometimes used synonymously with the Three Bureaus/Offices.

sānguān 三官: Three Bureaus. Also translated as "Three Offices/Officers." Three primary constituents of the universe. Heaven, earth, and water.

Sānqīng 三清: Three Purities. Also translated as "Three Pure Ones." Yuánshǐ tiānzūn 原始天尊 (Celestial Worthy of Original Beginning; highest/center), Língbǎo tiānzūn 靈寶天尊 (Celestial Worthy of Numinous Treasure; middle/left), and Dàodé tiānzūn 道德天尊 (Celestial Worthy of the Dao and Inner Power). Three primordial cosmic energies. Often discussed as the "high gods" of Daoism. Represented in anthropomorphized form as three old Chinese men. Connected to the Three Heavens.

sānshī 三尸: Three Deathbringers. Also translated as "Three Corpses" and also referred to as the "Three Worms" (*sānchóng* 三蟲). In early medieval Daoism, three biospiritual parasites believed to bring about disease and premature death. Later psychologized to indicate disruptive and harmful influences.

sāntiān 三天: Three Heavens. Yùqīng 玉清 (Jade Clarity; upper), Tàiqīng 太清 (Great Clarity; middle), and Shàngqīng 上清 (Highest Clarity; lowest).

sāntián 三田: Three Fields. Also referred to as the "three elixir fields" (*sān dāntián* 三丹田). In the more standard list, they include Qìhǎi 氣海 (Ocean of Energy; navel region; lower), Jiànggōng 絳宮 (Scarlet Palace; heart region; middle), and Zǔqiào 祖竅 (Ancestral Cavity; center of head; upper), with various name variants.

shàn 善: adept/adeptness. Also translated as "aptitude." More conventionally means "good/goodness" and "be good/skilled at." DTC preferred translation: "adept/adeptness."

Shàngqīng 上清: Highest Clarity. Also translated as "Highest Purity" and somewhat inaccurately referred to as "Máoshān 茅山 (Mount Máo) Daoism." Key early medieval Daoist movement emphasizing visualization and ecstatic journeying.

shén 神: spirit. May also mean "divine." Also occasionally translated as "daemon," which often indicates affiliation with the Graham school. May refer to divinities (outer and inner), spiritual capacities, and consciousness in a more abstract sense. Also used as an adjective ("divine/spiritual"). The third, highest, and most subtle of the internal Three Treasures. Sometimes designates Daoist body-gods.

shéntōng 神通: spirit pervasion. Also translated as "divine connection." Associated with the Indian and Buddhist Sanskrit *siddhi* ("accomplishment/attainment"), variously approximated as "numinous abilities," "paranormal abilities," and "psychic/supernatural powers."

shénxiān 神仙: spirit immortal/spiritual immortality. Also translated as "divine transcendent/divine transcendence." Often identified as the highest form of "immortality," that is, enduring, perhaps eternal personal post-mortem existence. More technically, the penultimate type or rank, just below "celestial immortals" (*tiānxiān* 天仙).

shèngrén 聖人: sage. The primary ideal of classical Daoism. Human beings who embody Daoist values and represent the Daoist community and tradition.

shì 士: adept. As a Daoist technical term, also translated as "practitioner." Originally designated a lower member of the aristocracy and feudal order, and thus rendered as "knight" and/or "retainer." Also used in the Ruist ("Confucian") sense of "scholar-official." As a Daoist category, individuals committed to cultivating the Dao and participating in the Daoist community. DTC preferred translation: "adept" or "practitioner."

shīfu 師父: master-father. Also translated as "teacher." Technically, a given Daoist's formal teacher or spiritual father/mother. Used by Daoists in a gender-neutral sense.

shījiě 尸解: corpse-liberation. Also translated as "escape/deliverance/liberation by means of a corpse-simulacrum." Lower form of "immortality" that involves using an object (e.g., a staff) as a substitute body to feign death. Usually refers to extended longevity on the earth.

shīyé 師爺: master-grandfather. Also translated as "grand-teacher." Technically, the teacher of one's formal teacher or spiritual father/mother. Used by Daoists in a gender-neutral sense.

shǒu 守: guard/guarding. Used as a Daoist technical term for meditation. Appears as *shǒucí* 守雌 ("guarding the feminine"), *shǒujìng* 守靜 ("guarding stillness"), *shǒuyī* 守一 ("guarding the One"), and *shǒuzhōng* 守中 ("guarding the Center").

shǒuyī 守一: guarding the One. Classical Daoist term for apophatic and quietistic meditation. Emphasis placed emptiness and stillness, with the resultant (non)experience of mystical union with the Dao-as-One (*yī* 一). Eventually used to refer to Daoist meditation in general, even including visualization.

shù 術: techniques. Often referred to as *dàoshù* 道術 ("techniques of the Dao") in order to distinguish Daoist methods from other types of practices.

shuìgōng 睡功: sleep exercises. May refer to recumbent Dǎoyǐn methods and/or actual sleep practice.

tàijí 太極: Taiji/Great Ultimate. Also translated as "Supreme Polarity." Yin-yang differentiation and interaction.

tāijié 胎節: embryonic knots. Also appears as *jiéjié* 結節. Technically refers to obstructions based on ancestral and/or karmic influences. Beyond ordinary and known conditions.

Tàiqīng 太清: Great Clarity. Also translated as "Great Purity." Key early medieval Daoist movement emphasizing external alchemy.

Tàishàng 太上: Great High. Also translated as "uppermost" and "supreme," with some overlap with *wúliàng* 無量 ("limitless"). More technically appears as an abbreviation for Tàishàng Lǎojūn 太上老君 (Great High Lord Lao), the deified Lǎozǐ 老子 ("Master Lao").

tāixī 胎息: embryonic respiration. One of the most renowned and influential Daoist respiratory techniques. Sometimes understood as Yǎngshēng;

at other times, located in internal alchemy. Usually involves the temporary and apparent cessation of normal respiration.

Tiānshī 天師: Celestial Masters. Also translated as "Heavenly Teachers." Most influential early Daoist movement and one of two forms of institutional Daoism surviving into the modern world. The pre-modern movement centered on the Zhāng 張 family. Emphasis placed on communal ritual and moral purity. DTC preferred translation: "Celestial Masters."

tiānxià 天下: all-under-heaven. Lit., "under-sky." Also translated as "world." The known world, especially the human socio-political realm. Cf. *shìjiè* 世界 ("world"), *tiāndì* 天地 ("heaven and earth"), *yǔzhòu* 宇宙 ("cosmos/universe"), and *zìrán* 自然 ("Nature").

tiānxiān 天仙: celestial immortal. Also translated as "heavenly transcendent." Sometimes used more technically as the highest form of immortality, but also synonymous with spirit immortal (*shénxiān* 神仙).

tóng 同: merge. Also translated as "identical" and "same/sameness." Process and state of being aligned and connected with the Dao, including in a state of mystical unity.

tōng 通: pervade/pervaded/pervasion. Also translated as "connect/connected/connection." May also be understood as "throughness." Process and state of being aligned and connected with the Dao, including in a state of mystical unity. DTC preferred translation: "pervasion."

wàidān 外丹: external alchemy. Also translated as "outer elixir/pill." Also referred to as "laboratory/operational alchemy." Refers to combining, refining, decocting and consuming elixir formulas consisting of diverse and various ingredients.

wànwù 萬物: myriad beings. Also translated as "myriad things" and "ten thousand things." Everything in existence.

wújí 無極: Wuji/Nondifferentiation. Also translated as "limitlessness," "non-polarity," and "non-ultimate." In Daoist technical usage, the cosmogonic (non)moment before the manifest universe based on yin-yang differentiation and interaction (Tàijí). DTC preferred translation: "Nondifferentiation."

wúlòu 無漏: non-dissipation. Lit., "without leakage." Related to conservation of vital essence, especially through sensory and psychological disengagement as well as celibacy, whether temporary or permanent. In internal alchemy (*nèidān* 內丹), usually understood as a prerequisite and foundation for more advanced training and attainment. Corresponds to the Sanskrit *anāsrava*.

wúwéi 無為: non-action. Also translated as "effortlessness" and "not-/non-doing." Uncontrived and naturally responsive modes of being and interacting. Usually involves non-interference and non-intervention. Classical and foundational Daoist approach, value, principle, practice, quality, and state/trait. Informed by and informing Daoist apophatic and quietistic meditation. DTC preferred translation: "non-action" or "nonaction."

xiāndào 仙道: Way of Immortals. Also rendered as "Way of Immortality" and "immortal path." May refer to external alchemy or internal alchemy.

xiānrén 仙人: immortal. Also translated as "ascendent" and "transcendent." Etymologically speaking, refers to beings (人/亻) living in the mountains (山). The character variant 僊 points towards a connection with birds/flying (䙴). The primary ideal of organized Daoism, especially among practitioners of external or internal alchemy. Usually refers to individuals who have successfully completed alchemical transmutation and achieved a non-dying, or at least eternal state of being. DTC preferred translation: "immortal."

xiāntāi 仙胎: immortal embryo. Also appearing as *shèngtāi* 聖胎 ("sacred embryo"). The transcendent spirit created through inner alchemical training. Sometimes indicates latency that develops into the Child/Infant (*yīng'ér* 嬰兒).

xiāntiān 先天: Prior Heaven. Also translated as "Anterior Heaven/proto-cosmic/prenatal." Generally understood as the cosmogonic moment(s) before the appearance of the manifest universe, but still related to emanation and differentiation. Corresponds to energy acquired from the cosmos and ancestors prior to birth ("prenatal qi") in human existence.

xiàng 象: appearance. Technically depicts an elephant. May also mean "emblem," "figure," "image," "shape," "symbol," and so forth. In Daoist technically usage, often refers to an appearance or object that not only represents, but also contains the presence of an associated being or energy. Also used to refer to the hexagrams of the ancient *Yìjīng* 易經 (Classic of Change).

xiāoyáo 逍遙: carefree ease. Also translated as "being carefree" and "free and easy." Also appears as *xiāoyáo yóu* 逍遙遊 ("carefree wandering"). Key Daoist approach, value, principle, practice, quality, and state/trait.

xiéhuì 協會: association. May also mean "organization" and "society." As used in the sense of "Daoist association" (*dàojiào xiéhuì* 道教協會), technically indicates institutional location inside the modern Chinese bureaucratic state and structure (People's Republic of China) and thus has a political association. The more traditional Daoist designation is *dàohuì* 道會.

xīn 心: heart-mind. Also translated as "heart" and/or "mind." May also mean "center" and "core." As the traditional Daoist view is psychosomatic and energetic, "heart-mind" is more accurate. The psychospiritual center of human personhood. Considered the storehouse of spirit. DTC preferred translation: "heart-mind."

xīnzhāi 心齋: fasting of the heart-mind. Also referred to as "heart-fast" and "mind-retreat" for short. Classical Daoist term for apophatic and quietistic meditation. Emphasis placed on disengaging sense perception and decreasing psychological agitation.

xíng 行: practice. More literally means "move" and "walk." In technical Daoist usage (via Buddhism), may also refer to "beneficial/good deeds" or "meritorious activity," especially actions that neutralize negative karma and increase positive karma.

xìng 性: innate nature. In the larger Daoist tradition, associated with the heart and spirit (*shén* 神). One's original and inherent connection with the Dao. Also the ground of one's being. Usually cultivated through stillness practice (e.g., meditation).

xìngmìng shuāngxiū 性命雙修: dual cultivation of innate nature and life-destiny. Psychosomatic cultivation. Integrated and holistic practice. Often explained as a balance of "stillness practice" (*jìnggōng* 靜功; meditation), focusing on the heart/innate nature/spirit, and of "movement practice" (*dònggōng* 動功; Yǎngshēng), focusing on the navel/life-destiny/qi.

xiūdào 修道: cultivating the Dao. *Xiū* 修 may also mean "mend" and "tend." Often invoked in English as "Daoist cultivation."

xiūjìng 修靜: cultivating stillness. Both intensive quietistic meditation practice and stillness as an all-encompassing existential approach.

xiūliàn 修煉/修鍊: cultivation and refinement. Or "cultivation-refinement." Sometimes approximated as "ascesis." Technically refers to Daoist alchemical training and transmutation. Often understood as shorthand for *xiūdào* 修道 ("cultivating the Dao") and *liàndān* 煉丹 ("refining the elixir").

xiūxíng 修行: cultivation and practice. Or "cultivation-practice." General Daoist term for "Daoist practice." Basically synonymous with *xiūchí* 修持, but the latter often includes "maintaining the precepts" (*chíjiè* 持戒). *Xiūxíng* also is used to translate the Indian Sanskrit *sādhanā* (spiritual discipline).

xiūzhēn 修眞: cultivating perfection. Also translated as "cultivating the real/true." Daoist alchemical training, especially internal alchemy (*nèidān* 內丹). Training regimens aspiring for complete psychosomatic transmutation, referred to as "perfection" (*zhēn* 眞/真). DTC preferred translation: "cultivating perfection."

xuán 玄: mystery/mysterious. Also translated as "dark" and "profound." Daoist (non)description of the Dao-as-Mystery. DTC preferred translation: "mystery/mysterious."

Xuánfēng 玄風: Mysterious Movement. *Fēng* 風 literally means "wind," and "current" by extension. One of the indigenous Chinese Daoist names for "Daoism."

Xuánmén 玄門: Mysterious Gate. Also translated as "Door/Gateway to the Mysterious." One of the indigenous Chinese Daoist names for "Daoism."

Xuánxué 玄學: Profound Learning. Also translated as "Dark Learning," "Mysterious Learning," and "Mystery Studies." Key early medieval Daoist quasi-salon and hermeneutic movement emphasizing reading and interpretation of the *Dàodé jīng* and *Zhuāngzǐ* ("Lǎo-Zhuāng Daoism"). Referred to as so-called ~~Neo-Daoism~~ in outdated and inaccurate Orientalist accounts of Daoism (avoid). DTC preferred translation: "Profound Learning."

yī 一: one/oneness/unity. Literally the number 1. May refer to the Dao (One), the process (unification), and the associated state (oneness/unity). Appears in important classical Daoist technical terms designating apophatic and quietistic meditation, including *bàoyī* 抱一 ("embracing the One"), *déyī* 得一 ("attaining/realizing the One"), *shǒuyī* 守一 ("guarding the One"), and *zhíyī* 執一 ("holding the One").

yángshén 陽神: yang-spirit. The transcendent spirit actualized and/or created through alchemical training and transmutation.

yǎngshēng 養生: Yangsheng. Lit., "nourishing life." Generally refers to health and longevity techniques. However, may also involve a larger repertoire, including dietetics and hygiene. DTC preferred translation: "Yangsheng."

yǐndé 隱德/陰德: hidden virtue. Exerting positive influence and effects and performing beneficial deeds without expectation of recognition or reward. Often considered a foundational and/or prerequisite for more advanced Daoist training.

yīnshì 因是: adaptive presence. Lit., "according with/following this/here." Also translated as "flowing cognition" (Harold Roth). Daoist contemplative state and trait, especially associated with embodied being-in-the-world.

yuánqì 元氣: original qi. Also translated as "original/primal/primordial breath." One of the purest and least differentiated forms of qi. Sometimes viewed as endowed, but generally understood as cultivated, actualized and embodied through Daoist practice. DTC preferred translation: "original qi."

yuánshén 元神: original spirit. Also translated as "primal/primordial spirit." The purest and least differentiated expression of spirit. Associated with the heart-mind and innate nature. Sometimes viewed as endowed, but generally understood as cultivated, actualized and embodied through Daoist practice. DTC preferred translation: "original spirit."

zàohuà 造化: transformative process. Also problematically translated as "creation" and inaccurately as "Creator." The universe as impersonal transformative process, especially as based yin-yang differentiation and interaction. DTC preferred translation: "transformative process."

zhāi 齋: fast/fasting. On the most basic level, actual dietary fasting. Also used by Daoists to refer to meditation. Most technically, purification rituals, which also are referred to as "fasts," "retreats," and even "levée" (via French *lever* ["rise"]) in the sense of formal court audiences. One of the two major forms of large-scale Daoist public ritual.

zhēn 眞/真: perfect/perfected/perfection. Also translated as "authentic/real/true." The character technically depicts a reaction vessel and/or alchemical crucible. For alchemical literature, "perfect/perfected/perfection" is the DTC preferred translation.

zhēnqì 眞氣/真氣: perfect qi. Also translated as "authentic/real/true energy." Generally understood as cultivated, actualized and embodied through Daoist practice. DTC preferred translation: "perfect qi."

zhēnrén 眞人/真人: Perfected. Also translated as "authentic/real/true being/person." One of the ideals of organized Daoism, especially among practitioners of external or internal alchemy. Usually refers to individuals who have successfully completed alchemical transmutation and achieved a non-dying, or at least eternal state of being. DTC preferred translation: "Perfected."

zhèng 正: align/aligned/alignment. May also mean "correct," "proper," "right," "upright," and even "orthodox." As a Daoist technical term, often refers to cosmological attunement and postural alignment, especially in formal meditation practice. DTC preferred translation (via Harold Roth): "align/aligned/alignment."

zhèngyàn 證驗: experiential confirmation. Also approximated as "signs of proof" and "verification." Beneficial and transformative effects of successful Daoist practice, often including numinous abilities (Skt.: *siddhi*). DTC preferred translation: "experiential confirmation."

Zhèngyī 正一: Orthodox Unity. Alternative name for Tiānshī 天師 (Celestial Masters) Daoism. Most influential early Daoist movement and one of two forms of institutional Daoism surviving into the modern world. The modern movement centers on various family lineages. Emphasis placed on communal ritual and moral purity.

zhǐ 止: pause/stop. Key Daoist approach, value, principle, practice, quality, and state/trait. Later used to translate the Buddhist Pali *samatha* and Sanskrit *śamatha*, "calm abiding" meditation. Also referred to as "cessation."

zhìrén 至人: utmost person. *Zhì* 至 also may be understood as "actualized," "complete," and "fulfilled." Sometimes used synonymously for *shèngrén* 聖人 ("sage"), and thus designates the classical Daoist ideal.

zhōng 中: center. May refer to the Dao (Center), the process (centering), and the state/outcome (centered). As a somatic location usually designates the heart region, but sometimes refers to the navel region.

zhújī 築基: establishing a foundation. Often used to designate the first, preliminary stage(s) of internal alchemy practice. Usually involves strengthening a root in virtue, including through hidden merit and good deeds, as the prerequisite for more advanced training.

zǐ 子: master/adept. Traditional designation (as suffix) for an elder and senior teacher (e.g., Lǎozǐ 老子 ["Master Lao"]) or (as prefix) for a disciple and student (e.g., Zǐkuí 子葵 [Adept Kui]).

zìrán 自然: suchness. Lit., "self-so." Also translated as "naturalness," "spontaneity," "thusness," and even "Nature." The Dao and reality as such. Being-so-of-itself. As-is-ness. DTC preferred translation: "suchness," recognizing that the latter also may invoke the Buddhist *rúlái* 如來 ("thus-come"; Skt.: *tathāgata*).

zuòwàng 坐忘: sitting-in-forgetfulness. Lit., "sit and forget." Also problematically translated as "sitting in oblivion." Referred to as "seated forgetting" or "forgetful sitting" for short. Classical Daoist term for apophatic and quietistic meditation. Emphasis placed on disengaging sense perception and decreasing psychological agitation, to the point of entering forgetfulness. From this perspective, *wàng* 忘 parallels *jìng* 靜 ("stillness") and *xū* 虛 ("emptiness").

Appendix 9

Foundational Readings of Daoist Literature in Translation

THE PRESENT APPENDIX OFFERS A concise, critical list of foundational readings of Daoist literature in reliable translation. These may be used to further one's translation facility and to deepen one's engagement with Daoist literature. Paralleling this translation primer as a whole, I focus on key works related to Daoist cultivation and refinement (*xiūliàn* 修煉/ 修鍊), with specific attention to foundational commitments, principles, qualities, values, views, and so forth. With the exception of the anonymous mid-fourth-century BCE *Nèiyè* 內業 (Inward Training), which is a recently rediscovered classical Daoist composition, the texts are organized chronologically.

Dàodé zhēnjīng (Lǎozǐ)
Nánhuá zhēnjīng (Zhuāngzǐ)
Nèiyè
Huáinánzǐ
Huángdì nèijīng sùwèn
Lǎozǐ míng
Lǎozǐ zhāngjù
Tàishàng huángtíng wàijǐng yùjīng (Huángtíng wàijǐng jīng)
Bàopǔzǐ nèipiān
Huángdì yīnfú jīng (Yīnfú jīng)
Tàishàng Lǎojūn shuō cháng qīngjìng miàojīng (Qīngjìng jīng)

Zuòwàng lùn
Wùzhēn piān
Chūzhēn jiè
Lóngmén xīnfǎ

For those who would prefer an alphabetical list, the fifteen texts are as follows:

Bàopǔzǐ nèipiān
Chūzhēn jiè
Dàodé zhēnjīng (*Lǎozǐ*)
Huáinánzǐ
Huángdì nèijīng sùwèn
Huángdì yīnfú jīng (*Yīnfú jīng*)
Lǎozǐ míng
Lǎozǐ zhāngjù
Lóngmén xīnfǎ
Nánhuá zhēnjīng (*Zhuāngzǐ*)
Nèiyè
Tàishàng huángtíng wàijǐng yùjīng (*Huángtíng wàijǐng jīng*)
Tàishàng Lǎojūn shuō cháng qīngjìng miàojīng (*Qīngjìng jīng*)
Wùzhēn piān
Zuòwàng lùn

If there are multiple translations, I have generally included what I consider to be the most reliable translation(s), obviously with a bias towards my own. The exceptions are Erkes' translation (1958) of the *Lǎozǐ zhāngjù* 老子章句 (Chapter-and-Verse Commentary on the *Lǎozǐ*; DZ 682; ZH 556) and Ware's translation (1966) of the *Bàopǔzǐ nèipiān* 抱朴子內篇 (Inner Chapters of Master Embracing Simplicity; DZ 1185; ZH 980). While pioneering and deserving recognition, both of these publications are outdated and often unreliable, and thus the primary Daoist texts deserve retranslation. In these cases, I have included unreliable scholarly translations because the texts themselves must be considered "foundational" from my perspective. The *Lǎozǐ zhāngjù*, which is the first commentary on the *Dàodé jīng* 道德經 (Scripture on the Dao and Inner Power) to provide chapter titles, is probably the most influential Daoist commentary and became a model for later installments. It provides insights into the text from an applied Daoist self-cultivation perspective, especially one informed by and informing Yǎngshēng 養生 (Nourishing Life; health and longevity practice). This might inspire deeper reflection on scripture study and exegesis as Yǎngshēng itself. The *Bàopǔzǐ nèipiān* is a key work of early medieval Daoism that is especially important for providing insights into Daoist religiosity, including Daoist alchemy, herbology, and minerology. For present purposes, it also illuminates the spectrum and diversity of lived Daoist practice (e.g., grain avoidance, meditation, qi ingestion). In any case, my brief annotations provide some key background information as well as point towards the contributions and limitations of the associated translation(s). This appendix may, in turn, be supplemented by my "Self-Study Guide to Daoist Scripture Study" (2022) and "Daoist Literature in Translation: An Annotated Catalogue" (2022), which is a revised, updated, and expanded version of my earlier "Daoist Texts in Translation" (2004).

DÀODÉ ZHĒNJĪNG 道德眞經: Perfect Scripture on the Dao and Inner Power: DZ 664; ZH 553. Also translated as the "Classic on the Way and Virtue." More commonly referred to as the *Dàodé jīng* and also known by its earliest title of *Lǎozǐ* 老子 (Book of Venerable Masters), which is more conventionally translated as "Book of Master Lao."
  A. Translated by D.C. Lau (1921–2010). *Chinese Classics: Tao Te Ching*. Hong Kong: The Chinese University Press, 1989 (1982). (historical)
  B. Translated by Wú Yí 吳怡. *The Book of Lao Tzu (The Tao Te Ching)*. San Bruno, CA: Great Learning Publishing Company, 1989. (philological)
  C. Translated by Michael LaFargue. *The Tao of the Tao Te Ching*. Albany: State University of New York Press, 1992. (practical)

D. Translated by Stephen Addiss and Stanley Lombardo. *Tao Te Ching*. Indianapolis: Hackett, 1993. (literary)
E. Selections translated by Louis Komjathy. *Handbooks for Daoist Practice*. 10 vols. Hong Kong: Yuen Yuen Institute, 2008 (2003). (Handbook 2) (literary/practical)

Anonymous multivocal anthology consisting of historical and textual layers dating from at least the fourth to the second century BCE. Contains the teachings and practices associated with various anonymous elders of the inner cultivation lineages of classical Daoism. Consists of 81 "verse-chapters" in the received (Wáng Bì 王弼) redaction. Traditionally attributed to the legendary Lǎozǐ 老子 ("Master Lao"; trad. dat. 6th c. BCE). However, revisionist scholarship requires a complete reimagining of received views, approaches, and interpretations. Key for developing a foundational Daoist view. For a select bibliography of translations see "On Translating the *Tao-te-ching*" (1998) by Michael LaFargue and Julian Pas. A complete translation that focuses on the contemplative characteristics of the text with attentiveness to the inner cultivation lineages of classical Daoism is currently being prepared by Louis Komjathy 康思奇 under the title *Dàodé jīng* 道德經: *A Contextual, Contemplative, and Annotated Bilingual Translation*, which is tentatively scheduled for publication by Square Inch Press by mid-2023. The versions by Ursula Le Guin (1929–2018) and Stephen Mitchell (b. 1943) as well as the adaptations of Wayne Dyer (1940–2015) and Benjamin Hoff (b. 1946) should be avoided, as they represent popular, Orientalist cultural appropriations rooted in hybrid spirituality and spiritual capitalism. They have little to do with the *Dàodé jīng* as such, which is a key work of classical Daoism and one of the most important scriptures in Daoist history. For critical discussions see Hardy 1998; LaFargue and Pas 1998; Komjathy 2004, 2014a; Siegler 2010; Carmichael 2017. For additional guidance see the "Self-Study Guide to *Dàodé jīng*" (2022) distributed by the Daoist Foundation 道教基金會.

NÁNHUÁ ZHĒNJĪNG 南華眞經: Perfect Scripture on Master Nanhua (Southern Florescence): DZ 670; ZH 616.
- A. Translated by Burton Watson. *The Complete Works of Chuang Tzu*. New York: Columbia University Press, 1968.
- B. Chapters 1–7 and selections from chapters 8–11, 13, 15, 22, 28–31, and 33 translated by A.C. Graham. *Chuang-tzu: The Inner Chapters*. New York: Mandala, 1981. Reprinted by Hackett Publishing Company, 2001.
- C. Translated by Victor Mair. *Wandering on the Way: Early Taoist Tales and Parables of Chuang Tzu*. New York: Bantam Books, 1994. Reprinted by University of Hawaii Press, 1998.

More commonly referred to by its earliest title *Zhuāngzǐ* 莊子 (Book of Master Zhuang), this is an anonymous/pseudonymous multivocal anthology consisting of historical and textual layers dating from at least the fourth to the second century BCE. It contains the teachings and practices associated with various anonymous, pseudonymous and named elders of the inner cultivation lineages of classical Daoism. The text consists of thirty-three prose chapters in the received (Guō Xiàng 郭象) redaction. The so-called Inner Chapters (chs. 1–7) are generally accepted as containing the teachings and writings of the text's namesake, the historical Zhuāng Zhōu 莊周 ("Master Zhuang"; ca. 370-ca. 290). Revisionist scholarship by A.C. Graham 葛瑞漢 (1919–1991), Liú Xiàogǎn 劉笑敢, Victor Mair 梅維恆, and Harold Roth 羅浩 identifies at least five distinct lineages or "schools" associated with a variety of chapters, which leads to a reorganization of the received text. In addition to providing entertaining stories and profound philosophical reflection, the text contains important information on the classical Daoist inner cultivation lineages, including specific inner cultivation techniques, apophatic and quietistic meditation in particular, and master-disciple dialogical exchanges. The latter became a major influence on the development of the Chán 禪 (Zen) Buddhist *yǔlù* 語錄 ("discourse record/recorded sayings") literary genre. The Watson translation, which is especially strong on the literary elements, tends to be the preferred one in Daoist Studies. Graham's translation is helpful for some philosophical insights, although it often uses idiosyncratic Sino-philological jargon that can be distracting, while Mair's translation is helpful for names and places. The *Zhuāngzǐ* also has now become appropriated in various Orientalist and academic publications, including repetitive edited volumes, by what may be understood as the "Zhuangzi Philosophy Industry" (ZZPI). For additional guidance see the "Self-Study Guide to *Zhuāngzǐ*" (2022) distributed by the Daoist Foundation 道教基金會.

NÈIYÈ 內業: INWARD TRAINING: Chapter 49 of the *Guǎnzǐ* 管子 (Book of Master Guan). Also translated as "Inner Cultivation" and "Inner Work."
    A. Translated by W. Allyn Rickett. *Guanzi: Political, Economic, and Philosophical Essays from Early China*. 2 vols. Princeton: Princeton University Press, 1985/1998. (Vol. 2, 39–55) (philological)
    B. Translated by Harold Roth. *Original Tao: Inward Training and the Foundations of Taoist Mysticism*. New York: Columbia University Press, 1999. (philological/historical)
    C. Translated by Louis Komjathy. *Handbooks for Daoist Practice*. 10 vols. Hong Kong: Yuen Yuen Institute, 2008 (2003). (Handbook 1) (literary/practical)

Dating from the mid-fourth century BCE and paralleling the *Lǎozǐ* 老子 (Book of Venerable Masters), this text survives as a chapter (ch. 49) in the *Guǎnzǐ* 管子 (Book of Master Guan), a textual collection traditionally ascribed to Guǎn Zhòng 管仲 (d. 645 BCE), but edited by Liǔ Xiàng 柳向 (77–6 BCE) around 26 BCE. It is often grouped with three other texts as the so-called "Techniques of the Heart-mind" (*xīnshù* 心術) chapters, namely, "Xīnshù shàng" 心術上 (Heart-Mind Techniques I; ch. 36), "Xīnshù xià" 心術下 (Heart-Mind Techniques II; ch. 37), and "Báixīn" 白心 (Purifying the Heart-Mind; ch. 38). Most likely dating to the mid-fourth century BCE, and thus possibly the oldest extant classical Daoist text, the *Nèiyè* is a manual of self-cultivation emphasizing dietetics, quietistic meditation, and mystical realization of the Dao. Like the texts of the inner cultivation lineages of classical Daoism in general, primary emphasis is placed on emptiness- and stillness-based meditation. The *Nèiyè* is especially important and helpful as a companion to the *Dàodé jīng*, often providing more technical details on cognate practices. Roth's translation is germinal, especially with respect to revisionist scholarship on classical Daoism and establishing a text-critical edition. However, it is sometimes deficient on the technical dimensions of Daoist apophatic meditation, especially the (mis)interpretation of qì 氣 as associated with "breath meditation." Komjathy's translation, which acknowledges its debt to Roth, is a literary and practical one, with the introduction discussing technical terminology in lieu of annotations. It is more reliable on the technical specifics of the associated Daoist practices.

Huáinánzǐ 淮南子: Book of the Huainan Masters: DZ 1184; ZH 978.
  A. Translated by John Major, Sarah Queen, Andrew Meyer, and Harold Roth. *The Huainanzi: A Guide to the Theory and Practice of Government in Early Han China, by Liu An, King of Huainan*. New York: Columbia University Press, 2010.

A collection of twenty-one essays edited in the second century BCE at the court and under the patronage of Liú Ān 劉安 (179–122 BCE), the Prince of Huáinán. It was submitted to Hàn Emperor Wǔ 武 (r. 140–87 BCE) in 139 BCE. From a revisionist perspective, the text is sometimes used as a convenient place-holder for the terminus of classical Daoism, but the latter actually flows into the *Shǐjì* 史記 (Records of the Historian; dat. ca. 94 BCE) and into various Fāngshì 方士 (lit., "formula masters"; magico-religious practitioners) lineages. The *Huáinánzǐ* is an anthology that contains material from a variety of historical periods and diverse religio-cultural movements, including some that might be labeled "Daoist" or "Daoistic." From a revisionist perspective, it may actually have been compiled and edited under the direction of Syncretic Daoists. Particularly noteworthy and influential in this respect are chapter one, titled "Yuándào" 原道 (Source-Dao/Dao-as-Source); the cosmologically-oriented chapter three, titled "Tiānwén" 天文 (Celestial Patterns); and the more practical chapter seven, titled Jīngshén 精神

(Concentrated Divinity/Quintessential Spirit). Also includes chapter twelve, titled Dàoyìng 道應 (Responding to the Dao), which is one of the earliest extant commentaries on the *Lǎozǐ* 老子 (Book of Venerable Masters). The Major et al. translation, which also is available in a selected edition (2012), builds on a variety of earlier publications focusing on individual chapters. While reliable and monumental, the translation often lacks literary readability, sensitivity, and musicality. The accompanying layout, although potentially viable, also at times detracts from the reading experience.

HUÁNGDÌ NÈIJĪNG SÙWÈN 黃帝內經素問: Yellow Thearch's Inner Classic: Basic Questions: DZ 1018; ZH 884. Abbreviated as *Sùwèn* 素問.
   A. Translated by Paul Unschuld and Hermann Tessenow. *Huang Di Nei Jing Su Wen: An Annotated Translation of Huang Di's Inner Classic—Basic Questions*. 2 vols. Berkeley: University of California Press, 2011.

Containing material dating from at least the second century BCE to second century CE, and edited in the eighth century, this is one of the most important early classics of classical Chinese medicine. It covers various aspects of Chinese medicine, including a codified system of correspondences focusing on yin-yang and the Five Phases (*wǔxíng* 五行) as well as important, practical information related to health, hygiene, and longevity, including Yǎngshēng 養生 (Nourishing Life; health and longevity practice). The DZ edition includes a commentary by Wáng Bīng 王冰 (Qǐxuán 啟玄 [Inspired Mystery]; fl. 760s), with a preface dated to 762. Wáng's edition represents one of the primary redactions of the primary source. Although not a "Daoist text" per se, there are some intriguing connections. In addition, for Daoists, it sets an important foundation of cosmological views and applications, including the possibility of attunement and harmonization. The Unschuld and Tessenow translation is a definitive Sino-philological rendering, although some readers may find technical renderings debatable and the overly sober, at times even stodgy English less than inspired/inspiring. More research on potential Daoist connections as well as influence on the later Daoist tradition is needed.

LǍOZǏ MÍNG 老子銘: Inscription on Laozi. Partially preserved in the *Hùnyuán shèngjì* 混元聖紀: Record of the Sage Chaos Prime: DZ 770; ZH 1148.
    A. Translated by Mark Csikszentmihalyi. *Readings in Han Chinese Thought*. Indianapolis, IN: Hackett Publishing Company, 2006. (105–12)

Dating to around 165 CE, this is an inscription on the legendary Lǎozǔ 老子 ("Master Lao") attributed to Biān Sháo 邊韶 (fl. 140s-160s). It commemorates a dream of Emperor Huán 桓 (r. 147–167) in which Lǎozǐ appeared to him. The inscription contains some of the earliest descriptions of Lǎozǐ's cosmicization and divinization, including associated Daoist visualization (*cúnxiǎng* 存想) practice. Csikszentmihalyi's translation is generally reliable, although it sometimes lacks sophistication with respect to Daoist technical terminology and the author has a variety of problematic (social constructivist) views concerning classical Daoism more generally.

LǍOZǏ ZHĀNGJÙ 老子章句: Chapter-and-Verse Commentary on the *Laozi*: DZ 682; ZH 556. Also later referred to as the *Dàodé zhēnjīng zhù* 道德眞經註 (Commentary on the Perfect Scripture on the Dao and Inner Power).
    A. Translated by Eduard Erkes (1891–1958). *Ho-shang Kung's Commentary on the Lao-tse*. Ascona, Switzerland: Artibus Asiae, 1958.

This commentary is better known by the name of its author, Héshàng gōng 河上公 (Elder Dwelling-by-the-River; fl. 160s CE?), concerning whom scant reliable historical information exists. Legend identifies him as a teacher of the Hàn Emperor Wén 文 (r. 179–157 BCE). This text is one of the earliest extant commentaries on the *Dàodé jīng* and probably dates from the second century CE, although some would date it as late as the sixth century. It interprets the *Dàodé jīng* especially in terms of

Yǎngshēng 養生 (Nourishing Life) practice and Hàn political concerns, specifically those of the so-called Huáng-Lǎo 黃老 school. It has been especially influential and even considered definitive in Daoist circles, including the important gloss of *zhìguó* 治國 ("govern the country") as *zhìshēn* 治身 ("regulate the self"). Erkes' translation is outdated and generally unreliable. A scholarly study, with translations of selected passages, appears in Chan 1991. A discussion and translation of the chapter titles is included in Louis Komjathy's *Dàodé jīng: A Contextual, Contemplative, and Annotated Bilingual Translation*, which is forthcoming (mid-2023) from Square Inch Press. Komjathy also is working on a scholarly translation of the *Lǎozǐ zhāngjù* for his ongoing Daoist commentary project.

TÀISHÀNG HUÁNGTÍNG WÀIJǏNG YÙJĪNG 太上黃庭外景玉經: Jade Scripture on the Outer View of the Yellow Court from the Most High: DZ 332; ZH 897. Abbreviated as *Huángtíng wàijǐng jīng* 黃庭外景經.

    A. Translated by Jane Huang. *The Primordial Breath: An Ancient Chinese Way of Prolonging Life through Breath Control*. 2 vols. Torrance, CA: Original Books, 1987/1990. (2.221–29)

Composed in heptasyllabic (seven-character) lines divided into three sections, this is a shorter text related to the *Huángtíng nèijǐng jīng* 黃庭內景經 (Scripture on the Inner View of the Yellow Court; DZ 331; ZH 896). Although the relationship is complex, it appears that the "Outer View" version predates the Shàngqīng 上清 (Highest Clarity) movement, probably dating to the third century, and originates in a currently unidentified earlier regional Daoist community. Read in concert, the "Inner View" version may be understood as a more elaborate and detailed expression of the "Outer View" version. Both describe the subtle anatomy and physiology of the human body, including its inner divinities. Huang's translation is technically a popular publication, but it is generally reliable. However, like such translations in general, it lacks necessary contextualization, annotation, and exegesis.

APPENDIX 9: FOUNDATIONAL READINGS 429

BÀOPǓZǏ NÈIPIĀN 抱朴子內篇: Inner Chapters of Master Embracing Simplicity: DZ 1185; ZH 980.

A. Translated by James Ware. *Alchemy, Medicine, and Religion in China of A.D. 320: The Nei P'ien of Ko Hung*. Cambridge, MA: M.I.T. Press, 1966.

Written by Gé Hóng 葛洪 (Bàopǔ 抱朴 [Embracing Simplicity]; 283–343), a Daoist alchemist, paternal grandnephew of Gé Xuán 葛玄 (164–244), and systematizer of the Tàiqīng 太清 (Great Clarity) movement. Called "inner" because chapters deal with more esoteric and important matters. Dating to 320, but first completed around 317 and revised around 330. A *summa* of fourth-century religious traditions and related methods. Provides information on the production of elixirs (*dān* 丹) through external alchemy (*wàidān* 外丹), also referred to as "laboratory/operational alchemy," which is the highest religious pursuit according to Gé. Contains information on Tàiqīng, including key figures, texts, methods, and so forth. Loosely linked with the Gé family lineage. Also details contemporaneous dietetic, exorcistic, and hygienic techniques. Ware's translation is somewhat outdated, but generally accurate on historical and literati dimensions, and sometimes on herbology and mineralogy. It is unreliable and almost completely deficient on Daoist views and terminology. For example, Ware renders *xuán* 玄 ("Mystery"), another Daoist (non)name for the Dào 道 (Tao/Way), as "God" and *zhēnrén* 真人 ("Perfected") as "God's Men." That edition also omits the various talismans. A complete, annotated literary and scholarly translation of the *Bàopǔzǐ nèipiān* is currently being prepared by the Daoist Translation Committee 道教翻譯學會, a collaborative collective being organized by the Daoist Foundation 道教基金會 and under the general editorship of Louis Komjathy 康思奇.

HUÁNGDÌ YĪNFÚ JĪNG 黃帝陰符經: Yellow Thearch's Scripture on the Hidden Talisman: DZ 31; ZH 642. Abbreviated as *Yīnfú jīng* 陰符經.

A. Translated by Louis Komjathy. *Handbooks for Daoist Practice*. 10 vols. Hong Kong: Yuen Yuen Institute, 2008 (2003). (Handbook 7)

Probably dating from the sixth century CE, this anonymous text is part of a corpus of works that became canonical in internal alchemy (*nèidān* 內丹) circles during the Sòng dynasty (960–1279), including in the Quánzhēn 全真 (Complete Perfection) movement. In fact, it became identified as one of the latter's three core scriptures, and retains this place in the contemporary monastic order. The scripture draws attention to cosmological principles and the process of cultivation based on stillness (*jìng* 靜) with a specific focus on decreasing sensory engagement and psychological agitation. Komjathy's translation is a literary and practical one, with the introduction discussing technical terminology in lieu of annotations. It also was included in his *The Way of Complete Perfection* (2013), with the associated commentary of Liú Chǔxuán 劉處玄 (Chángshēng 長生 [Perpetual Life]; 1147–1203), one of the members of the so-called Seven Perfected (*qīzhēn* 七真) of early Quánzhēn Daoism.

TÀISHÀNG LǍOJŪN SHUŌ CHÁNG QĪNGJÌNG miàojīng 太上老君說常清靜妙經: Wondrous Scripture on Constant Clarity and Stillness, as Spoken by the Great High Lord Lao: DZ 620; ZH 350. Abbreviated as *Qīngjìng jīng* 清靜經. Also referred to as the *Scripture on Purity and Tranquility*.

A. Translated by Louis Komjathy. *Handbooks for Daoist Practice*. 10 vols. Hong Kong: Yuen Yuen Institute, 2008 (2003). (Handbook 4)

An anonymous text probably dating from the eighth century, this is one of a group of Táng-dynasty (618–907) works that may be labeled "Clarity-and-Stillness Literature." Emerging under the influence of Buddhist insight meditation (Pali: *vipassanā*; Skt.: *vipaśyanā*) and expressing a form of wisdom (*zhì* 智) based on the practice of observation (*guān* 觀), the text combines the worldview of the *Dàodé jīng* 道德經 (Scripture on the Dao and Inner Power) with the practice of Daoist observation and the structure (as well as some content) of the Buddhist *Bōrě xīnjīng* 般若心經 (Heart Sutra of Perfect Wisdom; T. 250–257), with the latter also Romanized as *Pánruò xīnjīng*. It emphasizes the dual cultivation of clarity/purity (*qīng* 清) and stillness/tranquility (*jìng* 靜). The *Qīngjìng jīng* became identified as one of the three core scriptures of early

Quánzhēn 全眞 (Complete Perfection) Daoism, and retains this place in the contemporary monastic order. Komjathy's translation is a literary and practical one, with the introduction discussing technical terminology in lieu of annotations. It also was included in his *The Way of Complete Perfection* (2013), with the associated commentary of Liú Tōngwēi 劉通微 (Mòrán 默然 [Silent Suchness]; d. 1196), one of the less well-known senior members of the early Quánzhēn community.

Zuòwàng lùn 坐忘論: Discourse on Sitting-in-Forgetfulness: DZ 1036; ZH 992.
    B. Translated by Livia Kohn. *Seven Steps to the Tao: Sima Chengzhen's Zuowang lun*. Nettetal, Germany: Steyler Verlag, 1987. (77–111)
    C. Translated by Livia Kohn. *Sitting in Oblivion: The Heart of Daoist Meditation*. Dunedin, FL: Three Pines Press, 2010. (137–58)

Written by Sīmǎ Chéngzhēn 司馬承禎 (Zhēnyī 貞一 [Pure Unity]; 647–735), the Twelfth Patriarch of Shàngqīng 上清 (Highest Clarity) Daoism, this is a detailed manual on the practice of observation (*guān* 觀). Drawing upon and sometimes commenting on the germinal passage on *zuòwàng* 坐忘 ("sitting-in-forgetfulness") in chapter six of the *Zhuāngzǐ* 莊子 (Book of Master Zhuang), it provides guidelines for gradual progress towards mystical realization of the Dao (*dédào* 得道), with the path outlined in seven successive steps. Kohn's translation is a pioneering and key work in Daoist Studies, and includes translations of other, related Daoist meditation manuals as well. However, it problematically translates *wàng* 忘 (lit., "forget") as "oblivion," and thus obscures the connection of the contemplative state of "forgetfulness" with the associated *jìng* 靜 ("stillness") and *xū* 虛 ("emptiness"). The reissue edition (2010) also includes some questionable claims about popular presentations.

Wùzhēn piān 悟眞篇: Treatise on Awakening to Perfection. Contained in the *Xiūzhēn shíshū* 修眞十書: Ten Books on Cultivating Perfection: DZ 263, j. 26–30. See also *Dàoshū* 道樞: Pivot of the Dao: DZ 1017, j. 18.

A. Translated by Fabrizio Pregadio. *Awakening to Reality: The "Regulated Verses" of the Wuzhen pian, a Taoist Classic of Internal Alchemy*. Mountain View, CA: Golden Elixir Press, 2009.

Written around 1075, this is a seminal and highly influential internal alchemy (*nèidān* 內丹) text composed by Zhāng Bóduān 張伯端 (Zǐyáng 紫陽 [Purple Yang]; d. 1082), a central figure in the so-called Nánzōng 南宗 (Southern School). It is a poetry cycle divided into sets of sixteen, sixty-four and twelve verses describing the stages of alchemical practice in highly symbolic and esoteric language. It thus provides important insights into tradition-based, late medieval alchemical literary forms. Like his translations in general, Pregadio's rendering is reliable. However, it falls somewhere between a scholarly and popular translation, often lacking comprehensive annotations and exegesis. We still are in need of a complete scholarly translation of the latter, including intertextual comparison with Zhāng's *Jīndān sìbǎizì* 金丹四百字 (Four Hundred Characters on the Golden Elixir; DZ 1081; ZH 848).

CHŪZHĒN JIÈ 初眞戒: Precepts of Initial Perfection: JY 292; ZW 404.
A. Translated by Louis Komjathy. *The Way of Complete Perfection: A Quanzhen Daoist Anthology*. Albany: State University of New York Press, 2013. (326–60)

Compiled by Wáng Chángyuè 王常月 (Kūnyáng 崑陽 [Paradisiacal Yang]; 1622?-1680), the first Qīng-dynasty (1644-1911) abbot of Báiyún guàn 白雲觀 (White Cloud Monastery; Běijīng) and the founder of the official Lóngmén 龍門 (Dragon Gate) lineage, this is a collection of Lóngmén precepts (*jiè* 戒) and monastic codes. The namesake Ten Precepts of Initial Perfection (*chūzhēn shíjiè* 初眞十戒) parallel those found in the early eighth-century *Chūzhēn shíjiè wén* 初眞十戒文 (Ten Precepts of Initial Perfection; DZ 180; ZH 1316). The text is transmitted to ordinands of the first level of the Lóngmén lineage of the Quánzhēn 全眞 (Complete Perfection) monastic order and represents the order's most fundamental guidelines and practical precepts. It also includes conduct guidelines for women titled the *Nǚzhēn jiǔjiè* 女眞九戒 (Nine

Precepts for Female Perfected). Komjathy's translation is the only complete annotated scholarly translation of a traditional Lóngmén text. It also includes reproductions of the accompanying woodblock images of the associated material culture (e.g., ordination robes).

LÓNGMÉN XĪNFǍ 龍門心法: Core Teachings of Dragon Gate: ZW 201.
  A. Translated by Johan Hausen and Allen Tsaur. *The Dragon Gate's Core Methods*. Auckland, New Zealand: Purple Cloud Press, forthcoming.

Key work of the Lóngmén 龍門 (Dragon Gate) lineage of Quánzhēn 全真 (Complete Perfection) Daoism. It also is known in a slightly earlier, variant form as the *Bìyuàn tánjīng* 碧苑壇經 (Platform Sutra of the Jade Garden), a title inspired by the famous Chán 禪 (Zen) Buddhist *Liùzǔ tánjīng* 六祖壇經 (Platform Sutra of the Sixth Patriarch) associated with Dàjiàn Huìnéng 大鑒惠能 (638–713), the legendary founder of the so-called Sudden School. The *Lóngmén xīnfǎ* was written by Wáng Chángyuè 王常月 (Kūnyáng 崑陽 [Paradisiacal Yang]; 1622?-1680) as a primer and guidebook for late imperial Quánzhēn monastics, especially formal Lóngmén initiates. Wáng was the first Qing-dynasty (1644–1911) abbot of Báiyún guàn 白雲觀 (White Cloud Monastery; Běijīng) and the founder of the official Lóngmén lineage. Hausen's rendering is reliable, falling somewhere between a scholarly and popular translation. It contains some annotations. It also includes a commentary by Lǐ Xìngdé 李興德 (Xìng Dé; b. 1964), the abbot of Wǔxiān miào 五仙廟 (Five Immortals Temple) of Mount Wǔdāng 武當 (Shíyàn 十堰, Húběi) and Hausen's own master-father (*shīfu* 師父). It thus provides insights into a key traditional Lóngmén text as a living document being engaged and applied by modern tradition-based Daoists, both Chinese and Western. A list of the chapter titles of the *Lóngmén xīnfǎ* with English translations also is contained in Louis Komjathy's "Catalogue of Daoist Collectanea, Compendia, and Encyclopedias" (2022).

Appendix 10

Texts Included in *Primer for Translating Daoist Literature*

This appendix lists the texts included in this primer in alphabetical order according to Pinyin Romanization with lesson numbers in parentheses.

Bàopǔzǐ nèipiān 抱朴子內篇 (#3 and #13)
Bǎoshēng míng 保生銘 (#14)
Chóngyáng lìjiào shíwǔ lùn 重陽立教十五論 (#23)
Chūzhēn jiè 初眞戒 (#24)
Dàodé jīng huìyì 道德經會義 (#28)
Huáinánzǐ 淮南子 (#9)
Huángdì nèijīng sùwèn 黃帝內經素問 (#10)
Huángdì yīnfú jīng 黃帝陰符經 (#16)
Lǎozǐ 老子 (#7)
Lǎozǐ xiǎng'ěr zhù 老子想爾注 (#27)
Lǎozǐ zhāngjù 老子章句 (#25 and #26)
Lǚzǔ bǎizì bēi 呂祖百字碑 (#19)
Nèiyè 內業 (#6)
Tàishàng huángtíng wàijǐng yùjīng 太上黃庭外景玉經 (#12)
Tàishàng Lǎojūn jīnglǜ 太上老君經律 (#4)
Tàishàng Lǎojūn shuō cháng qīngjìng miàojīng 太上老君說常清靜妙經 (#17)

Wùzhēn piān 悟真篇 (#21)
Xíngqì yùpèi míng 行氣玉佩銘 (#5)
Yǎngxìng yánmìng lù 養性延命錄 (#15)
Zázhù jiéjìng 雜著捷徑 (#22)
Zhōng-Lǚ chuándào jí 鍾呂傳道集 (#20)
Zhōuyì cāntóng qì 周易參同契 (#11)
Zhuāngzǐ 莊子 (#2 and #8)
Zuòwàng piān 坐忘篇 (#18)

BIBLIOGRAPHY

Abram, David. 1996. *The Spell of the Sensuous: Perception and Language in a More-Than-Human World.* New York: Vintage.

Addiss, Stephen, and Stanley Lombardo. 1993. *Tao Te Ching.* Indianapolis: Hackett.

Baldrian-Hussein, Farzeen (1945–2009). 1984. *Procédés Secrets du Joyau Magique: Traité d'Alchimie Taïiste du XIe siècle.* Paris: Les Deux Océans.

Balfour, Frederic (1846–1909). 1894. *Taoist Texts: Ethical, Political and Speculative.* London/Shanghai: Trübner and Co./Kelly and Walsh.

Barnstone, Willis. 1993. *The Poetics of Translation: History, Theory, Practice.* New Haven, CT: Yale University Press.

Barrett, T.H. (Timothy). 1987. "Taoism: History of the Study." In *Encyclopedia of Religion,* edited by Mircea Eliade, vol. 14, 329–32. New York and London: MacMillan.

Bassnett, Susan. 1991. *Translation Studies.* London: Routledge.

Baudrillard, Jean. 1994. *Simulacra and Simulation.* Translated by Sheila Faria Glaser. Ann Arbor: University of Michigan Press.

Baudrillard, Jean, and Marc Guillaume. 2007. *Radical Alterity.* Los Angeles: Semiotext(e).

Baxter, William. 1998. "Situating the Language of the *Lao-tzu*: The Probable Date of the *Tao-te-ching.*" In *Lao-tzu and the Tao-te-ching,* edited by Livia Kohn and Michael LaFargue, 231–53. Albany: State University of New York Press.

Baxter, William, and Laurent Sagart. 2014. *Old Chinese: A New*

Reconstruction. Oxford and New York: Oxford University Press.

Benjamin, Walter. 1968. *Illuminations: Essays and Reflections*. New York: Harcourt, Brace, & World.

Benn, Charles. 1991. *The Cavern Mystery Transmission: A Taoist Ordination Rite of A.D. 711*. Honolulu: University of Hawaii Press.

Bensky, Dan, Steven Clavey, and Erich Stöger. 2004. *Materia Medica: Chinese Herbal Medicine*. 3rd ed. Seattle: Eastland Press.

Biguenet, John, and Rainer Schulte, eds. 1989. *The Craft of Translation*. Chicago: University of Chicago Press.

Bokenkamp, Stephen. 1983. "Sources of the Ling-pao Scriptures." In *Tantric and Taoist Studies*, edited by Michel Strickmann, 2.434–86. Bruxelles: Institut Belge des Hautes Études Chinoises.

———. 1986. "Taoist Literature. Part I: Through the T'ang Dynasty." In *The Indiana Companion to Traditional Chinese Literature*, 138–52. 2nd rev. ed. Bloomington: Indiana University Press.

———. 1997. *Early Daoist Scriptures*. Daoist Classics 1. Berkeley: University of California Press.

———. 2001. "Lu Xiujing, Buddhism, and the First Daoist Canon." In *Culture and Power in the Reconstitution of the Chinese Realm, 200–600*, edited by Scott Pearce et al., 181–99. Cambridge, MA: Harvard University Press.

———. 2021. *A Fourth-Century Daoist Family: The Zhen'gao, or Declarations of the Perfected, Volume 1*. Berkeley: University of California Press.

Boltz, Judith (1947–2013). 1986a. "Tao-tsang." In *The Indiana Companion to Traditional Chinese Literature*, edited by William H. Nienhauser, 763–66. 2nd rev. ed. Bloomington: Indiana University Press.

———. 1986b. "Taoist Literature. Part II: Five Dynasties to the Ming." In *The Indiana Companion to Traditional Chinese Literature*, edited by William H. Nienhauser, 152–74. 2nd rev. ed. Bloomington: Indiana University Press.

———. 1987a. *A Survey of Taoist Literature: Tenth to Seventeenth Centuries*. Berkeley: University of California, Institute of East Asian Studies.

———. 1987b. "Taoist Literature." In *Encyclopedia of Religion*, edited by

Mircea Eliade, vol. 14, 317–29. New York and London: MacMillan.

———. 1994. "Notes on the *Daozang tiyao*." *China Review International* 1.2: 1–33.

Bourdieu, Pierre. 1977. *Outline of a Theory of Practice*. Translated by Richard Nice. Cambridge and New York: Cambridge University Press.

———. 1988. *Homo Academicus*. Translated by Peter Collier. Stanford, CA: Stanford University Press.

Bradbury, Steven. 1992. "The American Conquest of Philosophical Taoism." In *Translation East and West: A Cross-Cultural Approach*, edited by Cornelia N. Moore and Lucy Lower, 29–41. Honolulu: College of Languages, Linguistics and Literature, University of Hawaii.

Brower, Reuben, ed. 1959. *On Translation*. Cambridge, MA: Harvard University Press.

Campany, Robert. 2002. *To Live as Long as Heaven and Earth: A Translation and Study of Ge Hong's Traditions of Divine Transcendents*. Daoist Classics 2. Berkeley: University of California Press.

Capitanio, Joshua. 2018. "Sanskrit and Pseudo-Sanskrit Incantations in Daoist Ritual Texts." *History of Religions* 57.4: 348–405.

Carmichael, Lucas. 2017. "The *Daode jing* as American Scripture: Text, Tradition, and Translation." Ph.D. diss., University of Chicago.

Chan, Alan K.L. 1991. *Two Visions of the Way: A Study of the Wang Pi and the Ho-shang Kung Commentaries on the Lao-Tzu*. Albany: State University of New York Press.

———. 1998. "A Tale of Two Commentaries: Ho-shang-kung and Wang Pi on the *Lao-tzu*." In *Lao-tzu and the Tao-te-ching*, edited by Livia Kohn and Michael LaFargue, 89–117. Albany: State University of New York Press.

Carré, Patrick. *Le Livre de la Cour Jaune*. N.p.: Éditions du Seuil, 1999.

Chén Guófú 陳國符. 1963. *Dàozàng yuánliú kǎo* 道藏源流考 (Study of the Origins and Development of the Daoist Canon). 2 vols. Běijīng: Zhōngguó shūjú.

Chen, Ping. 1999. *Modern Chinese: History and Sociolinguistics*. Cambridge and New York: Cambridge University Press.

Chén Yuán 陳垣 (1880–1971). 1988. *Dàojiā jīnshí lüè* 道家金石略 (Collection of Daoist Epigraphy). Edited by Chén Zhìchāo 陳智超 and Zēng Qìngyīng 曾慶瑛. Běijīng: Wénwù chūbǎnshè.

Cheung, Yat-shing, ed. 1992. *Literary Translation: A Reader's Perspective*. Proceedings from The Second International Conference on the Translation of Chinese Literature. Hong Kong: Hebei guoji huiyi zhongxin.

Clarke, J.J. 2000. *The Tao of the West: Western Transformations of Taoist Thought*. London and New York: Routledge.

Cleary, Thomas (1949–2021). 1986. *The Inner Teachings of Taoism*. Boston: Shambhala.

_____. 1987. *Understanding Reality: A Taoist Alchemical Classic*. Honolulu: University of Hawaii Press.

_____. 1991. *Vitality, Energy, Spirit: A Taoist Sourcebook*. Boston: Shambhala.

_____. 1999. *The Taoist Classics: The Collected Translations of Thomas Cleary*. 4 vols. Boston: Shambhala.

Cook, Scott. 2012. *The Bamboo Texts of Guodian: A Study and Complete Translation*. 2 vols. Ithaca, NY: Cornell University East Asia Program.

Csikszentmihalyi, Mark. 2006. *Readings in Han Chinese Thought*. Indianapolis, IN: Hackett.

De Bary, Wm. Theodore, and Irene Bloom eds. 1999. *Sources of Chinese Tradition*. Volume 1: From Earliest Times to 1600. 2nd ed. New York: Columbia University Press.

De Bruyn, Pierre-Henry. 2004. "Wudang shan: The Origins of a Major Center of Modern Taoism." In *Religion and Chinese Society*, edited by John Lagerwey, 553–90. Hong Kong: Chinese University Press.

_____. 2010. *Le Wudang shan: Histoire des récits fondateurs*. Paris: Éditions Les Indes savantes.

De Meyer, Jan. 2006. *Wu Yun's Way: Life and Works of an Eighth-Century Daoist Master*. Leiden: Brill.

De Wit, Han. 1991. *Contemplative Psychology*. Translated by Marie Louise Baird. Pittsburgh: Duquesne University Press.

Debord, Guy. 1970. *Society of the Spectacle*. Seattle: Red & Black Books.

Denecke, Wiebke, Wai-Yee Li, and Xiaofei Tian, eds. 2017. *The Oxford*

Handbook of Classical Chinese Literature (1000 BCE–900CE). Oxford and New York: Oxford University Press.

Despeux, Catherine, and Livia Kohn. 2003. *Women in Daoism*. Cambridge, MA: Three Pines Press.

Dippmann, Jeffrey. 2001. "The Tao of Textbooks: Taoism in Introductory World Religion Texts." *Teaching Theology & Religion* 4.1: 40–54.

Doniger, Wendy. 1998. *The Implied Spider: Politics and Theology in Myth*. New York: Columbia University Press.

Doniger O'Flaherty, Wendy. 1995 (1988). *Other People's Myths: The Cave of Echoes*. Chicago: University of Chicago Press.

Durrant, Stephen. 1991. "Packaging the Tao." *Rocky Mountain Review of Language and Literature* 45.1–2: 75–84.

Eco, Umberto. 2004. *Mouse or Rat? Translation as Negotiation*. London: Phoenix.

Eliade, Mircea. 1998 (1963). *Myth and Reality*. Prospect Heights, IL: Waveland Press.

Ellis, Andrew, Nigel Wiseman, and Ken Boss. 1989. *Grasping the Wind: An Exploration into the Meaning of Chinese Acupuncture Point Names*. Brookline, MA: Paradigm Publications.

Eoyang, Eugene and Lin Yao-fu, eds. 1995. *Translating Chinese Literature*. Bloomington: Indiana University Press.

Erkes, Eduard (1891–1958). 1958. *Ho-shang Kung's Commentary on the Lao-tse*. Ascona, Switzerland: Artibus Asiae.

Esherick, Joseph. 1972. "Harvard on China: The Apologetics of Imperialism." *Bulletin of Concerned Asian Scholars* 4.4: 9–16.

Esposito, Monica (1962–2011). 2013. *Creative Daoism*. Paris: UniversityMedia.

———. 2014. *Facets of Qing Daoism*. Paris: UniversityMedia.

Fang, Achilles. 1959. "Some Reflections on the Difficulty of Translation." In *On Translation*, edited by Reuben Brower, 111–33. Cambridge, MA: Harvard University Press.

Fukuoka, Masanobu. 1978. *The One Straw Revolution*. Emmaus, PA: Rodale Press.

Fuller, Michael. 2004. *An Introduction to Literary Chinese*. Rev. ed. Cambridge, MA: Harvard University Asia Center.

Gadamer, Hans-Georg. 2013 (1975). *Truth and Method*. Translated by Joel Weinsheimer and Donald Marshall. 2nd rev. ed. London and New York: Bloomsbury Academic.

Geertz, Clifford. 1973. *The Interpretation of Cultures*. New York: Basic Books.

Gerber, Leah, and Lintao Qi, eds. 2021. *A Century of Chinese Literature in Translation (1919–2019): English Publication and Reception*. London and New York: Routledge.

Girardot, Norman. 1972. "Part of the Way: Four Studies on Taoism." *History of Religions* 11.3: 319–37.

———. 1999. "'Finding the Way': James Legge and the Victorian Invention of Taoism." *Religion* 29.2: 107–21.

———. 2002. *The Victorian Translation of China: James Legge's Oriental Pilgrimage*. Berkeley: University of California Press.

Goldin, Paul. 2002. "Those Who Don't Know Speak: Translations of the *Daode jing* by People Who Do Not Know Chinese." *Asian Philosophy* 12.3: 183–95.

Goossaert, Vincent. 2022. *Heavenly Masters: Two Thousand Years of the Daoist State*. London and New York: Routledge.

Graham, A.C. 1981. *Chuang-tzu: The Seven Inner Chapters and Other Writings from the Book Chuang-tzu*. London: George Allen & Unwin.

———. 1989. *Disputers of the Tao: Philosophical Argumentation in Ancient China*. La Salle, IL: Open Court.

———. 1990 (1960). *The Book of Lieh-tzu: A Classic of Tao*. New York: Columbia University Press.

———. 1998 (1986). "The Origins of the Legend of Lao Tan." In *Lao-tzu and the Tao-te-ching*, edited by Livia Kohn and Michael LaFargue, 23–40. Albany: State University of New York Press.

Graziani, Romain. 2011. *Écrits de maître Guan: Les Quatre traités de l'Art de l'esprit*. Paris: Les Belles Lettres.

Grossman, Edith. 2010. *Why Translation Matters*. New Haven, CT: Yale University Press.

Hadot, Pierre. 1995. *Philosophy as a Way of Life: Spiritual Exercises from Socrates to Foucault*. Hoboken, NJ: Blackwell.
Hao Chunwen. 2020. *Dunhuang Manuscripts: An Introduction to Texts from the Silk Road*. Diamond Bar, CA: Portico Publishing Company.
Hardy, Julia. 1998. "Influential Western Interpretations of the *Tao-te-ching*." In *Lao-tzu and the Tao-te-ching*, edited by Livia Kohn and Michael LaFargue, 165–88. Albany: State University of New York Press.
Harper, Donald. 1998. *Early Chinese Medical Literature: The Mawangdui Medical Manuscripts*. London and New York: Kegan Paul International.
Hausen, Johan, and Allen Tsaur. 2021. *The Arts of Daoism*. Auckland, New Zealand: Purple Cloud Press.
———. Forthcoming. *The Dragon Gate's Core Methods*. Auckland, New Zealand: Purple Cloud Press.
Heidegger, Martin. 1977. *The Question Concerning Technology, and Other Essays*. Translated by William Levitt. New York: Harper Torchbooks.
Hendrischke, Barbara. 2007. *The Scripture on Great Peace: The Taiping jing and the Beginnings of Daoism*. Daoist Classics 3. Berkeley: University of California Press.
Henricks, Robert. 1989. *Lao-tzu Te-Tao Ching: A New Translation Based on the Recently Discovered Ma-wang-tui Texts*. New York: Ballantine.
———. 2000. *Lao Tzu's Tao Te Ching: A Translation of the Startling New Documents Found at Guodian*. New York: Columbia University Press.
Hervouet, Yves, ed. 1978. *A Sung Bibliography; Bibliographie des Sung*. Hong Kong: The Chinese University Press.
Heschel, Abraham Joshua. 2005 (1951). *The Sabbath*. New York: Farrar, Straus and Giroux.
Huang, Jane. 1987/1990. *The Primordial Breath: An Ancient Chinese Way of Prolonging Life through Breath Control*. 2 vols. Torrance, CA: Original Books, 1990.
Huang, Shih-shan Susan. 2012. *Picturing the True Form: Daoist Visual Culture in Traditional China*. Cambridge, MA: Harvard University Asia Center.
Hucker, Charles. 1985. *A Dictionary of Official Titles in Imperial China*.

Stanford, CA: Stanford University Press.

Ivanhoe, Philip, and Bryan W. Van Norden, eds. 2005. *Readings in Classical Chinese Philosophy*. 2nd ed. Indianapolis, IN: Hackett.

Jia, Jinhua. 2018. *Gender, Power, and Talent: The Journey of Daoist Priestesses in Tang China*. New York: Columbia University Press.

Jullien, François. 2003. *In Praise of Blandness: Proceeding from Chinese Thought and Aesthetics*. Translated by Paula Varsano. Brooklyn, NY: Zone Books.

Karlgren, Bernhard. 1957. *Grammata Serica Recensa*. Stockholm: Museum of Far Eastern Antiquities.

Katz, Paul. 1999. *Images of the Immortal: The Cult of Lü Dongbin at the Palace of Eternal Joy*. Honolulu: University of Hawaii Press.

King, Richard. 1999. *Orientalism and Religion: Postcolonial Theory, India and 'The Mystic East'*. London and New York: Routledge.

Kirkland, Russell. 1997. "The Historical Contours of Taoism in China: Thoughts on Issues of Classification and Terminology." *Journal of Chinese Religions* 25: 57–82.

_____. 2000. "Explaining Daoism: Realities, Cultural Constructs and Emerging Perspectives." In *Daoism Handbook*, edited by Livia Kohn, xi-xviii. Leiden: Brill.

_____. 2002. "The History of Taoism: A New Outline." *Journal of Chinese Religions* 30: 177–93.

_____. 2004. *Taoism: The Enduring Tradition*. London and New York: Routledge.

Kleeman, Terry. 1998. *Great Perfection: Religion and Ethnicity in a Chinese Millennial Kingdom*. Honolulu: University of Hawaii Press.

_____. 2016. *Celestial Masters: History and Ritual in Early Daoist Communities*. Cambridge, MA: Harvard University Press.

Knaul (Kohn), Livia. 1982. "Lost *Chuang Tzu* Passages." *Journal of Chinese Religions* 10: 53–79.

Knoblock, John, and Jeffrey Riegel. 2000. *The Annals of Lü Buwei: A Complete Translation and Study*. Stanford, CA: Stanford University Press.

Kobayashi Masayoshi. 1995. "The Establishment of the Taoist Religion

(*Tao-chiao*) and Its Structure." *Acta Asiatica: Bulletin of the Institute of Eastern Culture* 68: 19–36.

Kohn, Livia. 1987. *Seven Steps to the Tao: Sima Chengzhen's Zuowang lun*. Nettetal, Germany: Steyler Verlag.

———, ed. 1989. *Taoist Meditation and Longevity Techniques*. Ann Arbor: Center for Chinese Studies, University of Michigan.

———. 1993. *The Taoist Experience*. Albany: State University of New York Press.

———. 1998a. *God of the Dao: Lord Lao in History and Myth*. Ann Arbor: Center for Chinese Studies, University of Michigan.

———. 1998b. "The Lao-tzu Myth." In *Lao-tzu and the Tao-te-ching*, edited by Livia Kohn and Michael LaFargue, 41–62. Albany: State University of New York Press.

———. 1998c. "Taoist Scholasticism: A Preliminary Inquiry." In *Scholasticism: Cross-Cultural and Comparative Perspectives*, edited by Jose Ignacio Cabezon, 115–40. Albany: State University of New York Press.

———, ed. 2000a. *Daoism Handbook*. Leiden: Brill.

———. 2000b. "Research on Daoism." In *Daoism Handbook*, edited by Livia Kohn, xxvii-xxxiii. Leiden: Brill.

———. 2003. *Monastic Life in Medieval Daoism*. Honolulu: University of Hawaii Press.

———. 2004a (2001). *Daoism and Chinese Culture*. Rev. ed. Cambridge, MA: Three Pines Press.

———. 2004b. *Cosmos and Community: The Ethical Dimension of Daoism*. Cambridge, MA: Three Pines Press.

———. 2004c. *The Daoist Monastic Manual: A Translation of the Fengdao kejie*. Oxford and New York: Oxford University Press.

———. 2008. *Chinese Healing Exercises: The Tradition of Daoyin*. Honolulu: University of Hawaii Press.

———. 2009. *Readings in Daoist Mysticism*. Magdalena, NM: Three Pines Press.

———. 2012. *A Source Book in Chinese Longevity*. St. Peterburg, FL: Three Pines Press.

———. 2020. *The Zhong-Lü System of Internal Alchemy*. St. Peterburg, FL: Three Pines Press.

Komjathy, Louis. 2001. "Index to *Taoist Resources*." *Journal of Chinese Religions* 29: 233–42.

———. 2002a. "Changing Perspectives on the Daoist Tradition." *Religious Studies Review* 28.4: 327–34.

———. 2002b. *Title Index to Daoist Collections*. Cambridge, MA: Three Pines Press.

———. 2004. "Tracing the Contours of Daoism in North America." *Nova Religio* 8.2: 5–27.

———. 2007. *Cultivating Perfection: Mysticism and Self-transformation in Early Quanzhen Daoism*. Leiden: Brill.

———. 2008a [2003]. *Handbooks for Daoist Practice* 修道手冊. 10 vols. 2nd ed. Hong Kong: Yuen Yuen Institute 圓玄學院.

———. 2008b. "Mapping the Daoist Body: Part I: The *Neijing tu* in History." *Journal of Daoist Studies* 1: 67-92.

———. 2009. "Mapping the Daoist Body: Part II: The Text of the *Neijing tu*." *Journal of Daoist Studies* 2: 64-108.

———. 2013a. *The Way of Complete Perfection: A Quanzhen Daoist Anthology*. Albany: State University of New York Press.

———. 2013b. *The Daoist Tradition: An Introduction*. London and New York: Bloomsbury Academic.

———. 2014a. *Daoism: A Guide for the Perplexed*. London and New York: Bloomsbury Academic.

———. 2014b. "Title Index to the *Zhōnghuá dàozàng* 中華道藏 (Chinese Daoist Canon)." *Monumenta Serica* 62: 213–60.

———, ed. 2015. *Contemplative Literature: A Comparative Sourcebook on Meditation and Contemplative Prayer*. Albany: State University of New York Press.

———. 2017a. *Taming the Wild Horse: An Annotated Translation and Study of the Daoist Horse Taming Pictures*. New York: Columbia University Press.

———. 2017b. "'Names Are the Guest of Reality': Apophasis, Mysticism and Soteriology in Daoist Perspective." In *Ineffability: An Exercise in*

Comparative Philosophy of Religion, edited by Timothy Knepper and Leah Kalmanson, 59–94. New York: Springer Publishing Company.

———. 2018. *Introducing Contemplative Studies*. West Sussex, England and Hoboken, NJ: Wiley-Blackwell.

———. 2019. "A Daoist Way of Being: Clarity and Stillness (Qīngjìng 清靜) as Embodied Practice." *Asian Philosophy* 29.1: 50–64.

———. 2020a. "Teachings of the Venerable Masters: Laozi and the *Daode jing*." In *A Companion to World Literature*, edited by Ken Seigneurie et al., 153–65. West Sussex, England and Hoboken, NJ: Wiley-Blackwell.

———. 2020b. "Daoist Meditation." In *Routledge Handbook of Yoga and Meditation Studies*, edited by Karen O'Brien-Kop and Suzanne Newcombe, 189–211. London and New York: Routledge.

———. 2020c. "Daoist Body-Maps and Meditative Praxis." In *Transformational Embodiment in Asian Religions: Subtle Bodies, Spatial Bodies*, edited by George Pati and Katherine Zubko, 36–64. London and New York: Routledge.

———. 2021. "Daoist Meditation: From 100 CE to the Present." In *The Oxford Handbook of Meditation*, edited by Miguel Farias, David Brazier, and Mansur Lalljee, 310–31. Oxford and New York: Oxford University Press.

———. 2022a. "Research Guide to Daoist Studies." Daoist Studies Articles Online (DSAO) #1. Ravinia, IL: Center for Daoist Studies 道學中心.

———. 2022b. "Daoist Literature in Translation: An Annotated Catalogue." Daoist Studies Articles Online (DSAO) #2. Ravinia, IL: Center for Daoist Studies 道學中心.

———. 2022c. "Catalogue of Daoist Collectanea, Compendia, and Encyclopedias." Daoist Studies Articles Online (DSAO) #3. Ravinia, IL: Center for Daoist Studies 道學中心.

———. 2022d. "Daoist Studies." Daoist Studies Guides (DSG) #1. Ravinia, IL: Center for Daoist Studies 道學中心.

———. 2022e. "Daoism." Daoist Studies Guides (DSG) #2. Ravinia, IL: Center for Daoist Studies 道學中心.

———. 2022f. "Daoist Literature." Daoist Studies Guides (DSG) #3.

Ravinia, IL: Center for Daoist Studies 道學中心.

———. 2022g. "Classical Chinese." *Daoist Studies Guides* (DSG) #4. Ravinia, IL: Center for Daoist Studies 道學中心.

———. 2022h. "Title Index to the *Lǎozǐ jíchéng* 老子集成 (Collection on the *Lǎozǐ*)." *Supplements to Title Index to Daoist Collections* (STIDC) #3. Ravinia, IL: Center for Daoist Studies 道學中心.

———. 2022i. "Title Index to the *Dūnhuáng dàozàng* 敦煌道藏 (Dunhuang Daoist Canon)." *Supplements to Title Index to Daoist Collections* (STIDC) #4. Ravinia, IL: Center for Daoist Studies 道學中心.

———. 2022j. "Mountains in Early Quánzhēn Daoism." In *Buddhism and Daoism on the Holy Mountains of China*, edited by Thomas Jülch, 363–94. Melanges chinois et bouddhiques series. Leuven, Belgium: Peeters Publishers.

———. 2022k. "Religion, Animals, and Contemplation." *Religions* 13.5.

———. Forthcoming (2022). "*Nèidān* 內丹 Training According to the Qiānfēng 千峰 (Thousand Peaks) Sub-Lineage: Niú Jīnbǎo's 牛金寶 (1915–1988) Methods in Nine Stages." *Journal of Chinese Religions*.

———. Forthcoming (2023). *Handbooks for Daoist Practice* 修道手冊. Twentieth Anniversary Edition (TAE). Ravinia, IL: Square Inch Press 方寸書社.

———. Forthcoming (2023). *Dàodé jīng* 道德經: *A Contextual, Contemplative, and Annotated Bilingual Translation*. Ravinia, IL: Square Inch Press 方寸書社.

Komjathy, Louis, and Kate Townsend. 2022. *Entering Stillness: A Guide to Daoist Practice* 入靜指南. Ravinia, IL: Square Inch Press 方寸書社.

Kripal, Jeffrey. 2017. *Secret Body: Erotic and Esoteric Currents in the History of Religions*. Chicago: University of Chicago Press.

Kroll, Paul. 2017. *A Student's Dictionary of Classical and Medieval Chinese*. Rev. ed. Leiden: Brill.

Kuriyama, Shigehisa. 1999. *The Expressiveness of the Body and the Divergence of Greek and Chinese Medicine*. New York: Zone Books.

LaFargue, Michael. 1992. *The Tao of the Tao Te Ching*. Albany: State University of New York Press.

_____. 1994. *Tao and Method: A Reasoned Approach to the Tao Te Ching*. Albany: State University of New York Press.

_____. 1998. "Recovering the *Tao-te-ching*'s Original Meaning: Some Remarks on Historical Hermeneutics." In *Lao-tzu and the Tao-te-ching*, edited by Livia Kohn and Michael LaFargue, 255–75. Albany: State University of New York Press.

LaFargue, Michael, and Julian Pas. 1998. "On Translating the *Tao-te-ching*." In *Lao-tzu and the Tao-te-ching*, edited by Livia Kohn and Michael LaFargue, 277–301. Albany: State University of New York Press.

Lagerwey, John. 1992. "The Pilgrimage to Wu-tang Shan." In *Pilgrims and Sacred Sites in China*, edited by Susan Naquin and Chun-fang Yü, 293–332. Berkeley: University of California Press.

Lai Chi-tim 黎志添, ed. 2021. *Dàozàng jíyào tíyào* 道藏輯要提要 (Companion to the *Daozang jiyao*). 3 vols. Hong Kong: Chinese University of Hong Kong Press.

Lakoff, George, and Mark Johnson. 1980. *Metaphors We Live By*. Chicago: University of Chicago Press.

Large, Duncan, Motoko Akashi, Wanda Józwikowska, and Emily Rose, eds. 2019. *Untranslatability: Interdisciplinary Perspectives*. London and New York: Routledge.

Lau, D.C. 1975. "Translating Philosophical Works in Classical Chinese—Some Difficulties." In *The Art and Profession of Translation: Proceedings of The Asia Foundation Conference on Chinese-English Translation*, edited by T.C. Lai, 52–60. Hong Kong: Hong Kong Translation Society.

_____. 1989 (1982). *Chinese Classics: Tao Te Ching*. Rev. ed. Hong Kong: The Chinese University Press.

Ledderose, Lothar. 1984. "Some Taoist Elements in the Calligraphy of the Six Dynasties." *T'oung Pao* 70.4: 246–78.

Legge, James (1815–1897). 1962 (1891). *The Texts of Taoism*. 2 vols. New York: Dover Publications.

Little, Stephen, with Shawn Eichman. 2000. *Taoism and the Arts of China*. Chicago/Berkeley: Art Institute of Chicago/University of California Press.

Liú Míng 劉明 (Charles Belyea). 1998. *The Blue Book: A Text Concerning Orthodox Daoist Conduct*. 3rd ed. Santa Cruz, CA: Orthodox Daoism in America.

Liú Xiàogǎn 劉笑敢. 1994. *Classifying the Zhuangzi Chapters*. Translated by William Savage. Ann Arbor: Center for Chinese Studies, University of Michigan.

Lock, Graham, and Gary Linebarger. 2018. *Chinese Buddhist Texts: An Introductory Reader*. London and New York: Routledge.

Loon, Piet van der. 1984. *Taoist Books in the Libraries of the Sung Period: A Critical Study and Index*. London: Ithaca Press.

Lopez, Donald, Jr., ed. 1996. *Religions of China in Practice*. Princeton, NJ: Princeton University Press.

Mair, Victor. 1993. *Tao Te Ching: The Classic Book of Integrity and the Way*. New York: Bantam Books.

———. 1998 (1994). *Wandering on the Way: Early Taoist Tales and Parables of Chuang Tzu*. New York: Bantam Books.

Major, John, Sarah Queen, Andrew Seth Meyer, and Harold Roth. 2010. *The Huainanzi: A Guide to the Theory and Practice of Government in Early Han China*. New York: Columbia University Press.

Mander, Jerry. 1992. *In the Absence of the Sacred: The Failure of Technology and the Survival of the Indian Nations*. San Francisco: Sierra Club Books.

Mathews, Robert Henry (R.H.). 1943. *Mathews' Chinese-English Dictionary*. Rev. ed. Cambridge, MA: Harvard University Press.

McDowell, Edwin. 1988. "Translation of Ancient Tao Text Brings $130,000." *New York Times* February 16, 1988, C.18.

McLuhan, Marshall. 1967. *The Medium is the Massage: An Inventory of Effects*. New York: Penguin Books.

Miller, James. 2008. *The Way of Highest Clarity: Nature, Vision and Revelation in Medieval China*. Magdalena, NM: Three Pines Press.

Molendijk, Arie. 2016. *Friedrich Max Muller and the Sacred Books of the East*. Oxford and New York: Oxford University Press.

Mollier, Christine. 2008. *Buddhism and Taoism Face to Face: Scripture, Ritual, and Iconographic Exchange in Medieval China*. Honolulu: University of Hawaii Press.

Moore, Cornelia, and Lucy Lower. 1992. *Translation East and West: A Cross-cultural Approach*. Honolulu: University of Hawaii Press.

Needham, Joseph (1900–1995). 1956. *Science and Civilisation in China*. Volume II: History of Scientific Thought. Cambridge: Cambridge University Press.

Nietzsche, Friedrich. 1980. *On the Advantage and Disadvantage of History for Life*. Translated by Peter Preuss. Indianapolis, IN: Hackett Publishing.

———. 1997. *Untimely Meditations*. Edited by Daniel Breazeale. Translated by R. J. Hollingdale. Cambridge: Cambridge University Press.

Ōfuchi Ninji 大淵忍爾. 1978–1979. *Tonkō dōkei* 敦煌道經 (Dunhuang Daoist Scriptures). 2 vols. Tokyo: Fukutake shoten.

O'Neill, Timothy. 2013. "Xu Shen's Scholarly Agenda: A New Interpretation of the Postface of the *Shuowen jiezi*." *Journal of the American Oriental Society* 133.3: 413–40.

Pas, Julian (1929–2000). 1997 (1988). *A Select Bibliography of Taoism*. Saskatoon: China Pavilion.

———, with Man Kam Leung. 1998. *Historical Dictionary of Taoism*. Lanham, MD: The Scarecrow Press, Inc.

Petersen, Jens Østergård. 1995. "Which Books Did the First Emperor of Ch'in Burn? On the Meaning of *Pai Chia* in Early Chinese Sources." *Monumenta Serica* 43: 1–52.

Pellatt, Valerie, Eric Liu, and Yalta Ya-Yun Chen. 2014. *Translating Chinese Culture: The Process of Chinese-English Translation*. London and New York: Routledge.

Pregadio, Fabrizio. 1996. "Chinese Alchemy: An Annotated Bibliography of Works in Western Languages." *Monumenta Serica* 44: 439–76.

———. 2005. *Great Clarity: Daoism and Alchemy in Early Medieval China*. Stanford, CA: Stanford University Press.

———, ed. 2008. *The Encyclopedia of Taoism*. 2 vols. London and New York: Routledge.

———. 2009. *Chinese Alchemy: An Annotated Bibliography of Works in Western Languages*. Mountain View, CA: Golden Elixir Press.

———. 2011. *The Seal of the Unity of the Three: A Study and Translation of the Cantong qi*. Vol. 1. Mountain View, CA: Golden Elixir Press.

———. 2012. *The Seal of the Unity of the Three: Bibliographic Studies on the Cantong qi*. Vol. 2. Mountain View, CA: Golden Elixir Press.

———. 2019a. *Awakening to Reality: The "Regulated Verses" of the Wuzhen pian, a Taoist Classic of Internal Alchemy*. Mountain View, CA: Golden Elixir Press, 2009.

———. 2019b. *Taoist Internal Alchemy: An Anthology of Neidan Texts*. Mountain View, CA: Golden Elixir Press.

Pulleyblank, Edwin (1922–2013). 1984. *Middle Chinese: A Study in Historical Phonology*. Vancouver: University of British Columbia Press.

———. 1996. *Outline of Classical Chinese Grammar*. Vancouver: University of British Columbia Press.

Pym, Anthony. 2014. *Exploring Translation Theories*. 2nd ed. London and New York: Routledge.

Qīng Xītài 卿希泰, ed. 1995 (1988–1995). *Zhōngguó dàojiào shǐ* 中國道教史 (History of Chinese Daoism). 4 vols. Chéngdū: Sìchuān rénmín chūbǎnshè 四川人民出版社.

Ramsey, S. Robert. 1987. *The Languages of China*. Princeton. NJ: Princeton University Press.

Rèn Jìyù 任繼愈 (1916–2009), and Zhōng Zhàopéng 鍾肇鵬, eds. 1991. *Dàozàng tíyào* 道藏提要 (Synopsis of the Daoist Canon). Běijīng: Zhōngguó shèhuì kēxué chūbǎnshè.

Rickett, Allyn. 1985/1998. *Guanzi: Political, Economic, and Philosophical Essays from Early China*. 2 vols. Princeton, NJ: Princeton University Press.

Ricœur, Paul. 1970. *Freud and Philosophy: An Essay on Interpretation*. Translated by Denis Savage. New Haven, CT: Yale University Press.

Robinet, Isabelle (1932–2000). 1977. *Les commentaires du Tao to king jusqu'au VIIe siècle*. Paris: Mémoires de l'Institute des Hautes Études Chinoises 5.

———. 1984. *La révélation du Shangqing dans l'historie du taoïsme*. 2 vols. Paris: École Française d'Extrême-Orient.

_____. 1993. *Taoist Meditation: The Mao-shan Tradition of Great Purity*. Translated by Julian Pas and Norman Girardot. Albany: State University of New York Press.

_____. 1997. *Taoism: Growth of a Religion*. Translated by Phyllis Brooks. Stanford, CA: Stanford University Press.

_____. 1998. "Later Commentaries: Textual Polysemy and Syncretistic Interpretations." In *Lao-tzu and the Tao-te-ching*, edited by Livia Kohn and Michael LaFargue, 119–42. Albany: State University of New York Press.

_____. 1999. "The Diverse Interpretations of the *Laozi*." In *Religious and Philosophical Aspects of the Laozi*, edited by Mark Csikszentmihalyi and Philip Ivanhoe, 127–59. Albany: State University of New York Press.

Robinson, D., ed. 1997. *Western Translation Theory from Herodotus to Nietzsche*. Manchester: St. Jerome.

Robson, James, ed. 2014. *The Norton Anthology of World Religions: Daoism*. New York and London: Norton.

Roth, Harold. 1999. *Original Tao: Inward Training (Nei-yeh) and the Foundations of Taoist Mysticism*. New York: Columbia University Press.

_____, ed. 2003. *Companion to Angus C. Graham's Chuang Tzu: The Inner Chapters*. Honolulu: University of Hawaii Press.

_____. 2021. *The Contemplative Foundations of Classical Daoism*. Albany: State University of New York Press.

Rothenberg, Jerome, ed. 2017. *Technicians of the Sacred*. Berkeley: University of California Press.

Rouzer, Paul. 2007. *A New Practical Primer of Literary Chinese*. Cambridge, MA: Harvard University Asia Center.

Said, Edward. 1979. *Orientalism*. New York: Vintage Books.

Sailey, Jay. 1978. *The Master Who Embraces Simplicity: A Study of the Philosophy of Ko Hung (A.D. 283–343)*. San Francisco: Chinese Materials Center.

Saso, Michael. 1979. "Guide to the *Chuang Lin Hsu Tao-tsang*." *Journal of the China Society* 16–17: 9–28.

_____. 2016 (1978). *The Teachings of Daoist Master Zhuang*. 3rd ed. Los

Angeles: Oracle Bones Press.

Schafer, Edward (1913–1991). 1954. "Non-translation and Functional Translation—Two Sinological Maladies." *Far Eastern Quarterly* 13: 251–60.

———. 1966. "Thoughts about a Students' Dictionary of Classical Chinese." *Monumenta Serica* 25: 197–206.

Schilbrack, Kevin. 2002. *Thinking through Myths: Philosophical Perspectives*. London and New York: Routledge.

Schipper, Kristofer (1934–2021), ed. 1975a. *Concordance du Tao-tsang: Titres des ouvrages*. Paris: École Française d'Extrême-Orient.

———, ed. 1975b. *Concordance du Houang-t'ing King: Nei-king et Wai-king*. Paris: École Française d'Extrême-Orient.

———. 1981–82. "Les canons taoïstes des Song." *Annaire de l'Ecole Pratique des Hautes Etudes, Ve Section, Sciences Religieuses* 90: 115–19.

———. 1993. *The Taoist Body*. Translated by Karen C. Duval. Berkeley: University of California Press.

———. 1995. "The History of Taoist Studies in Europe." In *Europe Studies China*, edited by Ming Wilson and John Cayley, 467–91. London: Han-Shan Tang Book.

———. 2000. "Taoism: The Story of the Way." In *Taoism and the Arts of China* by Stephen Little, 33–55. Chicago/Berkeley: The Art Institute of Chicago/University of California Press.

Schipper, Kristofer, and Franciscus Verellen, eds. 2004. *The Taoist Canon: A Historical Companion to the Daozang*. 3 vols. Chicago: University of Chicago Press.

Schuessler, Axel. 2009. *Minimal Old Chinese and Later Han Chinese: A Companion to Grammata Serica Recensa*. Honolulu: University of Hawaii Press.

Schulte, Rainer, and John Biguenet, eds. 1992. *Theories of Translation*. Chicago: University of Chicago Press.

Seidel, Anna (1938–1991). 1969. *La divinisation de Lao tseu dans le Taoïsme des Han*. Paris: Publications Ecole Française d'Extrême-Orient.

———. 1970. "A Taoist Immortal of the Ming Dynasty: Chang San-feng."

In *Self and Society in Ming Thought*, edited by Wm Theodore de Bary, 483–516. New York: Columbia University Press.

———. 1989–90. "Chronicle of Taoist Studies in the West, 1950–1990." *Cahiers d'Extrême Asie* 5: 223–347.

———. 1997. "Taoism: The Unofficial High Religion of China." *Taoist Resources* 7.2: 39–72.

Sells, Michael. 1994. *Mystical Languages of Unsaying*. Chicago: University of Chicago Press.

Shahar, Meir. 2008. *The Shaolin Monastery: History, Religion, and the Chinese Martial Arts*. Honolulu: University of Hawaii Press.

Sharf, Robert. 2005. *Coming to Terms with Chinese Buddhism: A Reading of the Treasure Store Treatise*. Honolulu: University of Hawaii Press.

Shī Zhōurén 施舟人 [Kristofer Schipper] and Chén Yàotíng 陳耀庭, eds. 1996. *Dàozàng suǒyǐn* 道藏索引 (Index to the Daoist Canon). Shànghǎi: Shànghǎi shūdiàn chūbǎnshè.

Siegler, Elijah. 2010. "'Back to the Pristine': Identity Formation and Legitimation in Contemporary American Daoism." *Nova Religio* 14.1: 45–66.

Silvers, Brock. 2005. *The Taoist Manual: An Illustrated Guide Applying Taoism to Daily Life*. Eldorado Springs, CO: Sacred Mountain Press.

Sivin, Nathan. 1978. "On the Word 'Taoist' as a Source of Perplexity: With Special Reference to the Relations of Science and Religion in Traditional China." *History of Religions* 17: 303–30.

Smith, Linda Tuhiwai. 2012. *Decolonizing Methodologies: Research and Indigenous Peoples*. 2nd ed. London: Zed Books.

Soothill, William Edward, and Lewis Hodous. 1937. *A Dictionary of Chinese Buddhist Terms*. London: Kegan Paul.

Stanley-Baker, Michael. 2019. "Daoing Medicine: Practice Theory for Considering Religion and Medicine in Early Imperial China." *East Asian Science, Technology, and Medicine* 50: 21–66.

Steiner, George. 1992. *After Babel: Aspects of Language and Translation*. Oxford: Oxford University Press.

Strickmann, Michel (1942–1994). 1974. "Taoist Literature." In *Encyclo-*

pædia Britannica, vol. 17, 1051–55. 15th ed. Chicago: Encyclopædia Britannica.

Suzuki, D.T., and Paul Carus. 1973 (1906). *Treatise on Response & Retribution*. La Salle, IL: Open Court.

Tián Chéngyíng 田誠陽. 1995. "Zàngwài dàoshū shūmù lüèxī" 《藏外道書》書目略析 (Brief Analysis of the Contents of the *Zangwai daoshu*). *Zhōngguó dàojiào* 中國道教 (Chinese Daoism) 1995.1: 37–42 and 1995.2: 42–45.

Tsien, Tsuen-Hsuin. 2004 (1962). *Written on Bamboo and Silk: The Beginnings of Chinese Books and Inscriptions*. 2nd ed. Chicago: University of Chicago Press.

Unschuld, Paul. 1985. *Medicine in China: A History of Ideas*. Berkeley: University of California Press.

———. 1988. *Introductory Readings in Classical Chinese Medicine*. Dordrecht, Holland: Kluwer Academic Publishers.

Unschuld, Paul, and Hermann Tessenow. 2011. *Huang Di Nei Jing Su Wen: An Annotated Translation of Huang Di's Inner Classic—Basic Questions*. 2 vols. Berkeley: University of California Press.

Van Norden, Bryan. 2019. *Classical Chinese for Everyone: A Guide for Absolute Beginners*. Indianapolis, IN: Hackett Publishing.

Venuti, Lawrence. 1995. *The Translator's Invisibility: A History of Translation*. London and New York: Routledge.

———, ed. 2000. *The Translation Studies Reader*. London and New York: Routledge.

Verellen, Franciscus. 1995. "Chinese Religions—The State of the Field: Taoism." *The Journal of Asian Studies* 54.2: 322–46.

Vogelsang, Kai. 2021. *Introduction to Classical Chinese*. Oxford and New York: Oxford University Press.

Wang, Chengwen. 2010. "The Revelation and Classification of Daoist Scriptures." In *Early Chinese Religion*, edited by John Lagerwey and Lü Pengzhi, 2:775–888. Leiden: Brill.

Ware, James. 1966. *Alchemy, Medicine, and Religion in China of A.D. 320: The Nei P'ien of Ko Hung*. Cambridge, MA: M.I.T. Press.

Watson, Burton. 1968. *The Complete Works of Chuang Tzu*. New York: Columbia University Press.

———. 2013. *The Complete Works of Zhuangzi*. New York: Columbia University Press.

Weinberger, Eliot. 1987. *Nineteen Ways of Looking at Wang Wei*. New York: New Directions.

Wēng Dújiàn 翁獨健. 1935. *Dàozàng zǐmù yǐndé* 道藏子目引得/Combined Indexes to the Authors and Titles of Books in Two Collections of Taoist Literature. Harvard-Yenching Institute Sinological Index Series (HYSIS), no. 25. Běijīng: Yenching University.

West, Stephen. 1995. "Translation as Research: Is There an Audience in the House?" In *Translating Chinese Literature*, edited by Eugene Eoyang and Lin Yao-fu, 131–55. Bloomington: Indiana University Press.

Wieger, Leon. 1911. *Taoïsme*. Vol. I: *Bibliographie générale: I. Le canon (Patrologie), II. Les index officiels et privés*. Hien-hien (Ho-kien-fou): Imprimerie de al Mission catholique.

———. 1965 (1927). *Chinese Characters: Their Origin, Etymology, History, Classification, and Signification*. 2nd rev. ed. New York: Dover.

Wilhelm, Helmut (1905–1990). 1948. "Eine Chou-Inschrift über Atemtechnik." *Monumenta Serica* 13: 385–88.

Wilkinson, Endymion. 2018. *Chinese History: A New Manual*. 5th ed. Cambridge, MA: Harvard University Asia Center.

Wiseman, Nigel, and Feng Ye. 1997. *A Practical Dictionary of Chinese Medicine*. Brookline, MA: Paradigm Publications.

Wong, Eva. 1994. *Lao-tzu's Treatise on the Response of the Tao*. San Francisco: HarperCollins Publishers.

———. 1997. *Teachings of the Tao*. Boston: Shambhala.

———. 2000. *The Tao of Health, Longevity, and Immortality: The Teachings of Immortals Chung and Lü*. Boston: Shambhala.

Wong Shiu Hon 黃兆漢. 1982. *Investigations into the Authenticity of the Chang San-Feng Ch'uan-Chi*. Canberra, Australia: Australian National University Press.

Wu, Jianhsin. 2015. *The Way of Chinese Characters*. 2nd ed. Boston:

Cheng & Tsui.

Wu Jyh Cherng 武志成. 2015. *Daoist Meditation: The Purification of the Heart Method of Meditation and Discourse on Sitting and Forgetting*. Translated by Benjamin Adam Kohn. London and Philadelphia: Singing Dragon.

Wú Shòujū 吳受琚. 1981. *Sīmǎ Chéngzhēn jí jíjiào* 司馬承貞集輯校 (Critical Edition of the Collected Works of Sima Chengzhen). Běijīng: Zhōngguó shèhuì kēxuéyuàn yánjiū shēng yuàn 中國社會科學院研究生院.

Wú Yí 吳怡. 1989. *The Book of Lao Tzu (The Tao Te Ching)*. San Bruno, CA: Great Learning Publishing Company.

Xìng Dé 興德. 2021. *The Arts of Daoism*. Translated by Johan Hausen and Allen Tsaur. Auckland, New Zealand: Purple Cloud Press.

Yip, Wai-lim. 1993. *Diffusion of Distances: Dialogues between Chinese and Western Poetics*. Berkeley: University of California Press.

———. 1997. *Chinese Poetry: An Anthology of Major Modes and Genres*. 2nd rev. ed. Durham, NC: Duke University Press.

Yong, Heming, and Jing Peng. 2008. *Chinese Lexicography: A History from 1046 BC to AD 1911*. Oxford and New York: Oxford University Press.

Yuasa Yasuo. 1987. *The Body: Toward an Eastern Mind-Body Theory*. Translated by Nagatomo Shigenori and T.P. Kasulis. Albany: State University of New York Press.

———. 1993. *The Body, Self-Cultivation, and Ki-Energy*. Translated by Nagatomo Shigenori and Monte S. Hull. Albany: State University of New York Press.

Zhōu Yǒuguāng 周有光. 2003. *The Historical Evolution of Chinese Languages and Scripts*. Translated by Zhāng Lìqīng 張立青. Columbus, OH: National East Asian Language Resource Center, Ohio State University.

Zürcher, Erik. 1980. "Buddhist Influence on Early Taoism: A Survey of Scriptural Evidence." *T'oung Pao* 66.1/3: 84–147.

About the Author

Louis Komjathy 康思奇 (Xiūjìng 修靜 [Cultivating Stillness]; Wànruì 萬瑞 [Myriad Blessings]; Ph.D., Religious Studies; Boston University) is the Director and senior scholar-in-residence at the Center for Daoist Studies 道學中心, the education and research branch of the Daoist Foundation 道教基金會, and head archivist of its Daoist Studies Archive 道學檔案館. He began formal Daoist training in 1991, with early interests in quietistic meditation, mountain seclusion, movement practice, and scripture study, the *Dàodé jīng* in particular. After graduate studies from 1999–2005 and receiving his Ph.D., he lived and trained in China from 2005–2006. During this time, he was ordained as a 26th-generation Daoist priest (*dàoshì* 道士) in the Huàshān 華山 (Mount Hua) lineage of Quánzhēn 全眞 (Complete Perfection) Daoism under Chén Yǔmíng 陳宇明 (b. 1962), the former vice-abbot of Yùquán yuàn 玉泉院 (Temple of the Jade Spring), the base-monastery at Huàshān. In 2007, with his wife and fellow ordained Daoist priest and physician-teacher Kate Townsend 唐鄉恩 (Bàojìng 抱靜 [Embracing Stillness]; Wànqīng 萬清 [Myriad Clarities]), he established the Daoist Foundation 道教基金會, a US-based non-profit Daoist religious and educational organization dedicated to fostering authentic Daoist study and practice and to preserving and transmitting traditional Daoist culture. Now a leading Daoist scholar-teacher and translator for over a decade, he has published ten books and translated over forty Daoist texts to date, including as contained in *The Way of Complete Perfection: A Quanzhen Daoist Anthology* (State University of New York Press, 2013), *Taming the Wild Horse: An Annotated Translation and Study of the Daoist Horse Taming Pictures* (Columbia University Press, 2017), and *Dàodé jīng: A Contextual, Contemplative, and Annotated Bilingual Translation* (Square Inch Press, forthcoming

[2023]). He also is the featured Daoist scholar-practitioner in *Dream Trippers: Global Daoism and the Predicament of Modern Spirituality* (University of Chicago Press, 2017). With Townsend, he recently published *Entering Stillness: A Guide to Daoist Practice* 入靜指南 (Square Inch Press, 2022), a poetic and practical introduction to tradition-based Daoist practice-realization from an applied, committed, and lived perspective. He also serves as project manager and editor-in-chief of the Daoist Translation Committee 道教翻譯學會. He lives in semi-seclusion on the Northshore of Chicago, Illinois, where he listens to birdsong and walks with deer when not reading and translating Daoist literature.